ADVANCE PRAISE FOR
BACK TO BLAKENEY

"We are living in a time of growing inequality and class conflict. In the face of catastrophic climate change and increasingly extreme right-wing movements, young generations of activists are looking to craft an alternate future. But the burning question is how to turn progressive ideas into practical governance? *Back to Blakeney* provides a compelling primer in creating a focused and credible plan for social democratic change."

—Charlie Angus, author of *Children of the Broken Treaty*

"*Back to Blakeney* does two things exceptionally well—it sheds light on what was going on in social democratic Saskatchewan in the 1970s, while also providing ideas for how to confront the unsettling nation-wide, right-wing populism of today. The writers demonstrate Blakeney's exercise of power in building a more equal society: principled, consultative, pragmatic, and very competent. They also remind the reader of the important role public ownership in the resource sector can play, why tax reform and increases are now essential to expand the welfare state, and why a principled debate about the relevance of the notwithstanding clause will always be with us as a rights-based democracy. In short, it's an important, stimulating, and timely book."

—Ed Broadbent, former leader of the federal New Democratic Party

"This book makes a serious advancement to our collective understanding of political biography and Canadian and provincial politics from a historical perspective, and the implications of this biography and history for our understanding of Canada and Saskatchewan in today's world."
—Andrea Rounce, co-editor of *Disengaged*

"This collection of essays about the exemplary way in which Alan Blakeney practised and espoused the ideals of liberal democracy and social democracy is a timely reminder of what is at stake in resisting the current surge of right-wing populism. It tells us how Blakeney carefully balanced the leadership of cabinet, supported by a strong public service, with the participation of the public in shaping government policy. Other contributions project Blakeney's legacy into the future, showing how Canadian institutions can be made fairer, more inclusive, and more effective. For Canadians disturbed about existing trends in governance and politics, *Back to Blakeney* is essential reading."
—Peter H. Russell, author of *Canada's Odyssey: A Country Based on Incomplete Conquests*

"I can think of no other biographical work in this country that is so competent in its multifaceted approach to its subject."
—David Edward Smith, author of *The Constitution in a Hall of Mirrors: Canada at 150*

"This book, in memory of one of Canada's most creative statesmen, addresses the important issues of our time."
—Charles Taylor, author of *Reconciling the Solitudes: Essays on Canadian Federalism and Nationalism*

BACK TO BLAKENEY

BACK TO BLAKENEY

REVITALIZING THE DEMOCRATIC STATE

Edited by David McGrane, John D. Whyte, Roy Romanow, and Russell Isinger

© 2019 University of Regina Press

All rights reserved. No part of this work covered by the copyrights hereon may be reproduced or used in any form or by any means—graphic, electronic, or mechanical—without the prior written permission of the publisher. Any request for photocopying, recording, taping or placement in information storage and retrieval systems of any sort shall be directed in writing to Access Copyright.

Cover design: Duncan Campbell, University of Regina Press
Text design: John van der Woude, JVDW Designs
Copy editor: Dallas Harrison
Proofreader: Rhonda Kronyk
Indexer: Judy Dunlop
Cover art: Portrait of Premier Allan Blakeney, May 15, 1973. Provincial Archives of Saskatchewan, 72-1938-46.

Library and Archives Canada Cataloguing in Publication

Title: Back to Blakeney : revitalizing the democratic state / edited by David McGrane, John Whyte, Roy Romanow, and Russell Isinger.
Names: McGrane, David, editor. | Romanow, Roy J., editor. | Whyte, John D., editor. | Isinger, Russell, 1965- editor.
Description: Includes bibliographical references and index.
Identifiers: Canadiana (print) 20190113499 | Canadiana (ebook) 2019011360X |
 ISBN 9780889776418 (softcover) | ISBN 9780889776821 (hardcover) | ISBN 9780889776425 (PDF) | ISBN 9780889776432 (HTML)
Subjects: LCSH: Blakeney, Allan. | LCSH: Premiers (Canada)—Saskatchewan—Biography. | CSH: Saskatchewan—Politics and government—1971-1982. | LCGFT: Biographies.
Classification: LCC FC3527.1.B43 B33 2019 | DDC 971.24/03092—dc23

10 9 8 7 6 5 4 3 2 1

University of Regina Press, University of Regina
Regina, Saskatchewan, Canada, S4S 0A2
tel: (306) 585-4758 fax: (306) 585-4699
 web: www.uofrpress.ca

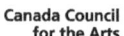 We acknowledge the support of the Canada Council for the Arts for our publishing program. We acknowledge the financial support of the Government of Canada. / Nous reconnaissons l'appui financier du gouvernement du Canada. This publication was made possible with support from Creative Saskatchewan's Book Publishing Production Grant Program.

This publication was made possible with the help of a grant from the Federation for the Humanities and Social Sciences, through the Awards to Scholarly Publications Program, using funds provided by the Social Sciences and Humanities Research Council of Canada.

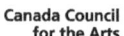   

CONTENTS

Acknowledgements **ix**

Introduction Looking Back to Allan Blakeney for the Sake of Democracy's Future • *David McGrane, John D. Whyte, Roy Romanow, and Russell Isinger* **xi**

Part 1
STATESMAN, PUBLIC ADMINISTRATOR, AND SOCIAL DEMOCRAT

Chapter 1 Principled Pragmatism: Allan Blakeney and Saskatchewan's "Resource Wars" • *Roy Romanow* **3**

Chapter 2 Pursuing Equality: The Political Thought of Allan Blakeney • *David McGrane* **15**

Chapter 3 The Blakeney Style of Cabinet Government: Lessons for the Twenty-First Century? • *Gregory P. Marchildon* **33**

Chapter 4 Experts, Politicians, and Public Opinion: Allan Blakeney and Unpacking Democratic Accountability • *Simone Chambers* **51**

Part 2
BLAKENEY'S CONSTITUTIONAL LEGACY

Chapter 5 Allan Blakeney and the Dignity of Democratic Debate on Rights • *Dwight Newman* **71**

Chapter 6 Allan Blakeney and Keeping Democracy's Promise • *John D. Whyte* **83**

Part 3
MEETING THE CHALLENGES TO THE DEMOCRATIC STATE IN THE TWENTY-FIRST CENTURY

Chapter 7 Is Democracy Compatible with Good Government? • *Michael M. Atkinson* 105

Chapter 8 Trust, Taxes, and Democracy in Canada • *Alex Himelfarb* 121

Chapter 9 Social Democracy and the Canadian Welfare State • *Nelson Wiseman* 135

Chapter 10 Because It's 2019: Gender, Canadian Politics, and the Democratic Deficit • *Melanee Thomas* 151

Chapter 11 The Duty to Consult: Creating Political Space for First Nations? • *Katherine Walker* 167

Chapter 12 Troubled Marriage: Liberal Pluralist Democracies and Religion • *Reg Whitaker* 185

Chapter 13 Federal Electoral Boundary Commissions: What's Right, What's Wrong, and What Can Be Done about It? • *John C. Courtney* 205

Chapter 14 Money Matters: A Democratic Assessment of Canada's Political Finance System • *David Coletto* 223

Conclusion Blakeney's Relevance to the Road Ahead 237

Endnotes 245
References 285
About the Contributors 317
Index 323

ACKNOWLEDGEMENTS

Following Allan Blakeney's death from cancer in April 2011, many people across Canada thought that his qualities, and the political benefits that they brought, deserved public recognition. The idea of a conference in his memory germinated during a brief conversation at Blakeney's funeral between Roy Romanow, a former cabinet colleague, and Russell Isinger, a former student assistant. Since Blakeney enjoyed his time in academia—in particular his time spent with students—a tribute to him seemed to be fitting. Subsequently, a conference was organized and held on November 6–7, 2015, at the University of Saskatchewan; this volume was the final result of many conversations, reflections, and questions regarding Blakeney's legacy to the democratic state in Canada.

Neither the conference nor this book would have been realized without the assistance of many people and organizations. The conference organizers, who then became the editors of this book, benefited from conversations with and contributions from numerous people; we are especially grateful to Sanjeev Anand, Michael Atkinson, Mark Carter, Brent Cotter, Joe Garcea, Dwight Newman, Dan Perrins, and Norman Zlotkin. We would also like to thank Mike Sibley, College of Law, University of Saskatchewan, for his expertise on administering financial accounts. Marnie Howlett, a graduate student in the Department of Political Studies, University of Saskatchewan, provided expert editorial assistance while getting the volume ready for publication. We are grateful for the generous financial support of the University of Saskatchewan Conference Fund; the College of Law, University of Saskatchewan; the Johnson Shoyama Graduate School of Public Policy, University of Saskatchewan and University of Regina; the Law Foundation of Saskatchewan; and the Broadbent Institute, Ottawa. Finally, we were touched by the support of the Blakeney family—Hugh, Margaret, Barbara, David, and Mrs. Anne Blakeney—and honoured to have Anne and Hugh in attendance at the conference.

INTRODUCTION

LOOKING BACK TO ALLAN BLAKENEY FOR THE SAKE OF DEMOCRACY'S FUTURE

David McGrane, John D. Whyte,
Roy Romanow, and Russell Isinger

Like ominous storm clouds on the horizon, right-wing populism is emerging as a major force in politics around the world. Its appeal arises from resentment of rapid social and economic changes experienced by many as displacement and loss. This ideology has the potential to lead to the weakening of our widespread political commitment to democracy's fundamental principle of the equality of all persons as politics becomes expressed in terms of the inferiority of some groups and identities and the superiority of others.

The great risk to the modern democratic state is the acrimony and disdain with which political differences are now expressed. The democratic virtue of searching for compromise and political reconciliation is being replaced by a politics of exclusion and delegitimation. This transformation weakens the practice of temperate democratic dialogue and justifies the abandonment of due process in favour of authoritarian rule by "strongman politicians."[1] This tendency is present in the political careers of many leaders, such as American President Donald Trump, Russian President Vladimir Putin, Turkish President Tayyip Erdoğan, Hungarian Prime Minister Viktor Orban, Brazilian President Jair Bolsonaro, and Philippines President Rodrigo Duterte. In the worldviews of such leaders, it is appropriate to manage state power by inflaming political sentiment, manipulating public opinion, denigrating political opponents and journalists, weakening constitutional limitations on political power, and characterizing minorities as threats to national well-being.

Canada is not completely immune to the growth of right-wing populism. It, too, is experiencing the politics of division. Some Canadian political voices cry for the barring of migrants and seek the removal of constitutional standards of due process.

Ontario Premier Doug Ford did not hesitate in threatening use of the notwithstanding clause after an Ontario court struck down his government's legislation to reduce arbitrarily the number of wards in Toronto from forty-seven to twenty-five just weeks before the municipal election. The initial court ruling found that this legislation altered the terms of democratic representation well after the election process was under way and therefore violated constitutional rights to free speech. Although a higher court in giving its decision on the collateral issue of stay expressed the view that, on appeal, the premier's actions could well be found not to violate the *Charter of Rights and Freedoms*, they reflected a ready willingness to act in disregard of Canada's liberal democratic values. Further, his assertion that "politically appointed judges" should not interfere with his "mandate from the people"[2] showed indifference to the rule of law. Politicians who had negotiated the inclusion of the notwithstanding clause in the *Charter* in 1981 condemned Premier Ford, saying that the clause was designed to be used only as a last resort after careful consideration and should not be used as a means of ill-considered circumvention of *Charter* protections.[3]

Maxime Bernier, a leadership candidate for the Conservative Party of Canada, lost the race and left the CPC to create a new, more right-wing, national party based on decreasing immigration. He warned Canadians that "extreme multiculturalism and the cult of diversity will divide us into little tribes."[4] He went so far as to label ethnic diversity a national weakness and argued in favour of removing persons who legitimately and legally immigrated to Canada but are then judged to be too slow in assimilating to Canadian culture.

These examples, in addition to less politically organized anti-immigrant and right-wing populist movements, suggest that some in Canada desire sharper political and social divisions. Right-wing populists appear bent on rewriting the rules of political practice at the expense of a political culture that celebrates diversity and conducts political competition with restraint and the acceptance that citizens can hold competing political positions.

Against the backdrop of Canada's aspiration to be a state that seeks to do good for its people, the narrowing of equal treatment and fair process represents a potential deterioration of democratic values in Canada. It is this trend, both within Canada and the wider world, that gives purpose to this volume of essays, which examine the legacy and political achievements of Allan Blakeney, who served as Saskatchewan's tenth premier from 1971 to 1982. The values that animated his career can stand as a model of governing on the basis of rigorous and balanced processes for policy analysis as opposed to pandering to temporary and shifting social passions. His career and legacy represent a sound alternative to right-wing populism.

Without doubt, Blakeney was a defining force in the treatment of dominant issues and innovations in Canadian politics during the second half of the twentieth century: publicly funded health care, appropriate taxation of non-renewable natural resource extraction, rebalancing federalism to overcome western Canadian alienation, and the reform and patriation of the Canadian Constitution. His political career was rooted in pragmatism, professionalism, and accommodation of society's many forms of diversity. Blakeney was a strong defender of the principles of democratic government and understood the basic commitments on which it depends for survival. He strove constantly to improve what could be called the "democratic state"—the set of government institutions that citizens consent to, trust, and perceive as legitimate to govern their lives, such as legislatures, courts, the cabinet, and the bureaucracy. As such, his career is a handbook for those interested in achieving good governance and the revitalization of the contemporary democratic state as an answer to right-wing populism and its promotion of irreconcilable division.

Naturally, Blakeney's political views were not beyond controversy. Some believed that he gave too little credit to private investment as an engine of social improvement. Others thought that his attacks on Supreme Court of Canada decisions limiting Saskatchewan's control over resources showed disrespect for the rule of law. His prioritizing health services and education as primary provincial needs caused some to wonder if other goals and values were being shortchanged. However, what was evident to most was the thoroughness of his analysis, his openness to other views, his ability to extend courtesy in debate, and his recognition that his government must serve the needs of the whole population with equal dedication.

The chapters in this book are divided into three parts. Part 1 examines Blakeney's political career and reflects on his legacy in terms of good governance and the democratic state. They look at who Blakeney was and what he stood for. The chapters in Part 2 look more specifically at his constitutional legacy, namely the notwithstanding clause. The chapters in Part 3 explore the challenges now facing the democratic state in Canada and review the strengths and weaknesses of contemporary Canadian democratic practices. They address many issues that have risen to importance since Blakeney was an elected politician and with which he would have expected governments to engage in order to develop policies that meet the changing needs of citizens. Each chapter contains concrete suggestions, inspired by Blakeney's career and by the principles by which he led his province, for revitalizing Canadian democracy.

The authors who contributed to this volume represent different fields of Canadian political science and have different political preoccupations. Some of them knew Blakeney, and others never met him. All of the contributors were encouraged both to reflect on his legacy and to evaluate the relevance of that legacy to the health of the elements of the Canadian democratic state, including issues such as ensuring social justice through the welfare state, government intervention in the economy, maintaining legal and constitutional structures that guarantee human rights, protecting the integrity of voting, encouraging excellence in public administration, and promoting political practices that have positive effects for the inclusion of minority political communities.

Some contributors concentrate on Blakeney himself and provide detailed portraits of Saskatchewan politics during his time in office. Others discuss current political issues and challenges. Some deal with broad theories of democracy, and others focus on the effectiveness and adequacy of concrete democratic practices within Canada. Despite these multiple levels of analysis, all of the chapters stem from the authors' belief that there is public benefit in reconsidering Blakeney's values, methods, and achievements. Blakeney's legacy can help us to think critically about the challenges now facing the Canadian democratic state and move towards its revitalization.

WHO WAS ALLAN BLAKENEY? WHAT DID HE STAND FOR?

Blakeney was brought up in a Conservative household in Bridgewater, Nova Scotia, but at Dalhousie University, where he earned his BA and later his LLB, he was captivated by the emerging thinking about the role of the state in the delivery of social programs necessary to meet basic human needs. After graduating from Dalhousie University, Blakeney went, as a Rhodes scholar, to the University of Oxford. His sojourn in Great Britain was two years after the end of the Second World War, at a time when socialist ideals served as a counterpoint to economic exploitation, the indifference of capitalism to the needs of the public, and disruptive colonialism. This reformist politics was an inspiration to many young people and Blakeney, too, found the new "left-wing" political atmosphere inspiring and heady. He came to see that what he wanted for his life's work was political engagement directed toward the noble goal of government meeting the needs of all and fulfilling the hopes of all for living with dignity.

Desiring to put the academic and political inspiration of Oxford into action, Blakeney moved to Saskatchewan in 1950 to take a position in the Cooperative Commonwealth Federation (CCF) government's civil service. He was elected for the CCF in a Regina riding in the 1960 provincial election and was quickly appointed to cabinet, serving first as education minister, then as provincial treasurer, and finally as minister of health, playing a central role in the creation of the first Medicare program in Canadian history. When the CCF lost power in 1964, Blakeney sat on the opposition benches and became the leader of the opposition New Democratic Party (NDP) in 1970. In the 1971 provincial election, the NDP was elected to government, and Blakeney became premier of Saskatchewan. His government was defeated in 1982. He served as leader of the official opposition until his retirement from active politics in 1988. Blakeney then spent over two decades at the College of Law at the University of Saskatchewan researching law, public policy, and politics until he died in April 2011 after a short battle with cancer.

His career brought him into close contact with most of the components of the Canadian democratic state: the legislature, the executive branch, the bureaucracy, crown corporations, and the judiciary. The first part of this volume explores Blakeney's legacy in relation to these sites of governing. It presents a portrait of him as a statesman, public administrator, lawyer, and social democrat. In each case, improving the functioning of the democratic state in Canada and seeking to make it more effective in meeting the needs of citizens were of paramount importance to him.

As a statesman, Blakeney was driven by the concept of the good state and by a sense of the beneficial outcomes that it could achieve for citizens within the context of democracy. For him, participation in democratic processes was the means to ensure a well-functioning government that provides a high quality of life for everyone. The chapter by Simone Chambers is an insightful comparison of Blakeney's views on democracy with the political thought of Jürgen Habermas. She contends that both Blakeney and Habermas saw democracy as a two-way communicative process between the governed and the governing. Through dialogues with citizens, the statesman both shapes public opinion and alters proposed policies according to public opinion. In his chapter, Roy Romanow examines a specific instance—Saskatchewan's nationalization of potash in the 1970s to create a publicly owned economic engine for the province. Blakeney's deeply held principles had to be reconciled with a difficult situation. As a statesman in a democracy, Blakeney adopted a form of "principled pragmatism" that consisted of creating a policy solution in line with his ideals but also achievable given the political, economic, and legal constraints under which he operated. For Romanow, the ultimate outcome of the Saskatchewan government's "resources war" with the Canadian federal government was a testament to Blakeney's political courage and his mastery of statecraft.

As a public administrator, Blakeney realized that achieving his social democratic goal of greater social justice required efficient government machinery within the state. During his time as a non-elected public servant in the CCF government under Tommy Douglas during the 1950s, and later as premier, Blakeney worked with a talented, motivated, and expert public service to create and implement numerous public policies that benefited the people of Saskatchewan. The fruits of his experience with public administration are contained in *Political Management in Canada*, which he co-authored with Sandford Borins.[5] This book has become a classic in the field of public administration and has been widely used by academics, senior managers, and elected politicians all over Canada.

Gregory Marchildon makes an important contribution to our understanding of Blakeney's views on public administration. He illustrates that Blakeney's approach to cabinet-style government, which Blakeney first experienced during his time in the Douglas government, was an important part of his government's ability to attain more just outcomes for citizens in Saskatchewan. The system of cabinet committees pioneered by Blakeney ensured the accurate identification of problems within Saskatchewan and guaranteed that well-designed programs were put in place to address those problems effectively. For Blakeney, social justice and efficiency in government went hand in hand because it was the duty of a democratically elected government to solve the problems of its citizens in the most effective manner possible and to increase the legitimacy of the government.

As a social democrat, Blakeney used the state to pursue equality within society. In his chapter, David McGrane depicts Blakeney's political ideas and practices as being organized around increasing all forms of equality—economic, social, legal, and regional—in society. For Blakeney, a truly democratic society required increasing levels of equality that would allow citizens to have the minimum standard of living required to fulfill personal potential and to participate in the politics of society. McGrane argues that Blakeney was convinced that democracy works better when society is based upon the bonds of cooperation and solidarity as opposed to promoting individualistic competition.

As a lawyer, Blakeney was intensely interested in constitutional questions, and he played a pivotal role in the patriation of the Canadian Constitution in 1982 as premier of Saskatchewan. Part 2 of this book examines his legacy in this area. Dwight Newman defends and supports Blakeney's advocacy of the creation of Section 33 (commonly known as the "notwithstanding clause"). Newman sympathetically describes the reasons for Blakeney's support for the notwithstanding clause both during constitutional negotiations and in his scholarly legal writings after he retired from politics. For Blakeney, citizens, through their representatives in legislatures, should retain authority over the Constitution and retain the ability in situations of crucial public interest to act as a check against exercises of democratically unaccountable power by the judges of the Supreme Court of Canada. Basic moral and social rights—such as access to medical care—should be implemented by committed governments and legislatures instead of activist courts. As such, Blakeney's defence of parliamentary supremacy was based on the premise that the rule of judges is a poor substitute for democratic exercises through which citizens can understand and debate rights and thereby shape the views of elected legislators through public pressure. Ultimately, Newman agrees with Blakeney's assertion that citizens and governments are better protectors of rights than are the courts.

In contrast to Newman, John D. Whyte disagrees with Blakeney's support of the notwithstanding clause. Whyte outlines Blakeney's broader conception of a human rights regime that depends on the social and moral dynamism of the people and their elected representatives as opposed to the values of courts and judges. Whyte then argues that a constitutionalized regime of human rights enforced by judicial elites is needed because the majoritarian tendencies of democracy can lead to unjust outcomes for vulnerable classes of citizens. For Whyte, a constitutionalized human rights regime allows statecraft to happen and democratic impulses to be expressed under a rights protection process that allows reasonable limits on rights to be set by elected representatives. He argues that judicial supremacy with respect to defining the essential content of fundamental rights is a democratically appropriate means to promote sound and just government.

So who was Blakeney, and what did he stand for? Parts 1 and 2 suggest that he was a statesman, public administrator, lawyer, and social democrat who believed in dialogue, pragmatism, equality, efficient government, and parliamentary supremacy, and his legacy to the Canadian Constitution is immense.

THE CHALLENGES OF GOVERNANCE, EQUALITY, DIVERSITY, AND FAIR ELECTIONS

From the perspective of what Allan Blakeney stood for and how he practised democratic politics, it is pertinent to ask what the challenges are that now face Canadian democracy, and how these challenges can be met. The chapters in Part 3 are the work of eight scholars from diverse backgrounds. Although these chapters discuss Blakeney's legacy in less detail than the earlier chapters, his career provides inspiration for these authors as they draw lessons from the time when Blakeney was premier of Saskatchewan. These scholars make parallels between his tenure in politics and the current situation of democracy in Canada and clearly identify the challenges facing the Canadian democratic state. These challenges can be grouped into four broad areas: governance, economic equality, diversity, and fair elections.

In the area of governance, there is an inherent tension between populism and technocratic expertise in the contemporary Canadian democratic state. Michael Atkinson observes that social democrats such as Blakeney must confront the argument that democracy can be an obstacle to good governance because it gives power to voters with inherent defects of knowledge about public issues and irrational biases, political parties that prefer to capture voters' anxieties rather than educate voters, and private companies that use their financial resources to manipulate elections and policy formation. Those who make a case for governments as positive forces in the lives of citizens need to find ways to address the deficiencies in the state caused by democracy.

The next challenge for the Canadian democratic state relates to the rise of economic inequality, a phenomenon that undoubtedly would have concerned Blakeney as a social democrat. Alex Himelfarb argues that taxes are a measure of how much citizens in a democracy trust each other and how much they trust governments to enact policies that will improve their lives. He makes the case that tax cuts have sapped the ability of the state to deliver social programs and other services that could decrease inequality. Higher and more progressive taxation would give people more confidence and trust in governments to solve problems related to rising inequality. If governments were to raise revenues in a fair manner, they would be able to reduce economic inequality while engendering a common purpose and common citizenship among Canadians. In short, Blakeney would have agreed with the sentiment "fair and progressive taxation=better democracy." Nelson Wiseman connects the welfare state to economic inequality. He makes the convincing case that the federal Liberal Party was gradually pushed over the course of the twentieth century to create a Canada-wide welfare state because of pressure from the CCF-NDP. In particular, CCF-NDP governments in Saskatchewan during the postwar era, in which Blakeney was a central actor, pioneered several innovative programs that forced the Liberals to follow their lead. Unfortunately, the retrenchment of the Canadian welfare state over the past three decades has led to a rise in economic inequality that threatens the postwar accomplishments of social democrats such as Blakeney.

The third challenge facing Canadian democracy outlined in Part 3 falls under the broad category of diversity. As premier, Blakeney faced a diverse Saskatchewan and a diverse Canada. He had to navigate through that diversity as he sought to find solutions to the problems facing his province and his country. Melanee Thomas notes that, though Blakeney's government made advances on legislation promoting women's rights, the nomination and election of women were not high priorities for the Saskatchewan NDP during the 1970s. Blakeney never had a woman in his caucus when he was premier, and there were no female NDP candidates in the 1978 provincial election. Thomas argues that increasing female representation in legislatures would be beneficial to Canadian democracy and explains how women are underrepresented in Canadian legislatures because of the gatekeeping function of parties reluctant to nominate women as their candidates.

Katherine Walker indicates that a key challenge facing the democratic state in Canada is redressing historical injustices done to Indigenous Peoples and promoting reconciliation between Canadian non-Indigenous governments and Indigenous nations. She explains that Blakeney was a key player in the process that entrenched Treaty Rights in Canada through his pressure to have Section 35 included in *The Constitution Act, 1982*. He also negotiated the "Saskatchewan Formula" for settling Indigenous land claims. Walker argues that the processes generated under the "duty to consult" doctrine, if fully implemented, could embody principles of treaty federalism, such as power sharing, interdependence, and intercultural dialogue. Yet, despite almost a decade of negotiations between the Saskatchewan government and Indigenous Peoples, a process for implementing a form of duty to consult agreeable to both sides has not been found.

In his chapter, Reg Whitaker discusses how religious diversity can create tensions within a democracy. He argues that competing religious metanarratives are bound to conflict and that the state ultimately must decide which fundamental interest must be granted priority in a liberal democracy. Secular social democrats have to deal with this fact whether they like it or not. How social democrats define themselves with respect to questions of religious accommodation and discrimination based upon religion is of great importance to the future of social democracy in Canada.

During his time as premier, Blakeney made a number of changes to how elections were regulated in Saskatchewan, such as introducing an independent electoral boundaries commission as well as spending limits and disclosure rules for donations that parties were obliged to follow. The final two chapters of the volume deal with ensuring fair elections. John Courtney evaluates the functioning of independent electoral boundaries commissions in Canada. He gives these commissions an "eight out of ten" because the public has become more involved, the process has become less partisan, and malapportionment has been reduced. Nonetheless, a key challenge for Canadian democracy is to make electoral districting even better by responding to public demands for transparency and non-partisanship as well as by beginning to use new communications technology such as social media. David Coletto deals with the inevitable, but potentially corrupting connection, between money and democracy. He argues that the quality of a democracy depends on how it handles the inflows and outflows of money needed for the functioning of election campaigns of political parties. He contends that the current Canadian model of low direct public funding combined with strict contribution limits encourages ideological polarization, the view of citizens as customers, and the erection of barriers blocking the success of smaller parties. In this situation, the democratic principles of fair electoral competition, political equality among citizens, and high-quality deliberation are endangered.

A BLUEPRINT FOR REVITALIZING THE DEMOCRATIC STATE

As his political career attests, Allan Blakeney was not content simply to identify problems in society. He actively sought solutions to problems that he saw. In the spirit of his principled pragmatism described in the opening chapter by Romanow, the contributors to this volume propose concrete actions and reforms. As opposed to ambitious and sweeping visions of change leading to the wholesale transformation of Canadian political structures, most of the authors opted to propose specific policy alterations to correct particular problems. Their approach is reflective of Blakeney's manner of pursuing his principles with incremental and carefully considered actions. Taken together, however, these reforms would entail a thorough rethinking of contemporary democratic practices in Canada and provide a blueprint to revitalize our democratic state.

The first set of policy prescriptions involves making the machinery of the Canadian government function more efficiently and democratically. Chambers proposes that royal commissions on precise topics could be used to enhance dialogues between citizens and their governments. Marchildon discusses how governments need to increase their research capacity and long-term visioning capability to engage in the type of evidence-based policy making that results in effective government programs. Atkinson considers how competition among policy actors could be fostered and how consultation with stakeholders could be enhanced to ensure that a diversity of ideas flow toward Canadian governments. Walker outlines changes to the duty to consult structures, such as allowing third-party facilitation, to reduce the crown's domination of consultation processes that are inattentive to Indigenous voices and concerns. Newman notes that traditions of parliamentary supremacy in Canada could be renewed if governments used the notwithstanding clause more frequently, especially in situations in which it is unlikely to cause much controversy. As such, use of the clause might come to be seen as more routine and less extraordinary.

A second set of prescriptions involves ensuring that increasing economic equality is a key mission of the democratic state. Himelfarb argues that Canadian governments should reconsider the unaffordable tax cuts recently implemented and focus on closing tax loopholes and combatting tax avoidance. The increased government revenue from these measures could be used for programs that redistribute society's wealth. Following the CCF-NDP tradition of thinking on the welfare state, Wiseman advocates a national child-care program and a national drug insurance program as ways that governments can increase equality in Canadian society. For his part, McGrane advocates universal benefits to reduce economic inequality, pay equity initiatives to decrease social inequality, and enhancements to equalization to promote regional fairness in Canada.

A third set of prescriptions emphasizes the structuring role that diversity plays in Canadian politics is provided. Whitaker is adamant that secular political parties cannot ignore the power of religion to provide a way to understand social reality for many citizens. Rather than running away from anything with a religious tinge, secularists must enter into dialogues with religious Canadians to create more harmonious democratic practices. Whyte points out that, in the age of Trumpism, there appears to be no guarantee that state discrimination against vulnerable and unpopular minorities will be stopped by a multitude of competing interests within a pluralistic democracy or by citizens who reflect on long-term national interests. In such a situation, an independent court system should be empowered to ensure that basic human rights are protected in the face of governments that might have been put in place by the majority of the population.

Finally, a fourth set of prescriptions deals with ways of strengthening Canadian democracy through alterations to the administration of elections. Coletto advocates several specific reforms to party financing: lower contribution limits, direct public subsidies to parties through the personal tax system, public funds tied to engagement in policy development, and start-up public funding for smaller parties. Similarly, Courtney and Thomas make several precise recommendations. Courtney suggests that the process for redrawing federal riding boundaries be reformed to reduce the population variance of ridings, enshrine public servants as ex-officio members of commissions, eliminate the final stage of objections by MPs, and create the opportunity for public input prior to the presentation of the first draft of the new electoral map. To increase women's representation in Canadian legislatures, Thomas calls for linking election expense reimbursements to the number of female candidates that a party runs and establishing clearer rules for the portrayal of female politicians in the media.

Allan Blakeney cared deeply about democracy and would have been alarmed at the rise of angry populism that seeks vindication through ignoring democratic values and institutions. In contrast, Blakeney sought to improve, not degrade, the functioning of the democratic state in Canada. A volume on his political and intellectual legacy and how it applies to the current challenges facing Canadian democracy is thus a fitting tribute to one of Saskatchewan's political giants and a personal friend of the editors. By looking back at his long and distinguished career, and by looking ahead to propose specific policy prescriptions, we hope this volume will spark dialogue, debate, and passionate discussion about how to revitalize the democratic state in Canada. Blakeney would not have wanted it any other way.

PART 1
STATESMAN, PUBLIC ADMINISTRATOR, AND SOCIAL DEMOCRAT

CHAPTER 1
PRINCIPLED PRAGMATISM
ALLAN BLAKENEY AND SASKATCHEWAN'S "RESOURCE WARS"

Roy Romanow

Having known and worked closely with Allan Blakeney for over five decades, I can attest that the phrase that best personifies him is "principled pragmatist." His principled pragmatism consisted of searching for policy solutions to problems facing society that were both in line with his principles and practically achievable given the political, economic, and legal contexts in which he found himself. In this chapter, I describe one example of his principled pragmatism—Saskatchewan's resource wars during the 1970s—that is especially exemplary of his approach to politics. Based upon my own experience as a member of his cabinet, I relate how the Saskatchewan government came to the decision to nationalize a significant part of the Saskatchewan potash industry. I outline six characteristics of his principled pragmatism that can be seen in how he handled the resource wars of the 1970s. Ultimately, I illustrate that Blakeney was equal parts principle and pragmatism, and it was this unique combination that made him a great Canadian statesman.

THE RISE OF THE RESOURCE WARS

The development and taxation of natural resources perennially result in conflict and disagreement among the provincial and federal governments, political parties, private companies, and interest groups. In the 1970s, following a sharp rise in commodity prices, issues stemming from taxation of the natural resource industries in Saskatchewan led to a "resources war" between Regina and Ottawa. As a result, the Province of Saskatchewan took an ownership stake in a number of potash mines through the Potash Corporation of Saskatchewan (PCS) and enacted legislation, though never used, allowing for the nationalization of the province's other potash mines. As the attorney general and deputy premier of Saskatchewan during this period, I contend Blakeney's ultimate decision to pursue public ownership was based upon a pragmatic solution—guided by his deeply held principles—to the problem of maintaining control of natural resources by the province.

Broadly speaking, Blakeney and his government firmly held to the principle that the province had exclusive constitutional jurisdiction over natural resources and that the benefits of their extraction should flow most significantly back to the provincial government and the people of Saskatchewan, their rightful owners. In this regard, Saskatchewan's control of natural resources was rooted in Section 92 of the *British North America Act, 1867* and in the Natural Resources Transfer Agreement (NRTA) of 1930. Symbolically, many people in Saskatchewan also viewed non-renewable natural resources as part of the "natural inheritance" of the province, and they believed the revenues received from natural resource extraction should be used for their benefit. The demand for provincial control of natural resources was also wrapped up in a feeling of alienation from central Canada, partly a result of Ottawa's retaining control of natural resources after Saskatchewan and Alberta became provinces in 1905 until the NRTA in 1930. As a result, when large and unexpected profits were generated by the natural resource industries in the 1970s, the government of Saskatchewan believed it had strong legal and political grounds for its actions in taxing the increased resource revenues.

For the Saskatchewan New Democratic Party (NDP), in particular, natural resources were seen as an important avenue for economic diversification, a goal that the NDP believed would be best achieved if the large majority of profits from this industry were funnelled back into the province. The Blakeney government regarded the development of the natural resource sector as a means of diversifying the economy beyond agriculture. Economic diversification was difficult because Saskatchewan had long had trouble attracting investment capital because of its long distance from ports and markets and its relatively small population. Over the years, tax breaks and incentives had lured multinational companies to build potash mines and drill oil wells, but progress had been slow and painful. Resource projects represented a needed stream of economic activity, which the Saskatchewan government hoped could be leveraged to develop other sectors and industries. Expanding beyond the traditional economic sectors of Saskatchewan was especially important considering the volatile boom-and-bust nature of commodity markets, often experienced with grain, oil, or potash.

Resource management and taxation remained important, but relatively low key, until the Arab oil embargo in 1973 on the United States and other industrial countries because of their support for Israel. Within a year, the price of oil had jumped nearly 400 percent,[1] yet the cost to produce a barrel of oil remained constant. For oil wells in Saskatchewan, most of which were profitable at three dollars a barrel, the huge and unexpected profits brought about by the embargo were a significant windfall. A similar escalation in potash prices was also resulting in windfalls. Therefore, the issue was how the provincial government, the federal government, and private enterprise should share in the benefits. Should the windfall accrue solely to companies licensed to extract the commodity? Should the province, which owns the resources, benefit to a greater extent? Or should Ottawa, with its responsibility for the national economy, take precedence?

In the case of potash, some important historical factors related to the development of the industry were at play. Before the rise in prices of commodities, attracting investment in potash mining required Premier Tommy Douglas to commit the province to low and stable royalty rates. This plan was so successful that a glut of potash production led the government of Ross Thatcher in 1969 to implement a controversial program of "pro-rationing" to suppress production through production quotas and to increase prices through a minimum selling price. Generally supported by the potash companies, this policy remained in place until the rise of potash prices in the early 1970s.

Forming the government in 1971, the Blakeney administration made reforms to the pro-rationing scheme, including introducing a pro-rationing fee of $0.60 per ton later raised to $1.20.[2] The government also mandated that production quotas be based upon a mine's overall capacity, not on contractual obligations, a policy designed to help ensure the viability of smaller mines that ran the risk of being run out of business by larger operations.[3] Central Canada Potash (CCP) strongly opposed our reforms to the pro-rationing scheme. It launched a court action to end pro-rationing, arguing that it had contractual export commitments to fulfill and that pro-rationing on the basis of capacity was preventing it from doing so. However, a strengthening market for potash rapidly saw the pro-rationing quota escalate from 40 percent of productive capacity in 1972 to over 68 percent by 1973 before the quota was finally abandoned in 1974.[4] Unwilling to give up its court action, even after the end of pro-rationing, CCP continued its legal battle, seeking $1.5 million in damages. The federal government, which argued that pro-rationing was a backdoor entrance into regulating interprovincial and international trade, unprecedentedly joined the company.[5] Premier Blakeney described the federal move to join the action as a co-plaintiff as "particularly disturbing" and a "betrayal on the part of the federal government."[6] Under these circumstances, even if CCP decided to drop its legal action, the federal government could continue to litigate the issue and challenge the province's jurisdiction over natural resources.

Even more contentious than pro-rationing was the Blakeney government's implementation of a "reserve tax" on potash in October 1974. The tax was intended to capture windfall profits for the provincial treasury for the benefit of Saskatchewan citizens, whom the government regarded as the true owners of the resource. The tax was charged on potash sold above $35.50, on a rising scale, adjusted for the costs of production for each operation.[7] Without the reserve tax, the rise in potash prices from $40 to $60 per ton would have increased provincial revenue by $2 million and resource companies' revenues by $131 million, according to some estimates.[8] The new formula would see the balance shift to $91 million for the province and $43 million for the companies.[9] At the same time, the province announced that it would participate in any new expansion of the potash industry through the establishment of a crown corporation. In both initiatives, Blakeney and his government held true to the social democratic principles of wealth redistribution from the private sector to citizens and the public ownership of a key industry.

The potash industry's reaction was immediate. Executives and spokespersons for the potash companies decried the Blakeney administration. Within months, the resource companies began advertising their plans to defer development until the "tax situation" was clarified.[10] From the perspective of the Blakeney administration, the potash industry on a whole had decided to escalate its opposition to the provincial government's policies rather than seek a constructive dialogue with the province. The resource companies went as far as delaying, and in some cases outright refusing, to pay their taxes, and they withheld important financial and operational information required to collect the reserve tax. By the middle of 1975, the companies were withholding approximately $30 million of their reserve tax payments.[11] Additionally, they had decided to challenge the reserve tax in court, arguing that it was unconstitutional.[12] Until the courts settled the matter, they would hold on to the cash. Legal threats persuaded many companies to pay their allotted taxes, but some continued to withhold them until the courts ordered them to make good.

At the same time, the federal government of Prime Minister Pierre Trudeau also believed that it had a right to a portion of Saskatchewan's windfall resource revenues. The federal government argued broadly that it had a responsibility to balance the economy of the nation from region to region, especially when resource-rich western Canada was profiting while the manufacturing sector in eastern Canada was struggling. On the oil front, the federal government used its powers of taxation to implement an oil export tax that eventually reached $5.20 on the wellhead price, using the money to subsidize domestic oil prices.[13] Later, in September 1973, the Trudeau government announced its plans to freeze the domestic price of oil and to introduce an export tax on western Canadian oil transported to the United States. By April 1974, the domestic oil price sat at $6.50, while the world oil price was nearly $10.50, the difference of $4.00 being collected by Ottawa through the federal export tax.[14]

Later, Ottawa squeezed all resource industries by announcing, in the November 1974 federal budget, the end to deductions of provincial royalties as an expense on federal tax.[15] Federal Minister of Finance John Turner argued that provincial resource taxes had distorted the meaning of a "bona fide royalty."[16] Premier Blakeney's view was that the federal tax was unfair to private companies and far too invasive into provincial control of natural resources. These and other efforts by Ottawa to capture resource revenues placed the federal and the Saskatchewan governments at odds. These taxation changes, coupled with confrontational court cases, amounted to nothing less than a federal-provincial "war" over who controlled natural resource revenues. For Blakeney, the principle of equality was at stake. The federal government was deliberately pursuing a set of policies that would deepen the inequality between western Canada and central Canada and rob the people of Saskatchewan of their constitutionally guaranteed jurisdiction over the resources they owned. Provincial control of natural resources was an important tool to reduce regional inequality, and to Blakeney it was unacceptable that Ottawa was taking that tool out of the hands of the people of Saskatchewan.

DEBATING THE "HOT OPTION": NATIONALIZATION AND POTASH

Above all else, Blakeney was a democrat. The 1975 election platform of the Saskatchewan NDP was entitled *New Deal '75*, and it argued that the biggest issue in the campaign was ensuring that the people of Saskatchewan benefited from the extraction of the province's natural resources instead of foreign multinational corporations or the federal government. The platform promised to increase provincial government revenues from resource royalties, "speed up direct government participation in the exploration for and development of potash and hard rock minerals," and "step up direct public participation in exploration for and development of oil, gas, coal and uranium."[17] For their part, the opposition parties were opposed to public ownership of the province's natural resources and pledged to lower resource royalties.

Following a hotly contested provincial general election, the NDP government was returned to office. Blakeney firmly believed that the 1975 election gave his government a democratic mandate to continue its policy of higher taxes on resource revenues, its legal efforts to protect its constitutional jurisdiction, and its exploration of ways to increase public ownership of natural resources. However, despite its democratic mandate to follow through with the plans outlined in the NDP platform based upon solid social democratic principles, the provincial government faced extreme pressure from multiple angles to reduce its level of taxation and its regulation of natural resources. In summation, Saskatchewan's ability to tax natural resources was being undermined, court cases were threatening to strike down the province's resource management laws, and resource companies were successfully denying the Saskatchewan government's access to their financial records. At the same time, the federal government had enacted onerous new taxation policies that essentially double-taxed the resource industry. In the face of these difficult circumstances, the Saskatchewan government's position remained clear: the minister in charge of resources, Elwood Cowley, stated that "the potash belongs to the people of Saskatchewan, and the profits from its extraction should go to them. If that policy of our Government slows development, so be it."[18]

The Blakeney government had a difficult decision to make. On one end of the spectrum, it could capitulate and allow the windfall revenues to flow to private capital and the federal government—essentially ceding its constitutional authority over natural resource regulation. On the other end, it could use its powers over property and civil rights, evident in Section 92(13) of the *Constitution Act*, to take an active ownership stake in potash development. Blakeney strongly believed that the duly elected government of Saskatchewan, as a principle of democracy, had the authority, duty, and legitimacy to defend its constitutional jurisdiction and represent the voices of its citizens.

The debates of the Saskatchewan cabinet on natural resources grew more lengthy and intense following the provincial election. By early August 1975, the majority of cabinet time each day was spent weighing options and searching for solutions. Ottawa's actions clashed with the vision of a balanced federation at the heart of Blakeney's understanding of Canada. His vision was rooted in the firm belief that political decisions made by elected representatives within the boundaries of the Constitution determined public policy. Respecting the Constitution and the authority that it bestowed on the representatives elected to provincial legislatures was fundamental to Canadian democracy. After two years of refusal by private companies and the federal government to respect this democratic principle, it seemed that the only adequate response was what came to be known as the "hot option": to put the operations of certain potash mines under public ownership. Whether or not to pursue the hot option became the focal point of intense debate within cabinet. Doing so meant that the provincial government would become a major and active player in the mining, production, and sale of potash, forcing Saskatchewan to assume ownership of existing potash mines in order to avoid the difficulties of starting mines from scratch. From the perspective of deeply held social democratic values and strongly held views on how Canadian democracy should function, the hot option appeared to be the correct course of action.

However, the major political, legal, and economic dangers were obvious. Politically, would the public accept expropriation as a valid response from the government? Would the resource issue override other important priorities of the government, such as health care and education? From a legal perspective, the public ownership option was attractive because Section 125 of the *Constitution Act* states that "no lands or property belonging to Canada, or any province, shall be liable to taxation."[19] The Saskatchewan government's interpretation was that this provision would shield the revenues of the proposed crown corporation, the Potash Corporation of Saskatchewan, from federal taxation. But would the courts come to the same interpretation? Did a province really have the constitutional power necessary to nationalize an industry whose products were almost exclusively exported? Could Saskatchewan design a legal framework for compensating companies for their expropriated mines that would be fair and stand up in court?

Economically, would other private industries in Saskatchewan restrict or withdraw investment? And could the provincial government successfully run a for-profit potash mine?

Premier Blakeney, however, was willing to take the political, legal, and economic risks if doing so meant gaining control of the destiny of the provincial resource industry. He reached this decision through a process of impeccable preparation, rigorous intellectual analysis, vibrant cabinet debate, his far-reaching understanding of Canadian federalism, and weighing all of the potential consequences of each recommended option. The differing voices in cabinet also came together when, late one evening in August 1975, they concluded that they were also willing to take the risk.

Blakeney immediately established two committees to pursue the nationalization of potash. I chaired the committee charged with sorting out the legal details of the legislation. Minister of Finance Elwood Cowley was tasked with planning the financing, creating organizational structures, building relationships with customers, and ensuring that the overall impact of the new crown corporation on provincial resources was positive. Every day of every week, and even late into the evening, the two committees gathered in their respective rooms in the basement of the legislative building. One of the first tasks was to convene expert advisers, such as Ken Lysyk, who later became a BC Supreme Court judge; the Toronto law firm of Davies, Ward and Beck; David Dombowsky, then head of the Crown Investments Corporation; Doug Fullerton, who worked on the nationalization of Quebec Hydro; and Michael Wilson, an adviser at Dominion Securities, who later became the minister of finance in the government of Prime Minister Brian Mulroney. Premier Blakeney often sat in on the meetings, offering his opinions and advice.

Cabinet's decision and the committee meetings were kept secret until the "Speech from the Throne" on November 12, 1975, laid out the plans: "My Government's objective is to assure the greatest possible benefits for Saskatchewan people by gaining effective control of the Saskatchewan potash industry through ownership."[20] The announcement stunned the Legislative Assembly, the people of Saskatchewan, and Ottawa. The president of the Canadian Potash Producers Association reacted by claiming to be "shocked and dismayed," noting that the "action appears to be totally arbitrary and unprecedented."[21] Many in the industry darkly predicted the death of potash mining in Saskatchewan. In the legislature, Leader of the Opposition David Steuart claimed that Blakeney was "a socialist and the idea of government ownership of all business is surely his eventual goal."[22] Industry pressure eventually led the American Department of State to file a formal complaint with the Canadian government. Trudeau firmly advised the Americans that this was a domestic dispute that would be resolved by Canadians.

As the attorney general, I piloted both the *Potash Development Act* and the *Potash Corporation of Saskatchewan Act* through the legislature. The opposition attempted to filibuster passage of the bills as best they could, forcefully challenging the government until late January 1976. The opposition argued that the government was reacting out of anger instead of reason. Above all, it argued that the province was making a mistake in seeking ownership of the mines rather than collecting tax revenue. The opposition believed that the capital costs of acquiring the mines would outstrip the gains in revenue and damage the province's business climate. The legislature, with its majority of NDP members, accepted that risk and passed the potash bills on January 28, 1976.

What were the reactions of the potash industry and financiers when the government set out to buy the first few potash mines? Quickly, the Duval Potash Company, mining just outside Saskatoon, was sold to the new PCS in August 1976. The deal for approximately $130 million saw PCS acquire nearly 15 percent of Saskatchewan's potash production.[23] Over the next two years, PCS added three more potash mines and a controlling interest in a fourth. The allegedly disastrous effects that the province's nationalization efforts would have on foreign investment in Saskatchewan were overblown, and financing for provincial bonds was secured from major global credit markets. In fact, Saskatchewan received more attractive interest rates from the hard-nosed bankers in New York than from those in Toronto.[24] Potash miners also accepted fair market value for their mines with relatively little complaint. Providing fair, if not generous, compensation for expropriation was designed to preserve business confidence, prevent possible trade repercussions, and demonstrate that the Saskatchewan government was acting with careful consideration and not anger. Indeed, in the end, these multiple buy-sell arrangements meant that the expropriation legislation was never utilized.

The two legal disputes brought forth by resource companies CIGOL (Canadian Industrial Gas and Oil Limited), which challenged oil taxes, and Central Canada Potash, which challenged pro-rationing, had less successful outcomes for the Saskatchewan government. In *CIGOL*, the Supreme Court of Canada declared large parts of Saskatchewan's oil taxes as indirect taxes and therefore *ultra vires*. In *Central Canada Potash*, it was ruled that the pro-rationing program infringed on the federal powers of trade and commerce found in Section 91(2) of the *Constitution Act*. The two decisions made it clear that, according to Canadian courts, Saskatchewan had limited control of its natural resources. And, with Prime Minister Trudeau pushing for constitutional change, the issue of natural resources became one of Saskatchewan's top priorities in the forthcoming patriation debates. As a result of Saskatchewan's insistence, Section 92a was added to the *Constitution Act* to solidify provincial control of natural resource regulation and taxation.

SIX PRINCIPLES OF PRINCIPLED PRAGMATISM

Saskatchewan's resource wars demonstrate that natural resource policy is an ever-present challenge to Canadian federalism. The Blakeney government's response to the potash issue was also an exceptionally bold initiative. Reflecting back, my own conclusion is that the fundamental reason for the decision to nationalize part of Saskatchewan's potash industry was based upon both practical and ideological considerations. Saskatchewan's government could not tax its own resources or completely regulate them when faced with the threat of intervention by Ottawa. With open hostility from potash miners and the federal government, pragmatism as much as principle demanded direct intervention. Certainly, Blakeney's social democratic values, and those of his cabinet, pushed the government in the direction of nationalization, but I believe that they were not the only driving force behind the decision to nationalize potash production. The hot option was a practical path forward as well.

The events of Saskatchewan's resource wars were important because they demonstrated the approach of a social democratic government to the management of natural resources in the Canadian federation. More specifically, these events demonstrated the principled pragmatism of Blakeney as a statesman, public administrator, lawyer, and social democrat. In reviewing his role in Saskatchewan's resource wars, it is possible to outline six characteristics of his principled pragmatism. Since three of these characteristics relate to his principled nature and three to his pragmatic nature, one could argue that Blakeney was equal parts pragmatic and principled. I will outline first the pragmatic characteristics before turning to the principled characteristics.

First, Blakeney worked within the scope of the law and the Constitution of Canada. To be sure, the Saskatchewan government disagreed vociferously with the decisions of the Supreme Court in the *CIGOL* and *Central Canada Potash* cases, but it always respected this institution and its decisions. The rule of law in Canada dictates that the Supreme Court is the ultimate arbitrator of the constitutional scope of authority held by each order of government. Once the court rendered its decision, Blakeney sought to enact public policy that realized his principles within the legal limits defined by the court.

Second, Blakeney's instinct invariably was to seek negotiated compromises and proceed in an incremental fashion. Blakeney tried to negotiate with the private resource companies and the federal government to find a compromise that best met the interests of all parties. Only when avenues of constructive dialogue were blocked, such as when potash mining companies declined to open their financial accounts for examination by the government, did he consider more dramatic measures, such as passing legislation allowing for expropriation. Even when armed with the powers of expropriation, Blakeney proceeded in a slow and cautious fashion. Instead of outright expropriation, he chose to use buy-sell arrangements that better reflected the economic norms in Canada and helped to ease the resistance of private companies to his chosen policy path.

Third, Blakeney approached these hugely important issues intellectually—in pursuit of lawful solutions—with careful consideration of the consequences. Contrary to what the opposition charged, he did not make rash decisions out of anger. Cabinet spent countless hours and late nights debating the hot option. Then, before publicly introducing the nationalization of parts of Saskatchewan's potash industry, Blakeney wanted everything to be meticulously prepared and every contingency to be explored. Hence, two planning committees, described above, were charged with designing the mechanisms for the entrance of PCS as a crown corporation into the potash market.

Now I turn to Blakeney's principled characteristics. First, Blakeney firmly believed in his duty to represent faithfully the desires of the Saskatchewan people as expressed through fair and democratic elections. In the 1975 election, Saskatchewan voters elected a majority government made up of representatives of the NDP, a party that had promised during the campaign to defend provincial control of natural resources, raise resource royalties, and increase public ownership of natural resources. Fulfilling his promises to voters made during election campaigns was an important principle for Blakeney. So Blakeney and his cabinet never seriously contemplated abandoning the Saskatchewan people's constitutional and economic claims as the owners of their natural resources entitled to get fair returns from the exploitation of those resources. Doing so would have meant abdicating their role as the democratic voice of Saskatchewan citizens and breaking a promise that they had made to the voters who elected them.

Second, Blakeney had deeply held social democratic principles, which meant that he had the philosophical underpinnings to consider public ownership in the resource sector as a valid policy option. When faced with the difficult circumstances of Saskatchewan's resource wars, Blakeney realized that the social democratic principle of public ownership of key industries that had been applied by social democrats in Saskatchewan and other parts of the world was a potential solution. He used his ideological principles as his guide to solve the challenges facing Saskatchewan during its resource wars, even if ideology was not his only consideration.

Third, Blakeney in his principled pragmatism exemplified courage, something difficult to measure. The events described above demonstrate his political courage to represent faithfully the democratic will of the people and to be true to his social democratic ideals. Despite immense pressure from several sources—Ottawa, business, the media, the opposition—Blakeney ultimately refused to compromise his fundamental principles. Rather, he embarked on a difficult journey to find a pragmatic way to act on those principles. In my estimation, this was his true essence as a great Canadian statesman. He took stock of what his principles were telling him to do and then, mindful of the consequences, proceeded to find practical compromises that would not abandon those principles. In this sense, Allan Blakeney always remained equal parts pragmatic and principled.

CHAPTER 2

PURSUING EQUALITY
THE POLITICAL THOUGHT OF ALLAN BLAKENEY

David McGrane

In many ways, Allan Blakeney was both a political thinker and a political practitioner. He thought hard about politics and created a substantial body of political thought, and as premier of Saskatchewan he had the opportunity to put his ideas into action. Relying on his archival papers and government documents from the 1970s, I assemble in this chapter a summary of his political thought from his speeches and examine how his government transformed those ideas in actual public policy.

My basic contention here is that Blakeney's political thought had three strands connected by the pursuit of growing equality in Saskatchewan society. The first strand is economic equality, embodied by his belief that expanding crown corporations, government intervention in the economy, and the welfare state would ensure that Saskatchewan citizens had the minimal level of material well-being needed to lead a civilized and satisfying life. The second strand is regional equality, apparent in his insistence that the benefits of economic growth should be evenly distributed across Canada's regions, leading Blakeney to embrace a distinctive left-wing version of western Canadian alienation. The third strand is social/legal equality, seen in his advocacy of liberal feminism, liberal multiculturalism, and

Indigenous self-determination to reduce inequities in society based upon gender and ethnicity.

How does this summary of Blakeney's political thought relate to the challenges facing Canadian democracy in the twenty-first century? I conclude the chapter by arguing that, in an unequal society, citizens do not have the material well-being, education, or security to participate actively in democracy. An unequal society encourages citizens to "check out" of politics, leaving it to elites who possess information, money, and privilege. The strengthening of Canadian democracy therefore requires a renewed commitment to greater equality within Canadian society, particularly through the strengthening of universal social programs.

ECONOMIC EQUALITY

Blakeney strongly believed that increasing economic equality was one of the primary tasks of government. The stated goal of his government's 1974 budget was the "narrowing of the gap between the rich and the poor to produce a better and more satisfying quality of life for all Saskatchewan citizens."[1] For Blakeney, greater economic equality would create the financial security necessary for citizens to live satisfying lives and have opportunities for self-development and happiness. His notion of economic equality had several affinities with the work of Sidney and Beatrice Webb, two founding members of the Fabian Society who exerted a strong influence on the British Labour Party at the turn of the twentieth century.[2] The Webbs outlined the concept of a "national minimum of civilized life" that would provide "sufficient nourishment and training when young, a living wage when able-bodied, treatment when sick, and modest but secure livelihood when disabled or aged."[3]

For Blakeney and the Webbs, the creation of a civilized and prosperous society requires that the government provide a minimum of material well-being so that its citizens can realize their individual potential and live satisfying lives within their communities. The latter part about community is important. Individuals are not provided with a minimal level of material well-being as a basis on which they can pursue their own selfish ends through competition with others to gain private profit in an unfettered free market. Rather, individuals develop themselves in order to contribute to the well-being of their communities, what Sidney Webb called their "humble function in the great social machine."[4] Reciprocally, the community gives the individual support to reach her or his highest level of self-development.[5]

Blakeney's finance minister, Ed Tchorzewski, echoed Webb's sentiments with reference to what he saw as Saskatchewan's founding values:

> Our grandparents had this vision when they first came to Saskatchewan. They set out to build a society based on cooperation, in which young and old alike can grow together, share together, and succeed together. Material success, yes! But with a purpose—a shared purpose. I believe that this vision can be summed up by saying that people come first. Not interest rates, not foreign exchange rates, not profits, but people— people come first.[6]

In this sense, equality creates community. Greater economic equality creates a situation in which everyone can participate fully in the community and have the tools to cooperate with others to make the community as strong as possible.

Given his strong belief in economic equality, the question facing Blakeney was how to find the public policy mechanisms by which he could achieve it. The first set of mechanisms was composed of initiatives to generate revenues for the government while redistributing wealth and ensuring that low-income and middle-income earners did not disproportionately pay for the cost of running the government. For that reason, progressive taxation using Blakeney's belief that "taxation should be based upon ability to pay" was considered a high priority.[7] One of the first actions of his government was to reduce property taxes that it thought were a regressive form of taxation. To compensate for the reduction in provincial government revenues caused by this drop in property taxes, the government increased the corporate income tax rate by 1 percent, increased taxes that private companies paid to extract natural resources (i.e., royalties), and raised the personal income tax rate by 3 percent.[8] At the same time, the Blakeney government took up ownership stakes in Saskatchewan's potash, uranium, and oil sectors, ensuring that greater portions of the profits from exploitation of natural resources went to the provincial government instead of private industry.

Stimulating economic growth was also seen as a way to increase government revenues in a way that would not lead to increased taxes on those who could not afford to pay them. Following Keynesian logic, the Blakeney government invested in the stimulation of demand through spending on public infrastructure such as highways, rinks, and bridges. At a first ministers' meeting on the economy in February 1978, Blakeney proposed that the federal government and provincial governments create jobs by undertaking energy projects, specifically power plants, heavy oil refineries, and pipelines, and reduce the personal income taxes of average citizens to give them more money with which to stimulate demand in the economy. He stated that,

> although Keynesian economics is no longer fashionable, surely Keynes was right to argue that a stimulation of demand will spur investment and employment and put our unused plants and our unemployed labour to work. Major cuts in government spending, or tax increases, while they may reduce government deficits, will certainly also reduce overall economic activity and produce a result precisely contrary to what is required.[9]

The Blakeney government was also aggressive in offering grants and loans to Saskatchewan's small businesses and farmers as a way both to stimulate economic growth and to redistribute wealth. During the 1971 campaign, he condemned the Saskatchewan Liberals, claiming that they would give millions to "big businessmen from New York" through low taxes on natural resources, and pledged that an NDP government would create a new department to provide technical assistance and grants to "the thousands of small businesses which play such an essential role in the economic structure of Saskatchewan."[10]

Blakeney firmly believed that the combination of progressive taxation, public ownership of natural resources, and increased economic growth because of Keynesian demand stimulation were the fairest ways to bring in greater revenues that the government needed to expand the welfare state. In particular, his expansion of the welfare state had two specific and interrelated aims. The first aim was the provision of a minimum material well-being to all Saskatchewan citizens at all stages of their lives. The Blakeney government's initiatives to achieve this aim included providing free dental care for children in schools, eliminating deterrent fees charged for visits to the doctor, creating universal prescription drug insurance, and expanding medical procedures covered by Medicare. It also substantially raised social assistance rates, created public housing with affordable rent, improved the guaranteed annual income program for seniors, and reduced nursing home rates. In the education sector, it established grants to ensure that kindergarten was offered on a province-wide basis and created need-based, non-repayable bursaries for university and technical institute students. Common to all of these social programs is that they provided a minimum level of government support for all citizens, thereby narrowing the gap between rich and poor and providing increased financial security to low-income earners and middle-income earners. They provided the material basis for a satisfying and civilized life for all citizens.

However, beyond just material security, the Blakeney government's second aim in expanding the welfare state was to create opportunities for Saskatchewan citizens to pursue self-development. In the 1975 provincial election, Blakeney promised to introduce a "comprehensive recreation plan... to make our leisure time more varied and rewarding."[11] The plan consisted of a package of increased funding for museums, heritage properties, archives, provincial parks, the fine arts, sports activities, and recreational facilities such as hockey and curling rinks. Other examples of the use of public resources to encourage individual self-development include the Blakeney government's expansion of the province's regional library system to cover the entire province, establishment of grants for non-profits offering recreational activities, and creation of a province-wide network of community colleges offering low-cost adult education. Individual self-development also became a guiding principle of Saskatchewan's social assistance regime. The Employment Support Program was created in 1973 to employ social assistance recipients in short-term community works projects in order to provide them with training and allow them to improve their employability. The program was voluntary and provided special features to facilitate participation, such as counselling, child care, and transportation. The Blakeney government also moved to sell hearing aids at cost, include chiropractic services under Medicare, and provide free prostheses, orthotics, wheelchairs, canes, crutches, and walkers to disabled people through its Saskatchewan Aid to Independent Living Program. This program allowed disabled residents of Saskatchewan to live more satisfying lives, pursue their own self-development, and integrate more fully into their communities. One might say that all of the programs outlined above were aimed at increasing what sociologists call "social capital": the knowledge of societal norms and interpersonal connections.[12] The acquisition of social capital increases earning potential and social mobility. In this way, the enhancing of social capital for Saskatchewan citizens meant a more economically equal society.

A final set of public policy mechanisms for creating economic equality included essential services provided at low cost through crown corporations and reforms to the Labour Code. Blakeney was a strong supporter of the crown corporations created by the T.C. Douglas government in electricity, natural gas, telephones, and bus transportation. For Blakeney, public ownership of services used by all citizens ensured that such services would be provided at the lowest possible cost and for the common good. Economic equality could be increased if these essential services were provided at affordable rates, and any modest profits went toward improving social programs. In terms of labour policy, economic equality was enhanced by a series of reforms that made unions easier to organize and improved labour standards to increase the minimum wage and better working conditions.[13] In short, Blakeney believed that increasing the number of unionized workers and broadening the scope of labour legislation could improve the financial security and quality of life of workers in Saskatchewan. Workers would be able to develop themselves and contribute to their communities as opposed to being oppressed by inhumane working conditions and low wages.

REGIONAL EQUALITY

For Blakeney, the pursuit of economic equality in Saskatchewan was hampered by the lack of regional equality in Canada during the 1970s. In a 1974 op-ed in the *Globe and Mail*, he wrote that Canada was undergoing a "crisis of regional inequality" and that Saskatchewan was a region "where incomes are below the national average and the costs of many essential commodities are above the national average."[14] The root of this crisis of regional inequality was that the so-called national policy of the federal government had been skewed in favour of eastern Canada (namely, Ontario and Quebec) and was unable to meet the economic development needs of the four western provinces. In particular, Blakeney's conceptualization of the historical roots of regional inequalities was based upon his understanding of Canadian Confederation as a two-part "bargain" between Saskatchewan and Canada. The first part of the bargain, as outlined in a speech to the National Farmers Union, was that "we would accept tariff protection of Eastern industry in return for fair freight rates and good rail service."[15] The second part of the bargain, asserted during his presentation to the federal government's taskforce on Canadian unity, was that, "when the rights of resource ownership were transferred to the Western provinces in 1930, those rights provided us with a source of revenue which might help compensate for the fluctuations of an agricultural economy and for the absence of a significant manufacturing industry."[16] Much of Blakeney's time as premier came to be consumed with pushing Ottawa to hold up its end of the Confederation bargain.

The complex details of the Blakeney government's decade-long fight with Ottawa over resource taxation and regulation of oil prices are covered elsewhere.[17] Thus, I will only briefly discuss Blakeney's main ideas in this area and how they relate to the importance of regional equality in his political thought. In the autumn of 1973, the federal Liberal government introduced a freeze on the price of domestic oil and an export tax on oil in reaction to the emerging Arab oil embargo, moves that the Alberta and Saskatchewan governments regarded as direct interference in provincial jurisdiction over resources.[18] When it came to the freeze on the price of domestic oil, Blakeney argued that the comfort of residents of eastern provinces was being prioritized over the prosperity of Saskatchewan. Comparing the financial well-being of residents of Ontario and residents of Saskatchewan, he wrote that in Ontario "some people may not be able to afford to buy as much gasoline as they need for their cars. But at least they have cars."[19] What Blakeney intended to impart by this sentiment was that the economic underdevelopment of Saskatchewan meant that its residents could not even afford to buy cars, whereas eastern Canadians were merely worried about the price of gasoline for the cars they already owned. For Blakeney, the federal government's moves on oil pricing reinforced the persistent and historical economic inequality between residents of eastern Canada and residents of Saskatchewan. A pamphlet widely distributed by the Blakeney government argued that, while Ottawa moved swiftly to lower the price of Saskatchewan oil for eastern Canadian residents when prices rose, it had never made an attempt to lower the prices of eastern Canadian goods bought by Saskatchewan residents such as lumber, automobiles, fertilizers, and farm machinery.[20] Nonetheless, Blakeney was not insensitive to the hardship of eastern Canadians and did not adhere to the mean-spiritedness displayed by many Albertans who proudly displayed during this time an infamous bumper sticker with the slogan "let the eastern bastards freeze in the dark."[21] As a solution to rising oil prices in the early 1970s, Blakeney argued that federal government subsidies to keep domestic oil prices below the world averages should be created and equalized throughout Canada based upon the ability to pay instead of forcing oil-producing provinces to bear the full burden of subsidizing oil-consuming provinces.[22]

In terms of resource taxation, Blakeney believed that Saskatchewan's natural resources were the property of the people of Saskatchewan, and therefore the benefits of resource extraction should accrue to them. The Blakeney government stated that "the people of Saskatchewan own the oil. We think that the people should get the benefit of high export prices."[23] Subsequently, the government embarked on a long series of legal battles with the federal government, oil companies, and potash companies over its attempts to increase royalties on natural resources to capture some of the profits from price increases in these commodities. Indeed, in the 1975 election campaign, the NDP platform argued that the biggest issue was ensuring that the people of Saskatchewan benefited from the extraction of the province's natural resources instead of foreign multinational corporations or the federal government.[24] The ultimate result of all of this jurisdictional wrangling over natural resource royalties was that the Blakeney government felt forced to nationalize parts of Saskatchewan's potash and oil industries to ensure that a reasonable portion of profits from the extraction of these resources was allotted to the people of Saskatchewan.[25] At the time, the Blakeney government pointed out that profits from these nationalized companies would be used to expand the welfare state, and therefore the federal government's interference in matters of provincial jurisdiction stood in the way of creating a more equal society in Saskatchewan.[26]

Although insisting that the federal government stay out of provincial jurisdiction over natural resources, Blakeney clearly saw that the overall weakening of the role of the federal government in the lives of Canadians was not the way to end regional inequality. He was far from a provincial rights advocate who sought to expand provincial jurisdiction in every area as a way to reduce regional inequality. In fact, his comments at the First Ministers' Conference on Energy in 1974 conveyed that a strong federal government could solve the problem of regional inequality in the Canadian federation. This sentiment was summed up in the concept of "Canadianism." At the conference, Blakeney defined Canadianism as

> a strong commitment by all Canadians to equality of opportunity for all Canadians, fair and equal access to social services for all Canadians, fair and balanced economic and social development for all parts of Canada. Saskatchewan recognizes that this requires a strong federal government with the money and the will to make this kind of Canadianism a reality....Some Canadians have at best been lukewarm to the concept of a strong federal government with the means and the will to remedy our present glaring regional disparities. We in Saskatchewan have consistently favoured this concept of Canada and Canadianism.[27]

In practical terms, Blakeney operationalized the concept of Canadianism by advocating increased federal government involvement and leadership in the areas of agriculture, economic development, and social services. When it came to agriculture, he believed strongly that the federal government was overinvesting in the development of eastern Canadian manufacturing and underinvesting in Saskatchewan agriculture. The key was not to get the federal government to transfer jurisdiction over agriculture to the provinces but to ensure that Ottawa lived up to its responsibilities and provided genuine leadership. Blakeney fought hard against the elimination of the Crow Rate, a subsidy paid to railway companies by the federal government since 1897 to reduce freight rates on eastbound grain. He argued that, to meet the economic needs of Saskatchewan, the federal government had to fund improvements to the Canadian railway system such as increasing mainline capacity and ensuring that branch lines were not abandoned.[28] The Blakeney government went as far as purchasing 1,000 hopper cars to be used by the railways free of charge to move grain within the western division. It argued that the Saskatchewan government could join forces with the federal government and provincial governments in the Prairies to pursue the eventual nationalization of the railway industry, and then "the only goal would be to increase Canadian exports, not to fatten the pocketbooks of corporate shareholders."[29] Other ideas that Blakeney had to enlarge the role of the federal government in agriculture were setting up a two-price system for wheat in which the domestic price would be one dollar per bushel higher than the export price, placing all grains under the Canadian Wheat Board, and converting a substantial portion of the defence budget into food aid for Third World countries. Although he was not successful in getting Ottawa to adopt these ideas, his government's continued lobbying of the federal government on the issue of grain income stabilization did lead to the Western Grains Stabilization Fund, which made payouts to farmers when their net cash returns for a certain grain fell below the five-year average.

By underinvesting in Saskatchewan agriculture, Blakeney held, the federal government was responsible for the reduction in incomes of small family farms, thereby undermining the financial security of Saskatchewan farmers. In this way, the federal government was acquiescing to the slow death of rural Saskatchewan through depopulation and the takeover of family farms by large agribusinesses to be run by a few hired hands. Blakeney genuinely believed that, because of federal policies, the survival of rural Saskatchewan was threatened and that immediate action was needed to protect the "social and cultural character of rural Saskatchewan" and to ensure "healthy rural communities—a social structure unique to Saskatchewan."[30] Thus, protection of the rural Saskatchewan economy through joint action by Regina and Ottawa was seen not just as an economic imperative but also as a means to protect Saskatchewan's unique cultural heritage.

Beyond agriculture, Blakeney pushed for a strong central government to manage the national economy in such a way that regional inequalities would start to disappear. His government's 1973 budget speech stated that "we need a national development policy which neutralizes the historic advantages awarded by successive old-line party governments to Central Canada."[31] At first ministers' conferences, Blakeney argued that the solution to regional inequality was a national economic policy that would focus on promoting economic development of the outlying regions of Canada through public investment.[32] Such public investment would include a federal program of subsidies to encourage western Canadian manufacturing and injections of federal funding for the construction of western energy projects, such as power plants, heavy oil refineries, and pipelines.[33]

Similarly, Blakeney wanted the federal government to take a leadership role in social policy. He was strongly opposed to the federal government's movement away from fifty-fifty cost-shared arrangements in program areas such as postsecondary education and health care and toward unconditional block funding.[34] The 1981 Speech from the Throne insisted that the Blakeney government's opposition to reduced transfer payments was "not just a fight over money, but also a struggle to maintain nation-wide standards in fields such as Medicare, which were pioneered by Saskatchewan people and of which we are justifiably proud."[35] Blakeney's fear was that shifting the costs of shared social programs to the provinces would lead to the erosion of national standards and the deterioration of those programs, particularly in have-not provinces such as Saskatchewan.[36] In this way, Ottawa's move away from cost-shared social programs would only accelerate regional inequalities because poorer provinces would not be able to afford the same levels of social programs as richer provinces.

Blakeney was concerned not just with economic inequality within Saskatchewan society but also with economic inequality among Canada's regions. The result was a distinctive form of left-wing western Canadian alienation.[37] Blakeney simultaneously fought against federal government intrusion into provincial jurisdiction over natural resources while urging Ottawa to take a leadership role in agricultural, economic, and social policies to reduce regional inequalities. His goal was not just more equality in Saskatchewan but also more equality in Canada. Indeed, for Blakeney, reducing regional inequality would increase the harmony and solidarity of the national community. This sentiment was seen in his reaction to the election of the Parti Québécois (PQ) in 1976. Shortly after the PQ came to power, Blakeney went on television to address Saskatchewan residents, arguing that

"Saskatchewan must continue to fight for fairer treatment of provinces and regions in our federal system....A Canada which provides greater prosperity throughout the nation will cut down sharply the separatist feeling in any part—including Quebec. Full employment and a fair shake for all regions means a unified country."[38]

SOCIAL/LEGAL EQUALITY

Blakeney saw three primary cleavages in Saskatchewan that caused pernicious social and legal inequalities: women versus men, Indigenous people versus non-Indigenous people, and Eastern European ethnic minorities versus the Anglo-Saxon plurality. He was keenly aware that prejudice and discrimination in Saskatchewan created situations in which women, Indigenous people, and Eastern European ethnic minorities could not fully participate in society and lead satisfying lives leading to self-development. Moreover, these inequalities made these groups feel excluded and angry, thereby eroding the solidarity and harmony of the broader community in which they lived. At times, social inequality was actually embedded in Saskatchewan's legal framework because of laws that treated one set of citizens versus another set differently based upon certain characteristics that they possessed. To achieve legal and social equality, the state had to treat all citizens in the same manner. In this sense, legal equality and social equality were two sides of the same coin for Blakeney. Growing legal equality could lead to real equality for these groups as they carried out their daily lives in Saskatchewan society.

As I have argued elsewhere, the Blakeney government's policy on women could be classified as "liberal feminism,"[39] which asserts that women are "as good as men," are entitled to the same treatment by the government as men, and should be given the opportunity to explore their full potential in equal competition with men.[40] Therefore, liberal feminism is interested in expanding women's legal rights and providing women with educational opportunities to allow them to participate fully in the labour market. The main idea is to treat women the same as men so that both sexes are playing on a level field.[41]

During the 1971 election campaign, Blakeney stated that "we have a long way to go—here as elsewhere in Canada—before we are able to say with honesty that women are treated with true equality."[42] In particular, he pointed out that women were discriminated against under the law in "many subtle ways" and that they "suffer[ed] other kind[s] of discrimination in employment because of their sex."[43] Here we can see his stress on legal equality—the state should treat all of its citizens the same—as opposed to substantive equality, denoting that citizens should be treated differently when appropriate to ensure that all enjoy equal results from their citizenship.[44]

Once in power, Blakeney's commitment to legal equality for women played out in a number of policies that his government adopted. For instance, it legislated that women and men could not be paid different rates for performing the same type of employment, and it ensured that property rights of men and women were made the same. His government also created the Human Rights Commission to ensure a process for complaints in the event of discrimination against individual women based upon their sex. Moves toward substantive equality, such as affirmative action with quotas, were not pursued. The only move toward recognizing that women had to be treated differently from men to ensure equality was the Blakeney government's establishment of unpaid maternity leave. However, it could be argued that even this measure was firmly liberal feminist in its intention to create more equal competition between men and women in the workforce by ensuring that women did not lose their employment because of pregnancy.

The Blakeney government's cultural policies are best described as adhering to an ethos of "liberal multiculturalism."[45] As articulated by Pierre Trudeau, it holds that, though there might be two official languages, legally there is no official Canadian culture, and no ethnic group takes precedence over another within the policies enacted by the state.[46] Individuals must be given the freedom to practise their homeland cultures and to experience the traditions of other cultures.[47] For such cultural freedom to be realized, the state supports the individual's choice to preserve their homeland culture and does not try to assimilate the individual into the dominant culture. Thus, the government has a responsibility to provide support for the preservation of homeland cultures, and members of cultural minorities have a responsibility to share their cultures with all of society in exchange for that support. Harmony among the different ethnicities living in a society is achieved by respecting individuals' right to choose their own cultural expression and by sharing minority cultures with the majority culture in order to generate acceptance of diversity among the public.

Although liberal multiculturalism is most associated with Trudeau and the policies of the federal government during the 1970s, Blakeney and his government were also at the forefront of this innovative thinking. Blakeney began his liberal multiculturalism from the claim that Saskatchewan developed a "distinctively Prairie culture from multicultural roots....Saskatchewan is the only Canadian province in which people of British descent and people of French descent together do not form a majority. We belong to neither of the two nations so often referred to in the current debate."[48] Yet he was aware that Eastern European ethnic minorities in Saskatchewan historically had faced discrimination and that the Saskatchewan provincial government had attempted to enforce assimilation by banning languages other than English from being spoken in public schools during the first half of the twentieth century. The actions of the provincial government had created social inequality in Saskatchewan, and these ethnic minorities were angry about historical injustices and now afraid of losing their cultural traditions.

At a conference of provincial government officials and representatives of ethnic minority groups in 1973, Ed Tchorzewski, Blakeney's minister responsible for multiculturalism, used excerpts from the United Nations Educational, Scientific and Cultural Organization's *Declaration of Principles of International Cultural Co-Operation* to argue that individuals and groups have the right to develop and preserve their cultures, especially their languages.[49] More importantly, he contended that governments have a "duty" to take measures to make it possible for ethnic minorities to preserve their cultures especially when they are in fragile states. To combat the social inequalities flowing from Saskatchewan's history, he stated that the Blakeney government would act decisively to recognize the contributions of pioneer ethnic groups that had too long been ignored and to secure the preservation of these pioneer groups' cultural heritage for future generations.[50]

In practical terms, the Blakeney government made the highly innovative move to provide a legal basis for multiculturalism, and in 1974 Saskatchewan became the first province to pass a multiculturalism act. Ontario was the next province to legislate such an act, but not until 1982, and the federal government did not pass its act until 1988. The *Multiculturalism Act* is an excellent reflection of the Blakeney government's conception of liberal multiculturalism that revolved around legal recognition of the importance of preserving and sharing the homeland cultures of Saskatchewan's pioneer ethnic groups. The act defines multiculturalism as the "recognition of the right of every community, whose common history spans many generations, to retain its distinctive group identity, and to develop its relevant language and its traditional arts and sciences, without political or social impediment and for the mutual benefit of all citizens."[51]

From this legal recognition of the right of all ethnic groups in Saskatchewan to preserve their cultures flowed a series of programs designed to give public funding to sustain the cultures of ethnic minorities. Throughout Blakeney's time in power, the *Multiculturalism Act* was used to provide legal authority to institute a program of grants to ethnic minority organizations to preserve their cultures as well as the teaching of heritage languages such as Ukrainian and German in public schools. In exchange for government support to maintain their cultures, ethnic minority organizations were required to educate the public about Saskatchewan's multicultural heritage through museum displays and annual "folk festivals" that received provincial government funding and were held in every major Saskatchewan city.

So Blakeney wanted to implement the liberal multiculturalism of the Trudeau government but to do so in a way that reflected local Saskatchewan circumstances and goals. In his speech to the 1973 multicultural conference, Blakeney stated that preserving and enhancing the province's cultural diversity can "create something which—in total—is distinctively Saskatchewan. We can preserve the old while we build the new."[52] Multiculturalism, along with collectivist values and agriculture, came to be considered one of the three principal components of Saskatchewan's identity. For instance, the Blakeney government held huge celebrations for Saskatchewan's seventy-fifth anniversary, honouring Saskatchewan's cooperative spirit, the health of the provincial agricultural economy, and, "above all else, the rich cultural diversity that has made Saskatchewan such an exciting place to live."[53] By ensuring that the province's established ethnic minorities felt at home, Blakeney thought that Saskatchewan was a better and more harmonious place to live, a province in which all felt that they belonged and that their contributions were valued. Indeed, he insisted that Saskatchewan demonstrates that "different cultures and languages can exist together....We show that the valuable traditions of all our many ethnic groups can be maintained and shared for the benefit of all."[54]

Finally, Blakeney believed in re-establishing Indigenous self-determination and giving Indigenous people in Saskatchewan more control over their lives and destinies. During the 1971 election campaign, he criticized the paternalism of the Liberal provincial government, "trying to tell Indian and Métis people what is good for them. The Premier is the Great White Father and Father Knows Best."[55] Blakeney pledged that his government would work toward solutions to the problems of Indigenous people in Saskatchewan by starting "where the Indian and Métis people are, and with them try to provide the resources and help to go in the direction they want to go."[56]

Two specific initiatives of the Blakeney government that encouraged Indigenous self-determination stand out. First, it worked to establish several Indigenous-administered and Indigenous-controlled institutions. Blakeney strongly believed in what was called at the time "Indian control of Indian education,"[57] and his government created some of the first Indigenous-controlled primary, secondary, and postsecondary institutions in Canada. At the same time, public funding was provided for the creation of Indigenous-controlled cooperatives, businesses, family services programs, and home construction initiatives.

Second, the Blakeney government tried to expand the land base under Indigenous control. Although groups of white settlers had their homesteading contracts with the crown respected, successive provincial and federal governments had failed to fulfill their contractual obligations under Saskatchewan's Numbered Treaties. Because of the research funding received from the Blakeney government, the Federation of Saskatchewan Indians (FSI) was able to determine the magnitude of Indigenous land claims within Saskatchewan. Instead of pursuing settlement of land claims through confrontational litigation, Blakeney decided to negotiate an agreement acceptable to Indigenous bands. After negotiations with the FSI and the federal government, the Blakeney government came up with the "Saskatchewan formula," which equalled 1.3 million acres, much more generous than the Manitoba and Alberta governments were willing to accept in their land claims. The Saskatchewan formula recognized the legal right of Indigenous people to the land that was owed to them under the treaties, thereby correcting a key legal inequality in provincial history.

Blakeney did not intend Indigenous self-determination to segregate First Nations from the broader provincial community. At a major Saskatchewan government–Indigenous conference held close to ten years after he came to power, Blakeney spoke extensively about finding "common ground" based upon "mutual self-interest" between Indigenous people and non-Indigenous people. He stated that Indigenous people benefit from cooperating with non-Indigenous people in the provincial government because their organizations are given resources to develop their communities. The benefit to non-Indigenous people of providing resources to Indigenous organizations is living in a society "where opportunities are open to all, where nobody is permanently caught in a cycle of poverty and unemployment." Blakeney was adamant that a stronger community results when Indigenous people, both individually and collectively, participate in the economic and social development of Saskatchewan. Providing Indigenous people with the means to engage in self-determination and self-development would result in a more prosperous and harmonious province in which "we're all better off."[58] Blakeney did not advocate a robust vision of Indigenous self-government and reconciliation as later found in documents in 1996 by the Royal Commission on Aboriginal People and in 2015 by the Truth and Reconciliation Commission. Indeed, several residential schools continued to operate in Saskatchewan during his time as premier, and his government continued various programs that encouraged the adoption of Indigenous children by non-Indigenous families (commonly known as the "Sixties Scoop").[59] Nonetheless, Blakeney did seem to express a sense that Indigenous people and non-Indigenous people needed to work together to find a way forward. Such sentiments might have acted as a harbinger of bolder action in the future.

DEMOCRACY AND EQUALITY

My reflections on the political thought of Blakeney and the policies of his government lead to the important conclusion that democracy and equality must go hand in hand. Indeed, a truly democratic society requires a growing level of economic, regional, legal, and social equality.

In terms of economic equality, a citizen needs a basic level of material well-being to participate in democracy. Someone who is homeless or forced to choose between paying rent and buying healthy food does not have the luxury of spending time thinking about politics. Further, participating in modern democracy requires more than just a full stomach and a place to live. One also needs political tools such as an internet connection, spending money to buy books to keep informed, and time outside employment to engage in the politics of the community. A basic level of material well-being, along with an appropriate level of leisure time for all citizens, is a necessity for any flourishing democracy.

Providing high-quality education to all citizens is undoubtedly a way to reduce the income gap between rich and poor, but it is also something that citizens need to participate effectively in democracy. Beyond reading and writing skills, the public education system can teach political literacy. It starts with a strong civic education curriculum taught at high schools well funded by provincial governments. But it must continue through affordable postsecondary education for children of low-income and middle-class families since universities and colleges are institutions that deepen the political knowledge of students and encourage them to think critically about politics. Through high-quality public education, citizens can come to understand the functioning of the basic institutions of democracy and gain the ability to discern how they can make social changes. They can understand the differences among the various political parties and political movements in their society so as to choose which ones they want to join. Without political literacy, citizens who try to participate in democracy are like pilots who try to fly with their eyes closed.

Regional equality is also an essential part of Canadian democracy in the twenty-first century. Having citizens of one region feel resentful about their unfair treatment compared with citizens of another is poisonous for democratic discourse in Canada. Over time, this politics of resentment creates deep divisions that eat away at bonds of solidarity and cooperation that should form the basis of any well-functioning country. Citizens of a region routinely treated unfairly might become so frustrated with having their concerns overlooked that they will stop participating in democracy and defer to elites in the metropole.

One possible solution to regional tensions in Canada is to try to force regions to give up their specific identities and sacrifice their particular interests to a singular national interest. Blakeney believed that Prime Minister Pierre Trudeau tried to impose this solution with the National Energy Program and certain elements of the various constitutional packages during the 1970s that sought to expand the scope of bilingualism. Suppressing regionalism in a country as vast and diverse as Canada could be seen as antidemocratic. Distinctive regions should be encouraged to cooperate with each other as opposed to being enveloped by a single national identity. Blakeney's alternative was for the federal government to find ways to even out regional inequalities in Canada, thereby leading to greater national unity. If that could be done, then regional resentment would ease, and compromises could be found that would make all of Canada's regions winners in Confederation. As such, regional equality could ensure the basis for democratic compromise.

When it comes to social/legal equality, citizens do not feel safe enough to participate in democracy if society marginalizes core parts of their identities. A society that routinely discriminates against women, visible minorities, Indigenous people, or members of the LGBTQ community does not create an atmosphere in which these groups feel comfortable participating in politics. If such participation means being exposed to disrespect and hatred, then it is only logical that many members of these groups will take a pass.

Ultimately, democracy is about more than voting. It is about citizen activation. It is about encouraging citizens to be politically active and politically aware on a routine basis. However, in an unequal society, citizens do not have the material capability, education, motivation, or security to participate actively in democracy and they believe that their participation will not make a difference. An unequal society discourages citizens from democratic participation and encourages them to leave politics up to elites who possess information, money, and privilege. Although it is difficult to prove a connection, it might not be a coincidence that voter turnout has consistently fallen in Saskatchewan since the 1980s.[60] And over the same period, the income gap between rich and poor in the province has widened.[61] It is not so much that the rich and elites in Saskatchewan are discouraging the poor from voting, but perhaps growing inequality is preventing the poor from attaining the education and financial security needed for participating in politics. Indeed, recent research illustrates that affluent citizens vote more than low-income citizens and that unconditional cash transfers from the government to poor households improve not only the socio-economic status of those households but also the likelihood that children living in them will vote when they grow up.[62] In this way, programs that reduce poverty could lead to long-term gains in voter turnout.

Looking back on his record in government in June 1983, Blakeney reflected that "what we aimed at was a province where all people had not only a 'fair share' of wealth, income, and opportunity, but also a share in making decisions which shape our lives."[63] Blakeney thus saw his legacy as both creating greater equality in Saskatchewan and providing improved opportunities for citizens to participate in democracy. As he worked to create a more equal society, he also worked to create a more democratic society. Canadian democracy certainly has many challenges as we approach the end of the second decade of the twenty-first century. One lesson that we can take from Blakeney's political thought is that a commitment to a more democratic society must be connected to a commitment to a more equal society. Initiatives to increase economic equality such as universal social programs, laws that reduce social inequality (e.g., employment equity), and budget mechanisms such as equalization that diminish regional inequality do more than just improve the quality of life of Canadian citizens. They improve the quality of Canadian democracy.

CHAPTER 3

THE BLAKENEY STYLE OF CABINET GOVERNMENT
LESSONS FOR THE TWENTY-FIRST CENTURY?

Gregory P. Marchildon

In this chapter, I reflect on how social democratic goals and policies are actually achieved on the ground. In particular, I examine the means used by Allan Blakeney and his cabinet government to translate his party's intentions and goals into workable policy programs that would change the economic and social directions of the province and influence progressive political change in the rest of Canada. I isolate Blakeney's unique contributions to the art of government and indicate why I think they succeeded in turning social democratic policy objectives into effective and sustainable programs.

The danger of such a focus is that it can reinforce the common perception of Blakeney as a technocrat—someone interested more in the techniques of government and its operations than in government as a means to the end of achieving a more equitable society. Underneath his rationally calculating exterior, Blakeney was passionately committed to the social and economic changes required to create the conditions that would give all citizens opportunities for meaningful lives. In rethinking the meaning of social democracy, the former leader of the federal New Democratic Party (NDP) and political scientist Ed Broadbent referred to the social democrat's "expanded notion of democratic citizenship"—expanded compared with the narrower focus of liberal democrats on formal equality as expressed in individual rights.[1] In contrast to liberal democrats, Blakeney emphasized the need for an activist state to redress, rebalance, and redistribute the existing distribution of rights and resources through major policy changes. But what truly distinguished Blakeney was his insistence on creating the efficacious state—one that would systematically generate and expertly implement major policy changes that would result in greater social and economic equality among all citizens.

Blakeney certainly mastered the machinery of government over his many years as a practising public servant, cabinet minister, and premier, and spent considerable time in his post-political academic life instructing and writing on the subject. He nonetheless viewed administration and governance as means to a greater end: to change what he had always viewed as an unsatisfactory and unfair status quo that perpetuated inequalities based upon wealth and social class. However, to build a more equitable society required an activist policy agenda, which in turn necessitated a purposeful and effective government led by a team of committed and disciplined cabinet ministers supported by a talented and sophisticated public service that, at the most senior level, was creative in terms of policy change and competent in terms of policy implementation and ongoing administration.[2]

Of course, Blakeney's style of government did not emerge in a vacuum. It evolved out of the practices, traditions, policy ambitions, and cabinet machinery established in the twenty years of Cooperative Commonwealth Federation (CCF) governments under Premiers Tommy Douglas and Woodrow Lloyd from 1944 to 1964.[3] These years formed Blakeney's apprenticeship in government, first as a senior civil servant and subsequently as a politician and minister. As a leader, Blakeney was also an anomaly relative to his social democratic mentors, colleagues, and successors in Saskatchewan. Unlike Douglas and Lloyd, he was originally a Maritimer who had not grown up with the progressive and populist political traditions of the Prairies. Moreover, his life in government began as a civil servant, not a politician. These differences would produce a governing style that differed from those of his CCF predecessors and his NDP successors Roy Romanow and Lorne Calvert.

I examine here the legacy that Blakeney inherited and carried forward into his government. I also describe his unique contributions to the art of governing and policy making that involved a departure from the Douglas-Lloyd government of 1944–64. Finally, I explore the lessons that we might draw from the Blakeney style of government for the twenty-first century in Canada.

INHERITANCE

A graduate of Dalhousie University's law school and a Rhodes Scholar at Oxford University, Blakeney was an intellectual who could easily have become a university professor early in his career—the vocation that he in fact took up after he left politics and enjoyed until the end of his life. However, for almost four decades, Blakeney worked through the government to achieve his social democratic vision of a better and more equitable society. Upon graduating from Oxford in 1950, he decided to use his considerable legal and analytical skills in Saskatchewan as secretary of the Government Finance Office (GFO), the provincial government's crown corporation holding company. In this capacity, Blakeney served as the lawyer for a number of the smaller crown corporations in the province. He was excited to be a part of the Douglas team and by the prospect of working with a group of individuals dedicated to major changes in terms of enhancing social and economic equality and modernizing the tools of government to achieve those changes.[4]

Blakeney remained in this position for the next five years and in the process learned much about the workings of cabinet government and how cabinet members and senior civil servants exercised the craft of governing and managing a provincial administration. He had the opportunity to work with a core of the most talented bureaucrats in the country, including George Cadbury (chair of the Economic Advisory Planning Board), A.W. (Al) Johnson (Treasury Board), Tommy Shoyama (Douglas's chief policy adviser), and Don Tansley (Treasury Board and eventual head of the Medical Care Insurance Commission), among many others. After the CCF was defeated in 1964, Blakeney's civil service colleagues went on to careers in other governments. Johnson, Shoyama, and Tansley ended up in Ottawa, where they served as deputy ministers in the Pearson and Trudeau governments. Affectionately known as the Saskatchewan Mafia, they influenced an entire generation of public servants in Canada by mentoring them in the systematic approach to policy formulation, decision making, and implementation that they had helped pioneer in the Saskatchewan government.[5]

Blakeney gained invaluable experience in the machinery of government during this period. As secretary of the GFO, he reported directly to Clarence Fines, the provincial treasurer (today called the minister of finance). In the process, he mastered the detailed preparations necessary to allow cabinet committees to work effectively. He absorbed the Douglas government's practice of requiring senior civil servants to put in writing not only their analyses but also the most viable policy options available in the circumstances and recommendations on the best policy options based upon all of the relevant policy factors. Ministers might not always accept the options or recommendations for good political reasons, including public acceptability, but Blakeney viewed this approach as creating a rigour and a disciplined accountability that he thought were essential to a well-functioning cabinet government.[6]

The Douglas government did more than any other postwar provincial government to modernize public administration in Canada.[7] The government's civil servants were instrumental in establishing and contributing to the Institute of Public Administration of Canada (IPAC). These government modernizers used the annual IPAC conference to discuss and compare innovative practices throughout Canada and beyond, and they regularly contributed articles that described their innovations in the annual IPAC conference proceedings.[8] Blakeney provided his own analysis of how best to organize and manage crown corporations in Saskatchewan in order to achieve a given set of policy objectives.[9] This was his reference point for the reorganization of the structures that he put in place to oversee and direct crown corporations when he became premier in the 1970s.[10]

In 1955, Blakeney became the secretary of the Saskatchewan Securities Exchange Commission. In the next couple of years, he would make a momentous decision. Despite his love of public administration and his preference for a life behind the scenes, he wanted a greater ability to effect change, which could only be done by becoming a cabinet minister and, eventually, the premier of the province. Of course, this meant becoming a politician. To facilitate this change, Blakeney began his transition out of the bureaucracy and into private legal practice. Doing so allowed him to seek nomination as a CCF candidate. Once he secured the nomination in a working-class area in Regina, Blakeney was elected in 1960, a campaign that became a de facto plebiscite on the government's plan for universal medical care insurance.[11] He would later describe the battle over Medicare between 1960 and 1962 as the most defining political experience of his life. This bitter struggle taught him the critical importance of maintaining unity within cabinet when a major policy change triggered powerful opposition.

Blakeney became one of the ministers whom Premier Lloyd most leaned on during this period. He became a central member of the inner committee of cabinet responsible for managing Medicare, including conducting negotiations with doctors, redrafting the legislation, and creating the necessary machinery to administer the new plan.[12] Blakeney was also responsible for leading the daily media conferences on behalf of the government during the height of the Medicare crisis.[13] After the strike ended, Lloyd appointed him as the minister of public health and gave him the responsibility to implement Medicare despite continuing opposition from many doctors.[14] Blakeney proved to be one of Lloyd's strongest ministers during the doctors' strike, and his reward was to gain even more responsibility after the strike.[15]

Unafraid of the controversy unleashed by Medicare, Blakeney was adamant about the need for the government to implement the policy despite the virulent opposition of the medical profession, the media, and almost the entire business and professional community in Saskatchewan. From his perspective, the art of governing a population, which included individuals and interest groups opposed to your political party's direction, required compromise at times, but he was more than prepared to fight when fundamental values were at stake.[16]

In the case of Medicare, two key issues could not be compromised. The first key issue was the need to alter the financing of medical care so that access would no longer be based upon the ability to pay for it. According to Blakeney, it was the mission of a social democratic government to civilize the market through regulation and taxation when possible or, when impossible, to take the more radical action of placing goods and services such as health care outside the logic of the market so that access would be based upon need alone.[17] The arguments for and against this policy had been reviewed extensively with the public for years, and the government had never been defeated electorally on the issue despite the consistent opposition of a vocal and influential minority.

The second key issue was that the CCF government had been re-elected on an explicit platform of introducing universal medical care insurance. To retreat from this promise because of the pressure of interest groups would have been a betrayal of the principle of democracy. In particular, the election of 1960 had become a de facto referendum on Medicare, and the CCF won the election despite vigorous and well-financed opposition.[18] In Blakeney's view, governments in the Westminster parliamentary tradition were elected periodically based upon explicit mandates, and in a representative democracy they had the legitimate right—and indeed should be expected—to carry out their platform promises irrespective of the opposition of a minority, no matter how powerful, wealthy, or influential. Moreover, in a representative as opposed to a direct democracy, the government had a responsibility to translate a particular platform objective into a detailed policy program without seeking consent through a plebiscite or referendum. It was enough to know that, if the majority of the public thought that the government had misinterpreted its mandate, it could be defeated in the next election.

Blakeney nonetheless implemented Medicare in a way that reduced both public and physician opposition to the program. He preserved the government's commitment to access medical care by establishing a single source of payment (public taxation) for Medicare, but he also oversaw administrative mechanisms that favoured existing modes of physician payment and delivery, a necessary compromise in his view but one that angered some in the left wing of the CCF who wanted to see major changes to how medical care was delivered.[19] Despite these efforts at compromise after the strike, the battle with doctors and the business and professional establishment cost the CCF government dearly in terms of polarizing the provincial population, and after two decades in power it was defeated in 1964.[20] Blakeney's role now shifted to that of opposition politician for the next seven years. Blakeney was so highly regarded by Lloyd that he was appointed deputy leader of the opposition.

As the finance critic, he used his insider's knowledge of the workings of the government to find weaknesses in the policies and management style of Ross Thatcher's administration. In particular, Blakeney saw how the Liberal premier was a poor delegator, unable to allow key ministers, their committees, and their civil servants to use their own judgment and make their own decisions.[21] This, in his view, weakened the capacity of the government to manage affairs properly much less make consistently good decisions.

When Lloyd stepped down as party leader in 1970, Blakeney was the first of four candidates to step into the leadership contest. With his years of experience as a member of the Legislative Assembly, minister, and deputy leader, he was regarded by everyone as the establishment candidate.[22] His position was solidly centralist from a social democratic perspective, and he was on record along with Douglas as supporting the Winnipeg Declaration of 1956, an effort both to modernize and to tone down the more radical elements of the original Regina Manifesto.[23]

Blakeney ran against candidates who represented the new Canadian left (the Waffle), the old socialist left forged in the 1930s, and the pragmatic centre-right represented by a young, charismatic, and telegenic Romanow. To the surprise of Blakeney, given the support of so many of the party's luminaries, he was narrowly defeated by Romanow on the first ballot. It took three ballots, but he finally emerged as party leader of the Saskatchewan NDP in large part because he was perceived by the new left as more acceptable than Romanow.[24] Blakeney had less than twelve months to prepare the party for the election of June 1971.

INNOVATIONS AS PREMIER, 1971–82

Organizational Innovations

When the election returns were finalized on June 23, 1971, Blakeney found that his party had won forty-five of sixty possible seats and 55 percent of the popular vote.[25] To train his cabinet members for their new roles and responsibilities, and to establish a proper relationship with the civil service, Blakeney brought in Tim Lee, the veteran cabinet secretary in the Douglas-Lloyd years, to explain how the system should work.[26] The upshot of the advice, in the words of Blakeney, was that he "wanted Cabinet to deal with policy and administrative detail, with recommendations, not with problems."[27] The recommendations and the analyses supporting them were to be prepared by an expert civil service so that ministers would have time and perspective to evaluate the policy options, bringing to bear their political expertise and knowledge.

Blakeney reinstituted the tradition of extensive planning under the aegis of cabinet committees with strong central agency support that had been the norm during the twenty years of CCF government between 1944 and 1964.[28] He went beyond the Douglas-Lloyd model when he shifted to a more premier-centred system. Central to this change was creating the post of deputy minister to the premier and making this individual the head of the public service. The most important change was to make this office responsible for advising Blakeney on the hiring, firing, and shuffling of deputy ministers, now within the purview of the premier. Prior to this change, the selection of deputy ministers had been largely up to individual ministers.[29]

Over time, all provincial governments altered their systems so that the premier's chief official also became the de facto chief operating officer of the government as a whole, but Blakeney was the first premier to introduce this centralized cabinet secretary approach. This innovation involved some trade-offs. On the positive side, it allowed the premier to exert greater discipline to ensure that the government's direction and priorities would be implemented despite the potential resistance of individual ministers, departments, and agencies. It allowed for more effective cabinet building in the sense that the choice of minister and deputy minister could be coordinated by the premier and the premier's chief official in a way to ensure complementarity of skill sets. It could also prevent ministers from overly controlling their deputy ministers and departments in a way that detracted from the collective mission and goals of cabinet.[30] Blakeney wanted his ministers to focus on the government's objective of achieving greater social and economic equality and to let the civil service concentrate on the administrative means required to implement and manage such changes. On the negative side, the change emphasized the collective responsibility of both ministers and deputy ministers to the detriment of individual departmental accountability. This was especially true because it accompanied the new practice of periodic cabinet and deputy minister shuffles. In the Douglas-Lloyd era, ministers and deputy ministers could remain in their respective portfolios for many years. However, in the Blakeney era, a minister or deputy minister could expect to change portfolios at least once in a four-year electoral term. At least for ministers, Blakeney thought, periodic shuffles were essential to ensure new energy and ideas and to encourage ministers to take their collective ministerial responsibilities seriously.[31]

Central to these organizational changes was Blakeney's philosophy of how the political and bureaucratic tiers of government needed to work together in order to achieve good governance based upon his ideal of the Westminster model. Blakeney worked these ideas into a speech that he repeated at almost every cabinet meeting. Over and over, he reminded his ministers that it was the job of the deputy ministers, not the ministers, to be the administrative heads of their respective departments: a minister's "job is to be a member of cabinet—to be part of the team that shapes the overall policy of the government, to defend that policy in public forums."[32]

In contrast to the general view of Blakeney as a technocrat, he also emphasized the critical political role that ministers played in the decision-making process, arguing that "we live in a democracy, not a technocracy." He "stressed the fact that what the bureaucracy felt was the best course of action from a technical point of view was only half the picture." Moreover, "if a course of action is technically sound but is not acceptable to the public, then it is a poor course of action." At the same time, Blakeney distinguished between less important policy issues on which a government should not expend precious political capital and more important policy issues, such as Medicare, that required "a pitched battle to win public acceptance," which sometimes occurred only years after their implementation.[33]

Blakeney also extended the cabinet system established in the Douglas-Lloyd era. Initially, he kept intact two of the three Douglas-era cabinet committees. The Treasury Board continued to perform the function of a cabinet committee that would make the first round of decisions on the budget, and it, along with supporting budget analysts from the Budget Bureau in the Department of Finance, comprised the government's main vehicle for controlling the expenditures of the executive government.[34]

The second committee was the Governance Finance Office Board, the committee of cabinet responsible for directing and controlling the expenditures of crown corporations in the province, a sector that rivalled in size—based upon the number of employees—the public service in executive government. However, the size and mandate of the GFO would grow substantially during the Blakeney era because of the growth in the government's ownership and control of natural resources, including the nationalization of the potash industry.[35] As a consequence, in 1978 the Blakeney government established the Crown Investments Corporation (CIC), a new holding company for the provincial government's larger public enterprises and its growing investment portfolio. Made up of cabinet ministers, CIC's board of directors not only governed the activities of CIC but also acted as a committee of cabinet.[36]

The Cabinet Planning Committee was the third and, in many respects, the most critical cabinet committee because it held responsibility for the policy direction of the government. This committee had a much broader mandate than the Douglas-era Economic Advisory and Planning Board since it took responsibility for all social as well as economic policy matters. The committee was supported by senior policy advisers working in the Cabinet Planning Secretariat in the Department of the Executive Council. Between ten and twenty senior policy advisers provided ongoing policy advice to the Cabinet Planning Committee. Although each department of the government was encouraged to set up its own policy and planning unit, with the result that the Blakeney government was widely regarded as the most policy competent provincial government in Canada, the Cabinet Planning Secretariat provided external support where it was needed.[37]

The central agency staff of the cabinet committees, in particular the Cabinet Planning Committee and Treasury Board, formed an expert elite within the Blakeney government. Occasionally, this fuelled the charge that these bureaucrats overly influenced cabinet decision making and acted as a Praetorian guard for the premier, sometimes acting against the interests of individual ministers and their departments. This view was reinforced by the fact that the Cabinet Planning Secretariat also had a coordinating role with the policy units in other departments, occasionally stepping in when policy and planning capacity was less than Blakeney expected or desired in the line departments.

Of course, these organizational changes were simply the means selected to implement an extremely ambitious policy program, much of which had been spelled out in the electoral platform of 1971. Cleverly titled *New Deal for People*, this twenty-one-page platform incorporated policies that had come up through the caucus and grassroots of the NDP during its years in opposition after the defeat of the Lloyd government. The platform policies were accompanied by 140 promises, and *New Deal for People* became known as the NDP government's "blueprint for the 1970s."[38] The most important promises were those aimed at altering the status quo in order to achieve greater economic and social equality, and most were achieved in large part because of the superb administrative ability of the Blakeney government.

Economic Development and Public Ownership

The Great Depression of the 1930s delivered a hammer blow to Saskatchewan that negatively affected the province both economically and psychologically for decades. The reliance on wheat, almost all of which was shipped to world markets, meant that the provincial economy was dangerously dependent on two highly variable factors: weather and the price of wheat.[39] Unwilling to wait for change through slow-moving market forces or a national policy of a federal government that seemed to be satisfied with the economic status quo of the Prairies, the Blakeney government intervened aggressively to diversify and deepen the Saskatchewan economy in an effort to improve economic opportunities and reduce income inequalities by creating an environment in which those with seasonal employment or limited education could get jobs in the sector. The obvious first step was to encourage development of the existing stockpile of non-renewable resources.

Oil and natural gas had been produced in the province for some time, but with the Organization of the Petroleum Exporting Countries (OPEC) crisis of 1973 the prices of these commodities began to rise sharply, and the Blakeney government—similar to the Progressive Conservative government in Alberta under Premier Peter Lougheed—raised taxation to divert some of the windfall profits from the oil and gas companies to provincial residents as well as to ensure that these resources would not be depleted too quickly. Passed in December 1973, the *Oil and Gas Conservation, Stabilization, and Development Act* would be contested by both the oil industry and the federal government.[40] From the OPEC crisis of 1973 to the *Constitution Act, 1982*, the government depended on a disciplined cabinet and an expert civil service not only to counter the oil industry and the government of Canada but also to be proactive.

An important part of the offensive strategy was to use direct state ownership of resources through crown corporations, a strategy previously avoided by the Douglas and Lloyd administrations.[41] By creating the Saskatchewan

Oil and Gas Corporation (SaskOil) in 1975, the Blakeney government obtained a publicly owned "window" through which to view the powerful industry. This action countervailed the industry's previous monopoly on information and gave cabinet and the civil service the data and evidence that they needed to regulate and tax private oil companies more effectively. SaskOil, with its cheeky motto "It can be done," was a small but effective poke in the eyes of powerful multinational oil interests.

The other two major resources were potash and uranium. Potash mining had begun in the 1960s but had been hampered by low world prices. This situation began to change in the 1970s as agricultural demand for the fertilizer made from this pink rock spiked upward. The first step was a review of the tax and royalty arrangements and the price cartel originally established by the previous Liberal government. The Blakeney government introduced a new tax and royalty regime that included a new reserve tax. Although all minimum price provisions were eliminated, the cartel-like rationing scheme was continued, a decision that Blakeney admitted, "in retrospect," was a "mistake."[42]

These events, including the subsequent legal challenge from Central Canada Potash, the one company opposed to the cartel, have been covered comprehensively in the chapter by Romanow in this volume. What needs to be emphasized is Blakeney's insistence on having his ministers and a select group of civil servants work full time for months to create effective policy options for cabinet so that it would have the raw material with which to make the best possible decision in the public interest.

Although not nearly as high profile as potash mining, uranium mining also involved contentious issues and raised major policy challenges and conundrums. Because of the historical connection of uranium to the nuclear arms race, there was strong opposition within the grassroots membership of the NDP to mining and exporting it. By the 1970s, major concerns had also emerged about the safety of nuclear reactor power plants and the difficulty of disposing of nuclear waste. Although Blakeney recognized these concerns, along with a majority of cabinet he thought that the advantages in terms of providing employment to northerners, the majority of whom were Indigenous, outweighed what he also saw as the "undeniable risks."[43] It did not help that the small amount of uranium mined in Saskatchewan before 1970 had been shipped to the United States, where it was used in the nuclear arms program.[44]

Here Blakeney and the party establishment found themselves at odds with many party activists. In his desire to create greater economic opportunities for Indigenous families living in Saskatchewan's vast north, Blakeney wanted uranium mining to proceed. In a failed effort to defuse the controversy, a party committee was established to report on the issue at the provincial NDP convention in 1976. This report precipitated a heated debate at the convention, and cabinet members had to use all of their political capital in order to prevent a call for a moratorium on uranium mining. Then, in his leader's speech to the convention, Blakeney promised to appoint a board of inquiry on the question of the new Cluff Lake Mine that ultimately would be led by Justice E.D. Bayda of the Saskatchewan Court of Appeal.[45]

When it reported in 1978, the Bayda Commission recommended that mining proceed subject to two conditions: first, that northerners, the majority of whom were First Nation and Métis, would be guaranteed 50 percent of the jobs created at the mine; second, that the revenues from mining be shared with northern communities.[46] The Blakeney government agreed with the first recommendation and made the northern hiring quota a requirement for all uranium mining in the future. However, it did not implement the second recommendation, preferring to rely on its existing social policies to generate greater income and self-sufficiency in northern Indigenous communities.[47]

Pursuing Greater Equality: Legal and Social Policy Innovations

The Blakeney government was elected on a promise of northern self-government and full consultation as part of a general effort to improve living conditions for the mainly Indigenous residents of northern Saskatchewan. As Blakeney described in a letter at the time to his old colleague Al Johnson, he viewed the marginalized position of Indigenous residents, and all the social pathologies accompanying poverty and racism, as the government's "major social problem" and its ability to "devise a strategy for dealing with the social ills" of Indigenous people as its most important challenge.[48] This strategy involved numerous policies and programs; however, few of them met the expectations of northern leaders, who expected revenue sharing from uranium mining and greater autonomy for Indigenous governments.

Blakeney, however, did not want to see the north divided along racial lines between Indigenous and white residents, on the one hand, and between First Nation and Métis communities, on the other. So he chose other means to achieve the government's objective, including the provision of funding to existing Indigenous organizations and northern communities. The most contentious of the new policies was the creation of a Department of Northern Saskatchewan with a head office in the northern community of La Ronge.

Although successful in redirecting the focus and resources from the south to the north, this initiative was widely criticized as an overly bureaucratic answer to the economic and social challenges of the north.

Less contentious and arguably more successful were the government's policies and programs in education. Community schools were established in the low-income neighbourhoods of Regina and Saskatoon that focused on the needs of inner-city Indigenous children. The Blakeney government set up programs to train Indigenous teachers. His cabinet also encouraged establishment of the Saskatchewan Indian Federated College, which, though affiliated with the University of Regina, had a mandate to educate postsecondary students in an environment that respected Indigenous knowledge and teaching methods.[49]

In health care, the Blakeney government immediately cancelled the deterrent fees on hospital and medical care services imposed by the Thatcher government to constrain the use of health services by Saskatchewan residents. Supported by the evidence of numerous experts, Blakeney argued that user fees mainly deterred the poor from accessing needed health services, a policy that by its nature created economic inequality. Supported by the Cabinet Planning Secretariat and a high-level policy team within the Department of Public Health, cabinet quickly introduced innovations that went beyond Medicare. The provincial government introduced one of the country's first public prescription drug programs, made universal so that it would act as an expansion of the existing Medicare program. Other provincial governments eventually adopted their own prescription drug programs, though most set up targeted rather than universal programs.

Even more innovative in terms of addressing both income and rural-urban inequalities was a dental program serving all school-aged children in the province. Delivered by dental nurses, known as dental therapists after 1981, this program provided prevention and basic treatment care in school-based facilities. As North America's first (and last) large-scale policy experiment of its type, the program was a major success in reversing what had been one of the provincial populations with the poorest oral health in the country to one of the best in less than a decade.[50]

Blakeney knew that both changing the configuration of legal rights and increasing access to justice were essential in generating greater equality. Women's rights were enhanced through a new property law that protected farm women in particular. A Human Rights Commission was established so that residents would be able to pursue and protect their rights in a low-cost and accessible forum. One of the country's first legal aid systems with staff lawyers was established so economically disadvantaged residents would have proper representation before the courts.

These initiatives had a common objective. They were intended not only to attenuate inequities created by a market economy but also to achieve greater economic and social equality.

CONCLUSION: LESSONS FOR THE TWENTY-FIRST CENTURY?

The reason that the word *technocrat* is so often applied to Blakeney derives from his close focus on the instruments of government and their effective use. To both friends and critics, this focus seemed to be obsessive at times. Blakeney required his ministers and senior public servants to consider carefully every viable avenue and option and the instruments that it entailed to achieve a given policy objective. He then forced his cabinet to review in a painstaking and lengthy process every possible scenario. Cabinet meetings would not end until he was satisfied that the best choice, judged on both policy and political criteria, to achieve the end desired—a progressively better society in which every resident would have the opportunity to live up to his or her full capacity—had been made.

In some cases, the decisions made by the Blakeney government upset the status quo and the positions held by powerful and highly organized forces in society, as the examples of public ownership of potash-mining enterprises and the children's dental plan illustrate. In these cases, Blakeney was a happy warrior, more than willing to take the offensive in contesting these interest groups to demonstrate that their positions were not consistent with the public interest of the majority of Saskatchewan residents, just as he did as a minister in the Lloyd government during the Medicare battle in the early 1960s.

A number of lessons can be derived from the Blakeney government. The first is as valid for the twenty-first century as it was for the twentieth century. The effectiveness of any activist social democratic government can be assessed only in terms of how successful it is in actually altering the status quo in order to achieve greater social justice. As described by one scholar-practitioner reflecting on the many innovations of the Blakeney government, this is the traditional social democratic perspective from which the state is used "to achieve greater control over the economic development of a province and greater justice and equality in its society."[51] However, Blakeney would have added that aspirations and ideals are not enough and that such an achievement is dependent on running an effective government.

Blakeney was highly traditionalist in his view of the merits of a Westminster parliamentary system. He thought that this form of government, more than any other, allowed for a smoothly functioning cabinet capable of translating the democratic aspirations of a majority of citizens into action. This meant making informed, evidence-based decisions using the resources of a highly competent and permanent public service in the Westminster tradition that, at the highest level, provides advice on a broad range of policy options to achieve the objectives set by the political tier of government.

Blakeney was a master conductor of the complex mix of actors, instruments, institutions, and conventions that make up modern government. Indeed, he was unusual in his great "interest [in] and concern for the organizational structure and administrative process of the Saskatchewan government and its public service."[52] He achieved greater self-determination of the economy by accelerating the growth of a more diverse economy mainly through non-agricultural resource development. Although he started from the solid foundation established by the Douglas and Lloyd administrations in which he served first as a public servant and later as a cabinet minister,[53] he added his own innovations to the machinery of government and encouraged a remarkable degree of policy innovation in the Saskatchewan public service.[54] This included changes in the regime of resource taxation and the creative use of public investment and direct state ownership.[55]

However, Blakeney went beyond the Douglas government in using direct state ownership of resources through crown corporations. SaskOil gave the Blakeney government a window through which to monitor the oil industry. The takeover of the potash industry triggered a battle with potash corporations, opposed to government control of production of the resource, but it marked the next stage in a constitutional battle with the federal government that would end only after passage of the *Constitution Act, 1982*. New mechanisms, including an enhanced crown corporation holding company, combined with a dedicated corps of public sector managers, many of whom were graduates of the famed Budget Bureau, delivered value for money as well as control to Saskatchewan residents.[56] Through his far-sighted stewardship, Blakeney demonstrated the effectiveness of public ownership and management. He proved that there could be a viable public option for any policy in dealing with private market forces.

Progress was also made on achieving greater equality through numerous social programs and legal initiatives. As discussed above, the children's dental program, the provincial prescription drug plan, legal aid for poor defendants, and a Human Rights Commission were major advances in Canada and, sooner or later, adopted in other jurisdictions. Such policies were conceived, refined, and ultimately implemented by a government that excelled in setting priorities, designing innovative policies and legislation, and effectively financing, implementing, and managing programs and regulations. As discussed in the preface of Allan Blakeney and Sandford Borins's book on effective statecraft, "the ultimate goal of any government is its policies, and these policies will influence whether it will be reelected or defeated, and whether it will be remembered for good or ill. However, it is management and organization that make policy development possible."[57]

Although Blakeney received what he wanted on resources in the new Constitution, he was forced to accept what he did not want—a constitutional *Charter of Rights and Freedoms*. His reasoning was simple. Democratically elected governments have more legitimacy than courts to make policy. Moreover, they have much greater expertise in matters of public policy than courts and can be more trusted to balance societal interests in determining policy changes. In addition, under a Westminster parliamentary system, unlike congressional-presidential systems such as in the United States, courts are not a third branch of the government and should have a role limited to administering and interpreting legal rather than policy matters. Finally, in his view, every Westminster parliamentary system has an unwritten constitution just as effective in protecting human rights as explicit constitutions in republican systems of government, such as the United States.[58]

However, Westminster systems evolve, and the adoption of a charter, though it has led to a more activist court, has not resulted in the wholesale reversal of policy as laid down by legitimately elected governments. Courts have ruled in some areas, such as Indigenous rights, where governments in Canada have stubbornly refused to make decisions. However, courts have done so carefully, leaving the manner of implementing policy change in the hands of governments. In the words of Kent Roach, this has generated a creative dialogue between courts and governments that has generally served the public well.[59]

Blakeney's unique contribution was to provide a model of the activist and efficacious state within the Westminster parliamentary tradition. In recent decades in Canada and elsewhere, there has been a retreat on both fronts. The role of the state has been minimized, a trend followed by even some ostensibly social democratic governments, and market forces have been emphasized. As a consequence, inequality has grown in most higher-income countries, including Canada. This development has created increasing dissatisfaction among those who have slipped in their socio-economic positions in recent decades, and it has led to a greater appetite for major change. The only question is whether that change will come from the social democratic left or from the far right on the political spectrum. For the left to become the favoured choice, social democrats will have to demonstrate their opposition to this dismal status quo and their willingness to push forward major changes that will fundamentally alter the existing distribution of economic and social rights.

At the same time, social democrats need to demonstrate their capacity to create and manage the efficacious state. In Westminster parliamentary systems, this means going back to the working principles and examples that Blakeney generated and refined decades ago. Consistent with the trend away from the activist state and toward a minimalist state, governments in Canada (and elsewhere) have gutted their policy capacities. To the extent that new policies are needed, their development has been increasingly outsourced to consultants and other external (non-state) policy experts. However, as Allan Blakeney demonstrated through his own government, the activist and efficacious state requires an innovative and expert public service led by a committed, disciplined, and visionary cabinet.

CHAPTER 4

EXPERTS, POLITICIANS, AND PUBLIC OPINION
ALLAN BLAKENEY AND UNPACKING DEMOCRATIC ACCOUNTABILITY

Simone Chambers

Allan Blakeney was both a policy expert and an elected representative. In the role of expert, he was accountable to the truth.[*] In the role of politician, he was accountable to the public. In this chapter, I investigate the tension between these two roles in light of evidence that the public rarely possesses the truth and indeed is often misinformed. Can elected representatives be responsive to public opinion while pursuing policies that they think are the most rational?[†] Yes, they can, but to understand

---

[*] By policy expert, I mean that Blakeney contributed to specialized academic debates about public administration. In the second section, I elaborate on the idea of experts, but in this context it refers to bureaucrats and technocrats. By truth, I mean a common sense and non-technical idea of correct answers according to accepted standards of science.

[†] A classic case here might be the tension between climate science that says we are causing global warming and a public that does not believe the facts. In this case, are representatives accountable to the truth or to the will of the people?

how this works we need to rethink ideas of democratic responsiveness in deliberative terms.

In what follows, I reinterpret some of Blakeney's key insights concerning accountability in the terms offered by the democratic and communication theorist Jürgen Habermas. Blakeney was not a philosopher, nor did he develop a normative theory of democracy. Nevertheless, he suggests a particular relationship between the public and elected representatives, especially ministers of the crown who stand more directly between bureaucratic experts and the general electorate, with regard to policy input. The two terms central to this discussion are "accountability" and "acceptability." Ministers are accountable to the public and constrained by what the public finds or can be persuaded to find acceptable. In fleshing out what might be entailed in this view—that is, what model of democracy might best support this relationship between the minister and the public—I draw some connections to deliberative democracy.

I begin by outlining how I use the term "deliberative democracy." This is to avoid confusion since the term has come to mean many things. I then sketch some ideas that Blakeney introduced in his two well-known keynote addresses to the National Conference of the Institute of Public Administration of Canada. Ministers are clearly expected to respond to public opinion on important policy matters, but Blakeney does not offer much detail in these writings or in his more extended treatment of public administration about this relationship or the normative standard of democracy that underpins it.

I then outline three models of the relationship between citizens and their representatives and ask which one best captures Blakeney's position. The first model is based upon responsiveness and has come to dominate the empirical study of democracy in the United States. Here citizens' preferences have or ought to have direct inputs into policy outputs. The second model is found in elite theories of democracy that limit citizen input to leadership selection during elections. Policy output is insulated from direct public opinion input. Neither model adequately captures the relationship between ministers and the public that Blakeney hints at in his writings. The third model is deliberative in that it represents interactions between elected elites and the public as a two-way communicative relationship. Elected officials not only listen to and respond to the public but also help to shape public opinion by persuasively defending policy outputs. I argue that the categories of public opinion formation and feedback loops as established by Habermas best articulate this ideal.

DELIBERATIVE DEMOCRACY

The view of democracy that I defend here is part of the growing field of "deliberative democracy," a rather large umbrella term that covers many varieties of democratic theory and practice.[1] For some, deliberative democracy is a form of decision procedure, mainly seen in mini-publics and small-scale forums in which citizens engage in face-to-face deliberation on issues and policies.[2] For others (and I include myself here as well as Habermas), it is a general paradigm through which to interpret and understand a democratic regime writ large.[3] In this case, it is called *deliberative* democracy not because citizens are expected to engage in high-end "deliberation" but because, in contrast to interest-based views of democracy, democratic legitimacy is assessed using a standard of justification or discursive accountability.

The claim here, then, is not that deliberative democracy is a new species of democracy; rather, it is a new way to study, evaluate, criticize, and perhaps improve the democratic systems that we have. All democracies at all times deliberate. In some general sense, all political regimes—unless they are truly just the results of arbitrary will (perhaps how we imagine a Caligula or a Nero to have ruled)—have a deliberative component in that some person or persons must weigh the considerations for and against policies and courses of action. In a deliberative *democracy*, that weighing involves input from and accountability to citizens. One way to understand the turn to deliberative democracy is simply as a turn to look at parts of democracy that have always been there but that we have not always paid attention to or thought important. Here we can think of deliberative democracy as bringing about a shift in the research agendas of both empirical and normative theories of politics. Rather than counting the votes, we look at opinion prior to those votes. Rather than viewing accountability as election turnover, we ask how elites respond to citizens and justify their policies. Rather than focusing on the fairness of the franchise, we turn to questions of voice and inclusivity of the public sphere. Rather than studying votes in Parliament, we study debates. These are some of the ways that a deliberative democracy paradigm is different from, say, a pluralist or economic model. We still look at the same democratic regime, but we ask different questions and suggest different improvements and enhancements.

The questions that interest me here focus on the public sphere and seek to analyze and evaluate the lines of communication that exist or could be created between citizens and their elected representatives. This perspective is what I call a talk-centric rather than a vote-centric view of democracy.[4] Of course, voting is an important exercise of democratic citizenship and is itself a form of communication. Powerful messages are sent and received through the voting booth, as the most recent Canadian election made clear. But voting in the democratic model that I present below is only one among many ways that citizens and their representatives communicate. Elections and referendums punctuate an ongoing "conversation," one might say, in which power holders are required to justify, explain, and defend their policy initiatives and legislative agendas in terms that citizens find acceptable and persuasive. Citizens, for their part, are encouraged to listen to their representatives and to talk about the policies presented by them in order to form considered opinions about public matters. This is an ideal of democratic communication, of course, that no existing public sphere fully achieves. Nevertheless, it is a useful ideal and often stands somewhere in the background of our praise of public figures who present substantive arguments in the public sphere as well as criticisms of public sphere actors (particularly the media) that appear to be distorting and sabotaging this ideal. It is also a normative ideal that is good to keep in mind when thinking about and designing citizen consultation.

MINISTERS AND THEIR RESPONSIBILITIES

I turn now to Blakeney's observations about the role and function of political elites or elected representatives in a well-functioning democracy. I claim that something like this communicative model is implied here. In 1970 and again in 1980, Blakeney delivered the keynote address to the National Conference of the Institute of Public Administration of Canada. In both sets of remarks, published soon after in *Canadian Public Administration*, Blakeney laid out the proper relationship among three sets of actors: the public, the minister, and the deputy minister. We could also say more generically citizens, representatives, and experts.[*]

The minister stands between the citizen and the expertise of his bureaucracy and mediates the relationship. Let me take the expert first, though I will have less to say overall about this relationship. Blakeney insists that

---

[*] As a parliamentarian, Blakeney believes that ministers are "accountable" to the legislature and that members of the legislature are accountable to citizens. Allan Blakeney and Sandford Borins, *Political Management in Canada* (Toronto: University of Toronto Press, 1989), 196. But he admits that this traditional view of accountability is shifting in such a way that governments speak (and really ought to speak) directly with citizens. Thus, his discussion of ministers includes their democratic obligations *qua* representatives.

the minister must resist identifying with the expert and indeed becoming an expert herself. This is tough to do. First, one wants to do a good job and might think that diving into one's portfolio in order to become an expert is what is called for in order to do a good job. Second, it is simply hard to hold out against the expert. As Max Weber famously said, "the power position of a fully developed bureaucracy is always great, under normal conditions overtowering. The political 'master' always finds himself, vis-à-vis the trained official, in the position of a dilettante facing the expert."[5] But ministers must resist the power and indeed the allure of expertise. Experts and bureaucrats are guided by the twin goals of truth and efficiency. Political representatives are primarily beholden not to truth and efficiency but to citizens, and they cannot do that job if they are guided by the internal imperatives of efficiency and even truth. This might seem to be strange at first because we want our representatives to tell the truth and to base policy on sound knowledge (i.e., the truth). But being beholden to the truth means that it takes priority. Here the justification for a course of action is simply that it is true or objectively valid. But possessing the truth does not transfer to one the right to impose that truth on others in a democracy. The reason to pursue a policy in a democracy cannot simply or solely be that it is the right, good, or true policy. Administrators can be more like scientists; indeed, they can do a terrible job if they are not like scientists. This functional division of labour between ministers and deputy ministers or representatives and experts is crucial. "The minister must not allow himself to be drawn into detailed departmental planning. If he does, he is effectively co-opted, and this renders it almost impossible for him to sense when the public is unhappy with the department's program."[6]

The minister, Blakeney tells us, cannot perform his function if co-opted by the administration. And what is that function? The minister must act as an interpreter: "First of all he should interpret and explain policies of the department to the public....The minister's second main function should be to interpret to his departmental officials public reaction to the department's policies and degree of public acceptance which they are receiving."[7] To perform this dual function, "the minister must be attuned to the views of the public.... To be attuned to public views, a minister must have time and he must have opportunity to consult, circulate and to listen. He must be in a position of receiving signals from both the general public and the particular publics."[8]

The appeal to the idea of interpretation (as well as ideas of receiving signals and listening) conceptualizes the function and role of the minister in terms of communication. Here we see the first similarity between Blakeney and Habermas. Communication and a certain type of functional analysis lie at the centres of both pictures of democratic accountability. The minister stands at the centre of a two-way communication, one flowing from the public to the policy choice and design and the other flowing from the administration to the public. A minister's first function is to interpret public opinions and public preferences so as to communicate them to policy experts and implementers. Her function is to "bring the public's influence to bear on… senior officials.…Clearly the public has a right to have some input not only on the 'what' but on the 'how' of policy."[9] The public should have "influence" and "input" but not control. Independence of the minister from administration and expertise allows her to perform the function of guiding and steering bureaucracies according to democratic inputs. Only in maintaining independence from the administration can the minister maintain her "capacity to criticize (policy) effectively in terms of its public acceptability."[10]

The second function of a minister reverses this flow. Here the job is to interpret policy to and for the public. This is to be distinguished from "selling" the policy.[11] Administrators like the idea of selling. But we live in a democracy and not, as Blakeney tells us, a technocracy. This means that public acceptability constrains and limits policy development "even though from a technical point of view, and in the eyes of the officials who designed them, the policies which the public reject happen to be superior."[12] Nevertheless, members of the public are not experts, so they need to have policies interpreted to them. The minister tells them what is happening and why. She connects the actions of the government to the preferences and interests of citizens and engages in a broad and ongoing enterprise of justification, explanation, and reason giving. This interpretive function can also be understood in educative terms. The minister's job is to inform and educate citizens about policy initiatives and proposals. But it is important that ideas of education respect citizens as sources of democratic sovereignty and autonomy rather than recipients of paternalistic guidance.

So information flows in from citizens to administrators and flows out from policy design and implementation to citizens. The elected representative, or in this case the minister in our system, is the clearing house at the centre of this process. This (here is a vital point) implies an ongoing relationship of communication between elites and citizens. This relationship might have intense moments during elections when whole policy platforms are presented and defended, but just as important is an ongoing interpretive enterprise that presents policy to citizens and then listens for reaction and reception. Again this is not presented as a cynical selling or focus group testing. Blakeney presents this as an essentially democratic function of elected elites.

In his more extensive treatment of public administration, Blakeney discusses a number of institutional venues in which to pursue consultations with citizens. Central among the options are royal commissions, which Blakeney again envisions as a form of two-way communication. These commissions canvass the public for input and explain government action and policy output to citizens in a more direct manner.[13] I return to the communicative function of royal commissions below.

Throughout both essays as well as in his later book on public administration, Blakeney regularly appeals to the idea of "public acceptance" of policy initiatives as a necessary (but not sufficient condition) of good government.[*] "Good decisions by governments are ones that the public agrees with or at least can be persuaded to accept. And that in order to achieve this public acceptance, it is often highly worthwhile to offer the general public, and other special publics, the political space to make themselves heard."[14]

I want to flesh out what might be entailed in this idea of public acceptance. I want to ask more specifically what the function or role of the public and public opinion is in this picture. Blakeney writes from the standpoint of public administration in a democracy and not from the standpoint of democratic theory per se. Therefore, he is concerned primarily with fleshing out the roles of ministers and administrators with only the occasional remark about citizens and citizenship. He leaves open how much input or what sort of input citizens are to have in the process. I introduce three models of democratic input and ask which one best fits Blakeney's position.

RESPONSIVENESS

Democracy means being systematically responsive to citizens' needs and interests.[15] Robert Dahl also notes that "a key characteristic of a democracy is the continuing responsiveness of government to the preferences of its citizens."[16†] Certainly, Blakeney's depiction of the minister as consulting, circu-

---

[*] "The likely level of public acceptance for a decision is one of the tests of whether the decision should be made at all." Blakeney and Borins, *Political Management in Canada*, 193.

[†] As Andrew Sabl notes, this sentence is ubiquitously quoted in responsiveness studies, but Dahl himself had a complex view of democratic quality that went far beyond pure responsiveness. Andrew Sabl, "The Two Cultures of Democratic Theory: Responsiveness, Democratic Quality, and the Empirical-Normative Divide," *Perspectives on Politics* 13, no. 2 (2015): 346.

lating, and listening to the public advocates a form of responsiveness. But what sort of form? That governments and policy outputs should respond to citizens' preferences is a common sense view of democracy. It brings together the twin insights that, on the one hand, good government rules in the interest of the governed and, on the other, the governed should have a say about what is in their interest. But this view runs into problems when it is understood in a narrow causal way and taken to be the exclusive standard of legitimate and justified policy outputs. This appears, however, to be the view of responsiveness that has come to dominate the empirical study of democracy in the United States.[17]

G. Bingham Powell, in his 2012 presidential address to the American Political Science Association, championed the idea of governing responsively and understood responsiveness as a type of congruence in which there is a good "fit between the preferences of citizens and the committed policy positions of their representatives."[18] "Congruence" or "fit" rather than "respond to" or "listen to" subtly shifts the relationship between citizens and elites from an active political relationship to a passive abstract relationship. "Congruence" and "fit" can be measured in a way that "listen to" cannot. Empirical social science, in seeking ways to measure responsiveness, has conceptualized it as a statistical relationship between public opinion data and policy output.[19] Rather than seeking descriptive analysis of the mechanisms that might facilitate responsiveness or studying how elites might translate the messages that they are getting from the public, research on responsiveness often simply matches public opinion data with policy output.

Although this model of responsiveness contains some problematic assumptions about what democracy should be doing, research on responsiveness has produced a number of important and interesting findings. For example, in the United States, studies show that the interests and preferences of the business community show a higher level of correlation to foreign policy than do the opinions of the general public,[20] and the opinions of wealthy constituents line up more closely with a US senator's voting record than do the stated opinions and preferences of poorer constituents.[21] These studies cause us to pause and look deeper into the determinants of legislative policy preferences. But we should not take these studies as offering a plausible or persuasive model of the ideal relationship between citizens' opinions and policies.[22] Responsiveness studies that claim to measure the quality of democracy imply that the closer the correlation between public opinion and policy output the higher up the democratic quality scale a government or regime climbs.

There is something problematic about thinking that democracy is working best if policy simply channels citizens' unfiltered preferences as measured by survey research. What is the problem with this view? There are two types of criticism of responsiveness.* The first focuses on the problem of survey research, and the second focuses on the problem of unfiltered preferences as determinants of policies.

The first type of criticism questions whether survey data actually can or do get at citizens' preferences in any deep sense. Responsiveness, as I noted, is underpinned by a common sense view of democracy in which a *well-functioning* democracy pursues policies that speak to the needs and interests of citizens generally (as opposed to, say, the top 1 percent). Many people have begun to question whether survey data can reveal the authentic needs and interests of ordinary citizens. Some argue that opinions and surveyed preferences are deeply endogenous.[23] The survey instrument itself might shape the outcome, and there is growing evidence that subtle shifts in how questions are framed can result in huge shifts in opinion.[24] Perhaps all polls are a type of push poll. This is just the tip of the iceberg when it comes to the instability of public opinion.[25]

Another line of research focuses on how framing, priming, and media presentation affect public opinion in ways that come close to manipulation.[26] So again we might ask whether survey responses to public policy issues are evidence of authentic interests and needs. Another set of studies shows that opinions on political matters almost never reflect interests or even political preferences. Citizens are moved by affective partisanship all the way down, one might say.[27] This line of criticism leads to the second reason to reject responsiveness. Here the argument is not simply that survey data do not get at true interests and needs but also that citizens are poor judges of their own interests and needs. They are uninformed and have weak cognitive skills. This line of criticism is more normative and challenges the fundamental principle of responsiveness. Good government rather than responding to the opinions and preferences of citizens should shield policy from such influence. This is often referred to as the elite theory of democracy. But before I discuss this theory, let me briefly ask whether responsiveness captures something of Blakeney's view.

His picture of the relationship between ministers and publics does not look much like responsiveness as it is measured in this empirical strand of research. First, Blakeney seems to think that actual consultation and not

---

* There are many more criticisms of pure responsiveness. See Sabl, "The Two Cultures of Democratic Theory."

survey data is how to understand the public's needs and interests. Second, the minister clearly plays a mediating and interpreting role between citizens' preferences and public policies. This implies that good policy will not be directly correlated to public opinion since it will have been translated and modified in the process of interpretation. So here we might think that Blakeney's view has affinities with a more elite view of democracy.

ELITE THEORIES OF DEMOCRACY

From Plato through Joseph Schumpeter to Philip Converse and Larry Bartels, many thinkers have questioned the fitness of citizens to shape policy. Schumpeter's view is widely shared: "The typical citizen drops down to a lower level of mental performance as soon as he enters the political field. He argues and analyzes in a way which he would readily recognize as infantile within the sphere of his real interest."[28] Bartels recently noted that the empirical evidence is overwhelming that "the political 'belief systems' of ordinary citizens are generally thin, disorganized, and ideologically incoherent."[29] The problem here is not simply that many citizens are ill informed. The problem is that, evident from both opinion surveys and votes, citizens do not appear to have stable or coherent preferences. Their preferences track partisan cues, group affiliations, and well-established mindsets.[30]

From this perspective, then, the responsiveness view of democracy has two problems, one empirical and one normative. First, as noted above, it is not clear that public opinion data accurately reflect the real interests, needs, and concerns of citizens. Second, it is not clear that policy ought to respond to the attitudes and opinions recorded in public opinion data. This issue then leads naturally to an elite theory of democracy in which citizens' input is restricted to choosing elites in competitive elections. This view of democracy "focuses on elections as mechanisms for leadership selection" and not policy determination.[31] To be clear, this is still a democratic theory in two senses: first, good government governs (ideally) in the interests of all (and not in the interests of elites only); second, majority elections and regular electoral turnover comprise the institutional bedrock of the system.

There are a number of versions of the elite theory of democracy, but perhaps the most influential in Canada has been the view of democratic representation put forward by Edmund Burke and generally known as the trustee model of representation.[32] Burke famously told the electors of Bristol that he was elected because he had good judgment, and he planned to govern based upon that good judgment and not on the opinions of the electorate:

Certainly, gentlemen, it ought to be the happiness and glory of a representative to live in the strictest union, the closest correspondence, and the most unreserved communication with his constituents....And above all, ever and in all cases, to prefer their interests to his own.... But his unbiased opinion, his mature judgment, his enlightened conscience, he ought not to sacrifice to you.[33]

Come election time, constituents might call their MP to account, but Burke again insisted that the standard that constituents ought to use is that of reason and judgment, not whether or not the MP did their bidding or voted in the way that they would have voted. In other words, Burke was fully committed to ruling in the interests of his constituents, but he was not convinced that their preferences were necessarily the best judge of those interests.

Burke defended an elite view of democracy based upon the twin pillars that natural law could furnish the right answers to political questions and that only a few exceptional and talented men (an intellectual and ethical aristocracy) were capable of discerning natural law. Good judgments were not widely or equally distributed among men. Modern defenders of elite theories of democracy tend to dispense with the natural law as well as the natural aristocracy argument but nevertheless insist, as Schumpeter does, that "democracy does not mean and cannot mean that the people actually rule in any obvious sense of the terms 'people' and 'rule.' Democracy means only that the people have the opportunity of accepting or refusing the men who are to rule them."[34]

Blakeney also uses the term "accept," and, as we saw, the pure responsiveness model does not seem to fit well with what he says about the public's role in policy development. Does this elite model fit any better? There are two ways in which what Blakeney says does not fit the elite model. The first is that his focus is not on the election of elites but on the development of policies. Although ministers mediate public opinion as opposed to simply responding to it, it would be inappropriate for them to think of their electoral mandates along the lines of a pure trustee model, in which citizens' only input is throwing the bums out (or not) at the next general election. There is some level of substantive input into the policy process itself outside the electoral cycle. And that input is some form of public opinion.

The second way that this elitist model does not fit is that Blakeney explicitly rejects technocracy (and by extension a Burkean idea of aristocracy). He might be the first to admit that there are right answers to thorny policy problems. He might also admit that knowledge and judgment of these right answers are not equally distributed among the population. But what Blakeney appears to reject is that either of these facts can serve as a reason to restrict or exclude citizens from the policy process.

Elected representatives function as an elite. They govern and set policy and guide the affairs of state not as delegates but as independent individuals elected to use their judgment and skill in political matters. The existence of such an elite does not make a democratic system elitist in an objectionable way, however. The view that elites need to limit the substantive influence of citizens because their opinions are of poor epistemic quality, or are unstable or otherwise unreliable, is objectionable. It is objectionable because it rests on a slippery slope to technocracy and guardianship. It also confuses good government with correct outcomes rather than with legitimate outcomes. Blakeney understood this distinction and sought a middle ground between correct and legitimate outcomes.

I have argued that Blakeney falls into neither the responsiveness camp nor the elitist camp, and one might ask about the populist camp since some have seen Blakeney as a prairie populist.[35] "Populism" is a tricky term. To the extent that it is tied to certain types of economic policy and substantive ideological positions on the right or the left as opposed to a view of how democracy is supposed to work, it is orthogonal to my distinction. However, to the extent that it is deeply suspicious of a political elite and favours procedural constraints (e.g., recalls and term limits) that move representatives toward the delegate spectrum, populism looks more like a form of responsiveness. But prairie populism in the Canadian context, unlike the American version, though suspicious of a "power elite," did not involve a significant rethinking of the role of the representative. The influence of money and business interests in the corridors of power was to be scrutinized but could be addressed by putting the right sort of people (sympathetic to the common citizen) in those corridors, not in limiting the role of the representative. In many ways, the Canadian parliamentary system has insulated Canadian politics from the most extreme versions of this delegate form of populism, and Blakeney was a very committed parliamentarian.

COMMUNICATIVE MODEL: TWO-WAY RESPONSIVENESS

There is no doubt that a pure responsiveness model suggesting that policy should be designed and shaped, as a direct response to the opinions of citizens as expressed in survey data, is a problematic view of the appropriate relationship between popular opinions and policies. But one can acknowledge this fact without rejecting responsiveness in its entirety: that is, without adopting an elite view that attempts to shield policy from citizen input. I call this the communicative model, in which responsiveness as a democratic ideal is retained but with two caveats. The first caveat is the insistence that survey data are neither the only nor the best way to get at the real interests, concerns, and needs of citizens. This caution does not reject survey research as a source of information on citizens' views and concerns. Rather, it suggests that survey data are among a number of sources of information and that we should understand preferences as endogenous within a process of communication. I come back to this point below. The second caveat is that responsiveness itself is understood not in a causal sense but in a communicative sense. The question posed to representatives is not "can we draw a direct line between public opinion and your policy choices?" but "can you communicate and defend your policy choices in terms of public opinion (broadly understood)?" Let me explain and elaborate these two points.

Sidney Verba has argued that survey data can help in some little way in making citizens at the bottom of the social-economic ladder more visible to policy makers and representatives. The poor and marginalized are underrepresented in traditional forms of participation (voting, letter writing, and so on). They often lack the resources, time, and opportunities to avail themselves of the standard means to communicate needs and preferences: "This means that governing officials receive more information about needs and preferences from some parts of the public than others."[36] Thus, survey data can furnish representatives with information about the interests and needs of citizens from whom they might not otherwise hear. But Verba's endorsement of responsiveness to public opinion does not suggest that representatives should mechanically react to that opinion; rather, Verba takes responsiveness to mean something like "respond to" or "answer" or "speak to" or "ask about." It is a communicative response that these data call for and not an immediate policy response. Part of that communicative response is also about preference clarification. If preferences are incoherent, or if survey instruments cannot really get at them without shaping and influencing them, then it makes no sense to take these data as the voice of the people. But from there elitist theorists jump to the conclusion that most theories of democracy are about the causal transmission of people's preferences, so most theories of democracy rest on thin ice. However, if we see public opinion data as the subject of conversation and the topic of deliberation rather than as crude input, then there appears to be an escape from the vicious circle of unstable public opinion.

Public opinion for Habermas is not aggregated survey data about what individual citizens think about public matters.[37] Public opinions are opinions about public matters that circulate in the public sphere. This of course includes survey data, for survey results are constantly being appealed to and cited in public debates. But survey data comprise only one element in the ongoing communicative process through which public opinions are constructed. "Considered public opinions," then, are opinions about public matters that have circulated in such a way that they have been subject to reflection, criticism, and serious consideration *as* public opinions.[38] In other words, considered public opinion is not simply opinion that has benefited from information, thoughtfulness, and the exchange of ideas. This is James Fishkin's model of deliberated opinion polls in which participants' opinions improve after information inputs, exercises that promote thoughtfulness, and exchanges with people who have different opinions.[39] These three dimensions of what is conducive to considered opinion are not absent in the model by Habermas, but a fourth condition is just as important: the public should reflect on public opinions *as public* opinions, those that have implications for public policy.

Let me illustrate what I mean. Consider the recent debates in the American public sphere regarding gay marriage. The public discourse and polled public opinion have shifted tremendously in the past ten years. According to the Pew Research Center, in national polls in 2005, only 34 percent of respondents were in favour of legally allowing gay marriage, and ten years later that number had jumped to 55 percent.[40] There is no consensus on what caused this shift, and my intention here is not to make any such causal claim.* But it is not implausible to suggest that part of the story might be about a shift in the discourse from gay marriage as a question of individual preference (how do you feel about gay marriage?) to gay marriage as a question of rights (is it fair to withhold this legal status from gay people?). This can be understood as a shift in framing. But I suggest that this shift can be understood as a shift in how citizens looked at their opinions. From this perspective, we see the public opinion shift as a move away from having an individual preference about something (recorded in opinion surveys) and toward thinking about

---

* Although there is a large amount of data documenting the shift in public opinion, there appears to be no consensus on what accounts for this historic and unprecedented shift. Often the vague determinant of "cultural shift" is invoked as the underlying causal factor. Dawn M. Baunach, "Changing Same-Sex Marriage Attitudes in America from 1988 through 2010," *Public Opinion Quarterly* 76 (2012): 364–78.

that individual preference *as a public opinion*: that is, a position taken by a public that justifies public policy. In this view, people might still find the thought of gay marriage personally distasteful but no longer see that as relevant to the public policy question.

Considered public opinions, then, are not simply or primarily the results of individuals who reflect on their own preferences or gain information about an issue; they are opinions considered as the opinions of the public, as opinions shared by a democratic public. Here elites, especially elected representatives, play a central role in translating polled opinion into considered public opinion by reframing it into policy proposals that are then fed back into the public sphere for debate and consideration. This feedback itself has (or can have) an influence on the very opinion from which it was drawn.

The reflective character of public opinion implies that the relationship between citizens and elites ought never to be understood in a unidirectional way. This view challenges a standard model of responsiveness common in democratic theory suggesting that elites, and especially representatives, should respond to and act on the preferences and interests that come directly from citizens.[41] It also challenges the elite models in which the directional flow of information and influence is reversed and elite discourse gives content and substance to democratic agendas ratified by voters. In the reflective model of considered public opinion formation, there ought to be an ongoing flow of information that circulates throughout the system and between elites and citizens mediated by a responsible media.[42] The system as a whole is supposed to produce considered public opinion, even if every actor within the system is not equally informed. In this picture, "knowledgeable elites" have the role of rearticulating opinions that flow in from civil society into recognizable policy options or indeed as public opinions. But then this rearticulation must flow back into public debate for scrutiny and discussion.

Habermas argues that the informal public sphere can generate legitimacy only if "autonomous audiences grant feedback between an informed elite discourse and a responsive civil society."[43] In his picture of public opinion formation, knowledgeable elites have the role of sorting through claims, ideas, interests, values, and aspirations that flow in from civil society and translating them into recognizable policy options to be debated and assessed. These public debates among information elites have the dual function of "laundering" the opinions and packaging them in propositions or policies that can generate a yes or no response. The debates bring reason and reasoning to bear on policy matters but also present public audiences with public opinions for scrutiny and assessment. There is a feedback loop that requires two-way responsiveness from all participants. Elites (especially representatives and deputies but also other information elites) need to be responsive to the problems, concerns, and interests of citizens, and citizens need to be responsive to the information and persuasive arguments presented by elites. Considered public opinion emerges from the feedback loop.

Habermas is a political philosopher who works with abstract and generalized concepts in order to lay out what he thinks are the major building blocks of a democratic system. In particular, he is interested in the relationship between the public sphere and government action. This relationship is conceived in communicative terms and works best when there exists a healthy feedback loop. Habermas is the first to admit, however, that our public sphere rarely works at its best, and this feedback loop often fails to appear. Nevertheless, we can see its outline in a number of places and institutional venues. I suggest that one place where the feedback loop can be seen is the royal commission as described by Blakeney.

He notes that most people think the primary function of a royal commission is to gather information that is then used in the design and implementation of policy. But Blakeney says that actually the larger and more important function reverses the flow of information and communication. Royal commissions offer articulations of policy that are then communicated back to the public. The communication, in turn, shapes public perceptions of the issues in question. Again we see the educative function of consultations. Blakeney offers a number of examples of this two-way responsiveness; I will discuss two of them here. In 1940, the Rowell-Sirois Royal Commission on Dominion-Provincial Relations recommended the introduction of equalization payments among the provinces. This policy was the result of collecting a great deal of information, much of which was economic but some of which was opinion/consultation based. Blakeney points out that the importance and influence of the commission did not end with the recommendation to adopt this policy. If anything, it was only the beginning. The importance and influence of the commission continued in how its recommendations filtered back to citizens to become a solid plank in Canadian public opinion. "So well established has the idea (of equalization payments) become that when the principle was included in the Constitution Act in 1982, virtually no public debate resulted."[44]

The second example that Blakeney gives is the institution of universal comprehensive medical insurance. The product of the Thompson Committee report from Saskatchewan and the Hall Royal Commission report at the federal level, the health-care system has come to be an integral part of Canadian infrastructure. It is also a fixed part of Canadian identity and public opinion. In speaking more generally about royal commissions, Blakeney says that "in some cases legislation flowed from these reports; in all cases the reports shaped the public dialogue."[45] Royal commissions not only consult the public but also influence and educate the public; they often "shape the public perceptions of issues and (inform) the subsequent debate."[46] This strikes me as exactly what Habermas is talking about when he calls for feedback loops between elites and public opinion formation.

I introduce Blakeney's discussion of royal commissions not to suggest that they hold the template for democratic renewal but to show that Blakeney understood citizen consultation as a two-way communication. Successful commissions hear from the public, but they also influence and inform public opinion formation. This was the hope of the Bouchard-Taylor Commission, for example. It set out to hear what Quebecers had to say about the accommodation of religious pluralism. But the commissioners were not court stenographers dutifully recording the opinions as input. The hope of the commission was that the public airing of opinions, a public debate about those opinions, and public engagement among people of different opinions would have a mitigating effect on some forms of religious intolerance as well as move public opinion forward toward a consensus. In this way, public policy develops hand in hand with public opinion formation. This view of democracy, then, encourages diverse forms of citizen consultation as a significant supplement to elections and opinion surveys. The model of two-way communication that I have been outlining here suggests that, rather than focusing on electoral turnout and whether representatives keep their electoral promises, we should be interested in studying the types of conversation that develop between elections and are incorporated into the policy process.

CONCLUSION

Allan Blakeney and Jürgen Habermas share two things (in addition to being social democrats). The first is the idea that representatives and political elites stand between citizens and experts and play a mediating role. Both have strong convictions that modern reason, science, and policy expertise can untangle thorny policy challenges and move us closer to the "right" answer. Both acknowledge, however, that democratic accountability requires that policy be justified to and accepted by citizens even when they do not have the expertise to judge policy fully. This leads to the second idea that Blakeney and Habermas share. Both understand the mediating role of representatives as a two-way communication—what Habermas calls feedback loops and Blakeney calls interpretation—between public opinion and government policy. Representatives are neither delegates enacting the preferences of citizens nor trustees acting simply in the best interests of the public with little or no direct input from the public. They are instead tasked with listening to and consulting the public in order to translate the authentic interests and concerns of citizens into policy options and then presenting those options back to citizens for their assessment and acceptance (or rejection). This is often a long-term process that cannot be measured in one or even two election cycles, as the two royal commissions introduced above make clear. This process is best understood as a communicative and not a causal one.

PART 2
BLAKENEY'S CONSTITUTIONAL LEGACY

CHAPTER 5

ALLAN BLAKENEY AND THE DIGNITY OF DEMOCRATIC DEBATE ON RIGHTS

Dwight Newman

It is an honour to participate in this volume on Allan Blakeney and democracy. I first joined the faculty at the University of Saskatchewan College of Law in 2005. Over the subsequent years, I had the privilege of speaking often in our faculty lounge with Blakeney in his role as scholar-in-residence and of being able to draw on him as a guest speaker in my first-year constitutional law class each year. The conversations that arose often related to constitutional jurisdiction over natural resources and, indeed, were the initial seeds of my book on that topic.[1] They also often related to various features of Canada's constitutional amendments in 1982, including the *Charter of Rights and Freedoms*, and it is an aspect of this latter topic that I address here. I argue in defence of a Blakeney position that many Blakeney supporters have often opposed.

Having referred to the past, though, I want to start this chapter in the future—not in some distant utopian or dystopian science fiction but in a plausible near-term future. Suppose that it is 2023. One of the cases that the Supreme Court of Canada hears that year is a constitutional challenge to Medicare arising from a case brought by Brian Day's Cambie Surgery Clinic and heard at trial in a set of proceedings beginning in 2016. The case concerns an argument that Section 7 of the *Charter* concerning "life, liberty and security of the person" is violated by denials of access to private health care.[2] The court has decided in favour of that argument. In doing so, it has drawn on the judgment of Chief Justice Beverley McLachlin and Justice John Major in the 2005 *Chaoulli* case,[3] which identified a breach of Section 7 of the *Charter* in a system that imposed excessive wait times on patients without permitting alternatives. That judgment was supported by only four out of nine justices, but a fifth justice did draw the same conclusion based only upon Quebec's separate *Charter*. However, the court has also drawn on other cases concerning the ever-expanding Section 7 of the *Charter*, including the Insite drug injection site, the legalization of prostitution, and assisted dying.[4] In effect, two Canadian symbols—the *Charter* and Medicare—have met on a battlefield.

This day was foreseen. Over several pages of his memoirs, Blakeney discusses the judicial expansion of Section 7 of the *Charter* that took place rapidly after it was enacted, in judicial defiance of the intention of the drafters.[5] Chief Justice McLachlin's view of Section 7 in the 2005 *Chaoulli* decision, he recounts there, amounted to an unintended judicial implementation of a view that "the courts would use the words in section 7 to erect some general supervisory role over all governmental activities."[6] Decisions made about Medicare significantly affect the life and security of each individual, and McLachlin's view on Section 7, as I have described it elsewhere in articles shortly after the court's Section 7 decisions on injection sites and assisted dying,[7] tends to apply a highly individualistic analysis. Within this analysis is a judicial tendency to identify significant adverse effects from the legislation on just one individual and then to strike it down on the basis of gross disproportionality between these effects and the typically underdeveloped aims of the legislation. So in this situation envisioning a plausible future, suppose that Medicare's restrictions on private medical care have now run afoul of the court's interpretation of the *Charter*.

The question both for social democrats and for others is whether in this scenario—whether ultimately realized in that exact form or not—it would or would not be legitimate within Canadian constitutionalism to contemplate the use of the notwithstanding clause in Section 33 of the *Charter* so as to override such a judicial interpretation. Can there be a debate on the merits of the policy issue and use of Section 33, or is that discussion simply off limits?

The Section 33 clause permits Parliament or provincial legislatures to enact any given piece of legislation notwithstanding the rights guarantees contained in Section 2 and Sections 7 through 15 of the *Charter*, subject to that use being renewed every five years.[8] That five-year term corresponds to the maximum term of a Parliament or Legislative Assembly and thus effectively asks for each new Parliament or Legislative Assembly to reconfirm any such use. The sections referenced relate to the fundamental rights, legal rights, and equality rights that affect everyone, but the clause does not allow an override of democratic rights themselves (Sections 3 through 5), mobility rights (Section 6), language rights (Sections 16 through 23), or Indigenous rights (Section 35, outside the *Charter* itself).

Premier Blakeney was one of the main proponents of this notwithstanding clause, but it had flowed from an approach to constitutionalism different from that of the federal New Democratic Party and many of his own supporters. Here I revisit his reasons for supporting the notwithstanding clause and argue that they reflect his broader democratic commitments and fit with certain strands of broader democratic theory that often receive inadequate attention in academic and elite discourse.

In his later years, Blakeney offered an extended scholarly account of the notwithstanding clause.[9] I will draw here on his defence of the clause and build upon it, showing how his argument fits with a broader argument about democratic theory. In doing so, I offer three arguments on why the notwithstanding clause ought to be considered a vital defence of the democratic traditions to which Blakeney was committed and that have been imperilled by governments that sacrifice democracy to the *Charter*. First, I draw on his argument concerning conflicts of rights that arise from judicial enforcement of the *Charter*. Second, I draw on an argument from a leading political theorist, Jeremy Waldron, that I suggest fits as a logical extension of Blakeney's argument. Third, I suggest that an underlying element of both of these aspects concerns the diminishment of citizens themselves if they do not maintain authority over the Constitution relative to the nine elite lawyers who make up the Supreme Court.

BACKGROUND: DELEGITIMATIONS OF THE NOTWITHSTANDING CLAUSE

In more recent decades, the Section 33 notwithstanding clause has been seen in some quarters as something not to be contemplated, so much so that Prime Minister Paul Martin in the 2006 federal leaders' debate suddenly indicated his intention to press for repeal of the clause. This debate posture was startling in many respects, not least in suddenly focusing on an issue not at the forefront of public attention at the time. Nonetheless, Martin seems to have thought that there was some traction to be gained on the issue.

As members of a brokerage party, the Liberals had actually politicked with the notwithstanding clause before this moment. Interestingly, the only two prime ministers known to have promised to use the notwithstanding clause in some circumstance were Paul Martin and Pierre Trudeau, notwithstanding the general opposition both purported to have to the clause on other occasions. Martin had promised in 2003 that he would consider using the notwithstanding clause to protect the right of religious freedom in the context of legislating same-sex marriage.[10] Trudeau, in private communications with the Catholic archbishop of Toronto, made a definitive commitment to use the clause to prevent the courts from dictating abortion policy were they ever to strike down Canada's abortion law.[11] This sort of posturing on these issues might strike some as one reason to be concerned about the notwithstanding clause, and indeed the possibility of politicking on rights is part of the case that a defence of the clause must meet.

The argument for the notwithstanding clause is not particularly popular in the circles of constitutional law academia. It would be overly cynical to suggest that this is perhaps partly because constitutional law academics prefer that their views on the interpretation of rights prevail over those of the public. It also would be a mistake to suggest that there have been no defences of the clause, for some academic constitutionalists have both offered accounts of it in at least partly favourable terms and shown, at a practical level, that the clause has been used more than sometimes assumed.[12] Moreover, recently, Guillaume Rousseau has offered a distinctive account of the clause among Quebec constitutionalists who see it favourably.[13]

Nonetheless, the dominant trend in academic commentary has surely been skeptical of the clause.[14] In a later iteration within this vein, in a 2007 article, Professor John D. Whyte—who, along with Howard Leeson and Roy Romanow, worked alongside Blakeney during the patriation debates—argued that the notwithstanding clause had fallen into disuse and become less than legitimate.[15] In effect, Whyte argued, the notwithstanding clause had ceased to be part of Canada's political and constitutional culture. Also making a normative argument against the clause, Whyte reiterated broader themes of its critics, expressing concerns about the imposition of majoritarian positions and the absence of potential for judicial mediation if subject to legislative override. However, Blakeney maintained his position on the provision and published a reply in 2010 in which he defended the clause.[16]

One important final piece of background is that the notwithstanding clause was not some spur-of-the-moment invention during the final round of constitutional negotiations with the premiers in late 1981. It had been under discussion at the first ministers' meeting in February 1979 and again in mid-1980, meaning that there had been preliminary discussion that, as Barry Strayer puts it, made it "available" as a concept during the final discussions in November 1981.[17] Moreover, it did not simply originate in these discussions with the premiers but tracked text from the *Canadian Bill of Rights*, a quasi-constitutional statute enacted by the John Diefenbaker government in 1960.[18] It also built upon the same concept present in other related instruments, notably the *Alberta Bill of Rights* and the *Quebec Charter of Human Rights and Freedoms*.[19] The historical grounding of the clause has been unappreciated in much analysis and discussion of it and ought to receive more attention, along with the views of proponents of the clause during the negotiations, like those of Blakeney.

BLAKENEY'S ARGUMENT FOR THE NOTWITHSTANDING CLAUSE

Let us consider, then, Blakeney's argument in his 2010 article.[20] His argument implicitly rests on the view that there are moral rights—morally justified entitlements, whether or not they appear within the law—that go beyond legal rights embodied in the *Charter* and that we should be concerned with conflicts between moral rights and with not giving the upper hand to some rights over others simply because they are in the *Charter*.

Blakeney explicitly cites the example of a moral right to basic health care. He notes that this right is not in the text of the *Charter*. But he adds an important further element, suggesting that such a right cannot properly be put in the text because its proper enforcement is not through the courts.[21] Although his 2008 memoirs hint at his possible support for a positive social charter at some stage of Canadian development,[22] Blakeney seems to have had deeper concerns about such an idea at the time of the negotiations and subsequently. Indeed, contrary to recent tendencies in contexts such as the South African Constitution, in his 2010 article he suggests that any protection of such rights might give rise, at most, to a non-justiciable constitutional clause.[23]

Blakeney does not provide in that piece an extended account of the nature of moral rights that might properly compete with legally entrenched rights in the decisions of governments. He takes as a given, though, that there might be such rights, thus recognizing that the scope of rights can extend beyond those rights given specific legal expression. Such a position effectively recognizes that there might be fundamental interests of individuals that give rise to duties in governments, whether or not those interests are already reflected in particular legal norms.[24] These moral rights might be such that they can be implemented through a wide variety of different policies. However, their status as rights identifies them within the context of a government that operates in a democratic tradition as having a particular priority, such that morally they ought to be implemented, even in the context of competing distributive claims. Blakeney uses the example of basic health care and suggests that governments ought to implement it through policy in priority over merely distributive choices. But saying as much does not avoid all of the complex considerations that can arise when rights are in conflict with other considerations, as Blakeney recognizes.

According to him, the *Charter* not only actually but also inherently leaves out some moral rights. His argument is that legislators and governments need to be able to work out ways of implementing those rights without interference from the courts' interpretations of those rights within their *Charter* ambit. In some circumstances, Blakeney argues, the defence of a basic moral right that is not in the *Charter* might even require the limitation of a right that is.[25] Sometimes Section 1 of the *Charter*, which permits limitations on rights subject to a justification analysis, will be a sufficient means of finding an appropriate reconciliation. However, Blakeney argues, sometimes legislators might need to be able to act despite an interpretation by the courts operating within their limited perspective. The means of doing so, when necessary, is the notwithstanding clause.[26]

Another key supporter of the notwithstanding clause in the patriation negotiations in 1982 was Alberta Premier Peter Lougheed. Like Blakeney, Lougheed offered a more recent explanation of his support of the clause. Much of his argument focuses as well on potentially different interpretations of rights.[27] Although some of his concern no doubt stemmed from different ideas about the appropriate interpretations of certain rights, the coalescence of his argument with Blakeney's highlights the deeper democratic roots of their political statecraft.

The published version of Blakeney's 2010 article was significantly shorter than the manuscript that Blakeney submitted to the journal. The shortening might have been justified on standard editorial and stylistic grounds but arguably had the unfortunate side effect of diminishing somewhat the historical record on Canadian constitutionalism. Fortunately, the original version that Blakeney submitted still exists and was provided to me by the journal. In that version, Blakeney roots his thinking in an even more extended reflection than in the final version on the origins of the Canadian system of government, tracing (albeit briefly) the continuation in Canada of ideas from Greek and Roman democracy, the British parliamentary system, and various other aspects of the historical development of democratic government. Although accepting of the wider recognition in recent decades of the role of rights entrenchment in ensuring the better protection of some rights, Blakeney constantly returns in the longer manuscript to certain themes. They indicate that rights are complex, that they cannot be adequately reflected in lists of textually enumerated rights that might be enforced by judges, and that there must be room for the possible interaction of parliamentary views on rights with judicial views on rights.

Blakeney offers a scholarly account, albeit without necessarily referencing directly the pertinent writings on constitutional theory that ground his view. His vision is rooted, of course, in long traditions of political thought and was no doubt informed in some respects by his years at Oxford University. Yet it is also an account that fits with political practice. Indeed, Blakeney's memoirs reflect his participation in the constitutional talks in 1982 grounded in very similar ideas concerning the role of democracy and parliamentary sovereignty in advancing the interests of citizens and the social democratic vision.[28]

Insofar as Blakeney's thought and practice reflected these ideals, they might well help to demarcate some distinctive aspects of social democratic thought on the Prairies, where Blakeney had moved immediately after his years at Oxford to participate in the policy process within the Tommy Douglas government.[29] The ideals of Canada's prairie social democracy have been of widespread interest and deeper engagement,[30] so this particular thought must remain a side note here. More significant for my purposes is the second claim, that Blakeney's thought on the notwithstanding clause, even if not directly citing the scholarship, is consistent with a broader trend in scholarship on political theory, particularly as embodied in the work of Waldron.

DEMOCRATIC PARTICIPATION AND THE NOTWITHSTANDING CLAUSE

Jeremy Waldron now holds a University Professorship at the New York University School of Law but recently occupied the Chichele Professorship of Social and Political Theory at Oxford University, which has also hosted intellectual luminaries such as Sir Isaiah Berlin, Charles Taylor, and G.A. Cohen. Waldron is one of the world's most prominent legal and political philosophers, and some of his work has shown why legal philosophy justifications of the role of courts in reviewing legislation for compliance with constitutional rights are subject to fundamental objections from political theory on democracy. Waldron's thought, I suggest, has a closer fit with Blakeney's conception of the notwithstanding clause—and, indeed, with his broader political thought on democracy—than might have been realized. Whyte's article,[31] to which Blakeney responded,[32] engaged with Waldron but in relation to a book chapter in which Waldron commented directly on the notwithstanding clause.[33] However, his comments there were relatively limited and might not have fully reflected other aspects of how his own political theory might have further things to say on the notwithstanding clause.

In his classic piece "A Rights-Based Critique of Constitutional Rights," Waldron argues that placing some rights beyond democratic discussion has the procedural effect of diminishing another basic right, that of democratic participation.[34] There is, Waldron suggests, the basic right "of ordinary people to participate on an equal basis in public decision-making,"[35] and this is a core right within a democratic tradition, what he is ready to call "the right of rights."[36] This deeper theoretical underpinning on democracy and judicial review has much to say on the notwithstanding clause in line with Blakeney's thought.

In Canadian circumstances, if judicial rights outcomes are taken as determining questions of policy on which there would have been reasonable room for disagreement, then the views of judges are substituted for democratic dialogue and equal participation in public decision making. Without the notwithstanding clause, judicial decisions are final. The clause effectively serves as the last bulwark for what Waldron calls the right of rights.

Blakeney's 2010 argument highlights one of the bases giving rise to the potential for reasonable disagreement on the proper scope of judicially enforced rights. There will be moral rights beyond those in the list enumerated for judicial enforcement whose fulfillment might well be in some tension with those rights subject to enforcement through the courts. Blakeney's exposition of one of the bases on which Waldron's issues arise responds to the natural counterargument that arises to Waldron. The counterargument of some would be, of course, that ordinary men and women cannot be trusted to have dialogues on rights, that they act tyrannically through majorities to oppress their fellow citizens.

However, Blakeney's point that democratic dialogue can be responsive to social needs on moral rights not enumerated among those judicially enforceable has significant bite against this point, for likely those affected by social and economic policies are equipped to have dialogues on some of their consequences. Judges, drawn from the confines of a legal elite, might not have a better understanding of some of the real circumstances of the lives of their fellow citizens, and the law reports themselves are replete with problematic decisions.

Blakeney was not ignorant, of course, of concerns about how majoritarian democracy might abuse minorities. Rather, like Waldron, he always saw more potential in parliaments to protect minorities than those who have pushed for a larger role for the courts. Both draw on a deeper tradition of thought on parliaments that sees their open forum as one in which all interests can be put forward and in which there can thus be deep respect for minority rights. When properly functioning, parliaments allow full discussion of issues and represent fully the people—more so than courts given the ability to trump parliaments or any other single branch of the government. Here there is an implicit invocation of a deeper current of thought on parliaments, almost lost in the contemporary Canadian context, in which the ideal nature of the parliamentary institution has almost been forgotten, yet scholars writing on both pre-Confederation political dialogue and the debates on Confederation itself have recently done much to revive it.[37]

In some senses, Blakeney's argument fits with the stream of political theory represented by Waldron's thought, with Waldron thus being a worthwhile extension to Blakeney. Yet Blakeney's argument can offer a grounded perspective that is a worthwhile extension to Waldron. In any event, though Blakeney does not cite extensive scholarly literature, his argument is grounded in a solid stream of political theory on democracy and parliamentary supremacy.

EMPOWERING THE CITIZEN WITHIN ACCOUNTS OF DEMOCRATIC THEORY AND JUDICIAL REVIEW

Many constitutionalists effectively presume that citizens act in a way exogenous to the nature of the constitutional system itself. Such a view gives rise to the concept of constitutional design. Whyte, among others, employs that concept in suggesting that the tendencies of majorities to oppress the interests of minorities gives reason both for the entrenchment of constitutional rights and for the illegitimacy of the notwithstanding clause.[38] In some respects, democratic theorists such as Waldron or even democratic practitioners such as Blakeney have been too ready to acquiesce in these assumptions, effectively accepting that the question is what majorities tend to be like and then simply substituting a different exogenous answer on this point.

At the same time, though, the argument that democratic processes allow dialogues on rights can reflect a different relationship between citizens and processes than might first be assumed. Indeed, the nature of citizens' participation might be considered endogenous to the processes adopted for their participation.

In simple terms, the more one presumes the inability of citizens to be called on to engage in responsible discussions on rights and deep questions of morality, the more that inability can result. When citizens are told that they are expected to vote with their middle-class pocketbooks and to let the experts resolve questions about rights, that expectation can further a culture of political consumerism rather than a culture of democratic and moral discourse.

To say as much is to make an empirical claim, admittedly without providing the evidence for it, particularly a claim more difficult to prove in light of the removal of assumptions based upon exogenous variables that it would recommend to any empirical analysis. As an empirical claim, it would be subject to further testing. However, it has a basic salience with significant work on concepts such as trust and social capital, with some of that work increasingly showing negative effects on trust and social capital from the circumstances and policies of the contemporary Western state.[39] So, for the moment, relying on a claim that meets with agreement from political practitioners seems to be as safe as not.

That citizens face the responsibility of the role is not always as easy to facilitate, but it is vital. As Blakeney puts it,

> if citizens are encouraged to believe that somehow a constitution protects them and they no longer need to be vigilant about how our political system works, either to protect personal rights and freedoms or otherwise, then we will all be the poorer. If voters depart from the idea that democracy is about free people governing themselves and that constant vigilance is the price of liberty...then liberties are endangered.[40]

Telling people what the Supreme Court has said about rights, and perhaps even distorting it for one's own ends, are in many respects easier than talking with fellow citizens. In certain respects, it is easier to work one's will through legal manoeuvres than to persuade people around kitchen tables and on coffee row in advance of parliamentary debate. But each such act diminishes democracy. Each such act takes away from the moral responsibilities of citizens and thus from their inclination and effort to live up to them. Only in placing those responsibilities on the *demos* will the *demos* live up to those responsibilities.

The truth that Blakeney recognized is that judicial power degrades democracy and that the notwithstanding clause meaningfully protects it. The ultimate responsibility to make decisions on rights recognizes the dignity of fellow citizens in a way that ever-hollower judicial words about dignity cannot because it asks citizens to live out their lives in dignity rather than merely telling them about dignity.

So ultimately I stand with Blakeney on the claim that an effective, usable notwithstanding clause that allows a legislative override of rights better respects rights and democracy than its absence. This has not been a popular position in the legal discourse of Canadian elites. But it offers legitimate political choices about how to defend conflicting rights in the potential future scenario that I described at the outset of this chapter, maintains the fundamental right of democratic participation, and furthers a culture in which democratic participation remains expected rather than a quaint provision of a text ultimately to be forgotten.

The resulting prescriptions are more complex, though, than they might appear at first. It might be important for governments to find ways deliberately to use the notwithstanding clause, precisely to avoid arguments of its possible fall into disuse.[41] The clause has been used more than sometimes realized,[42] including the recent use in Saskatchewan in the context of a complex debate about religious schools and a trial decision that would have caused immense disruption while the government awaited an appeal decision in the case. The Doug Ford government came close to using it in Ontario recently as well, with its use avoided by the Court of Appeal staying a trial decision that would have disrupted a municipal election process—albeit in circumstances of complicated things one might say about the underlying decisions. However, arguments concerning its disuse continue to surface,[43] such that deliberate efforts to use it would be constructive in ensuring its survival.

Moreover, there are instances when its use would be relatively uncontroversial, and there is reason to begin with those uses. For example, the newly elected federal government applied to the Supreme Court of Canada in early 2016 for additional time to develop a careful implementation of the court's decision on assisted dying, on which the court had granted a suspension that did not give enough time in practical terms for parliamentary consideration of the issue, as pointed out by at least one constitutional scholar and by one of the justices of the court itself.[44]

Even such uncontroversial uses of the clause would have the salutary effect of immediately making clear that it is indeed something for Parliaments and Legislative Assemblies to contemplate. The likely effect is that they would become more engaged in discussing other rights outcomes where parliamentary interpretations of particular rights clauses differ from judicial interpretations. Over time, prudent use of the notwithstanding clause could increase, placing again more responsibilities on Parliaments, Legislative Assemblies, and citizens.

Yet there are powerful reasons in advance of or alongside such prescriptions to legislators for there to be much expanded discussion on democracy and the nature of parliamentary supremacy and Parliaments' duties to respect the rights of minorities. To the extent that those traditions have become submerged in an era of courts that assume judicial supremacy and others that acquiesce to it, parliamentary traditions and democratic traditions must be revived. The conference from which this book has stemmed is one contribution to this effort, but there must be much wider discussion and education on the democratic and parliamentary traditions that Blakeney held dear.

In a world in which democracies have occupied only a small fraction of space and time, the ideal of maintaining democratic traditions is one about which Blakeney's constitutional thought has much to teach us. His constitutional statecraft in support of the notwithstanding clause should remind us of some of the often forgotten value of that constitutional provision's abiding role in relation to democratic and parliamentary practice.

ACKNOWLEDGEMENTS

I am grateful for questions and discussions at the Blakeney Conference on Democracy from various individuals, including Brian Beresh, Sarah Burningham, Simone Chambers, Hugo Cyr, Dave McGrane, Ken Norman, Pat Paradis, Frank Quesnel, Reg Whitaker, John Whyte, Wanda Wiegers, Nelson Wiseman, and Norman Zlotkin.

CHAPTER 6

ALLAN BLAKENEY AND KEEPING DEMOCRACY'S PROMISE

John D. Whyte

There are competing views of the primary condition for achieving democratic governance. The first view is that both the holding of political power and the policies adopted by those with such power can be fully legitimated by the people of the state who give their consent through the mechanism of fair elections. Under this conception of democracy, holding and exercising political power is licensed through electoral success. The second view, perhaps less frequently recognized, is that the exercise of political power must be conditioned by the complex structure of attitudes, norms, and mechanisms designed to ensure that the primary condition that the power be based upon is the people's consent is genuinely, and comprehensively, satisfied. These two conditions of democracy are closely interrelated and, if seen to build upon each other, suggest that the bare practice of holding elections will not, on its own, meet the challenge of sustaining democracy's claim to legitimacy. Under this elaboration, democracy depends on following various norms of restraint and decorum that govern political debate over the choice of a state's political actions. Differing political preferences require that opinions be considered through open and respectful processes and that political resolutions occur through established formal law-making processes. Furthermore, policy choices and political actions need to avoid the suppression of political activity. They must not create discriminations, and they need to respect foundational commitments to due process and the fair treatment of individuals and groups.

Under these conditions, state action is to be taken within established constitutional—or quasi-constitutional—limits on political choices and be made subject to structures for holding democratic power holders to account for their choices. Implementation of state policies should be performed by politically independent and neutral governmental agencies and must be subject to the rule of law as administered through independent judicial review of governmental action. As Alexander Hamilton and James Madison stated in 1788, "in framing a government...the great difficulty lies in this: you must first enable the government to control the governed; and in the next place oblige it to control itself. A dependence on the people is...the primary control on the government; but experience has taught mankind the necessity of *auxiliary* controls."[1]

At its heart, democracy is a moral response to the totalitarian rule of a single person who has prevailed over all other competitors for power, or rule by a narrow and publicly unaccountable coterie of persons that has seized political privilege, or by someone who bases the holding of political authority upon an inherent entitlement or a God-given mandate. Democracy therefore entails political involvement of, and control by, the people of a state or at least by its enfranchised population, and it depends on ongoing reliable public information about the affairs of state. The ideal of legitimating power through popular consent can readily be corrupted if there are no substantive and procedural restraints on the exercises of power that will check claims of political power and clearly establish what holders of power are able to do and how they must do it. The statecraft challenge in a democracy is to establish a regime of political power based upon majoritarian rule that will avoid tyranny and prevent the exclusion from political participation of segments of the public through governmental adoption of unjust and discriminatory actions.

Although we often consider the "will of the people" to be the paramount condition of democracy, more so than the integrity of a complex political structure that restrains power, neither can claim to be the uniquely foundational idea of democratic government. For instance, in the formation of the Canadian nation in the 1860s, the idea of procedural and substantive restraints on government power was heavily adopted to help protect existing political communities. This was done through the constitutional structure of federalism under which constitutional protections were adopted to prevent provincial or national majorities from acting against the core interests of regional, religious, and linguistic minority populations. Furthermore, the significant constitutional separation of the three traditional branches of government—executive, legislative, and judicial—was established to ensure compliance with these limits on the exercise of political power.[2]

Constitutionalism is the principle designed to provide limits on power that reflect long-term, and possibly permanent, national commitments and concerns. However, national stability also depends on a nation's capacity for making changes to its constitutional regime. Nations periodically sense the need to develop new processes of political accountability, new constitutional protections for vulnerable communities, and the recognition of new values and practices. The actions of self-determining nations in revising constitutional conditions for the exercise of political power—both legally established conditions and those formed through convention—is as healthy for sustaining a good fit between political imperatives and government practices and structures as it is inevitable. It is the case, however, changes to the constitutional structures will normally be controversial since they produce shifts in power, create constitutional complexity, and abridge established political practices and prerogatives that the nation's population has grown used to and sees as both vital and sufficient to guarantee national well-being and identity.

Notwithstanding the rarity and controversy of making constitutional changes, significant and nationally redefining reforms to Canada's Constitution were adopted in 1982. Not surprisingly, some reforms were strongly contested.[3] For example, some government leaders considered that recognition in the 1982 constitutional amendments of Indigenous Rights would likely lead to the undue hampering of legislative prerogatives with respect to lands, regulations, and programs, whereas leaders of Indigenous governments and organizations (and many other citizens) considered the proposed form of recognition of Indigenous Rights to be unduly vague and likely to produce only weak reforms that would have uncertain (and likely minimal) effects. Likewise, some governments saw the process for making future constitutional amendments established in 1982 as undermining the foundational principle of Canada as having two founding peoples. Other governments saw in the amending formula that was adopted a far better reflection of federalism—one that would measure the support of the people as represented by both orders of government, recognize disparities in the sizes of provinces, and give provinces formal equality in measuring provincial consent. These amendments altered the conditions for the exercise of important political authority, and they produced a considerable degree of public attention.

However, the greatest degree of controversy generated by the 1982 constitutional amendment process came from the federal government's proposal to entrench, through the Constitution, basic human rights. This proposal raised directly and forcefully the question of whether the Constitution should establish essential conditions of liberty and justice for persons and groups that courts would enforce against parliamentary and legislative decisions that limited these values.

ADOPTION OF THE *CHARTER OF RIGHTS AND FREEDOMS*

As noted, the enactment of a constitutional human rights regime for Canada was the most contested feature of the 1982 constitutional reforms, and the subsequent history of the application of the provisions of the *Charter of Rights and Freedoms* has confirmed the importance of this reform. Placing the *Charter* in the Constitution has had a dramatic impact on government policy and on national political culture. Constitution-based judicial review of legislative policies has been a constant feature of Canadian governance since Confederation—preserving the structure of federalism and the independence and jurisdiction of superior court. However, the addition of the protection of human rights to the constitutional limits placed on governmental authority has driven Canadian courts, especially the Supreme Court of Canada, into the emotional centre of Canadian politics, subjecting public regulation to moral limits based upon basic concepts such as liberty, equality, and personal integrity and engaging the Constitution in the nation's treatment of its deepest social and personal concerns.

For more than a decade, Prime Minister Pierre Trudeau had put at the centre of his agenda for constitutional renewal the entrenchment of human rights, and from the earliest days of this proposal a majority of provinces opposed the idea. Neither the perennial rounds of federal-provincial negotiations on constitutional reform nor the clear growing public sentiment in favour of constitutional rights brought government parties closer to resolution or led to greater flexibility in their positions. After repeated failures to get federal-provincial agreement for a package of constitutional reforms, including the *Charter*, in October 1980, Trudeau decided to proceed on the basis that it would be constitutionally permissible for Canadian constitutional amendments to be enacted by the British Parliament acting on the request of the federal government alone, without the concurrence or consent of provinces. The strict legality of this process for bringing about constitutional amendment was affirmed, in due course, by the Supreme Court of

Canada, which, in a majority opinion, stated that provincial participation in requests to Britain for amendments was not a requirement under Canadian constitutional law.[4]

However, the court's opinion did not make securing constitutional amendments easier. Many members of the British Parliament believed that a unilateral federal request from Canada to Britain to enact amendments failed to respect the federal structure of Canada's Constitution. This view was bolstered by the collateral opinion of the Supreme Court of Canada that the constitutional convention in Canada was that Canada could not properly ask the United Kingdom Parliament to amend the Canadian Constitution without the substantial support of Canadian provinces.[5] Although the British government accepted Trudeau's claim that the British Parliament *could* enact amendments on the basis of a request of the Canadian government acting without provincial concurrence, many British parliamentarians considered it wrong to proceed over substantial provincial opposition. British parliamentarians opposed enacting constitutional changes over provincial objection so strongly that Prime Minister Margaret Thatcher informed Trudeau that he would need to base his request for British parliamentary implementation of the proposed amendments on broader provincial support before she would be willing to introduce the necessary implementing legislation. As a result, in November 1981, Trudeau was forced to convene a further federal-provincial conference, which, once again, would strive to find a plan to which both orders of government could agree. Since at this point there was general agreement on most of the other elements of the federal plan, the question of the constitutional entrenchment of human rights and the issue of the most suitable formula for future constitutional amendments took centre stage at this meeting. As before, the discussion on these matters, especially the constitutional recognition of basic fundamental human rights, was acrimonious and unproductive and federal-provincial agreement on constitutional reform seemed doomed. However, on November 4, 1981, the attorneys general from Canada, Saskatchewan, and Ontario, stepping away from the futility and anger of the first ministers' formal session, came to an agreement on terms that they believed represented an honourable compromise on the two outstanding issues of human rights and the constitutional amending formula.

With respect to human rights, the proposal of the attorneys general was that a full list of human rights and minority community protections be included in the new Constitution. But with respect to the three most basic, or universal, rights (freedom of religion, speech, and assembly and association; due process in decisions affecting vital personal interests; and equal protection of the law and equal rights under the law), it was provided that any legislature—provincial or federal—would be allowed to immunize its legislation from the judicial application of these protections simply through enacting that its legislation would apply and be constitutionally valid notwithstanding the constitutional provisions recognizing these rights. The textual implementation of this proposal is known as "the notwithstanding clause." This proposal broke the decade-old logjam over the constitutionalization of rights and, as a result, agreement on a limited package of constitutional reforms was reached. All of the governments, except that of Quebec, accepted these reforms at the November 1981 federal-provincial meeting. Soon after, the Canadian Senate and House of Commons approved the proposed constitutional amendments and passed a resolution asking the Parliament at Westminster to enact Canada's new Constitution. This Constitution was enacted and proclaimed in force in Canada in April 1982. In this way, Canada came to adopt a form of constitutional recognition for basic freedoms, due process, and equal treatment of the law; more firmly, the new Constitution entrenched, without the possibility of legislative override, democratic rights and constitutional protections for historical minority communities. This achievement was widely celebrated, not only because it largely—except for the notwithstanding clause—brought Canada within the modern constitutional orthodoxy of protecting basic rights and liberties, but also because it brought about the uncompromised capacity of Canada to amend its Constitution and, thus, achieved national self-determination for the first time in the nation's history. While it is the case that the identity of, and the terms of succession to, the Canadian head of state are typically determined outside Canada, Canada does have the power to bring this arrangement to an end through a unanimously approved constitutional amendment.

The sense of celebration over the *Constitution Act, 1982* and the *Canadian Charter of Rights and Freedoms* must be tempered, however, by Quebec's decision not to support the November 1981 constitutional accord. These important constitutional amendments were made without the unanimous consent of Canada's provincial governments. This failure represents an especially dark cloud since Quebec is the provincial inheritor of one of Canada's founding peoples. This taint on the legitimacy of the 1982 constitutional reforms has not greatly faded with time; it continues to represent one of the nation's most pronounced elements of division.

THE NOTWITHSTANDING CLAUSE

The notwithstanding clause was seen as a victory for those provinces that had opposed entrenching constitutional rights. Prime Minister Trudeau feared that this element of the *Charter* would lead to the erosion of the most important feature of constitutionalism—the protection of citizens from oppressive policies of the state. As a result of this compromise, the Constitution does not entrench, in the literal sense, the basic human rights of liberty, due process, and equality. It does create a constitutional presumption that executive action or legislation that abridges these rights would be unconstitutional, but it allows that presumption to be overridden by an explicit legislative measure declaring that an act, or a part of an act, shall not be subject to the courts' nullification by applying the *Charter* sections that recognize these rights.

During the period of federal-provincial constitutional politics leading up to the 1982 amendments, the most articulate opponent of the entrenchment of rights was Premier Allan Blakeney of Saskatchewan. He insisted that the supremacy of Legislative Assemblies and Parliament provided the safest and most accountable form of government for regulating personal conduct and ensuring personal well-being. For this reason, Blakeney was, and remained, a strong supporter of the notwithstanding clause.[6] It reflected his view that the collective wisdom of the people, measured in free elections and reflected in legislation, is a better and safer basis for holding elected governments accountable and for holding their coercive powers in check than is judicial application of the general and indeterminate texts of constitutionalized rights. However, this had not been his view with respect to conflicts between the Constitution and the decisions of legislatures in other contexts. In conflicts over the application of the constitutional division of legislative powers, Blakeney had aggressively used the courts to challenge erroneous claims of constitutional powers. In that context—admittedly a very different context—he accepted the necessity of this element of judicial control of popularly elected legislatures and relied on the principles of constitutional limits on legislatures and governments to protect provinces and minority communities from overbearing political ambitions of legislative majorities. Furthermore, Blakeney was not opposed to the judicial enforcement of constitutional terms that guaranteed the role of courts in preserving the rule of law.

He was not, however, convinced that judicial supremacy with respect to basic human rights was an appropriate means for promoting liberal democracy. This view was based, in part, upon his confidence that democratic populations will make wise choices, if not in every moment of political difference or conflict between competing interests, then at least over a longer period of debate and reflection. Blakeney believed that the population of a democratic state would not unreasonably cling to ignoble purposes or ungracious attitudes toward minority communities or those whose speech, personal practices, and attitudes are at odds with the community's ideas of "sound" thinking and "responsible" behaviour. He held that, when the public bore the ultimate responsibility for preserving the good state, it would accept different identities, languages, values, and practices and recognize the social enrichment that comes from the acceptance of diverse communities. Blakeney believed that legislators are capable of recognizing the commonality that lies below division: the human need to be treated justly and not be made a victim of state favouritism and discrimination. He considered the historical Saskatchewan experience of accommodation of ethnic diversity, early recognition of human rights, and adoption of policies of social support for all citizens as proof of the inexorable tendency in democratic politics toward granting equal justice to all.

On the other hand, Blakeney was concerned that, generally, judges were socially and economically situated to reflect the values of the privileged. Therefore, under a regime of entrenched rights, a pattern would emerge of courts' applying rights in a manner that favoured those in society who were already favoured and ignore those for whom state protection ought to be more compelling. He also feared that, once a decision relating to a constitutional right was made, it would become fixed and could not be altered as social values changed and as new social imperatives emerged. Blakeney had greater confidence in the social and moral dynamism of the people than in the values of courts and judges. His view reflected a historically located cultural assessment of judges and jurists as well as his own cynicism about (some) judges' social understanding and intellectual subtlety. He held that, since legislatures were comprised of people from many walks of life, this gave them greater social wisdom than could be found in courts made up of persons bound by the experiential limitations of lawyers. He believed that the diversity of members of legislatures would lead to wiser and more inclusive accommodation of social differences.

Blakeney worried that constitutional texts that set out human rights would necessarily be so general that they could not adequately restrain discretionary judicial power—that the indeterminacy of rights language would invite a broad and unrestrained exercise of personal convictions and biases, not principles of law. In short, judges' limited social experience would limit judicial understanding and the nature of constitutional texts would enable activist decisions.

Beyond these functional concerns, Blakeney feared the impact on democracy of the growing influence on government decisions and actions of strongly empowered experts and the waning influence of the wisdom and instincts of the people. This development, he thought, weakened political engagement by removing from citizens many questions of social and personal significance. Blakeney feared the consequences of removing from public and political discourse choice about the most needed social programs. His view was that democracy depends on the people's confidence in open processes in public government far more than on the solutions advanced by intellectually sophisticated specialists. He thought that removing political choice from the electorate would cause citizens to doubt the legitimacy of government and its roles of regulation and social support.[7]

Blakeney strongly objected to the narrow conception of rights that had animated the development of the constitutional recognition of rights. He saw the rights being proposed as negative rights—those that curtailed the government—and not positive human rights essential to well-being. He feared a regime in which the negative rights in the Constitution would operate to restrain government programs designed to meet people's basic needs and protect the socially and economically vulnerable. His enthusiasm for the notwithstanding clause was based upon its vital role in forestalling attacks on programs that, he feared, would be based on the *Charter*'s protection of personal liberties, or on its higher commitment to formal equality and equal treatment, or on economic conceptions of due process. Ultimately, the process of constitutional reformation culminating in the 1982 constitutional amendments adopted the Blakeney view on the centrality to Canadian constitutionalism of parliamentary sovereignty through inclusion of the notwithstanding clause and the ability that it gave legislatures to enact laws that could violate core provisions of the *Charter*. This political victory, however, has not been matched in the political life of the *Charter*. Only twice in thirty-six years has it been used to remove an apparent or a judicially determined abridgement of a *Charter* right: first, freedom of association in the context of a labour strike, and second, freedom of speech in the context of regulating commercial signs. And, for over a quarter of a century, it has not been used at all to block rights claims. There have been other threats to enact the override clause, but apart from the cases mentioned above and Quebec's omnibus override legislation enacted immediately following patriation, these pieces of legislation have not been put into effect. Thus, it might be thought that

Canada has achieved de facto, or conventional, entrenchment of constitutional human rights[8] with the legislative override seeming to stand outside a common conception of how the Canadian state operates. It could be the case that the idea that the legislative body of a democratic state holds the power to determine conclusively the legitimacy of its laws as they relate to individuals' basic rights, due process, and the rights of vulnerable minorities might have lost currency in a nation that seeks to practise liberal democracy. It might no longer be possible to square the older political culture of unchecked majoritarian control of human rights with current conceptions of the just state. However, the claim that the legislative authority granted in the *Charter*'s notwithstanding clause has become spent through a long history of non-use was weakened by the rejuvenated currency of the clause in 2018. Quebec's premier threatened to use it to protect proposed legislation that would ban religious dress in the public sector from being challenged under the *Charter*'s protection of religious freedom. Saskatchewan enacted a notwithstanding clause to prevent the *Charter*'s protection of freedom of religion from being applied to the province's funding of religious schools. This legislation was not proclaimed in force. Ontario introduced legislation to block challenges, based upon the *Charter*'s protection of freedom of expression, to the legislative amendment of municipal electoral constituencies in mid-election. This legislation was never enacted.

Political expiration of the constitutional power to override the *Charter*, if it were to occur, could also result from the structure of the constitutional text. The 1982 Constitution contains provisions that clearly protect human rights from oppressive policies of governments, but it also contains an interpretive clause that invites courts to hold in favour of governmental regulations and their restrictions on rights whenever a case can be made for the impairment of the right, on the basis that reasonable accommodation of governmental policy is necessary in order to protect a highly valued social or public goal. It might be that there has developed—or will develop—the view that, if a government believes that there is good reason to limit a *Charter* right, it should make that case, not as a matter of legislated edict by a body generally under governmental control, but before a court where governmental and legislative claims of necessity, or proportionality between right holders and public interest, can be examined critically and neutrally.

From Blakeney's perspective, including the notwithstanding clause in the 1982 Constitution reflected fears that courts could make decisions that eroded the capacity of legislators to adopt socially beneficial (or necessary) policies. It is a common concern in constitution making that the powers and protections being adopted will prove to hamper governments in responding to dire conditions and existential threats. This sort of fear arose with respect to provisions of the 1867 Constitution; as a result, that Constitution included special and irregular powers allowing Parliament to override provincial powers, and to displace provincial laws, when Parliament considered doing so to be necessary for the national good. Such federal powers are no longer exercised and, as a matter of constitutional convention, no longer available. The political reality is that the deeper value, over time, becomes maintaining government legitimacy by adhering to basic constitutional structures and not the usurpation of power based upon the claim that constitutionally assigned powers are inadequate or are being exercised irresponsibly. Mature liberal democratic nations do not enable the usurpation of established powers and structures, even when their constitutions grant that capacity.

Characterizations of the virtues of government institutions, estates of power, and social effects of regulation are inevitably based upon personal ideas about appropriate power and authority—ideas about the right roles for and the right structures of government. Blakeney subscribed to a particular ideal of ultimate authority in democratic government, and he held a particular belief about the social tendencies of those with the privileges of wealth and political and social status. But, in truth, there is no final answer to the questions of either ultimate state purpose or necessary and prudent political structures. In structuring political accountability in particular, the tension between respect for the wisdom of the majority in determining what best serves the polity and fear of political harms to the state when individuals and minority communities are tyrannized by majorities is constant and basic. Blakeney joined this foundational debate and brought to it both established principle and conviction. He also brought a specific sense of the right lesson to draw from the history of democracy and of the terms under which it will produce a sound political practice for nations and their peoples.

DEMOCRACY AND ENTRENCHED RIGHTS

Democracy is political theory's best answer to the problem of the legitimacy of political power. The moral challenge is inherent in the exercise of coercive power by states: the power to compel citizens to act in prescribed ways and to impose penalties and punishments when they fail to comply with laws and orders. The legitimating condition ascribed to democracy is based upon the consent that the members of the state, in aggregate, give to the actions of the state. Although this notion of consent does not include the consent of each individual to state restrictions on his or her freedom, democracy is rooted nevertheless in the core idea of personal autonomy, and it is that ethical assumption that justifies the requirement that there be a general public consent to actions of the state.

All states, including democracies, must take corporate actions that will necessarily abridge the preferences and impair the liberties of the many persons who have not given their approval to the states' political rulers or consented to their rules and orders. This tension between personal freedom and state order is inevitable. The absence of personal consent to power has troubled political philosophy for millennia. Long before liberalism became an established political philosophy, the idea of a free citizenry, and the cognate idea of political self-determination, emerged as a conception of the essence of humankind. Free choice as an essential human value has driven the growth of democracy and, simultaneously, its refinement into liberal democracy. Thus, democracy has become increasingly controlled by an array of conditions for the exercise of political power, including restrictions on governmental interference with liberty and other protections against state rule.

The moral issue in democratic government arises from the combination of diversity in interests and preferences and the necessity in governance for unity of state purposes and methods. This tension cannot be resolved by assuming away diversity of personal and community identity; by denying the social relevance of factors such as ethnicity, religion, sexual orientation, and (dis)ability; or by minimizing the variety of human needs, conditions, and preferences. Recognition of such differences fuels much democratic political theory and discourse, and the accommodation of such differences shapes much public policy. Democracies wisely do not assume an exhaustive commonality in organizing state practice and regulating conduct. Nor do they assume that every element of governance should be made contingent on the precise condition of each person. We do not, for instance, apply different rules of highway use for those whose lives are governed by frenzy compared with those whose habits are to plan ahead and remain calm.

The aspiration of liberal democracy is to achieve a workable balance between addressing personal conditions and needs and valuing uniformity of regulation for all people and all circumstances. The moral challenge is in reconciling the presumption that a state's power properly applies generally, even to those who have not consented to it (or to its exercise), and the contrary idea that, when individuals' moral entitlements are not taken into account, any law may impose unjust burdens on some persons in some situations. In resolving this tension, democracies, like strong forms of despotism, can adopt the sets of resolutions that create tyrannies, unjustly taking away valued liberties, basic well-being, equal respect, and personal dignity. Although democratic majorities might claim that granting exemptions from the law, for whatever reason, will violate both democracy's efficacy and its commitment to equality, it takes no imagination to recognize that legitimating all exercises of state power, no matter the case or circumstance, on the basis of majoritarian consent, will bring about the exercise of this power that deserves fear and condemnation as an imaginable form of political oppression. Democratic governments that base legitimacy solely on majoritarian support can deprive people of property, possessions, liberty, family, dignity, voice, and even life without the restraints of justice or due process. They can become the embodiment of political tyranny.

This potential outcome of democratic government does not arise only in states that have cynically used the label "democratic" in order to legitimate to their citizens, and the world, their exercise of state power that represses and victimizes minorities, the economically exploited, and political opponents. In all democracies, there can be strong factions that pursue specific political and economic interests, condemn some part of the population to destitution, seek favour for their ethnic and religious communities, harbour deep grievances against minority communities, and attempt to punish those whom they think have undeservedly benefited from favourable treatment. Such factions can gain power and exercise it against groups that the state had sought to include in national well-being.

A democratic state will value, of course, the principle of the general application of laws—the ideas of equal justice and commitment to the equal dignity of all. But working out these ideas needs to be tempered with the recognition of distinct histories and circumstances. This requires the subtle calculus of meeting both justice and political stability. In this process, there is always the possibility that democratically chosen governments will abandon the protection of minorities and allow the interests of the majority faction to prevail. It is not surprising that the currency of democratic competition then becomes anger over the failure of governments to accommodate diverse interests, markedly distinct conditions, or differing historical experiences of groups and peoples.

Intense competition between communities—and communities of interest—that turns destructive is a long-standing concern for democracies. One response to this concern about the vulnerability of democracy comes from debates on the adoption of the new United States Constitution agreed to at the convention held in Philadelphia in 1787. The new Constitution required ratification from the thirteen states of the United States, but this was not a certain thing. Those who wished to keep substantial powers in the hands of the former colonies fiercely opposed it. The case for adopting the new Constitution was made in essays collected together as *The Federalist*. James Madison, one of the authors of these essays, in "The Federalist No. 10," pointed out the risk to democracies of strong political factions, which he described as "a number of citizens...united and actuated by some common interest, that, if pursued to the exclusion of compromise, will injure the interests of others... and, ultimately, would destroy the polity as much as any unchecked tyranny would do."[9] He feared that "measures are too often decided, not according to the rules of justice and the rights of the minor party, but by the superior force of an interested and overbearing majority."[10] For Madison, the essential condition of democratic government was the ability to check the tendency of majorities to sacrifice weaker parties, unpopular persons, and causes with limited appeal. The route for checking the effects of majority factions that Madison favoured was to take advantage of the barriers to constructing a majority-fuelled program for political domination that, he argued, would be present once the polity became the size and diversity that the new republic was bound to become. If this essential restraint on the majority is to be effective, he argued, then the republic's governing role must be large and significant; only in a large and politically powerful republic with widespread public functions could partisanship be defeated by the competition among a population with diverse conditions, interests, and passions, and as a result the population would come to recognize the need for compromise.[11]

However, we cannot look at America (or Canada) today and be persuaded that oppressive factionalism and unjust majoritarianism will necessarily be defeated by the size and complexity of the nation or by the power of its central government. Perhaps size and national complexity provided a check against majoritarian tyranny in the 2015 defeat of the Conservative Party, stopping the apparent march of ideologically driven policies and the abridgement of democratic structures. And an anti-Trumpian mobilization in America could well demonstrate the inherent possibility of marshalling wider national interests to defeat factional hostility toward members of vulnerable communities. Nevertheless, in nations around the globe, the capacity to muster political idealism through accommodating national complexity and thereby guarantee to all the universal entitlement to full and equal participation in the benefits and protections of the state is highly questionable.

Although diversity and complexity in large nations can provide an answer to the deadly effects of majoritarian partisanship and the use of power to serve special interests, there is no reason to be confident that the iterative and complex policy processes of the modern democratic state will result in the correction of policies oppressive to unpopular minorities or the politically vulnerable. There is no certainty that state discrimination against vulnerable and unpopular minorities, imposed with the consent of a popular majority, can be reversed through the operation of a multitude of competing interests or through the process of citizen reflection on deeper and long-term national interests. Of course, social values do change, and the sense of appropriate restrictions on minorities does adapt, over time, to new conceptions of accommodation and new appreciations of the harms of injustice. But the ravages of exclusion and unjust treatment by the state are immediate; the subsequent development of a widespread appreciation of the injustice that oppressive policies have imposed on minorities often takes decades. As well, champions of justice face dangers, and fighting for justice takes rare political courage. Not only does the organic political development of popular recognition of harms to minorities take time, but also the period of experiencing oppression by distinct communities embeds deep social and economic marginalization that cannot be expunged simply by the later removal of oppressive measures and dwells in the polity as a social pathology. The harms to societies of victimized communities live on for generations, perpetuating exclusion and little opportunity and imposing on a nation the ruinous burdens of continuing unresolved intersocietal conflict.

There are other reasons for the lack of confidence in the tolerable timeliness of the development of political sensitivity to the long-term injuries to individuals and minorities imposed by oppressive regimes, such as colonialism, slavery, or simply highly structured cultural exclusions based upon race, gender, poverty, and sexual orientation. There is reason to believe that in political discourse—and in electoral mandates and subsequent state policies—there is no strong basis for faith in the development of a nuanced understanding of the character and interests of the groups or peoples (or, in Canada, the nations) that comprise the nation. This might be a reflection of the limited rhetorical possibilities in national elections; too easily they become centred on a singular or homogeneous national issue. The search for a politically compelling national interest drives political competition away from the nation's diversity, complexity, and specific needs and toward the adoption of simple national visions that can confirm the aspirations of many but leave behind the concepts of recognition, accommodation, and compromise. Instinctual appeals to a nation's general character—or its current grievances and needs—easily displace recognition of national complexity.

A further reason to be skeptical of the sufficiency of elected leaders and legislatures to secure stable and just nations is that we know from international studies of democracies that they are prone to failure when they become led by "strongman" rulers. These rulers—and in the world there have emerged many authoritarian elected national leaders—have two chief aims. They are to suppress political criticism and dissent and to retain power by disabling political opposition, especially from minority communities—typically, ethnically defined minority communities—and from an effective civil society. Enduring and just democratic states depend on a convergence of good state attributes such as the free and active political voices of diverse elements of the nation, the absence of an epidemic of violence, universal social welfare entitlement, control of corruption, and an inclusive and active civil society.[12] The last feature is particularly important to protect democracies from political repression of reformist political action and debate. The destructive imperative of the strongman state is to represent the elements of civil society and minority ethnic communities as subversive, corrupting the authority of the formal state. In such states, minority communities are campaigned against as promoting secessionist sentiment and threatening to break apart the nation. The suppression of voices from minority populations and from civil society serves to entrench existing power structures and is designed to do so in addition to rendering the state—democratic or not—static and unresponsive. Effective democracy simply cannot tolerate the suspension of the population's engagement with political reform. In this context, the preference for waiting for the development of greater political tolerance is mistaken; it defeats sound democratic practice and conduces to the brutal rotation of political supremacy, each stage of which is conducted through the suppression of all opposition. The failure to protect minorities, whether political or ethnic, produces instability that disables nations and oppresses citizens. Such suppression needs early and effective checking.

The claim of efficacy in resisting tyranny through a process of political enlightenment, without the aid of a regime of constitutional protection, is based upon seeing national integrity as deeply dependent on the strongest possible condition of state solidarity. There is, therefore, fear of weakening national stability through adopting legal protection for liberties and political entitlements of individuals and groups. However, a more serious peril to state stability is injustice to groups and individuals that is not redressed and the resulting isolation and demonization of minorities. The effects of this sort of national exclusion come quickly but heal slowly. The amelioration of the victimization of groups, or of those who campaign for political or social reform, through the development of social enlightenment, is a positive development wherever and whenever it occurs. It would be an error to deny that there have been such transformations in Canada's relationships with vulnerable minorities and dissident political movements. For those who suffer from oppression, the organic enlightenment arising from majorities who gain a broader perspective and greater maturity is a painfully slow transition from injury to redress. Although a nation can gain awareness of the unjust suffering of the politically vulnerable, we are in a far superior moral state when we choose to learn of our oppressions from the timely authoritative vindication of principles of justice that the nation has constituted and granted formal recognition and respect to those citizens through effective remedial orders.

The robust form of control of oppressive state policies that has emerged in democratic state formation since the middle of the twentieth century is the inclusion in national constitutions of both substantive and procedural limits on government and legislative action and the enforcement of these limits through an independent legal process. In the process of progressive nation building among a nation's historical communities and its diverse populations, we offer each other guarantees—essential guarantees of the continuance of distinctiveness and the affirmation of legitimacy. Such guarantees appear in constitutional texts. Constitutional law administered through an independent court system operating within a developed separation of powers is an effective way to preserve these essential elements of just and stable nationhood against abridgement by national majorities.

Canada, for example, has seen the costly consequences of denying, for centuries, the place of law in giving protection against national majorities.[13] Specifically, we have seen unaccountable governmental policies that have come close to destroying, for Indigenous nations, hope for and trust in the Canadian nation. Our history makes it difficult to place great hope in political goodwill, the longer-term calculation of national benefit, or a growing commitment to reflect honour in intersocietal dealings as persuasive instances of demonstration of the reforming virtues of majoritarianism, especially when that principle remains mired in the tropes of colonialism.

Canada's political history, at the level of overt national formation and definition, more so than in the context of ordinary political competition, has often acknowledged the limitations of political discourse and protracted reflection in correcting policies that would be oppressive to minorities. At Confederation in 1867, Canada adopted the idea of a French nation that would be made immune—at least in the important ways of preserving language, culture, and legal system—to the potential insensitivity and indifference of the national majority. The same degree of lack of confidence in the justice capacity of electoral politics is now evident in the recent experience of conducting relations between Indigenous and non-Indigenous people on the basis of legal inference from treaties with First Nations and on constitutional rights, not on the basis of political sensitivity to the terms and spirit of treaties. The notions of Indigenous Title, honour of the crown, the duty to consult, and the recognition of a regime of multiplicity of nations with governing capacity acting outside the pervasive authority of the Canadian state are all products of a justiciable relationship, not of incremental goodwill. In these areas, constitutionalism, in the context of recognizing a diversity of identities and creating a capacity for communities' continuance, is based upon constituting legal restraint and guaranteeing the powers that allow intrastate communities an effective measure of self-rule.

Apart from these largely prudential arguments for creating legal checks on the exercise of legislative and executive power, constitutional theorists sometimes justify constitutional restraints by arguing that they share a common ground of legitimacy with other majoritarian processes of law making. National majorities are as entitled to adopt basic principles of the state that will bind its operations through its many turns and seasons as they are to make laws that satisfy immediate needs and enact policies designed for current contexts. The argument is this: in self-determining nations, people are not limited to adopting policies that respond only to current situations. They are entitled to adopt more far-reaching and enduring policies that govern the very processes of law making or establish conditions that the exercise of government power must satisfy.[14] They can enact and make enforceable the higher law of the state's purposes and limits. It is anticipated in state formation that existing communities—whether political, ethnic, or both—will adopt legal and constitutional protections to preserve some traditional self-governing capacities and autonomy of cultural markers. These protections, when conceded, become an expression of majority will to accept limitations on majority power far into the constitutional future.

CONCLUSION

Perhaps the soundest democratic justification for constitutional protections and limits based upon forms of human rights and minority rights might be that they create a constructive *modus vivendi* with respect to questions to which there might be few morally trumping positions or prudentially superior answers. In particular, these are the questions that animate the broadest and deepest values of the population and touch on every person's idea of the good and in respect to which there is little reason to believe that common positions will be achieved through political dialogue, no matter how broad the citizen engagement. These are questions about things such as the integrity of identity, faith, just and equal treatment, reasonable accommodation, and personal expression. A regime of articulated rights will not deliver members of a nation from many of the losses of value and personal autonomy that politics imposes on many people all the time. And there are not state principles that will satisfy the moral understanding of each citizen. Nevertheless, the orderly and principled resolution of conflicts over state authority can underscore the core idea of liberty, and it will affirm the democratic ideal of citizen participation in acts of personal self-determination.

Our guiding understanding of society is that it is founded not on universally subscribed beliefs but on diversity. In the face of such diversity, our basic political good can be grounded not on arriving at the right answers to all of society's challenges but on peaceful coexistence even when there are deep disagreements. We can give up the idea that there is one way of life best for all. The entrenchment of human rights has a clear prescriptive appearance, but its prescription is simply to respect the right that needs to be taken account of: the right to make a claim that will be heard in a context in which there is restraint and decorum; an opportunity to check lies, misrepresentations, and false claims; the chance to present evidence to challenge exaggerations; and the insistence that preferred outcomes be justified by analysis and evidence. The entrenchment of rights guarantees equal voice and equal status to the politically less significant. It provides visibility of the humanity that lies behind contested interests, the primacy of due process over power, equal respect for the pleas of the mightiest and the weakest, and dignity and respect for parties regardless of claim or outcome. These are the qualities of justice and humanism that prevent our inevitable conflicts over what we regard as foundationally important from becoming moments of division and conflict and even national disintegration. Rather, they can become moments of national affirmation and solidarity. These moments can be seen as states of national life that are more profoundly important to our living together peaceably than is ruling the people of the nation through the will of the majority or its elected representatives.

PART 3

MEETING THE CHALLENGES TO THE DEMOCRATIC STATE IN THE TWENTY-FIRST CENTURY

CHAPTER 7

IS DEMOCRACY COMPATIBLE WITH GOOD GOVERNMENT?

Michael M. Atkinson

Liberal democracy, when it functions well, ensures that the personal and political agendas of those who govern are constrained by law and disciplined by free elections. And, though liberal democratic governments are expected to supply public goods to meet the needs of citizens, the principal virtue of liberalism is that it allows autonomous individuals to create their own versions of the good life, typically in the context of an open market economy.

Social democracy endorses these values but offers an alternative combination. Social democrats imagine the good life primarily in terms of the things that we enjoy together. Accordingly, social democratic governments seek social justice, not just private freedoms and procedural protections. For them, the pursuit of social justice requires a modern state capable of good government: that is, government able to produce desired collective outcomes.

Allan Blakeney was one of those social democrats intent on demonstrating that the government could be harnessed to do much more than simply make the world safe for the market economy. Blakeney believed that a well-designed government, operating with a well-developed plan, could accomplish far more than most liberal democrats were willing to concede, especially for those who failed to prosper in so-called self-regulating markets.

Standing squarely in the way of this social democratic vision is the view that democratically elected governments, social democratic or otherwise, are either incompetent or corrupt and perhaps both. Since at least the turn of the twenty-first century, the decline in public support for democratically elected governments across Organization for Economic Cooperation and Development (OECD) countries has become a well-worn theme in studies of public opinion.[1] Governments, it seems, are not trusted to do the "right thing" anymore.

This disdain for government has not, to date, spilled over into an open rejection of democracy, but public opinion specialists have begun to detect attitudes that are not entirely reassuring. In exploring the sources of disillusionment, researchers have found a new breed of critical citizen, people with high expectations and high standards for performance.[2] Although the nostrums of liberal democracy—political freedom and political equality—continue to receive their support, the actual institutions of government—parliaments, the legal system, and the civil service—are increasingly seen as underperforming.[3]

Such is the tenor of our times that there is considerable support for the idea that we would be better off collectively if experts or business people were in charge of government. In Saskatchewan, over 40 percent of respondents to a 2011 election survey thought that public policy decisions should be made by independent, non-elected experts. A massive majority, 87 percent, wanted public officials to "stop talking and take action."[4] It is not that citizens despair of elections as such; they simply want the people whom they elect to stop bickering over what they believe should be commonsensical solutions to public problems.[5]

Among students of democracy, a tension is also emerging. On one side of the discussion are those who believe that democracy is a universal value toward which humankind as a whole is striving. At the end of the twentieth century, Amartya Sen put it this way: "While democracy is not yet universally practiced, nor indeed uniformly accepted, in the general climate of world opinion, democratic governance has now achieved the status of being taken to be generally right."[6] On the other side of the discussion are those who sense that democracy might be entering a period of existential struggle.[7] The assumption that democracy will always survive its shortcomings has been described as a "confidence trap." For David Runciman, "democracies survive their mistakes. So the mistakes keep coming....At some point the repeated failings of democracy will catch up with it."[8]

If the social democratic project is to survive, let alone thrive, then it will need to confront directly the argument that democracies have a built-in propensity to be incompetent.[9] This argument, outlined below, is frequently followed by advice that is anathema to social democrats, namely that—since democratic governments are subject to problems of competence—they should be less ambitious. Smaller government implies less scope for error.[10] It also implies fewer opportunities for rent seeking: competition among politicians, voters, interest groups, and bureaucrats for artificially contrived benefits.[11]

If the deficiencies of democracy mean that good government is small government, then social democrats will be obliged to rethink their preference for collective goods supplied by a large and strong state apparatus. This is far from a given, but make no mistake: the challenge to democracy is serious. What follows is a sober assessment of that challenge and a consideration of how to meet it.

DEMOCRACY AND GOOD GOVERNMENT

Almost all justifications for democracy are rooted in the beneficent consequences of democratic procedures.[12] For liberal democrats, the consequences of most importance have been the protection of personal liberties, the development of personal autonomy, and the guarantee of peaceful political transitions.[13] These justifications are heavily procedural. They focus on how well democracies protect citizens by limiting the reach of government and obliging it to follow rules that restrict arbitrary action.

Bad government, from the liberal perspective, manifests itself in the abuse of power or, more precisely, the private appropriation of public assets without the commensurate provision of public welfare. In short, bad government is corrupt government. Why so many countries seem to be rooted in bad government is a matter of extensive conjecture,[14] but introducing the electoral institutions of democracy has not proven to be a particularly effective antidote. It seems that the relationship between corruption and democracy is not linear: adding more democracy does not reduce corruption. Where economic development is stunted, it appears that democracy aggravates the search for good government rather than facilitating it.[15] Democratic reforms reduce corruption only after the problems of poverty and deprivation have been addressed.[16]

So how does democracy perform as a means of alleviating deprivation and increasing standards of living? This question is of particular concern to social democrats since the strength of social democracy lies in its willingness to attend directly to public needs, particularly the needs of the most disadvantaged. Unfortunately, it seems that democracy's track record in producing good public outcomes is not much better than its ability to prevent the abuse of power. Soren Holmberg and Bo Rothstein find only weak or sometimes even negative correlations between standard measures of human well-being and democracy.[17] Rothstein, in particular, argues that democracies have a weak record when it comes to infant mortality, poverty, income inequality, access to safe water, life expectancy, and other similar indicators.[18] Democracy might not stand in the way of improving social and economic conditions, but it is not clear that it has much to do with providing them either. The most comprehensive study of the effects of democracy on economic development concluded that there is no appreciable difference between democracies and non-democracies in terms of growth in per capita income.[19]

In the search for good government defined as good outcomes, a much stronger case has been made for the rule of law, the protection of property rights, and a professional public service.[20] According to this line of argument, good government depends less on politicians and political competition than on the quality of civil servants, professional bodies, and law enforcement officials.[21] Rules are what matters, including rules that limit the flexibility and scope of democratically elected politicians.[22] From this perspective, it is not electoral democracy that produces good government but rules that encourage an efficient use of public resources and protect citizens from the energy-sapping practices of clientelism and favouritism. Good governments install and adhere to a norm of impartiality, one that obliges them to treat citizens equally and ignore extraneous politically driven considerations.[23]

A procedural rule such as impartiality takes us back to the liberal version of good government, protection from the abuse of power. Other rules, aimed at the economy, explicitly promote limited government. These rules, many inspired by Douglas North's analysis of economic development,[24] require governments to protect private property and guarantee contracts. Good governments instill confidence that they will not confiscate assets or use the resources of the state for narrow political ends. Discipline is the key prescription, and rules requiring the independence of central banks, adherence to fiscal targets, and neutral regulatory agencies are all consistent with it.[25] Democracy, on the other hand, is not a requirement.

So has democracy contributed nothing to environmental protection, public pensions, Medicare, and early childhood benefits? None of these policies is uncontested, but they do represent examples that social democrats can point to as rendering significant societal, not just personal, benefits. Then there are the regulatory successes that receive little or no notice because we take for granted that the roads we drive on, the foods we consume, and the water we drink are all safe. To be sure, regulatory failures exist, but typically they are not systemic. Are all of these achievements in spite of, rather than because of, democracy?

In the "in spite of" camp are those who believe that democratically elected governments are inefficient, wasteful, and incapable of learning from mistakes.[26] They might be impartial in their dealings with citizens and even beneficent in their intentions, but they are incompetent: that is, they are unable to make and implement correct decisions. Some of these critics follow the lead of Friedrich Hayek and argue that governments, democratic or otherwise, are incapable of assembling the knowledge required to maximize public welfare.[27] Others believe that democratically elected governments systematically underestimate the economic constraints associated with producing good outcomes.[28] With few exceptions, these critics of government are persuaded that the demands of democratic politics are frequently inconsistent with good public policy. For them, the formula "good politics, bad policy" is a rule-of-thumb explanation for why bad things happen in the public realm.

Could we have more intelligent government, including a better supply of high-quality public goods, if decision making were better insulated from the pressures of democracy? Put a bit more forcefully, are the demands of citizens so incoherent, and the behaviour of politicians so myopic, that democracy is actually a threat to good government?

A CLOSER LOOK AT DEMOCRATIC DEFICIENCIES

If government is to be entrusted with divining and implementing the collective will, then it should possess more than minimal intelligence. In other words, anyone who sees democratic government as a vehicle for improving social welfare must argue that democracy is a more intelligent (*smarter* is the word often used) form of government than the rest.[29] The key premise of this epistemic approach is that, independent of procedures, a right choice or correct outcome exists, and democratic decision rules will track it.[30] The overriding decision rule in a democracy is that governments must decide questions of law and policy by taking account of the formally expressed opinions of equally empowered citizens.[31] Deliberation followed by majority voting is the classic format, and (for better or worse) electoral institutions are the core institutional manifestation of democratic practice.

Unfortunately, the idea that voting can reveal an intelligent public will has some critical problems. Since 1951, when Kenneth Arrow produced the Impossibility Theorem, it has been widely conceded that aggregating individual preferences into a collective decision that meets standard rational criteria is a logically impossible proposition as long as there are more than two choices.[32] Contemporary students of vote aggregation have pressed the matter further, discovering that serial decision making using majoritarian rules can also lead to incoherent outcomes.[33] Put bluntly, the populist view of democracy, in which majority rule yields the "will of the people," is logically incoherent.[34] The response to these challenges has been either to ignore them, on the ground that they seldom produce the advertised dysfunction,[35] or to overcome them by reducing policy disagreements (via agenda setting or deliberation) to a single dimension.[36] Manipulation of this kind is not particularly easy or particularly democratic.

The problems of vote aggregation have not disappeared, but they have been joined by two different arguments against democracy. Both assert that, regardless of how votes are aggregated, elected democratic governments cannot devise good public policy. The first argument asserts that democratic citizens do not have stable policy preferences to aggregate, and the preferences that they do have are frequently divorced from well-established facts.[37] The second argument claims that their agents, elected politicians in particular, are susceptible to serious biases, some of them induced by the requirements of democracy itself. Together these arguments suggest that it is far from likely that democracy will yield intelligent government.

Let us begin with the deficiencies of democratic citizens. A main line of attack against democracy as a source of intelligent government has aimed at showing that voters have neither the requisite knowledge nor the interest required to form and convey policy preferences. Worse, in the eyes of some observers, voters are not only uninformed but also misinformed, so the policy positions that they endorse are unlikely to produce good policy or good government.

Since the 1960s, we have come to appreciate that the level of public affairs knowledge among ordinary voters is surprisingly low. A comprehensive examination of political knowledge—general political and economic facts and campaign promises—yields discouraging results. Civic literacy is generally poor and not improving; younger voters are even less knowledgeable than older voters.[38] In the 1990s election studies in Canada, even with "generous coding," less than half of the sample could come up with the correct answers for a large majority of questions testing fundamental knowledge. More disturbing is the discovery that it is not uncommon for voters to attribute policy positions to the wrong political party.[39]

In spite of these depressing findings, knowledge deficits are not completely debilitating. Knowing the name of the current minister of finance (which only 37 percent of respondents could manage in the 1997 election study) is not a prerequisite for sound views on economic policy.[40] And, though voters might struggle with discrete facts, it is still possible to imagine them using policy principles to inform their electoral choices.[41] As long as any errors that result are randomly distributed, there might not be much to worry about. The so-called magic of aggregation will produce a result that approximates an informed choice. Even though they represent a small minority, voters who are better informed are those around whom decisions converge. Additionally, political parties provide cues that allow voters to short-circuit their knowledge deficiencies,[42] while competition of all kinds, whether among political parties or contending interests in a policy debate, is a boon to the information deprived.[43]

Whether these compensating mechanisms work, specifically whether they make up for a lack of fundamental knowledge, is an open question. In a democracy, it is critical that voters not only have preferences but also can connect them to parties and leaders. Knowledge is critical in establishing that linkage.[44] In their devastating assessment of the populist theory of democracy, Christopher Achen and Larry Bartels argue that electors are much more inclined to vote based upon their group identities rather than their policy preferences.[45] Jennifer Hochschild and Katherine Levine Einstein call those who follow group cues and ignore the facts "the active misinformed."[46] Because these voters are both attentive and ignorant, they are difficult to persuade. Media fragmentation produces "echo chambers," and the rise of "fake news" accusations prompts the question of what counts as facts in a "post-truth" world. Political parties are of limited assistance. Rather than correcting voter misapprehensions, parties are more inclined to reinforce the prejudices of their electoral bases. For politicians, it is more important that party supporters move from being active to inactive than from being misinformed to informed. Evidence from Canada suggests that, even when groups or parties attempt to correct misperceptions, intervener cues do not close the knowledge gap between the better informed and the poorly informed, and the latter do not follow the behaviour of the former.[47]

The danger, then, is that voters will be systematically wrong in at least two ways. First, they will base their decisions on widely shared but incorrect information. American scholars have estimated the size of this effect by comparing beliefs to "known facts," and the results are not encouraging for democrats: for example, the American public regularly (and significantly) overestimates welfare funding, foreign aid included, and underestimates the costs of Social Security.[48] Second, voters often fail to understand the mechanisms by which economic growth, urban peace, and positive healthcare outcomes are produced. Differences of opinion on these topics might cancel one another out if they were distributed around an expected value of the correct answer. But they are not, at least according to some theorists.[49] For example, Bryan Caplan argues that voters are systematically ignorant about the market, irrationally prefer protectionist policies to free trade, and strangely seek to preserve labour (a "make work bias").[50] As long as democratic politicians pay attention to voters' preferences, according to this perspective, giving voters what they want will result in poor public policy.

Increasing political competition does not help because, as Caplan argues, the well-oiled machinery of political competition ends up working in reverse: that is, pandering to incorrect policy theories.[51] Moreover, because these policy theories make voters "feel good," they resist rational discourse.[52] For the average voter, political irrationality has little or no cost, even if the collective outcome is wealth destroying. Without being overly judgmental, Paul Quirk observes that "ordinary citizens do not have incentives to improve their understanding of public policy, unless they happen to find it interesting. Their lack of information reflects, in the end, their lack of any strong motivation to make careful or accurate judgments."[53]

Aside from the deficiencies of voters, consider the deficiencies of politicians. Even assuming a well-intentioned, other-regarding political elite (a rare assumption in contemporary academic studies), the demands of political competition oblige politicians to factor personal interests into policy decisions. These interests have been modelled in a variety of ways, most prominently by presuming that politicians prefer to retain public office and thus act in ways that will increase the probability of re-election. According to this argument, attention to the electoral cycle induces a form of policy myopia in which short-term opportunism drives out policies with long-term benefits.[54] The result is a propensity to underinvest in non-targeted public goods and to burden future generations with the costs of current consumption. In the case of public finance, for example, policy myopia induces a deficit bias in which governments lavish attention on the current electorate at the expense of the long-term needs of citizens. This is a case of the "good politics, bad policy" phenomenon mentioned earlier.

Once again, optimistic theories of democratic competition hold that, as long as entry into the political arena is unobstructed, policy entrepreneurs will offer superior alternative policies that voters will eventually endorse.[55] But free entry into politics is a strong assumption. Besides, since all policies create vested interests of some description, there is considerable friction in the system. These vested interests are a key source of policy stability or, put another way, a key obstacle to change. Stability is the norm, and even when change comes it is shaped by vested interests. As Terry Moe argues, "reforms are often adopted not because they genuinely solve social problems, or even because they make logical sense, but rather because the prevailing constraints of power happened to make *those* incremental gains possible."[56]

Governments fearful of backlash from vested interests do not learn well. Because there are few policy experiments, politicians have no basis on which to reject the claims made by current beneficiaries that change would be problematic.[57] Democratic governments might fare better than others in facilitating change were it not for the oversized ability of the affluent to reach the centres of political power. Research in the United States has confirmed that policy makers pay more attention to upper-income voters than to anyone else.[58] Meticulous assessments of policy change reveal that business groups in particular enjoy enormous influence, whereas the preferences of median-income voters barely register. In a recent comparison of preferences and policy outcomes in the United States, Martin Gilens and Benjamin Page came to the following conclusion: "When the preferences of economic elites and the stands of organized interest groups are controlled for, the preferences of the average American appear to have only a minuscule, near-zero, statistically non-significant impact upon public policy."[59]

These results might come as a relief to those who doubt the wisdom of average voters, but a political system in which the interests of affluent citizens and corporate donors are systematically overrepresented in public policy will have a hard time meriting the description "democratic."[60] If the biases of government are located in a biased power structure, one that privileges the interests of capital over those of labour and concentrated wealth over distributed consumption, then perhaps democracy itself cannot be blamed. Then again, democracies are prized for their ability to achieve political equality by correcting malpractice. Democratic innovations can reduce power asymmetries and improve political access, but innovation in democracies requires some measure of voter demand, which in turn presumes a substantial measure of voter competence. We are back to the first objection to democracy as a source of intelligence.

Those who wish to make a positive case for the intelligence-producing effects of democracy have their work cut out for them. But the picture is not as bleak as one might assume. In fact, in the past decade or longer, the epistemic perspective mentioned earlier has been developed and refined, specifically the view that democracies, for all their deficiencies, offer a particular form of wisdom. This argument is especially important for social democrats whose ideological agenda is at odds with the idea that democratic governments are intrinsically inept and democratic voters routinely stupid.

AN EPISTEMIC CASE FOR DEMOCRACY?

The claim that democracy is a competency-enhancing form of government must either deal directly with the alleged deficiencies of voters and politicians or find a means to circumvent them. The oldest and strongest case for the intelligence of democracy has its roots in the "wisdom of the crowd" argument. The claim that majority voting by political equals who possess no more than modest intellectual endowments could result in good policy decisions was made centuries ago by the Marquis de Condorcet. His Jury Theorem is premised on the idea that, when voting by simple majority rule, a group of voters is more likely to choose the correct outcome than any individual voter. This propensity for correctness increases with the size of the group, assuming that the group is not dominated by a faction of likeminded people.[61] As long as voters act as individuals and perform better than random (e.g., a coin flip), a large number of less competent (but better than random) voters will come to the correct decision more likely than a small number of more competent voters.

If collective competence improves with a broader electorate, it also improves with a more diverse electorate. When everyone operates with the same models of how the world works, the collective wisdom of the group will be no better than the sophistication of the people in it. Required, in addition to a modest level of individual competence, are diverse interpretations of the world. A diversity of experience, identity, and reasoning, it is argued, contributes to better collective outcomes,[62] but what is really important is cognitive variation in the models that people employ in interpreting how the world works or how it should be understood.[63] This perspective is summarized in the "Diversity Trumps Ability Theorem," which maintains that given the right conditions a "randomly selected collection of problem solvers outperforms a collection of the best individual problem solvers."[64]

Even its proponents concede that this argument, at the least, is counterintuitive: "You are better off with a random group of people who think differently than with a bunch of Einsteins! Who would have thought?"[65] Of course, for the theorem to work, the average voter must be able to recognize the correct answer more than half of the time. In addition, the decision structure needs to be binary—a right answer and a wrong answer—and issues need to be decided *seriatim*, one after the other. Defenders of the epistemic version of democracy argue that these requirements are not as imposing as they might appear.[66] Many decisions rendered by majority rule are binary in character, and, as long as they can gather information as required, voters are unlikely to be worse than a random process at making the right choice. People do not need to be geniuses, but they need to be "smart enough" to handle what the problem requires.

These arguments, and the research that supports them, will be reassuring to democrats who believe that, far from being a threat to good government, democracy can make a net contribution to more intelligent decisions. But there are serious objections to this rosy picture.

First, only some issues of collective choice allow a single correct decision and only then in retrospect. Estimations by large groups in information markets—movie box office receipts, crop yields, and elections—frequently average out to the correct answer, but democratic decision making is not just about weighing the evidence and making a good guess. Frequently, the facts themselves are in dispute, and what is required is an assessment of risk.[67] Non-experts are good at evaluating some risks but bad at evaluating others. They frequently choose to employ what has been called "hybrid epistemologies," whereby conventional standards of evidence are used to decide some issues but intuition or the path of revealed truth is used for others.[68] This propensity means not that people lack competence overall, and this is the spirit of some of the recent critiques of rationality in voting, but that their competence is likely to vary from issue to issue. Unfortunately, this uncertain application of reason is troubling for making correct decisions. As Jon Elster observes, "mechanisms for collective wisdom may be compared to alchemy—they turn lead (mediocre individual judgment) into gold (good collective judgment). Yet the individual judgments have to be at least mediocre rather than poor."[69]

Second, politics, democratic or otherwise, does not unfold in the orderly manner that epistemic models presume. Specifically, many democratic decision-making bodies—legislatures, committees, and forums—do not decide issues one at a time. They typically take up a host of issues at once and often seek agreement by bargaining gains and losses.[70] "Partisan mutual adjustment," the phrase that Charles Lindblom uses to describe how issues are often resolved in democracies, involves rationally adapting preferences based upon existing options and anticipating the actions of others.[71] This strategy typically produces what Lindblom describes as "disjointed problem solving" and incremental changes to existing policies.[72] Epistemic accounts of democratic decision making afford little room for bargaining even though politics in democracies is replete with it. What role is there for bargaining when there are right and wrong answers that can be divined by appropriately diverse decision-making bodies?

Third, and perhaps of most importance for social democrats, the value of epistemic democracy appears to be fully realized only in small-scale ventures, including participatory budgeting, consensus conferences, citizen juries, and deliberative polls. Each of these innovations is aimed at raising the level of sophistication among voters in advance of a vote. British Columbia's citizen forum, charged with sifting through alternative electoral processes and offering a considered proposal, is a case in point. These are admirable efforts to apply the insights of deliberative democracy, but few of them are premised purely on epistemic grounds, and all of them involve bounded decision situations. Transferring the practices of democratic decision making to national or provincial political institutions has not been a popular project. Hélène Landemore claims, for example, that smaller settings, such as local councils, have "a certain deliberative purity, which often gets lost in national legislatures, as interests, partisanship, and ideological posturing obscure the purely argumentative content of many debates."[73]

Yet tackling the topic of good government while ignoring national institutions is not a particularly satisfying political strategy in a world of spillover effects, economies of scale, and international competition. Besides, critics of democracy, such as Daniel Bell, have already agreed that if democracy has a role it is in localized communities. According to Bell, democracy belongs not in national institutions but "at the bottom."[74] This view has much in common with those who suggest either radical decentralization or simply a withdrawal of government in favour of the market.[75]

Whatever appeal libertarian solutions might have for epistemic democrats, social democrats are unlikely to be moved. Too many of the victories of the welfare state—public education, public pensions, progressive taxation, and social welfare—have been enacted by nationally organized political parties working through national legislatures. Allowing these public goods to be provided by local authorities that compete with one another to attract wealth and investment is not a formula likely to endear itself to social democrats. And, though some epistemic democrats seem to be prepared to concede that small-scale competitive jurisdictions are an attractive option, the reform of national institutions based upon epistemic principles need not be a pipe dream.

Consider the idea that in most democracies the core institutions of government typically contain what Adrian Vermeule calls "epistemic bottlenecks."[76]

Legislative institutions are a case in point. Traditionalists aside, it is hard to argue that parliamentary institutions, as currently designed, tap the full potential of a cognitively diverse body of independent thinkers. What goes on in these assemblies is mostly set piece debates followed by entirely predictable votes as opposing parties whip their supporters into place and present as solid a wall of opinion as possible. Behind-the-scenes decision making is monopolized by select committees of ministers or, in a worst-case scenario, the prime minister on his or her own. The epistemic advantages of democracy are seldom on display.

On the contrary, such wisdom as might exist in a chamber of independent, cognitively diverse legislators is significantly reduced by allowing smaller groups to monopolize decisions. When small, homogeneous groups control the agenda or dictate the outcome of votes, any claim that democracies are inclined to wisdom by virtue of their epistemic qualities is severely diminished. Although legislatures are typically small relative to democratic electorates, they are large enough to capture many of the epistemic advantages of democratic deliberation.[77] To realize those advantages requires more diverse legislative bodies with expanded authority over public policy.

What about the executive institutions of the modern state? Do they constitute epistemic bottlenecks as well? State bureaucracies are demonstrably not majoritarian institutions, and the discourse that occurs in them is heavily constrained by hierarchical norms. Do bureaucracies that operate in democratic systems draw any epistemic sustenance from their democratic contexts? Or are bureaucracies inevitably rigid, rule bound, and beyond the reach of the epistemological advantages of democracy?

The reason for posing the question this way is that, though politicians and voters are favourite targets of critics of democracy, much of the literature on good government lays the blame for its absence squarely at the feet of unresponsive and unaccountable bureaucratic agencies. Those who work in these agencies are frequently assumed to labour under the constraints of principal-agent models in which agents seek to maximize their own values (budgets, discretion, income, etc.) rather than pursue the goals of their principals (e.g., politicians or voters). This simplified portrayal of bureaucratic behaviour is an overstatement at best that does not provide much, if any, scope for recruiting the epistemic advantages of democracy. It is, however, a popular perspective nurtured in part by well-cultivated images of rent-seeking bureaucrats.[78]

An alternative view of bureaucracy, one that emphasizes the willingness of public servants to seek the public interest independent of political directions or personal interests, suggests a different route to good government. In this version of bureaucratic behaviour, innovation in bureaucracies depends on the capacity of democracy for reflexivity, willingness to experiment, and adjustment of direction based upon evidence.[79] Bureaucrats, in this model, evaluate the results of policy and suggest alternative ways of thinking about problems. Democracy encourages this kind of experimentation because, as John Dewey argued, it embodies a commitment to problem solving by citizens in interaction with politicians and other state actors.[80] Like other versions of epistemic democracy, the Deweyan experimental model depends on diversity and deliberation as a means of arriving at intelligent decisions.

Bureaucracies are not majoritarian institutions, but that does not mean that they are ineligible to contribute to creative problem solving using methods that respect research, observation, and inference. Public servants in Saskatchewan, such as Al Johnson and Tommy Shoyama, were creative experimenters. If bureaucrats seldom display creativity,[81] it is not because they are incapable of being imaginative. The obstacles to intelligent government inside the state cannot all be traced to the deleterious effects of democracy. However, if governance in modern bureaucracies is an extension of partisan political contestation and little else, then we deprive ourselves of much of its epistemic capacity.

CONCLUSION

I have considered here the untidy relationship between democracy and good government and reviewed a list of objections to the idea that democracy can help governments to make intelligent public policy choices. The main arguments against this idea focus on the ignorance of voters, the venality or incompetence of politicians, and the rigidity of bureaucrats. These arguments underpin the preference of many liberals, and all libertarians, for governments that are not just limited but also small and restrained.

Social democrats, who typically seek to make government a bold and ambitious innovator, need to reflect on democracy's weakness and defend its epistemic value. Reflecting on its weakness means abandoning the comforting idea that voters are much moved by policy considerations and that, in electing social democratic governments, they are endorsing an active, interventionist state. The evidence is overwhelmingly otherwise. Democratic elections produce governments, not policy mandates, and there is no way of extracting clear policy directions by aggregating votes. The epistemic value of democracy lies less in the inherent wisdom of the electorate than in the opportunities that democracy affords governments to draw widely on opinion and expertise. How well governments seize these opportunities depends entirely on them.

As for the epistemic value of democracy, here are three ways, touched on above, in which democracy can contribute to sound public policy. First, the opportunities for policy experimentation are far more evident in democracies than in closed, authoritarian societies. Democracy presumes competition, which obliges politicians to advocate objectives and canvass the means of achieving them. The merits of these ideas are inevitably challenged, and policies are regularly revised. Smart policy choices are not guaranteed; however, where competition is genuine and authority is shared or fragmented, the prospects for experimentation are enhanced. In a country such as Canada, where authority is distributed between national and subnational governments, the opportunity to try new policies, and to learn from mistakes, has allowed the pioneering of ideas that would otherwise struggle to achieve a national consensus.

Second, democratic norms encourage organization in civil society and the engagement of voices beyond the corridors of power. As we have seen, epistemic democrats contend that the more diverse these voices the more reliable the overall policy advice. The strong state that social democrats advocate cannot afford high barriers to entry if diversity is to be encouraged. There must be ample opportunity to organize politically, and broad, meaningful consultation must accompany major policy initiatives. Partial interests will always find expression in democracies, but the prospects for intelligent decisions increase as the inputs become more diverse. Democracy is far more likely to produce diverse inputs than any other form of interest aggregation.

Third, and more controversially, democracies have a superior capacity to recruit leaders who exhibit good judgment. The contrary view, that democracies select poor leaders, can be traced back as far as Plato,[82] and the rise of democratically elected authoritarians confirms this concern. But research shows that democracies (albeit with some conspicuous exceptions) tend to select educated leaders with more intense commitments to the public interest. Better-educated leaders are inclined to focus on broadly based policies rather than indulge political clients or sectional interests. The result is better performance, at least in terms of economic growth.[83]

It is dangerous to move from the general to the specific, but Allan Blakeney's turn as premier of Saskatchewan provides a pointed illustration of how democracies get the leaders they need, when they need them. Roy Romanow's description (in this volume) of the Blakeney government captures the essence of the argument. Democratic leaders have much more robust ideas of the public interest than do leaders selected via other mechanisms. Political competition, aided by well-constructed electoral institutions, obliges these leaders to reach beyond their bases to secure power. When that happens, these leaders are all the more attentive to the future constellation of interests and opinions.

Romanow describes Blakeney's style of leadership as "principled pragmatism," a phrase that captures the qualities that democracy induces. Principles of social justice are what define the social democratic approach to governing; pragmatism is what democratic governance demands. Democracy privileges pragmatic solutions because pragmatism, like democracy, accepts the inevitability of conflicts over values. Democracy gives pragmatic leaders the scope to navigate these conflicts and pursue broadly acceptable policies by paying close attention to feedback from a variety of sources. So, though the populist expectation that in a democracy policies will reflect the preferences of the majority is highly problematic, at least some of democracy's epistemic qualities are still on offer. To build upon those qualities, and achieve "smart" and competent government, requires principled and pragmatic leadership. Blakeney's time in office is a case in point.

CHAPTER 8

TRUST, TAXES, AND DEMOCRACY IN CANADA

Alex Himelfarb

One might well wonder what a chapter on taxes is doing in a volume dedicated to the memory of Allan Blakeney, former premier of Saskatchewan, and his commitment to strengthening democracy. But how we think about taxes is a reflection of how we think about government and the relationships of citizens to one another and the state. Our willingness to pay taxes is a measure of how much we trust one another and our political institutions and therefore how much we can accomplish together. Absent social and political trust, democracy—or at least Blakeney's noble vision of it—cannot flourish.

The essence of democracy for Blakeney can be summed up in his phrase "a fair share for all in a free society."[1] Democracy, he understood, is not simply about how we choose our government but also about what happens between elections, the extent to which we protect individual freedoms and minorities, and how we ensure that everyone pays and gets his or her fair share. He understood that citizens' commitment to democracy depended in large part on their belief not only that they have an equal voice in choosing their representatives but also that their government is in fact there for them, for the many, not just the powerful few. A few years after leaving office, Blakeney was clearly concerned, telling an interviewer, for example, that we should be troubled by the steady decline in voter participation, by what it signalled regarding the health of our democracy, and by what it portended for the future.[2] He was right to worry.

For decades, most or at least many scholars believed that mature democracies such as ours—with a robust civil society and relative wealth—were pretty much immune from threat. Citizens might have been upset about the government of the day or about particular policies and institutions but were, the argument goes, thankful that democracy gave them the opportunity to hold governments to account, throw them out when necessary, and put in a new lot. But recent evidence puts in question this assumption and allows for no sense of complacency about the future of democracy. For example, Roberto Foa and Yascha Mounk, concerned about the growing popularity of right-wing populism, authoritarianism, and nativist alternatives, started some time back to measure public support for democracy.[3] Their latest findings indicate a worrying decline in commitment to democratic institutions and in confidence that democracy can deliver:

> What we find is deeply concerning. Citizens in a number of supposedly consolidated democracies in North America and Western Europe have not only grown more critical of their political leaders. Rather, they have also become more cynical about the value of democracy as a political system, less hopeful that anything they do might influence public policy, and more willing to express support for authoritarian alternatives.[4]

The authors do not suggest here that democracy sits on some precipice ready to fall over the edge. But they do warn of erosion, what they call deconsolidation, and the opening that it creates for what have hitherto seemed to be unthinkable alternatives. We have seen concretely in the United States and in much of the world the political risks when people lose trust in their democratic institutions, how vulnerable they can be to antidemocratic options, to nativism and authoritarianism. The authors warn that we not take for granted support for our democratic institutions and urge that we carefully examine the factors that might be undermining democratic participation and trust.

I explore here one potential factor, specifically the relationship between democracy and taxation or, more precisely, decades of tax cuts and the austerity that inevitably follows. Much has been written on the impacts of austerity on inequality, health and well-being, and more recently economic performance. But little attention has been given to its impacts on politics, on trust in and commitment to representative democracy. One major exception is the collection of articles compiled by Wolfgang Streeck and Armin Schäfer that explicitly, and depressingly, addresses "politics in the age of austerity."[5] Their focus, however, is on Europe, particularly Greece, Spain, and Ireland, where cuts to services were sharp and devastating and the role of external institutions—the European Commission and the International Monetary Fund in particular—put in question the capacity of national democracies to make decisions on behalf of their citizens. The conclusion of this important volume is nonetheless instructive beyond Europe: when people believe that vast market forces or the interests of the rich and powerful have captured the government, when people come to view the democratic process as more or less irrelevant to the needs of the many, they increasingly opt out or act out and can become more vulnerable to the appeal of non-democratic solutions.

Clearly, austerity in Canada has not been anywhere near what Greece, say, has had to endure, and in Canada it has been largely self-inflicted through decades of unaffordable tax cuts. Nonetheless, I explore how, here as elsewhere, the unholy duo of tax cuts and austerity is also leading many to lose trust that the government is there for them or even that it is capable of achieving much. In turn, this leads many to question whether their votes matter, whether any government that they might choose is truly able or willing to represent their interests. Why trust, why play, why vote, why participate if the game is rigged?

There are hopeful signs too, of course, signs that some people, not yet cynical, are fighting to "unrig" the game, to revitalize democracy. However, if we are to reverse the vicious circle of austerity and democratic decline, if we are to reclaim Blakeney's noble vision of democracy, a key place to start is with a new and honest conversation about taxes.

HOW DID WE GET HERE?

It is certainly not news that there has been a profound loss of trust in government and political institutions almost everywhere, especially since the late 1970s.[6] The World Value Survey shows that trust in political and democratic institutions has declined in most advanced democracies over the past twenty years, and Canada is no exception.[7] And trust matters. Absent trust, people are less likely to comply with the rules and less likely to invest time and effort to make short-term sacrifices for longer-term benefits.

Of course, less deference to authority and a healthy skepticism of the government of the day are good. But some degree of trust—in one another and in our institutions—is a prerequisite for collective action. Ample research has shown that without trust we can find ourselves in what game theorists call a social trap, unable to cooperate with others even when doing so is clearly in our interest.[8] Without trust in others and in our shared institutions, we are on our own to a considerable extent, our sense of the "collective" increasingly limited to our personal relationships. The decline in trust over the past few decades has meant a weakening of our collective toolkit at the very time when, arguably, our collective action problems—notably climate change and growing inequality—are particularly acute.

There is no shortage of data indicating that the majority of Canadians still want what people wanted when Blakeney was premier—a living wage, a secure job, a safe community, greater equality, opportunities for the young, a just and fair society, a healthy environment, and strong social programs.[9] What seems to have changed is how little we trust that our democracy can deliver this kind of future. What has changed is not so much what we want of government as what we think is possible.[10]

No doubt this is at least part of the reason that we have witnessed declines in Canadians' participation in voting and party politics.[11] Although the 2015 federal election saw a bump in voter participation, we probably ought not to celebrate that still over 30 percent of eligible voters stayed home.[12] Why vote if you do not believe that much good can come of it?

One way to tell this story of declining trust is through the lens of taxes. After the defeat of the Conservative government in 2015, John Ibbitson argued that Stephen Harper had profoundly altered Canada's political landscape.[13] Of course, Ibbitson understood that many of the specific Conservative policies implemented over the previous decade would be undone by a new government—and this is exactly what has been happening. But, Ibbitson argued, the Harper government's enduring legacy, what no party seems to be ready to reverse, is deep tax cuts and what they portend for the role of government.[14] He might have been right.

One of the Harper government's first policy moves was to cut the Goods and Services Tax (GST) by two cents between 2006 and 2008. The politics of the cut were easy. That is what the Conservatives had promised during the election. And most people—economists excluded—hated this particular tax, which they were reminded of each time they made a purchase. Perhaps more surprising about this expensive tax cut was that there was virtually no political pushback. No party asked the government to defend the decision, to explain the benefits. Most disturbing, nobody asked about what we lose when we take $14 billion out of the federal treasury every year (yes, at least $14 billion is more or less what two cents of GST is worth). Nobody asked what this might mean for our resilience in tough times, for the quality and availability of our public services, for the integrity of our public institutions, for our choices for the future.

All parties, it seems, had developed an allergy to taxes. Taxes had become a political no-go zone. The political punditry were pretty much in agreement that a politician who dared to suggest any tax increase would most surely lose votes. Indeed, any mention of taxes—other than tax cuts—would be suicidal. The "tax and spend" days were over, smaller governments our inevitable future.

Taxing and spending have indeed taken a hit over the past two decades. Taxes as a proportion of our economy hit their peak in Canada in the mid-1990s. Since then we have been on what one of my colleagues called a "tax jihad." The last Conservative federal budget projected federal taxes and spending to hit lows that we had not seen for seventy years, before we had Medicare and mass education. In the early 2000s, the Liberal government cut taxes, according to its own estimate, by $100 billion over five years.[15] The Conservative government followed suit, accelerating the corporate tax cuts that the Liberals had initiated and implementing a number of "boutique" tax measures, which cut federal revenues by additional tens of billions of dollars on top of its costly GST cut. Canada is now below the OECD average in how much tax revenue it collects (as a percentage of the economy).[16] And still not much political pushback.

Nor is our tax allergy confined to the political right. Survey data suggest that relatively few Canadians share the view of the Fraser Institute that almost any tax is bad, a drag on the economy, and an unjust constraint on our freedom.[17] Most Canadians value the public goods and services that their taxes buy. They understand that taxes are necessary. In fact, according to the same surveys, many Canadians say that they would even be willing to pay more taxes—but only if they could trust that the money would not simply be squandered by governments that had lost their trust and only if they believed that everybody was paying her or his fair share.[18] Most believe, however, that neither condition is being met. So they continue to vote for the next tax cut, and politicians continue their reluctance to change the tax conversation.

This is not to say that there ever was a time when people simply loved to pay taxes. In the almost thirty years of my career as a public servant, I never met a politician who thought that raising taxes would be a political winner. Over 500 years ago, Machiavelli warned the prince not to be too generous to the people lest he have to raise their taxes and risk their wrath.[19] On the popularity of taxes, one can say that not much has changed. Which of us ever really enjoys paying the bills, and, after all, taxes are how we pay the bills for those things that we have decided to do together because we could not do them at all or as well alone.[20]

But something has changed. During the 1960s and 1970s, Canadians kept voting for governments, like Blakeney's government in Saskatchewan, that raised taxes. They no doubt grumbled, but they knew what their tax dollars were buying. Governments of all stripes were putting in place new infrastructure. They were building the key elements of the welfare state, bringing Medicare to all Canadians, strengthening income supports, expanding access to education. Canadians could see what their tax dollars were delivering, and they liked it. Perhaps because we put no prices on these services and governments, for some time now, have stopped building, we take all of this for granted. Who of us ever asks how much it costs to light our streets or ensure that our water, medicine, and food are safe?

Undoubtedly, a major reason for our rejection of taxes, public spending and government regulation—even when tax, spend, and regulate are exactly what all governments do—is that the very idea of government has been under attack for decades. What some refer to as the neoliberal counter-revolution, ushered in by Ronald Reagan in the United States and Margaret Thatcher in the United Kingdom in the 1980s, redefined government as the problem rather than our major tool for collective progress. This new framework offered less government, more market, less public, more private. Competition in a "free market," rather than human attempts at planning, was viewed as the source of well-being. In some respects, then, the market was the "true democracy" in which people were able to make free choices. Economist Bryan Caplan stated baldly what few others today would say out loud: what we need is less democracy, more market.[21] But Caplan was simply echoing what critics of the welfare state had been saying for decades: the danger was not too little democracy but, in the words of Samuel Huntington, "an excess of democracy."[22] Huntington and his colleagues argued that what was needed was more public apathy, lower public expectations. That is precisely what underlies the now conventional wisdom that what we need is less collectivism, less "interference" in the market, less government. "Faceless bureaucrats," "bloated bureaucracy," "needless red tape" became the new language to describe labour rights, social justice, environmental protection, and public service.

At the same time, however, the political leaders of the day understood that people had come to value, even if take for granted, the public goods and services that governments were providing. Perhaps people were ready to cut government in some abstract way, but they were far less likely to support a party that ran on less health care or higher tuition or weakened social security. The way to handle this paradox? Start with tax cuts, not service cuts, and convince voters that these tax cuts are free, more change in their pockets at no cost to their quality of life. The attack on taxes depended heavily on magical thinking, convincing people that there is indeed a free lunch. As one political commentator put it, the idea was to pretend that we can have both Swedish-style services and American-style taxes.[23]

Initially, politicians promised that tax cuts would generate so much economic activity that they would pay for themselves, but the enormous deficits that the Reagan government racked up soon put the lie to that. Today the promise is typically that tax cuts would be paid for by eliminating waste and corruption, draining the swamp, derailing the "gravy train," privatizing public services, and selling off private assets. As economist Robert Reich once stated, the greatest accomplishment of those on the right was that they managed to equate government with waste and inefficiency and to portray the private sector as the model of efficiency.[24]

The idea that "big government" was the problem entered more slowly and with less ferocity in Canada than in, say, Reagan's America or Thatcher's Britain—perhaps Canadians were more comfortable with the notion of "peace, order, and good government," less individualistic, and more attached to their public services. However, all of this notwithstanding, in Canada, as elsewhere, citizens came increasingly to see government as overhead, waste, something foreign and apart, something that should always be made smaller. And, to be fair, governments themselves helped the cause. Every government scandal, every auditor general report on inefficiency, every news report on the personal spending habits of public officials fed distrust and consolidated the notion that tax cuts could indeed be free.

Of course, Canadians are right to demand better of their governments. Every instance of waste and misspending not only deprives public services of needed resources but also fritters away public trust. But media coverage and deliberate misrepresentation from organizations such as the Fraser Institute have led many to exaggerate what proportion of total spending is, in fact, "wasted." Research and successive reports of parliamentary budget offices and their equivalents repeatedly demonstrate that there is never enough "gravy" to pay for the tax cuts, that promises that tax cuts will have no real consequences on public services are never fulfilled. Never. And never do critics address the often higher costs of privatization or private-public partnerships that inevitably accompany tax cutting. Nor do they ask about the financial and human costs of market failures when governments lack the resources to regulate the private sector effectively. Think of the financial catastrophe of 2008 or the devastating Gulf oil spill or the Walkerton water tragedy for starters.

Yes, it is important to demand less waste, greater efficiency, and more transparency of governments. No organization—public, private, or in between—is perfectly efficient; all are managed by perfectly imperfect people. There will always be examples proving that more needs to be done. And there is always more that can be done. But this is separate from assuming that efficiencies will pay for all of the tax cutting and therefore that tax cuts will have no consequences on public services. All the tax cutting inevitably does have consequences: in a word, *austerity*.

AUSTERITY IN CANADA

Some no doubt will dispute use of that word to describe what has been happening in Canada. As stated previously, Canadians certainly have not experienced anything close to the cuts that the Greeks have had to endure since the 2008 financial meltdown. Austerity in Canada has come in increments, in slow motion. In part, that is because Canada went through a version of austerity—when no other country was doing so—over a decade before 2008. We had already made deep cuts in the 1990s to government services, our system of redistribution, and the federal share of funding for health and social development, the consequences of which are still being felt. By the time the meltdown hit—and it did not hit us as badly as many—we were in good fiscal shape, running annual surpluses, low and declining debt to gross domestic product, the fiscal envy of most other rich countries.

Unlike in Greece and other European countries, the second round of austerity in Canada was largely self-imposed. When the Conservative government took power in 2006, it inherited a surplus of over $13 billion.[25] This means that clearly there was no great spending problem. The federal government was taking in much more revenue than it was spending. Nor was there great pressure to reduce taxes after the record-breaking cuts of the Liberal government that preceded Harper's victory. Nonetheless, tax cuts—deep tax cuts—were precisely what we got. Indeed, because of these tax cuts, Canada was seemingly heading toward a structural deficit even before the big 2008 recession hit.

Austerity was not simply the consequence of these unaffordable tax cuts; it was, arguably, their purpose, the justification for governments to reduce their footprints and impose service cuts that people might otherwise not accept.

Here is how it works. First make annual balanced budgets a fetish, the major criterion by which to judge government performance (we should welcome the current Liberal government's challenge to this particular orthodoxy). Of course, governments must be fiscally responsible, but few economists would argue that annual balanced budgets comprise a sensible fiscal anchor. Indeed, when balanced budgets become more important in assessing our governments than, say, the health of our environment, or human health, or the level of unemployment, or the extent of inequality, something is seriously out of whack. Nonetheless, that is, until recently at least, where we have been.

Once balanced budgets are established as the sacred duty of all governments, and debts and deficits are portrayed as the greatest risk to our future, the government then cuts taxes with the promise that doing so will have no consequences for public services. Indeed, tax cuts (along with trade deals) are portrayed as, or more accurately substitute for, an economic plan, with promises of innovation and productivity increases that will fuel economic growth, the benefits of which will trickle down to the many.

Those tax cuts, despite the promises, eventually and inevitably create a deficit—in our case amplified by the recession and bailouts that followed the 2008 financial crisis. The deficit is then treated as the major problem to be solved, leaving "no alternative" to cutting or squeezing public services, at least until the budget is once again balanced. At which point the process is repeated. Tax cuts, deficits, spending cuts, balanced budget, more tax cuts, more deficits, more spending cuts, et cetera. Government's footprint is gradually reduced, its role is gradually changed, and the costs of the tax cuts, bailouts, and financial crisis are socialized, passed on to those who least can bear them.

Austerity in slow motion is of course harder to detect. Opposition is slower to arise. Some will deny that it is happening at all. Spending might still rise in absolute terms, though not nearly as quickly as population increase and economic growth demand. Like taxes, federal spending as a portion of the economy declines to levels not seen for decades, and public servants comprise a shrinking proportion of the labour force, despite prevailing myths. The consequences play out over years, so we often fail to make the connection with the prior tax cuts. How many of us link rising tuition, stagnant wages, record-breaking household debt, longer wait times, environmental degradation, traffic gridlock, deteriorating infrastructure, unenforced regulations, and higher user fees with the decades of tax cuts that made these inevitable? Instead, the failure of governments to address these issues, and the erosion of public services that we count on, amplify our distrust of government and our skepticism about what our tax dollars buy. Indeed, American pundits had a phrase for this cycle of erosion and distrust: "starve the beast."[26]

As the public sphere shrinks, we question its value to us. Families are increasingly left to fend for themselves to pay tuition or find child care or plan for retirement or even pay for health care—the out-of-pocket costs of health care are at their highest since Canada introduced Medicare. For most of us, the value of the few dollars of extra cash that we get from the latest tax cut is dwarfed by what is lost. That is particularly so since corporations and the rich have been the biggest beneficiaries of the changes to our tax system. So we have some cause to think that we might be paying more than our fair share (though most of us still pay less than those in many other rich countries) and getting less in return. Confidence in government is sapped. Hunger for more tax cuts grows.

With austerity comes reluctance to invest in the future even as we continue to take for granted the benefits that we derive from the investments of previous generations more willing than we are to pay taxes. It is evident that low inflation, tax cuts, deregulation, weaker unions, and smaller governments—the package, apparently, that the "market demands"—have not produced the growth or innovation promised. Significantly, the research arm of the International Monetary Fund, which promoted austerity everywhere, has finally recognized that it significantly oversold its benefits and underestimated its human and economic costs.

Mariana Mazzucato, among others, argues provocatively that ambitious governments—those willing to tax and spend—are crucial for fostering innovation.[27] We could be building the clean and green technologies and infrastructure of the future—and the jobs that would be created by doing so—but we are not. We could be dramatically increasing our investment in science and basic research—arguably the most important sources of innovation in the long term—but we are not. Austerity feeds short termism, leaving future governments and future generations to bear the costs. It undermines trust not only of government but also of the future. Of course, governing means choosing, but austerity profoundly narrows the choices and, over time, stunts the political imagination and narrows our sense of what is possible together.[28]

AUSTERITY, INEQUALITY, AND DEMOCRACY

Austerity also inevitably contributes to greater inequality. It weakens our redistributive programs, welfare and employment insurance, and social programs designed to reduce inequality or mitigate its impact. In the neoliberal frame, inequality is not only inevitable but also desirable and efficient, the benefits supposedly trickling down to the many. Instead, austerity yields what I have called elsewhere a "trickle-down meanness."[29] Its consequences are heaviest for those who arrived last in the labour market, young people and women, and for the most vulnerable, those most dependent on public services: the poor and unemployed, people of colour, people with disabilities, refugees and migrant workers, veterans, and prisoners. And our misguided "tough on crime" policies mean ever more prisoners, disproportionately Indigenous, even as crime rates have been declining for decades.

Canadians might take false comfort from comparisons with the United States which has the highest level of inequality, however one measures it, of all rich countries. But the gap between the rich and the rest has been widening in Canada too, and we are lagging behind most other wealthy countries in reducing poverty. Our performance with respect to Indigenous justice and child poverty has been shameful, though the Canadian Child Benefit is a welcome and long-overdue, if partial, response to the latter.

More than a couple of decades back the sociologist Herbert Gans asked whether citizens could ever find common purpose or any sense of common citizenship in the face of extreme inequality.[30] Rich and poor do not experience the same Canada. They do not breathe the same air or see the same problems. They live in different neighbourhoods, separated by more than geography. They do not interact as neighbours. They attend different schools and churches. Professor David Hulchanski at the University of Toronto provides detailed evidence of how Toronto, for example, is polarizing in exactly this way, becoming a "city of disparities," two very different and separate Torontos.[31]

Furthermore, as Miles Corak has shown, extreme economic inequality undermines equality of opportunity.[32] Inheritance becomes the only dependable path to economic success. Simply put, if the rungs of the ladder are too far apart, then it becomes almost impossible to climb up the ladder. So the poor and those living paycheque to paycheque start to believe that the system is rigged.

As historian Tony Judt warned, extreme inequality is corrosive, leading inevitably to feelings of superiority and inferiority and a breakdown in solidarity.[33] The rich too often come to believe that they are the job creators and that they deserve all they have. Less dependent than the rest of us on public services, they can effectively secede from society—or at least think they can. So why pay taxes? And, with extreme inequality, their voices carry great weight. If money always talks, then massive amounts of money talk even more loudly.

Increasingly, then, we see taxes on corporations and the rich decline and government's footprint get smaller. This is not to say that the austerity agenda is some libertarian utopia of voluntarism and a disappearing state. Government still matters—some taxes are necessary—but its role or purpose shifts away from the welfare state with its focus on social justice and opportunity to the security state with its emphasis on surveillance and punishment. Cynically, one might say that the primary role of government has become protection of the market and those who benefit most from it. The result? Massive increases in incarceration, the creation of an underclass excluded from social and economic opportunities, and an increasingly intrusive state, ever more foreign, remote, something outside us. Here in Canada, intrusive counterterrorism legislation, a decade of "tough on crime" laws, and increased reliance on incarceration—even for many who have never been convicted of a crime—demonstrate that this is not some remote dystopian future. This, Ibbitson says, is the second pillar of the Harper legacy, and again no party seems to be ready to reverse course.[34]

CONCLUSION: TAXES AND DEMOCRACY

And so we come full circle. If the system is rigged, then why participate, why vote? If we believe that government is not there for us, that there is really not much that government can or should do to help us, that we are pretty much on our own, and that there really is no alternative, then why participate, why vote?

About eighty years ago, Antonio Gramsci wrote that there are moments in history when confidence in the prevailing order has disintegrated but no new consensus has formed, what he called "interregnum," when the old world is dying and the new world is not yet born, a time of "morbid symptoms."[35] Gramsci was writing during such a time, so he well understood the stakes. As the Brexit vote in the United Kingdom, the electoral victory of Donald Trump in the United States, and the threat of authoritarian nativist parties throughout Europe attest, these are dangerous times. Joseph Stiglitz talks about "globalization's new discontent."[36] Chris Hedges warns that we have entered a revolutionary moment.[37]

Andrew Potter recently offered a provocative and insightful view of two very different orientations to politics: we can find ourselves along a continuum from cynic to naïf. For the naïf, politics is a contest of ideas, a conversation about our future.[38] Policy platforms and debates are what matter most. Our votes are decisions about the future of our country. For the cynic, politics is primarily about the exchange of power, the circulation of elites, "throwing the bums out," and replacing them with another set of bums. Policy platforms are pretty much marketing tools. In the end, whoever wins must contend with the diverse interests of the electorate and make the necessary compromises and trade-offs, or they will be replaced. Politics is the art of the possible.

The cynics have been on the ascendancy. But where are we when all politics is practised within a shrunken version of what is possible? And what if that shrunken politics is increasingly irrelevant to an increasingly restive electorate? If people lose trust in their democratic institutions and the governments that they yield, then we should not be surprised when many turn to strongmen (yes, usually men) who seem to transcend government and promise to bring it and the detested elites to heel, "saviours" who will protect their interests against "the other." Mistrust and skepticism make fertile ground for right-wing populist demagogues. If we cannot renew our democratic institutions, and if we cannot restore citizens' trust that things can be made better for the many while protecting individual freedom and rights of minorities, then Blakeney's vision of democracy as a "fair share for all in a free society" will seem impossibly naive.[39]

If we are even to begin to turn this around, a good place to start would be to change the Canadian conversation on taxes, to end austerity, and above all to reverse growing inequality. This, clearly, is no easy task. The backlash and controversy that still linger from recent attempts by the federal government to close just a couple of the many loopholes in our tax system are reminders that tax remains politically explosive terrain. But it is terrain that must be crossed.

At a minimum, governments should stop making things worse by continually pursuing unaffordable tax cuts. And they should collect what is owed, reviewing domestic policies and international agreements to close loopholes that allow for the loss of tens of billions through tax evasion and avoidance. The leaking of the Panama Papers and Paradise Papers show just how easy it is for the rich to find ways of avoiding paying their share, undermining the legitimacy of our tax system. Public anger has led to welcome government investments in enhanced tax enforcement. More is needed.

Furthermore, immediate steps should be taken to make our tax system more progressive. Recent data show that Canada is not as effective at mitigating market inequalities as it used to be and as are many other rich countries. We have room and reason to move.

More than that, it is time for a fundamental review of our tax system to bring it in line with our changing demography and labour market and, above all, to ensure that it is fair and adequate for the environmental and social challenges before us.

Potter's cynics might roll their eyes, but there is nothing naive or outdated in Blakeney's view of what democracy can be. We are witnessing the dangers that arise when people lose trust and hope, when cynicism prevails. The stakes are high. If we are to recover Blakeney's hopeful vision, however, we need to be willing to pay the freight. It's time for a different conversation on taxes. It's time to reconnect taxes to the common good.

CHAPTER 9

SOCIAL DEMOCRACY AND THE CANADIAN WELFARE STATE

Nelson Wiseman

Social democracy seeks to extend democracy from the political realm to the economic and social spheres. For social democrats, social programs are an underpinning of Canadian democracy. For Allan Blakeney, this meant the "pursuit of the objective of fair shares for all in a free society."[1] Industrialization, urbanization, and the dislocations of war and the Depression expanded the role of the state in providing social security, but social democrats like Blakeney were in the vanguard of those calling for comprehensive universal social programs. They continuously sought to counter poverty and to maximize welfare in the interests of producing a more egalitarian society in which social cohesion and solidarity prevailed.

Although social democrats have never held national power, their ethical judgments and ideals have been pivotal in the creation, evolution, and defence of the Canadian welfare state. They laid its intellectual and operational groundwork and were the first to push for the programs that came to constitute the welfare state: primitive old age pensions in the 1920s, unemployment insurance and family allowances in the 1940s, hospital insurance in the 1950s, medical insurance and a universal pension plan in the 1960s, social housing in the 1970s, and elder care, child care, and pharmacare subsequently. Indeed, one New Democratic Party (NDP) member of Parliament has claimed that hers is *The Party that Changed Canada*,[2] and party leaders have cited the welfare state as its signal achievement.[3]

In many respects, Canadian politics and social policy have mirrored those of Western Europe more closely than those of the United States.[4] Europe's socialist governments have shaped policy; in the United States, socialism has had little purchase, and the liberal party there, the Democrats, have appropriated social policy prescriptions as their own radical ideas. In Canada, social democrats have been less powerful than those in Europe, but they have not been as impotent as those in the United States. To be sure, the welfare state is a common feature of all modern Western societies, but in the United States it has been detached from any socialist moorings; in Canada, it is tethered to them. Introduction of the Medicare program in Saskatchewan, for example, in which Blakeney played a key role, served as a template for a national program that became a national totem, "the most widely embraced symbol of the Canadian identity,"[5] and Canadians voted Medicare's father, Tommy Douglas, as "the greatest Canadian."[6]

IDEOLOGY AND WELFARE

Conservatives, liberals, and socialists view social welfare through different ideological lenses. Classical conservatives look to voluntary charitable efforts to aid the needy if family members, friends, and neighbours fall short. If inadequacies persist, then such conservatives, as opposed to many contemporary neoconservatives, are prepared to use the state to help fill the void. They are willing to do so in the interest of maintaining social order and harmonizing the interests of different classes. The role of the state, however, is to be minimal and marginal. Philosophical liberals, like classical conservatives, look first to the philanthropic provision of social welfare. Reacting to the paternalism and authority of the classical conservative state, liberals are leery of state power and champion self-reliance. The limitations of the liberal creed of laissez-faire, however, have led liberals, who remain reluctant statists, to acknowledge a role for government in helping to equalize opportunities for individuals.

Social democrats are suspicious of the outcomes produced by the "invisible hand" of the liberal's idealized market. They seek to deploy state power and establish high-quality universal social programs as remedies for social problems and to produce more egalitarian outcomes. Some social democrats favour nationally centralized, top-down management of programs; others favour more participatory, self-managed, and decentralized organizational forms. Both liberals and social democrats are committed to enhancing progressively the human experience, but their rationales differ: liberals accept a welfare floor to compensate for the failure of individuals in the marketplace because of illness, disability, or access to education; social democrats see a welfare safety net as a matter of social rights. For the latter, true personal liberty exists only in a context of social equality.

Canada and the United States share British parentage, but Canada's ties to Britain help explain its more collectivist approach to social policy. Looking to Britain's Conservatives,[7] Canada's Conservatives twinned the interests of labour and capital in the 1870s and pioneered trade union legislation.[8] Looking to Britain's Liberals,[9] Canada's Liberals supplemented their business liberalism with welfare liberalism.[10] And, looking to Britain's Labour Party, Canada's social democrats drew on its program of social security.

The policy attitudes of partisan liberals, conservatives, and social democrats highlight the much stronger attachment of the last group to the welfare state. Surveys of party activists at NDP, Liberal, and Conservative conventions in the 1980s revealed that relatively few NDPers thought that recipients abuse welfare programs. NDPers were the most consistent in their attitudes; a majority of them opposed means tests to access welfare programs in contrast to the partisans of the other parties. Two percent or less of the NDPers supported decreased funding for education, housing, welfare, or health; the attitudes of Conservatives were polar opposites, and the attitudes of Liberals fell in between.[11] Such differences make the Liberals susceptible to pressure by social democrats or "contagion from the left."[12] These attitudes have not changed over the decades. The overwhelming majority of NDP activists in a 2009 survey thought universalism was important in health and pension programs and that talk of welfare abuse is exaggerated.[13] Most Conservative voters in 2015 wanted less welfare spending, most NDP voters wanted more, and Liberal voters were more evenly divided.[14]

Liberal governments created the federal programs that constitute the modern welfare state, but it was social democrats who led and helped them to do it. As centrists ambiguous and ambivalent about their ideology but decidedly opposed to socialism, Liberals adopted welfare legislation in part to undercut support for the Cooperative Commonwealth Federation (CCF) and its successor, the NDP. The parties developed an "antagonistic symbiosis," with the Liberals relying on the CCF-NDP for innovative policy ideas and the CCF-NDP depending on the Liberals to implement them.[15] For Liberal Prime Minister Louis St. Laurent, the CCF was composed of "Liberals in a hurry."[16] For CCFers, the Liberals were reluctant collectivists susceptible to pressure.

ORIGINS AND FOUNDATIONS

The Canadian welfare state emerged as a product of the country's political culture, institutions, and interplay of its political parties. Fledgling socialist parties had debuted in the late nineteenth century when debate swirled about whether regulating factory conditions, minimum wages, public health, and compulsory education was consistent with the prevailing belief in laissez-faire. Many non-socialists, including one-time Prime Minister Charles Tupper, supported social security measures such as life insurance but, as in his case, relented in the face of opposition from private corporations.[17]

As factories proliferated and industrialization proceeded, compensation for workplace injuries became a cause shared by organized labour and social democrats. Canada's labour-socialists pointed to New Zealand, which adopted such legislation in the 1890s, and Britain, which did so in 1906. Most of Canada's provinces followed suit, creating government insurance funds that assumed liability when employers defaulted or were insolvent. In contrast, most states in the United States relied exclusively on private casualty or mutual assistance firms. Unlike the American courts, which struck down compulsory compensation laws, Canada's courts upheld them.[18] These differences in jurisprudence spoke to Canada's stronger collectivist political culture, its greater receptivity to statism and socialism. J.W. Longley, Nova Scotia's Liberal attorney general in the 1890s, noted that regulatory laws are "socialistic" by nature and that "both Socialism and Individualism are consistent with true liberalism."[19] A related sentiment appeared in *Queen's Quarterly*: "Socialistic schemes are the attempts of men to better their lot in life. This desire is natural and the aim praiseworthy....Almost the whole machinery of civic government is socialistic in...[a] limited sense."[20]

The Methodist Church in Canada led the charge for an unemployment insurance program after Britain adopted such a program in 1911.[21] A tribune for the poor, labour-socialist leader and former Methodist clergyman J.S. Woodsworth used his parliamentary platform and the pages of *Canadian Forum* to make the case for unemployment insurance.[22] Liberals and Conservatives dismissed it as a municipal issue and disruptive to the labour market. However, promising social reforms—including old age pensions and health and unemployment insurance—William Lyon Mackenzie King won the Liberal leadership in 1919. Once King became prime minister, Woodsworth and Labour MP William Irvine pressed him on welfare issues, but he claimed that his government's minority status kept him from acting. After King secured a majority government in 1926, he brought in a rudimentary pension program in response to pressure by the Labour MPs.[23] Although they supported his pension program, social democrats were not satisfied because it was means-tested and dependent on provinces sharing the cost. Nevertheless, social democrats took credit for the program, and it set a pattern for the rest of the century: Liberals would introduce welfare programs only after prodding by social democrats. Woodsworth also fought in Parliament for the belief that "a wage sufficient to provide for a reasonable standard of living should constitute a legal minimum."[24]

In many respects, Britain and the United States showed Canada its social policy future. This was logical. Many Canadians looked to Britain as a cultural and political model while they simultaneously drifted into the economic and cultural orbit of the United States. The New Deal's social welfare measures in the United States in the 1930s reverberated in Canada. In that decade, the CCF emerged against the backdrop of the Depression, and in the 1940s the Canadian welfare state emerged in a setting of war and the high point of popularity for the CCF.

As many Canadian academics and intellectuals in the 1930s shifted from humanistic and religious studies to a more scientific orientation,[25] the appeal of the religiously driven social gospel, which had impelled social democrats in the first quarter of the century, faded.[26] Social democrats adopted the idea of social planning in an increasingly secular society. Never as fervent as their American counterparts in defending laissez-faire, Canadian academics became more favourably disposed to mitigating the negative effects of capitalism. Mainstream economic theory began to incorporate concern for the amelioration of social conditions while the climate of opinion among both elites and the broader public changed. Popular thinking began to accept that the destitute were not necessarily accountable for their condition and that social welfare was not necessarily demeaning. There was a shift in public consensus on the role of government and the entitlements of persons. The grimness of the Depression led even Conservative Prime Minister R.B. Bennett to suggest that preserving capitalism required some redistribution of wealth.

The appearance of the CCF and the spectre of socialist electoral gains elicited a response in Quebec. Circulation of the party's founding Regina Manifesto so concerned Jesuit Joseph-Papin Archambault that his organization, École sociale populaire, produced a Programme de restauration sociale articulating the social doctrine of the Catholic Church. Archambault, fearing that atheistic socialism could become an alternative to the natural piety of capitalism, became the province's chief herald of the 1931 papal encyclical *Quadragesimo Anno*, which declared the church and other community organizations duty-bound to protect the community's weakest members.[27] The church, however, retarded the role of the Quebec provincial state in alleviating poverty. As well, Quebec had secured a legal opinion from future Prime Minister Louis St. Laurent that the 1927 old age pension program was an unconstitutional violation of provincial jurisdiction and opposed the program, only signing on to it nearly a decade after all of the provinces west of it had done so.[28]

The change in public attitudes from thinking that individuals and voluntary associations were solely responsible for social welfare to believing that the state had some obligation to provide assistance dovetailed with the ascent of the CCF as a political force. The party's brain trust, the League for Social Reconstruction (LSR), which modelled itself on Britain's Fabian Society, produced books that made the case for social security in the context of economic planning.[29] The LSR shared with the Fabians a non-doctrinaire, non-utopian orientation, faith in "the inevitability of gradualness," and belief in the iterative enhancement of social welfare.[30] This outlook led the LSR to propose insurance against illness, unemployment, accident, and old age and the provision of publicly administered medical and hospital services to attenuate "the common man's normal state of insecurity and hardship."[31] To the LSR's historian, "the major impact of the League, accompanied by the policies of the CCF, was the birth of the Canadian welfare state."[32]

With the Depression highlighting the plight of the unemployed, Labour MP A.A. Heaps repeatedly called for unemployment insurance.[33] The CCF's Regina Manifesto promised it, and future Saskatchewan Premier Tommy Douglas studied it as a PhD student. After the United States adopted and Bennett's government introduced such a program in 1935, King's newly elected Liberal government referred it to the courts, which struck it down as beyond Ottawa's jurisdiction. This frustrated social democrats dedicated to national programs. Acknowledging that it was beyond their financial capacities, the provinces finally agreed unanimously to transfer constitutional responsibility for unemployment insurance to Ottawa in 1940. Similarly, Ottawa gained responsibility for old age pensions a decade later. As centralists, social democrats welcomed both developments.

Writing in the field of social work as empirical academic pioneers rather than as idealists, leading LSR members Harry Cassidy and Leonard Marsh, both CCFers, sketched blueprints for the welfare state that was to emerge during and after the war.[34] Michael Bliss deemed Marsh's *Report on Social Security for Canada* "the most important single document in the history of the development of the welfare state in Canada."[35] Cassidy, the founding dean of the School of Social Welfare at the University of California, Berkeley, and the British-born Marsh had undertaken research for Liberal Sir William Beveridge. Admirers of his report,[36] Cassidy and Marsh saw social welfare as buttressing the liberal and socialist ideal of the emancipation of individuality and the free development of personality. They believed that education, research, and technology combined with planning fostered social welfare.

The CCF pursued welfare reforms in a manner akin to pulling teeth from the governing Liberals. Unlike classical liberals, content to attempt to provide equal opportunities for individuals, social democrats aspired to the equality of conditions. Despite the rhetorical flourish of the concluding sentence in the Regina Manifesto—"No CCF Government will rest content until it has eradicated capitalism..."—both the CCF's parliamentary party and its extra-parliamentary brain trust, like social democrats in the rest of the world, were always resigned to humanizing capitalism rather than eliminating it.[37] They believed that gradualism would eventually yield transformative change. The approach of the CCF, like those of Cassidy and Marsh, was functionalist: a belief that intelligent adaptations of the prevailing system could remedy problems.[38] Scandinavians formulated this idea as "functional socialism."[39] The CCF, and then the NDP, drew increasing attention to Sweden's welfare system as a template for Canada's system.

Social democrats had long advocated family allowances; Woodsworth was the only MP to speak in support of a 1929 motion proposing them,[40] the 1942 CCF convention adopted a resolution favouring them, and the BC CCF proposed that provinces introduce them if Ottawa did not.[41] After Marsh's report recommended family allowances, a wider public debate ensued; the Canadian Congress of Labour and the majority of the country's professional social workers endorsed them.[42] Having been unsympathetic to a family allowance program in the 1930s, King unveiled such a program in the run-up to the 1945 election when the federal CCF was a more serious competitor for office than at any time in its history. After an amendment by CCF MP Stanley Knowles,[43] and after an appeal by future Quebec CCF President Thérèse Casgrain, the family allowance went to mothers rather than fathers.[44]

EXTENSION AND CONSOLIDATION

A broad consensus arose that a welfare state ought to emerge from the warfare state, as the CCF had been advocating. The imperatives of war had validated the efficacy of economic and social planning, and Canada's alliance with the Soviet Union quieted antisocialist feelings. As support for the party grew between 1942 and 1944, the book *Make This Your Canada* by CCF national secretary David Lewis and party chairman Frank Scott became a national bestseller.[45] The CCF, which had no representation in Ontario's legislature, came within four seats of winning the provincial election and, within a week, won two federal by-elections in previously held Liberal prairie ridings. Ten months later the CCF won power in Saskatchewan. Party strength in British Columbia led the Liberals and Conservatives to coalesce, and the Manitoba party captured as many votes as the governing Liberal-Progressives in 1945. To blunt the popularity of the CCF, the Liberals and Conservatives responded with similar welfare proposals. In the Ontario election of 1943, for example, the Conservatives had promised mothers' allowances, pensions, "the fairest and most advanced labour laws," and "economic and social security from the cradle to the grave."[46]

Universal social programs extended the universal commitment that war had required in the form of mass production and mass participation. A series of reports during the war, including those by Cassidy and Marsh and studies of health insurance and housing, had addressed anticipated postwar problems. Simultaneously, the federal bureaucracy turned to Keynesianism, which advocated government spending to stabilize economic conditions during recessions. King's Liberals campaigned in the 1945 election on the slogan "A New Social Order for Canada": one of social security. Not to be outflanked, the federal Conservatives offered a "People's Charter," which recognized "the right of every worker to a fair day's pay...[and] of every citizen to security against loss of income arising from accident, sickness, loss of employment, old-age or other disability."[47] Both "old line parties," as the CCF characterized them, pledged social security without socialism.

Thus, the CCF's welfare state vision helped to shape the public policy agendas of its adversaries. The party's electoral prospects were dashed, however, when a smear campaign succeeded in associating the party with communism and atheism. To be sure, the CCF shared some welfare policy objectives with the Communist Party; women from both parties, for example, rallied to expand child-care services and to save from closure the daycare nurseries created during the war.[48] Opponents of the CCF, however, turned the social gospel's Christian and compassionate justification for social welfare on its head. A prominent advertisement in the *Globe and Mail* scorned the CCF as being incapable of embracing the "Christian way of life" and of being "tied hand and foot" to the Communist Party.[49] A Conservative poster similarly asserted that "Religious Socialism and Christian Socialism are expressions implying a contradiction in terms."[50]

Ironically, as the CCF faltered during the Cold War and the onset of postwar prosperity, its campaign for a social welfare state became part of the popular zeitgeist. Even conservative business circles accepted social security as "a first charge on the nation's wealth," with the *Globe and Mail* editorializing that "only when the majority of people have been assured a comparatively high standard of living, with security against unemployment, old age and sickness, is a surplus available for any other purpose."[51] The CCF transformed itself into the NDP in 1961, but its founding program continued the CCF's promise of "comprehensive social security."

The Douglas CCF government in Saskatchewan had groomed a cadre of professional public administrators, including Blakeney, in tune with social democratic objectives.[52] Blakeney was subsequently elected, played a pivotal role in the creation of Medicare, and was subsequently appointed minister of health to administer the program. Ottawa's Liberal government in the 1960s enlisted some of Blakeney's public administration colleagues, notably A.W. Johnson and Tommy Shoyama, to aid in the construction of additional national welfare programs. They included the national Medicare program, the Canada Pension Plan (CPP), the Canada Assistance Plan, and the Guaranteed Income Supplement for retirees ineligible for CPP benefits, programs that Liberal Prime Minister Lester Pearson termed measures "to complete the welfare state."[53]

As leader of the new federal NDP, Douglas relocated to Ottawa and leveraged the party's position in a string of minority Parliaments to press the party's welfare agenda. When Ontario Premier John Robarts, who represented London and its outsized insurance industry, objected to the CPP, and fought Medicare as a "Machiavellian scheme" and one of Canada's "greatest political frauds,"[54] Douglas urged Pearson to stand firm: "Damn the torpedoes, full speed ahead."[55] The NDP also made the case for social housing. Until then, housing policy had focused almost exclusively on the private ownership sector.

Before the 1960s ended, the essentials of the national welfare regime were in place, with the NDP repeatedly calling for the enhancement or extension of benefits such as lowering the age of eligibility for the old age pension.[56] In the minority Parliament of 1972–74, the NDP used its positional advantage, as it had earlier, to persuade the Liberals to augment pensions and family allowances—the latter were almost tripled—and to back down on restricting eligibility for the old age pension.[57] Over NDP objections in majority Parliaments since then, a child tax benefit has replaced family allowances, and old age pensions are no longer universal since they are subject to being clawed back.

PROVINCIALIZING AND DEFENDING

Provinces are constitutionally responsible for social welfare. Since the 1950s, provincial capacities for and public expectations of health and welfare programs have grown dramatically. Such programs now define the primary policy role of the provincial state. As late as mid-century, provincial revenues equalled less than a third of Ottawa's revenues, and Ottawa accounted for three-quarters of all public expenditures on health and welfare.[58] Today provincial expenditures well exceed federal expenditures, and most of the federal expenditures are for health and welfare programs in a context in which Ottawa cost-shares programs with the provinces but does not deliver services. Welfare programs are also Ottawa's largest budgetary expenditure, largely in the form of direct payments to individuals and provinces with few conditions attached.

Saskatchewan is particularly significant in Canada's social welfare story since it served as a laboratory for innovative programs eventually adopted by other provinces and the federal government. Deliberately and systematically, the Douglas CCF government embarked on a strategy of wholesale social reform with "socialized medicine" as its priority. Douglas was particularly sensitive to the issue: as a child, he had been spared amputation of a leg only because his family had agreed to allow medical students to observe his surgeries in exchange for his free treatment.[59] A former social gospel preacher, Douglas considered public health care as the "inalienable right of being a citizen of a Christian country."[60] Under Saskatchewan's *Hospitalization Act* of 1946, the province covered virtually all hospital costs and relieved municipalities of paying for indigents. By the mid-1950s, four provinces had followed Saskatchewan's model. Parliament passed a federal *Hospital Insurance Act* modelled on it in 1957, and by 1963 it covered 99 percent of Canadians.[61] Medicare replicated this "demonstration effect" after Saskatchewan established a publicly funded and administered comprehensive scheme in 1962 in which Blakeney played a key role, one of the "two or three personal high notes" in his political career.[62] For him, it was an issue of social justice as well as social security, a concrete manifestation of the CCF's winning slogan in 1944, "Humanity First."[63]

As they attained power in more provinces, social democrats shifted their preference for centrally administered national programs to more decentralized local control of programs but not to devolving power to the provinces. In the 1970s, NDP governments in Saskatchewan, Manitoba, and British Columbia created some new welfare programs and expanded existing ones. Under Blakeney's premiership, a children's dental program and a prescription drug program were introduced, "the germ of a program that would work well for all of Canada."[64] In Manitoba, the NDP introduced Canada's first provincial home-care program for seniors, a model for programs in other provinces. The Manitoba NDP also eliminated Medicare premiums, subsidized prescription costs, expanded public housing, and launched a guaranteed income pilot project known as Mincome.[65] In subsequent decades, and despite the province's "have-not" status, the Manitoba party created a child-care regime "characterized by more social solidarity than in other English provinces,"[66] and it spent more per capita on early childhood education and daycare than any other province except Quebec.[67]

In British Columbia, Dave Barrett's NDP government launched no fewer than eighteen new programs, including "the most significant change in welfare policy...arguably over the entire postwar period."[68] The NDP decentralized, coordinated, and incorporated citizen participation in social service delivery. In just three years, the NDP government increased welfare rates between 20 and 40 percent.[69] Barrett, as well as Manitoba NDP Premier Greg Selinger and former federal NDP leader Audrey McLaughlin, were trained social workers, a group overrepresented among social democratic supporters and generally sympathetic to and vested in the welfare state.

The harsh realities of governing have resulted in some dissonance between NDP provincial governments, whose positions are more complicated, and the federal NDP, which has never governed. As one example, Manitoba Premier Ed Schreyer spoke of "able-bodied welfare recipients" who produced "a profound seething resentment against the whole welfare system." It was "unrealistic and unfair" of them, he said, to refuse jobs 100 miles away when others were prepared to take them.[70] In contrast, federal NDP leader David Lewis lambasted the Liberals at the same time for fuelling a backlash against welfare recipients.[71] Like Schreyer, Mike Harcourt's NDP government in British Columbia in the 1990s adopted an image of toughness with abusers of welfare, and Bob Rae's NDP government in Ontario hired hundreds of workers to review the province's 690,000 welfare cases in a bid to snare those cheating the system.[72] All three premiers consolidated their provincial welfare regimes in a context of fiscal constraint and federal cuts to provincial transfers.

Ontario's NDP government relieved municipalities of welfare costs as those costs rose by more than double the rate of inflation between 1990 and 1993. Subsequently, the government lowered or eliminated the income taxes of many on low incomes, but it also reduced transfers to schools, universities, and hospitals.[73] The NDP also considered but did not act on a proposal to tie welfare benefits to recipients' efforts to find employment.[74] Revising its welfare policies, the Ontario NDP alienated some of its erstwhile supporters. Some assumed that, since women comprised approximately 42 percent of the cabinet, more positive policy outcomes would follow for women. Although child-care spaces were added, parental leave was extended, and the minimum wage was raised, the presence of so many female ministers did not keep the government from imposing limits on some welfare programs.[75]

Social democrats continue to champion standardized and enhanced universal national welfare programs and seek to entrench them as quintessentially Canadian values. This is not, however, an article of faith across the political spectrum. When the Liberal government of Lester Pearson insinuated in the 1960s that welfare programs might be subjected to needs tests, Stanley Knowles, the longest-serving CCF-NDP MP, described the idea as "affronting human dignity."[76] When the Liberal government of Pierre Trudeau reduced family allowances in the 1970s, the NDP called for their doubling.[77] Similarly, in the 1980s, the NDP opposed the Conservative government's clawback of the old age pension and family allowance benefits, which eliminated their universality.[78] Although NDP efforts fell short, the party contributed to strengthening public resistance to the wholesale dismantling of social programs.[79]

The experiences of provincial NDP governments with privatization reveal both similarities to and differences from their federal kin. Privatization gained increasing attention in the 1970s in a milieu of federal cuts to provincial transfers, fiscal pressures, and growing demands on welfare services. These factors led to the privatization of more social services, but NDP governments responded differently from their partisan rivals. Unlike the Conservatives, they did not engage in restraint gleefully. They opposed for-profit privatization and looked more kindly at non-profit privatization delivered by non-governmental organizations.

In Saskatchewan and British Columbia, NDP governments in the 1970s favoured the voluntary sector for delivering public/private social services.[80] More focused on economic policy than on social policy, Blakeney's government supported the federal Liberal policy of wage controls and dropped its statist bias in service delivery in favour of community-based delivery. Although it fell short on some commitments, for example delivering only a quarter of the daycare spaces that it had promised[81] and being characterized as dabbling in the issue,[82] Blakeney's government remained insistent on the principle of universality. Under even more extreme fiscal pressure than in the 1970s, Roy Romanow's NDP government in the early 1990s rationalized social programs, cut spending on both education and health, and closed over fifty rural hospitals.[83] Manitoba's NDP government contracted out child welfare services but restricted contracts to the non-profit sector and actively discouraged for-profit proprietary operations.[84]

An intriguing proposal by Ontario's NDP government was to incorporate a "social charter" into the Constitution. It would have enshrined positive rights to social programs in the *Charter of Rights and Freedoms* alongside the negative liberties there.[85] Based loosely upon a European Union charter, it would have obliged the federal government to guarantee social rights, including health care, employment, and shelter. The proposal came to naught, but it reflected the continuing association of social democracy with social welfare.

The federal NDP has consistently called for more resources for what it has deemed malnourished social programs such as pensions, income supplements for seniors, maternity leave benefits, unemployment insurance, and social housing as well as for more cash transfers to provinces for the social programs they deliver. During the Brian Mulroney and Jean Chrétien administrations, the NDP pushed back against retrenchment of the welfare state, but its leverage was limited because they led majority governments. The influence of the NDP reasserted itself, however, when Paul Martin led a Liberal minority government in 2005; in exchange for propping it up, the party under Jack Layton extracted over $4 billion in spending for affordable housing, more pension protection for workers, and transfers to the provinces to reduce tuition fees as an addition to the Canada Millennium Scholarships that the Liberals had created.[86] Since then, the party has promised to reintroduce a federal minimum wage, create a national daycare and early learning program, create a caregiver tax credit, and offset prescription costs.[87] These are the most urgently needed additions to the contemporary welfare state.

CONCLUSION

By the 1990s, Canada, with one of the lowest rates of poverty among seniors in the world, had avoided the extremes of rising poverty and inequality. In good measure, this was because many Canadians consider universal social benefits as more than citizenship entitlements; they consider them as part of their national identity. Three-quarters of Canadians positively consider the social democratic ideal of more equitably redistributed income and wealth, seeing it as a societal virtue.[88] Provincial CCF-NDP parties have been in the forefront, building and defending the welfare state. They have won more than two dozen elections and governed for almost seventy-five years.

Reflecting the relative strength of social democracy, Ontario, British Columbia, Saskatchewan, Quebec, and the Yukon, whose populations constitute over three-quarters of Canadians, all had social democratic governments in 1995. Since then, Manitoba, Nova Scotia, and Alberta have also elected NDP governments. In a comment on the success of social democracy, Mulroney decried social welfare programs as contributing to "the tragic process of the Swedenizing of Canada" before he became the Conservative leader;[89] once on the hustings seeking office, however, he spoke of those programs as a "sacred trust not to be tampered with."[90]

In the twenty-first century, the unwavering commitment of social democrats to social justice and a fairer distribution of the fruits of economic growth continues to differentiate them from philosophical conservatives and liberals. Globalization, however, challenges social democracy's social welfare agenda. Social democrats are now often on the defensive, seeking to shield and stabilize demand-driven social programs such as health care. In this context, social democrats have scaled back attempts at economic restructuring and settled for fostering a private investment climate favourable to generating the revenues necessary to sustain the welfare state.[91]

With the influx of immigrants from the global South, the entry of unprecedented numbers of women into the paid labour force, and a heightened consciousness of Indigenous people's issues, social democrats have added diversity to their conceptions of class and democracy. Social democrats have long seen women, some ethnic groups, and racial minorities as being shortchanged, but in recent decades they have determined that the lower status of such groups cannot be ascribed solely to the capitalist market economy. They have come to see racism and patriarchy as being less connected to capitalism than they had imagined. In recognition of the "collective cultural rights for minorities," social democrats have come to identify with the welfare needs of equity-seeking groups and drawn special attention to them.[92]

Changing workplace patterns—more women in the labour force, more part-time employment, and fewer stable, well-paying jobs with benefits for the less educated—have put pressure on Canada's social welfare architecture. With fewer workers eligible for employment insurance benefits and extended health-care benefits than in the past, with the increasing use and cost of drugs in medical treatment, and with little government support for growing numbers of caregivers for the ill and disabled, social welfare policy requires redesigning.[93]

The middle class has grown and benefited in recent decades from the welfare state. Because it is the primary beneficiary, it has developed an interest in defending that state.[94] This has led the NDP to make more electoral appeals to this class because, in a liberal democratic regime like that in Canada, "there is more consensus about welfare between better-off sections of the working class and the middle class."[95] This has led Marxists such as Adam Przeworski to write of "class compromise."[96]

As opposition parties, social democrats will continue to press for a compassionate social welfare agenda. With a Liberal majority government once again in Ottawa, the NDP is back to its traditional role of pushing the Liberals leftward. Whether Prime Minister Justin Trudeau will turn to the NDP's ideas like King turned to the CCF's ideas remains an open question. In power, the actions of social democratic governments—Blakeney's and Romanow's governments are examples—are mediated by fiscal realities and globalization pressures. Globalized finance, trade, manufacturing, and communication might limit the ability but not the will of social democrats to resist assaults on the welfare state. Nor will such forces restrain the aspirations of social democrats to rebuild it.

CHAPTER 10

BECAUSE IT'S 2019
GENDER, CANADIAN POLITICS, AND THE DEMOCRATIC DEFICIT

Melanee Thomas

Although he was one of Canada's greatest premiers, Allan Blakeney might not be best remembered as a paragon of diversity. His government admittedly generated important policy "firsts" for women in Saskatchewan; for example, his government established a legal framework for gender-based pay equity in 1971, set up a task force to study how the recommendations from the Royal Commission on the Status of Women could be implemented in Saskatchewan, and created the first Advisory Council on the Status of Women in the province's history.[1] That said, under Blakeney's leadership, the Saskatchewan New Democratic Party (NDP) not only failed to elect a single woman to office but also failed to nominate as many women as the Liberals or Conservatives throughout the 1970s. In fact, the NDP nominated no women as candidates for the 1978 general election, and women's issues "disappeared from the NDP's discourse and platforms" in the late 1970s and early 1980s.[2] If one identifiable group of citizens—women—appear to have been systematically excluded from participation in a government, then what does that mean for Blakeney's legacy?

I argue in this chapter that, in general, the systematic underrepresentation or (at times) full exclusion of women in Canadian politics is a strong indicator of democratic deficit and malaise. More specifically, this lens helps us to place Blakeney and his accomplishments in a historical context, but it also helps us to identify ongoing issues in contemporary Canadian democracy.

I explore here gender and Canadian democracy in four steps. First, I outline what gender-based representation is and why it matters in the Canadian context. Second, I outline how many, and which types of, women are elected representatives in Canada. Third, I analyze why women's representation is so much lower than their demographic weight by framing women in elected Canadian politics in terms of supply and demand. Although there are credible and serious problems with the supply of women who can be presented as candidates, the balance of evidence shows that the real barriers are created by the lack of demand, especially from political parties, for women in politics. And fourth, I examine what happens to women once they are elected, showing that the treatment of many women in politics reflects deep-seated sexism. Although Blakeney could have been forgiven for being lukewarm on gender issues in politics, no one in Canadian politics in 2019 can justify being lackadaisical on the issue.

WHY DOES DIVERSITY IN REPRESENTATION MATTER?

It would be unfair to suggest that Canadians are unconcerned about diversity in political representation. Indeed, they appear to approach the world from a reasonably feminist viewpoint. In 2011, almost 75 percent of Canadians rejected the idea that Canadian society would be better off if more women stayed at home. Nearly 66 percent disagreed that equality has been achieved between women and men in Canada, and a slim majority (52 percent) agreed that more should be done for women. Importantly, 60 percent of Canadians thought that the best way to protect women's interests is to increase their presence in Parliament.* Given these data, it seems to be fair to conclude that most Canadians agree with the basic democratic principle that women ought to have the same rights and opportunities as men.

Yet women are arguably the most underrepresented identifiable group in Canadian politics. Although they comprise over 50 percent of the general population, their average proportion across federal and provincial legislatures in Canada in 2016 was approximately 27 percent. This means that women's

---

* These data are from the 2011 Canadian Election Study (CES). More information about CES data can be found at http://www.queensu.ca/cora/ces.html.

political representation was about half of what it should have been given their proportion of the population. However, when asked directly if their current level of representation in the House of Commons—far below women's demographic weight in the population—was a problem, 70 percent of Canadians said that it was a minor problem if a problem at all.* This presents a paradox: if so many Canadians acknowledge that gender inequality exists and that the best way to address it is to elect more women to political positions, then why do so many Canadians refuse to identify women's underrepresentation as a problem, let alone a problem that ought to be taken seriously?

This might have been the paradox that Blakeney himself faced: although it is fairly easy to identify that women experience inequalities relative to men, it is far more difficult to achieve consensus on when those inequalities are political and when they merit a political solution. In the literature, there are three particularly compelling arguments for increasing women's presence in politics. The first is related to equity and justice; the second is based upon policy-relevant information that women bring to politics; and the third shows that women, in fact, are better representatives for women than are men.

One way to evaluate how good a job a legislature, such as the House of Commons or the Saskatchewan Legislative Assembly, is doing is to ask how well it matches the population that it represents. When there is a mismatch between the composition of the legislature and the population, the legislature is unrepresentative.[3] By this standard, all legislatures in Canada are unrepresentative because they are doing a poor job of representing the diversity of the Canadian public. This is perhaps perplexing, for there are no formal legal barriers preventing any identifiable group of Canadians from fully exercising their democratic rights.† Given that such barriers could not be justified in Canada now, there is no good or just reason why historically excluded groups should not now be present in politics in numbers proportionate to their demographic weights. That historically excluded groups such as women continue to be underrepresented suggests that there are strong informal barriers that continue to prevent them from entering electoral politics.

Critiquing the House of Commons for its composition might be justifiable from an equity perspective, but for those who might prefer to assess a legislature on its actions this critique is admittedly weak. As a result, it is worth

---

* These data are from the 2004 CES.

† The last formal barrier was removed in 1960, allowing Indigenous Peoples to vote in federal elections without relinquishing their treaty status.

asking if and how a legislature might act differently if more women (and other historically excluded groups) were included in larger numbers. Research suggests that legislatures do act differently when they are gender balanced and that women are best represented by women for several reasons. First, women have been excluded from politics based upon erroneous ideas about their inability to rule.[4] Arguably, their continued exclusion from politics rests, in part, on stereotypes informed by past legal barriers suggesting that women are not "as good" at politics as men. Thus, increasing women's presence in politics now might help to correct these stereotypical assumptions. Certainly, the proliferation of women in premiers' offices between 2010 and 2016 helps to show that women can, in fact, "do politics" as well as men.

Second, diverse representatives bring experiences to legislatures that are useful for deliberation and policy processes. This information helps to show which policies are good for Canadians as a whole and which are better for some groups instead of others.[5] Importantly, because groups that have been excluded historically, such as women, are diverse, this information function justifies why each group must have representatives present in a legislature in proportion to its weight in the population. This reflects the reality that white women have experiences different from those of immigrant women, who have experiences different from those of Indigenous women, who all have experiences different from those of various other groups and types of men. These different experiences produce a variety of politically relevant attitudes and policy preferences.[6] This information can be crucial for government policy, for the political executive in Canada is primarily drawn from members of the legislature.

Third, research shows that even with their low numbers women in Canadian politics advocate for gendered policy considerations and women's concerns more than their male peers.[7] Yet studies also show that Canadian politics constrains women's ability to act for women, even in key political roles. Part of the reason is that men in politics react differently to women in positions of leadership than they do to men in the same roles. For example, in some contexts men become more hostile to women in politics as their numbers increase,[8] whereas in other contexts men can alter their motivations and policy decisions when they work with women.[9] Decision rules are key: when operating under majority rules, women need to form a majority before they achieve speaking time or influence equal to that of men. However, when groups tasked with political decision making are required to operate unanimously, a woman's ability to provide information and affect outcomes is considerable.[10] Thus, under Canada's majoritarian legislative rules, these results suggest that women's influence in Canadian politics will increase considerably only when women and men are equally present.

WOMEN IN CANADIAN POLITICS

The few times when women are equally present in politics compared with men—notably in parity cabinets comprised of equal numbers of women and men—one of the most prominent critiques raised is that ministers should be appointed on "merit" rather than gender.[11] This argument is predicated on the erroneous assumption that, by representing gender, some other characteristic, such as judgment or policy knowledge, might not be represented. In other words, suggesting that gender does not merit representation is like suggesting that women are not (as) qualified (as men) to be representatives.

This view runs counter to the Canadian Constitution. Section 3 of the *Canadian Charter of Rights and Freedoms* stipulates that "every citizen of Canada has the right to vote in an election of members of the House of Commons or of a legislative assembly and to be qualified for membership therein."[12] This is an important frame for any discussion of historically underrepresented groups or political representatives who might appear to be "atypical" because of past exclusions. In Canada, the highest law of the land asserts that all citizens are *qualified* to be elected representatives.

This has not always been the case. White women in Canada were first granted a provincial franchise in 1916 in Manitoba; they did not receive the federal franchise until 1920. White women finally received the provincial vote in Quebec in 1940. For women of colour, the franchise was slower in coming. Japanese and South Asian women could vote in federal elections in 1947, and race was eliminated as a ground for exclusion from federal elections for non-Indigenous Canadians in 1948. However, Indigenous Peoples, including women, were not granted the unfettered right to vote in federal elections until 1960.[13] Thus, with the removal of these formal barriers, and the adoption of the *Charter* rights noted above, there remain no formal legal barriers to women's participation in Canadian electoral politics.

WHICH CANADIANS ARE ELECTED REPRESENTATIVES? WHICH WOMEN?

Given the absence of formal barriers, and the clear statement in Section 3 of the *Charter* that all citizens are qualified for elected office in Canada, how well does the current House of Commons reflect the Canadian population?

Of the 338 members of Parliament (MPs) elected to the 42nd Parliament, 26 percent are women (*n*=88), 14 percent are visible minorities (*n*=46), and 3 percent are Indigenous.[14] In contrast, 51 percent of Canadians are women, 19 percent are visible minorities, and 4.3 percent are Indigenous.[15] This means that Canadian women's representation in the House of Commons is half of their demographic weight, whereas both visible minorities and Indigenous people are represented at about 70 percent of their respective demographic weights. Importantly, women's underrepresentation extends to visible minority and Indigenous MPs. Far more white women than women of colour are elected as MPs.

Women in the House of Commons also come from considerably different occupational backgrounds than their male peers.* Most MPs who are men are in business or law prior to election. Women MPs, in contrast, are more likely to be teachers and community activists.[16] This trend is reflected at all levels of government: even in municipal politics, women are most likely to participate in school boards, whereas men are more likely to sit on public utilities boards and municipal councils.[17]

Indeed, women, visible minorities, and Indigenous Peoples would all be more present in Canada's representative institutions if they were randomly selected from the population instead of through general elections. These large differences at the federal level, and their replication in provincial legislatures and municipal councils, suggest that informal barriers continue to prevent these identifiable groups from fully participating in Canadian politics.

WHY ARE THERE SO FEW WOMEN? SUPPLY VERSUS DEMAND

If both research and public opinion suggest that the best way to protect the interests of women (and other historically excluded groups) is to elect more of them to Parliament, then why is Canada so slow to elect more women?

---

* Canada's MPs are also older than Canadians: the average MP is fifty-three years old, though women MPs are slightly younger (fifty-two). See Parliament of Canada, "Members of the House of Commons Average Age: Current List," 2015, http://www.parl.gc.ca/parlinfo/lists/ParliamentarianAge.aspx?Menu=HOC-Bio&Parliament=&Chamber=03d93c58-f843-49b3-9653-84275c23f3fb&Section=Default&Gender=F&Name=&Province=&Party. The average Canadian is only forty years old, though women's average age (forty-one) is higher than men's (thirty-nine). See Statistics Canada, "Annual Demographic Estimates: Canada, Provinces, and Territories," Statistics Canada, Demography Division, 2012, http://www.statcan.gc.ca/pub/91-215-x/91-215-x2012000-eng.pdf.

Although more women have been elected to the House of Commons over the past twenty years (from fifty-three in 1993 to eighty-eight in 2015), the rate of change has been very slow at less than 1 percent per year.[18] The answer to this question is typically framed in terms of supply and demand, and the presence of informal barriers to women's political participation suggests that powerful factors could be restricting both the supply of women willing to stand as candidates and MPs and the demand from political parties and the public for women as elected representatives.

Potential Problems with Supply

There are three classic factors cited that diminish women's political participation and, by extension, the number of women candidates: socio-economic resources, political engagement, and family life.

Historically, socio-economic resources have been highlighted as the most important barrier to women's political participation and election. The earliest studies of individual-level political participation found that higher levels of education, income, and occupation were associated with higher levels of political participation. These studies also noted that women participated in politics at considerably lower rates than did men. They concluded that, as women's level of socio-economic resources caught up to men's, so would women's political participation.[19]

However, in Canada, women have made great socio-economic gains over the past few decades but remain underrepresented in politics. They are now more likely than men to earn university degrees.[20] Women's labour force participation has doubled since the 1970s, and women are now considerably more likely to be professionals and managers than they were in the past, though this progress is strongly conditioned by the economic field.[21] Women admittedly lag behind men in terms of earned income, as their median income is about two-thirds that of men,[22] and the gender pay gap is more acute in Canada than it is in other countries.[23]

Still, if socio-economic resources caused women's lower levels of political participation, then gaps in participation should have closed steadily over time as women's socio-economic resources increased. This has simply not been the case. Women are admittedly more likely than men to vote, but this appears to be more because women are more likely than men to see voting as a duty rather than a choice.[24] Women are still far less likely to engage in other forms of political participation, such as taking out a party membership, donating to a political party, or seeking a nomination for elected office.[25]

Income arguably remains a strong secondary individual-level barrier because of the absence of campaign finance regulations in some municipal and provincial jurisdictions. Similarly, though there are spending limits on federal nomination contests, these limits are high at approximately 20 percent of the electoral district's campaign spending cap.[26] Although it is not known how many candidates for nomination self-finance their campaigns, it is known that they typically fundraise from friends and family members.[27] This suggests that women might struggle more than men to fund a competitive nomination campaign not only because women have fewer financial resources of their own, on average, but also because their networks (presumably full of other women) have access to less money than many men's networks.

Although these financial barriers might be especially acute for some women, few nomination contests in Canada are actually contested, for the overwhelming majority of candidates for public office are acclaimed.[28] Given this, the perception that money matters a great deal in Canadian politics, especially for nomination and election campaigns, might do more to reduce the supply of women willing to participate as candidates than the gender gap in income and financial resources. And overall, given the significant change in women's socio-economic resources over time in Canada, other barriers must be at work.

Political engagement is likely a key factor that reduces the supply of potential women candidates. Women are less likely than men to be politically engaged, for women are significantly less interested in and knowledgeable about politics compared with men.[29] Women are also less likely than men to be confident in their political abilities.[30] These gender gaps in political engagement (particularly in political self-confidence) have been linked directly to women's lower levels of political ambition.[31] It is plausible that these factors lower the number of women prepared to stand for election, or to respond positively, were a party to try to recruit them as candidates.

Importantly, with the exception of income, women's lower levels of socio-economic resources cannot explain why women are less engaged with politics compared with men.[32] That said, higher levels of income boost men's, but not women's, confidence in their political abilities. Similarly, lower levels of income reduce women's, but not men's, political self-confidence.[33]

Apart from this, it is not clear why Canadian women are less engaged with politics than Canadian men. One plausible reason might be that there continue to be too few women in politics to act as role models for women in the public. When women's presence in a national legislature increases, so does women's self-reported interest in politics in general.[34] This effect has yet to be found in Canada,[35] and it is not clear if that is because Canada has too few women in the House of Commons to produce such a role model effect or if Canada's executive-focused federal institutions are such that this effect is not found unless the prime minister and/or key cabinet ministers are women.

Family responsibilities are another important factor that might reduce the supply of women candidates, though the reasons why are not straightforward. Parental or marital status does not have a direct negative effect on women's political engagement or political ambition.[36] Yet women perceive that family responsibilities comprise a substantial barrier to their political participation.[37] This perception is hardly surprising given that women who work full time outside the home spend double the hours on child care compared with their male peers.[38] What remains surprising is that, on average, this does not appear to have a direct negative effect on women's political participation.

Instead, women who choose to enter politics seem to acknowledge and address strategically a "double bind." They must be successful both in their political and civic activities and in their roles as wives and mothers. Stated differently, for women to "be successful public citizens, [they] must also be successful private citizens."[39] As a result, women who decide to engage in community or political activities do so with considerable supports from their spouses, friends, and extended support networks.[40] Interviews with potential candidates in the United States show that politically active women report that they "wouldn't be able to do anything like run [for office] without the backing of...husband[s] and friends."[41] In Canada, women MPs appear to be less likely to display their family status to constituents compared with MPs who are men.[42] The latter show photos of their children on their websites or their holiday cards in a variety of social and family contexts (e.g., at home, playing hockey). In contrast, only three women MPs showed photos of their children on their websites (all Conservative MPs with adult children), and even then these photos were exclusively professional, showing women with their children in their parliamentary offices or during a swearing-in ceremony. This might explain why men (but not women) report that "it is usually accepted and understood that the business of being an MP involves your whole family," and studies on political marketing are clear that showing their families is a common way for men in politics to cue that they are "normal."[43] Women MPs were more likely to receive comments from constituents about "who's looking after the children?!"[44] This double standard might act as a chilling effect for women who might otherwise be keen to stand for election.

A fourth factor helps to restrict the supply of women willing to participate in politics, but it also helps to structure and restrict demand for women to participate in politics from parties and other gatekeepers. The idea that politics is a "man's game" is pervasive and helps to create stereotypes that form a key barrier to women's political participation. The stereotypes of women in politics are different from both stereotypes of women in general and stereotypes of men in politics. Women in general are stereotyped as compassionate, warm, and empathetic; men in politics are stereotyped as competent leaders. Few of these positive traits of women or of male politicians are applied to women in politics. Instead, women in politics are more likely to be stereotyped negatively as uptight, dictatorial, or ambitious.[45] This leads women's qualifications to be discounted systematically. When this happens, women's desire to participate in politics is also systematically eroded and undermined,[46] thus reducing the supply of women available for politics.

Potential Problems with Demand

Stereotypes of women and politics also structure how the public and political parties seek women for political participation, especially as nominated candidates and elected officials.

It is difficult to find evidence showing that these stereotypes directly prevent voters from supporting women candidates. Indeed, studies find that voters are as, if not more, likely to support women compared with men.[47] However, research does show that stereotypes of women in politics lead voters to seek more information about a woman candidate's competence and issue positions,[48] in part because stereotypes suggest that women ought to be less competent at politics than men. The difficulty is that the information voters seek about women in politics is not neutral. Although the media cover women in politics far more now than they did in the past, the coverage that women in politics receive is typically more negative than that of men in politics.[49] Worse, the content of negative coverage of women is disproportionately focused on their character, whereas the content of negative coverage of men is focused more on their credentials.[50] This creates systematic problems, as research shows, for voters' perceptions of a candidate's character are important for their vote choices.[51] Thus, these stereotypes and negative media coverage can contribute to the public perception that politics is a man's game that women are less capable at and contributes to the idea that women's underrepresentation in Canadian politics is unproblematic, as noted above.

Political parties also use these ideas to assess whether or not women are potentially viable candidates for public office. Most parties set the rules for nominating candidates centrally but then leave the process of selecting candidates to local electoral district associations (EDAS). These rules vary considerably across parties. The federal Conservatives, as well as other parties on the political right in Canada, only task their local EDAS to find the "best possible" nominees.[52] Stereotypes of women and politics might structure how local party members assess which potential candidates are the best. In contrast, the NDP explicitly requires EDAS to search for women and other diverse candidates;[53] as a result, the party typically nominates more women candidates than do other political parties.

Still, there are troubling trends across all political parties that highlight how women's underrepresentation in Canadian politics persists. Women are systematically recruited as party members and as potential candidates at a lower rate than men. Women are more likely than men to be asked to join a party to support someone else's nomination bid.[54] Importantly, women are more likely to be recruited as candidates when party gatekeepers, such as the riding association president, are women.[55] When women are recruited as candidates, research in Canada shows, nearly every political party disproportionately nominates women in ridings that the party cannot win. A majority of women candidates are thus sacrificial lambs.[56] The effect of this systematic bias is considerable: if the Conservative Party nominated as many women to safe seats in 2011 as it did men, then 25 percent of the House of Commons would have been women in the Conservative caucus alone. Similarly, in 2015, despite their unexpected seat gains, women comprised a smaller portion of the Liberals' caucus than of their nominated candidates, the Conservatives nominated a smaller proportion of women candidates than they had in 2011, and only the NDP nominated and elected at least 40 percent women candidates.[57] This suggests that, like the Canadian public, Canadian political parties typically do not prioritize the recruitment of women as candidates, nor do they prioritize the nomination of women as candidates in winnable ridings. In this sense, perhaps little has changed in this regard in Canadian politics since Blakeney was premier in Saskatchewan.

What Matters More, Supply or Demand?

The key to assessing what suppresses women's political participation and representation (supply or demand) is to ask which lens most plausibly explains why women are so chronically underrepresented in Canadian politics. Here the analysis is different for elections contested by parties and for elections contested without a party system.

When parties help to organize candidates for election, as is the case for all federal and provincial elections in Canada, as well as some municipal elections, the demand for women candidates from political parties can easily be quantified. Any party that wishes to field a gender-balanced slate of candidates to voters simply needs to recruit women to fill half of the available candidacies. At the federal level, the available candidacies are the seats in the House of Commons; in the provinces, the available candidacies are the seats in the Legislative Assemblies. Thus, for the 2015 federal election, because there were 338 seats in the House of Commons, any federal party that wanted to field a gender-balanced slate of candidates to Canadian voters would have had to recruit 169 women from coast to coast.[58] Similarly, in Saskatchewan, parties that wish to nominate as many women as men would need to find thirty or thirty-one willing, qualified women across the province to fill half of the legislature's sixty-one seats.

Although the systemic barriers that stifle the supply of women candidates noted above are formidable for many women, it is ridiculous to suggest that all federal political parties are simply unable to recruit a mere 169 women to stand as candidates. Or, to put it differently, it is implausible to suggest that these women do not exist. Rather, it is far more likely that those who recruit candidates for political parties systematically exclude sufficiently qualified women, are unwilling to put in the time required to convince women to stand as candidates, or some combination of the two. As a result, it is appropriate to conclude that the problem rests with the demand for women as candidates and not with the supply of available, qualified women. Framing women's underrepresentation as a problem of supply misidentifies the problem as that of individual women who lack ambition and/or skill; rather, the problem is that of political parties that do not attempt to recruit the small number of women required to reach parity at federal and provincial levels. Voters are also to blame for not demanding that parties recruit the women needed to achieve parity.

Evidence from other provinces, notably from New Democrats such as Rachel Notley (Alberta, 2015), John Horgan (British Columbia, 2017), and Andrea Horwath (Ontario, 2018), highlights how, if directed to by the leader, a party can overcome the challenges that women in politics face in becoming candidates. And the relatively low numbers of women elected in Canadian municipalities further demonstrate the potentially positive role that parties can play in increasing women's representation. As of 2015, women comprised 28 percent of all municipal councillors in Canada and only 18 percent of mayors.[59] This might be why the Federation of Canadian Municipalities is advocating that local governments address barriers to the participation of women in local government and other decision-making processes.[60] Local governments are challenged to generate more demand for gender-equitable politics, though whether that challenge is accepted is ultimately the decision of each municipality.

GENDER AND "DOING POLITICS"

Why might parties and the public fail to demand that more women be presented as candidates or elected as representatives, especially when, as noted above, research shows that women's presence in legislatures does change policy? Sexism—that is, prejudice and discrimination based upon gender—is arguably the main culprit. This is shown by the considerably different experiences of women in politics compared with those of men.

As noted above, research shows that men in politics react differently to women in positions of political leadership or key legislative roles than they do to their male peers.[61] Research also shows that, once women are elected, they are bounded by restrictions not applied to men. Much of this comes from the media. Women in Canadian politics are far less likely than men to be associated with images of power.[62] News coverage of women politicians focuses far more on their appearance, personal relationships, marital status, and parental status than it does of men.[63] And the negative media attention that women politicians receive is often more focused on their character than on their competence, whereas the reverse is the case for men.[64] This can affect vote choice, for research shows that voters' assessments of political elites' character matter significantly more for their vote than do their assessments of their competence.[65]

These gender differences in how women and men in politics are presented by the media lead women to make strategic decisions about how they communicate with the media and their constituents. Men can and often do present their families as a strategic or branding cue, whereas women candidly report that they cannot do likewise.[66] This issue of family life is exacerbated by the fact that few legislatures (if any) in Canada as well as worldwide make any provision for parents to balance work and family life. For men, this is seen to be less problematic, for it is often assumed that they have a partner at home who ensures that family responsibilities are met. Women, in contrast, are held to a different standard. Although several high-profile women have given birth while holding elected office in Canada, including Sheila Copps, Christy Clark, and Pauline Marois, there are rarely any maternity or parental leave provisions for elected representatives.[67] Similarly, child-care facilities on Parliament Hill do not accept infants; in the past, this situation has led to at least one seeming ejection of an MP for bringing her infant with her to vote on a motion in the House of Commons.[68] It is not uncommon for women who seek political office to be asked by the media and voters who will care for their (older) children, and it is not uncommon for women to be castigated as "bad parents" if they pursue political careers.[69] Women also voice safety and security concerns about their children given the public profile of their political work; men never raise comparable concerns in interviews.[70] Instead, male MPs report that their constituents are happy to see their families grow and change over time, candidly observing that the context is simply more hostile for their female peers.[71]

Although not studied as systematically as more conventional media coverage, evidence suggests that women in Canadian politics face pernicious sexism and threats online in ways that men do not. Some media reports compile examples highlighting how hostile social media can be for women, for it is not uncommon for them to be subjected to sexualized insults as well as violent, sexualized threats.[72] In addition, the reaction politicians receive from identifying with ideas and policies can be dramatically gendered. The first minister for the status of women in Alberta was dismissed and, at times, castigated for leading a ministry designed to "build feminism in Alberta."[73] In contrast, when Justin Trudeau self-identified as a feminist, the United Nations credited him with igniting a positive global movement.[74] This suggests that even supporting the idea of gender equality in politics can be positive for men in ways not mirrored for women.

Given this, the democratic deficit in gender and politics is multifaceted. Women already in politics are treated differently and held to different standards by the public and the media than are men. Parties are seemingly unwilling to recruit women as candidates, though few are required to be nominated at rates equal to men. And, though members of the public do not appear to discriminate overtly against women candidates at the ballot box, they do not seem to be willing to demand that parties present them with more women to vote for or even to identify women's underrepresentation as a problem. Although this might have been understandable in the context of the 1970s, shortly after the release of the report of the Royal Commission on the Status of Women, it certainly is not justifiable now.

Ameliorating the Gendered Democratic Deficit

Given the systemic barriers that continue to suppress women's representation and participation in Canadian politics, what could Canadian politics look like if they were ameliorated? The result is clear: women would be present in all representative institutions at their demographic weight (50 percent), and they would be as diverse as women in the Canadian population. Every category of women—young or old, visible minorities, Indigenous or white—would be systematically present at their demographic weight. Furthermore, parity cabinets would be the norm instead of the exception, as is currently the case, and party leaders would be as likely to be women as they are to be men. Simply put, Canadians should be able to look at their representatives and see themselves easily, quickly, and consistently. Given the current context and the systemic barriers that need to be overcome, we have a long way to go to achieve this.

Several potential solutions will help to get us there. First, party leaders could follow Rachel Notley from the Alberta NDP, who simply asked that her party recruit an equal number of women and men as candidates. Organizers report that this was not a hard quota but something that the leader asked to be done (and it was).[75] Similarly, the Conservative Party doubled the number of women nominated as candidates in the short time between the 2006 and 2008 federal elections, which suggests that Stephen Harper demanded that his party nominate more women as candidates. When the party leader demands gender equality, that is in fact what she or he gets. Party leaders could thus be asked to justify why their parties failed to recruit women in equal numbers to men. If Blakeney had been asked that question prior to the 1978 election, then his party might have found women to nominate as candidates.

Given the key role that political parties play in selecting candidates for public office, and given how few of them appear to put in the necessary effort to recruit the fairly small number of women required to achieve parity, some penalty or incentive might be required to ensure that more women are presented to voters for election. Quotas for women's representation are not unheard of in single-member plurality electoral systems, but they tend to be less effective than they are under other institutional arrangements, such as list proportional representation.[76] Instead, Canada has a history of using campaign and party finances as incentives for parties to engage seriously with citizens.[77] This can be extended to the equity and diversity of any party's nominated candidates: for example, parties that nominate candidates who, on balance, look like Canadians could receive larger election expense reimbursements than do parties that choose the status quo.* Although cyn-

---

* A private member's bill recently before the House of Commons proposed to amend the *Canada Elections Acts* to do just this; the bill was defeated. See https://openparliament.ca/bills/42-1/C-237/.

ical, it is reasonable to expect that party leaders would demand their parties recruit women from the ample supply available to serve as candidates if doing so were linked directly to the money that parties receive from the public purse.

Second, given the disparity in how women and men are covered in political news, ameliorating the democratic deficit requires that media in Canada first follow, and then amend, the requirements set out by their own profession. Currently, *The Canadian Press Stylebook* directly addresses how to avoid perpetuating sexism in the media. The rule is to ask "would this information be used if the subject were a man?" and requires that gender-neutral language be used in reporting.[78] These are good things. However, the stylebook can be critiqued for making too many allowances for "appropriately" commenting on a woman's appearance in a news story as well as for its recommendation that social media and online comments comprise an acceptable gauge of how people are reacting to news events. In addition to the research highlighted above about how women in politics are covered differently from men with respect to their character and competence, research shows that these online reactions are more abusive and disruptive when the journalist who wrote the article is a woman, the subject of the article is a woman, or the topics covered are of particular interest to women.[79] Given this finding, norms for how gender is approached in political news need to change.

Third, initiatives such as those offered by the Federation of Canadian Municipalities highlighted above could be expanded, both for municipal politics and for other levels of government. The Alberta government, among others, is moving in this direction by indicating that it will populate agencies, boards, and commissions with diverse representatives, even if doing so means that sitting members will not be renewed when their terms expire.[80]

Fourth, though this initiative might sit uncomfortably for some, it leads to perhaps the most effective solution. Instead of asking why women should be equitably present in politics, it is useful to rephrase the question around why some groups (e.g., men) "merit" such dramatic overrepresentation in politics. When seen through this lens, it is difficult to imagine an argument in favour of men's overrepresentation that does not rest on problematic assumptions about why men are "better" than women at politics. In other words, requiring skeptics to defend why men should be overrepresented might help to highlight the deep sexism that can prevent some from viewing women's chronic underrepresentation in Canadian politics as a problem.

CHAPTER 11

THE DUTY TO CONSULT
CREATING POLITICAL SPACE FOR FIRST NATIONS?

Katherine Walker

It is difficult to pinpoint a current Canadian democratic challenge facing Indigenous* Peoples. Arguably, politics have been challenging since 1867 when the sovereignty of settler peoples was made absolute and the nationhood of First Nations was negated by their enumeration as subjects under federal jurisdiction. At the same time, democratic relations became strained when the history of alliances and treaties between Indigenous nations and Britain was replaced with the "official history" of Canada as a tale of two nations: the British and the French. The legacy from the trail of oppressive "Indian" policy over roughly the past 150 years could be held up as an ongoing democratic challenge for First Nations—one that seemed

---

* By the term "Indigenous," I mean the descendants of nations that occupied certain lands prior to the arrival of European colonizers, settlers, and state powers and the peoples united internationally under this political identity. As such, it includes Métis, Non-Status Indians, Inuit, and First Nations. The term "Aboriginal" refers specifically to the "Indian, Inuit, and Métis Peoples" legally recognized in Section 35 of the *Constitution Act, 1982*, while the term "First Nations" refers only to "Indians" legally recognized under the *Indian Act of 1876*.

to culminate in the White Paper in 1969 and its plan to wipe the Canadian slate clean of any political and legal status for Indigenous Peoples. More recently, the social movement Idle No More, co-founded by four women living in Treaty 6 territory, called attention to how Indigenous Peoples continue to be challenged by certain A/acts of Canadian "democracy." In effect, Indigenous Peoples have long struggled to address "the Canada problem" or the challenge of transforming Canada into a place that enables Indigenous Peoples to live "in distinct communities with the ability to make decisions on the important aspects of their lives and which lives up to its many promises."[1]

The legal "duty to consult" is often viewed as key to addressing this challenge because it supposedly mandates shared decision making among federal and provincial governments and First Nations* when an Indigenous or Treaty Right might be infringed as well as purports to affirm and implement these rights. But the degree to which this duty actually restrains unilateral crown decision making or affirms rights entrenched in Section 35 of the *Constitution Act, 1982* is the subject of much debate. One could argue that the constitutional protection of Indigenous and Treaty Rights created a de facto division of powers among Parliament, Legislative Assemblies, and Indigenous Peoples[2] or that it merely created some "political space" for Indigenous Peoples in Canadian federalism—a relatively small space at that.[3] The Supreme Court of Canada's articulation of the duty to consult is significant within Indigenous legal discourse because it seeks to define the parameters of the political space afforded through the constitutional protection of Section 35 rights. In this chapter, I argue that the duty to consult falls short, both in theory and in practice, of fulfilling the type of federal relationship set out in the treaties and that a forum more conducive to affirming and implementing inherent collective and Treaty Rights in Saskatchewan might be provided through the Office of the Treaty Commissioner (OTC). I begin by outlining the principles of treaty federalism, including an examination of the role that Allan Blakeney's government and First Nations in Saskatchewan played in advancing these principles in the 1970s. I then apply the treaty federalist framework to the duty to consult and the current relationship between First Nations and the Saskatchewan government.

---

* A marked limitation of this research is that, though the duty to consult and to accommodate pertains to all Indigenous Peoples, here I deal only with the obligation to First Nations.

TREATY FEDERALISM

Defined in broad terms, treaty federalism is a "nation-to-nation" model of governance based upon treaty making between diverse nations within a clearly defined federal structure.[4] The process of treaty making consists of intercultural dialogue that involves the reciprocal and rational exchange of ideas that balances the autonomy and interdependence of the nations. The conditions for this dialogue or its federal structure are based upon *mutual consent* and *mutual recognition of and respect for nationhood*.[5] In discussing and agreeing to a treaty, the parties must consent to it if it is to be deemed legitimate—this is one reason that treaties have representative signatories. Consent is also the basic principle of legitimate governance in any democratic system. A treaty recognizes that peoples living together in the same territory are interdependent and thus must work out a mutually beneficial arrangement. This interdependence is based upon mutual recognition of and respect for nationhood, whereby no single nation is regarded as possessing absolute sovereignty or power over the other or the land and its resources. Instead, the separate laws, systems of governance, and jurisdictions of each nation are recognized and respected, while mutual areas of concurrent and shared jurisdiction are agreed on. On an ongoing basis, when disputes arise regarding the interpretation of a treaty, the same process of intercultural dialogue based upon the principles of treaty federalism must be utilized to resolve the dispute.[6] The norms of treaty federalism are the same norms that treaty First Nations apply to their federal relationships with the crown in Canada today.

Treaty federalism is significant in Canada because this mode of federalism predates the Constitution and provides constitutional legitimacy for the existence of Canada. It is rooted in the fact that, when settlers arrived, the land now commonly regarded as Canada was not *terra nullius* or "nobody's land" but occupied by Indigenous Peoples with their own laws, governments, cultures, and customs. Through treaty making, agreements or treaties were forged between First Nations and settler peoples for how to share jurisdiction peaceably while maintaining separate but equal spheres of governance in accord with the laws and will of their respective peoples.[7] In effect, First Nations did not "join" Canadian federalism; instead, they existed as sovereign nations that had relations with the British crown.[8] When the Constitution was repatriated in 1982, the delegated powers of the British crown were officially transferred to Canada but with the provision in Section 35 that existing Indigenous and Treaty Rights were recognized and affirmed. Without treaties, settlers were unlawful squatters on Indigenous lands—so the legitimate Constitution of Canada depended on the negotiation of treaties.

However, once treaties were signed between First Nations and the crown, issues with their interpretation and implementation ensued almost immediately.[9] The problems arose from the fact that, despite apparent assurances to the contrary, European signatories to the treaties "always" had "the clear intention of asserting dominance and control, blended with the recognition that particular Indigenous nations presented an obstacle to this goal."[10] Non-Indigenous signatories *masked* their conception of the treaties as formal Indigenous surrenders of land and jurisdiction in exchange for certain rights and a circumscribed sphere of jurisdiction limited to reserve lands.[11] At the same time, First Nation signatories maintained their autonomy or inherent right to self-determination and other pre-existing rights and never consented to the blanket sale of the land.[12] As James Henderson notes, "the First Nations' relationships with the land have always defined their identity, their spiritual ecology and their reality. The sale of the land, the sale of the rights of future generations, is beyond the linguistic comprehension of most Aboriginal languages."[13] The avowed, agreed upon understanding at the time of treaty signing must prevail.[14]

For the most part, Indigenous Peoples have been powerless to formally contest interpretive control over the treaties by the Canadian state through the mechanisms of federalism.[15] But a mounting "reinterpretation" of the treaties outside state processes in the past three decades suggests that the prevailing crown interpretation of the treaties is too narrow and that a fuller reading that captures the true nature or "spirit and intent" of the treaties is more accurate and leads inevitably to their being implemented as constitutional accords.[16] The Supreme Court of Canada has enshrined such a reinterpretation in its common law. The courts have stipulated that "a generous and liberal" approach to interpretation must be used and that "extrinsic evidence," such as oral history, must be considered in addition to the written text itself.[17] To do otherwise might compromise the "integrity and honour" of the crown because it would entail a failure to fulfill promises that caused a First Nation to sign a treaty.[18]

Drawing on its twenty-year involvement in political and scholarly work on treaties in Saskatchewan, the federally mandated OTC holds the position on the treaty covenant made between Canada and First Nations that, to date, the crown (federal and provincial governments) has benefited immensely from the treaties while First Nations have not: "The objective of the Crown, to settle and prosper on this new land without conflict from First Nations, has been achieved. Those of the First Nations, to share economic prosperity with the new society, secure a brother-to-brother relationship with the Crown, continue to nurture their communities and protect their right to govern themselves, have not."[19]

Despite its issues with interpretation and implementation, treaty federalism offers a basis for structuring relations between First Nations and the crown in a way that does not attempt to subvert or circumscribe differences dating back to the time of treaty making; rather, it embraces and builds upon them. It also offers a way forward, based upon the principles of *mutual consent* and *mutual recognition of and respect for nationhood*, that balances separate and shared areas of jurisdiction.

APPROACHING CONSULTATION IN SASKATCHEWAN

During the 1970s, when Allan Blakeney became premier of Saskatchewan, federal and provincial governments still largely ignored the inherent collective and Treaty Rights of Indigenous Peoples. Far from recognizing the principles of treaty federalism, the provinces regarded all lands and resources as falling fully within their authority and jurisdiction, as per the Natural Resources Transfer Agreement (NRTA) of 1930. There was no consultation with Indigenous Peoples regarding how the provincial crown allocation and use of lands and resources would affect their rights. Instead, federal and provincial governments largely rode roughshod over the rights and interests of First Nations and Métis with all the tools of the state at their disposal. Métis scholar Howard Adams described Saskatchewan as a virtual "prison of grass" for First Nations and Métis because they had little institutional means to break free from the chains of systemic colonial domination.[20] Despite the widespread systemic disadvantage, First Nations in Saskatchewan were politically active in protecting their sovereignty and Treaty Rights. All but four were signatory to one of the six historical Numbered Treaties covering the entire land mass of the province. This shared history is the foundation of unity among the First Nations, bringing them together for the common purpose of honouring the treaties.[21]

During his tenure as premier from 1971 to 1982, Blakeney adopted fundamental democratic practices and principles that aligned with many of the tenets of treaty federalism. These were part of his "principled pragmatism" approach to leadership.[22] Blakeney the pragmatist understood that the lives of Indigenous and non-Indigenous peoples were *interdependent*, while the principled part of him insisted on *mutual* benefits. Common ground was to be pragmatically worked out within critical and sometimes competing institutions of democratic governance: the rule of law, negotiation and compromise, and informed decision making. The principles that guided Blakeney in navigating these processes were a faithful representation of the majority will of the Saskatchewan people, a commitment to social democracy or the extension of equality to the economic sphere, and a courageous spirit that defended an unpopular course of action because he believed that it was the right thing to do.

So how did Blakeney extend his principled pragmatism to his relationship with Indigenous Peoples? According to his memoir, his approach began with his democratic faith in *all people*, including Indigenous people, based upon the belief that "society is wiser to rely upon the inherent good sense of the mass of the people" than on technocrats or experts.[23] He eschewed a paternalistic approach and instead sought to learn from Indigenous people through *meaningful consultation* or *intercultural dialogue*. He contrasted his approach to that of the government of Ross Thatcher: "The government did what it thought best. It did little to find out what Aboriginal people thought was best for them."[24] Blakeney also understood the inherent injustice of relying solely on a Saskatchewan majority opinion, for he understood that those in power tend to exercise that power to serve themselves or the groups or classes that vote for them, which means that the legitimate rights of Indigenous people and powerless minorities are ignored.[25] For him, a people's lack of self-determination or a locus of democratic accountability to a distant majority constituted colonialism. For example, Blakeney stated that "in 1971 northern Saskatchewan represented a classic case of colonialism and underdevelopment. Organizations and people from outside controlled almost everything in the North—government, the education system, businesses, and the churches."[26] However, he failed to see the same colonial structures in relation to First Nations in central and southern Saskatchewan.

Following the process of intercultural dialogue meant Blakeney largely diverged from other government leaders of his day by supporting the implementation and protection of Indigenous and Treaty Rights. Primarily through direct dialogue with the Federation of Saskatchewan Indians (FSI, now the Federation of Sovereign Indigenous Nations) leader David Ahenakew and others, Blakeney came to understand that First Nations sought to address colonialism by strengthening and validating Indigenous identity and accessing the local economy—and that both aims would require education.[27] Accordingly, his government worked with First Nations to enact a number of policies to achieve these ends: affirmative action programs that mandated the inclusion of Indigenous people in workplaces; local hiring via surface lease agreements with uranium companies whereby 50 percent of the workforce was to be drawn from the predominantly Indigenous population of northern Saskatchewan; and the establishment of the Saskatchewan Indian Federated College (now the First Nations University of Canada) and the Native Law Centre at the University of Saskatchewan.[28] The FSI also identified that funding for research on treaty obligations and a communications program to educate the entire public about Indigenous issues was needed, and both initiatives received support from the Blakeney government.[29]

Arguably, the path that Blakeney pursued often went beyond consultation to include First Nations in shared political and economic decision making on key issues. Such a road was often unpopular with the Saskatchewan majority because it meant giving up some of the privilege and power it enjoyed under an unequal, colonial relationship. Two pieces of policy in particular attest to Blakeney's approach.* The first was the successful negotiation of the "Saskatchewan Formula" with First Nations as part of the Treaty Land Entitlement (TLE) Agreement. The TLE arose from the fact that First Nations had not been allocated the reserve lands that they were entitled to under the terms of the historical Numbered Treaties. The Blakeney government could have taken a minimal, legalistic approach to fulfilling entitlements, as was the case in some other provinces, but in consultation with First Nations readily agreed that the spirit and intent of the treaties should be honoured, which entailed a "generous" approach that would also support economic development for First Nations.[30] The actual generosity of the agreement is questionable given that, even with the additional TLE lands, the total land base for First Nations would constitute less than 1 percent of land within Saskatchewan,[31] an insufficient amount to support First Nations based upon an agricultural economy. In addition, the fact that unilateral provincial jurisdiction over lands and resources violated the terms of the treaties was never put on the political agenda. Regardless of the differing views, First Nations

---

* Although I am focusing on the explicit approach of Blakeney and others in his intimate circle (e.g., Romanow), other conflictual policy approaches were pursued by the NDP government during the same time frame. For example, a clear policy of the criminalization of Indigenous people was also exhibited, with rates of policing targeting Indigenous people and subsequent incarceration rates increasing substantially from 1974 to 1982. See Jim Harding, *Social Policy and Social Justice: The NDP Government in Saskatchewan during the Blakeney Years* (Waterloo, ON: Wilfrid Laurier University Press, 1995).

and the province came to a tentative agreement on TLE in 1976, well ahead of all other jurisdictions.

But it turned out that the issue of generosity would further undermine the process of finalizing and implementing the agreement: Blakeney met with opposition from cabinet ministers, farmers, municipal officials, as well as procrastinating federal bureaucrats who considered the Saskatchewan Formula too generous.[32] Provincial NDP polls commissioned at the time indicated that overall "people thought the government was doing too much for Indians."[33] Despite the widespread, largely racist opposition, Blakeney actively worked to persuade citizens, provincial and federal bureaucrats, and government officials to honour the TLE agreements, including making certain unoccupied provincial crown lands available for purchase. In many cases, TLE lands and funds have resulted in considerable economic development for both First Nations and local municipalities in Saskatchewan. Unfortunately, there are still many outstanding issues concerning implementation of the agreements that have yet to be worked out with the current provincial government.[34]

The other noteworthy policy achievement during his time in office was the inclusion of Section 35 in the repatriated Constitution, which recognizes and affirms existing Indigenous and Treaty Rights. Although Blakeney played no direct role in this section's development, he pushed for its inclusion when constitutional talks unexpectedly reopened for final negotiations.

In the late 1970s, Indigenous Peoples were formally excluded from Canadian negotiations to repatriate the Constitution. Determined to secure some measure of constitutional protection of their rights and interests, Indigenous leaders used other local, national, and international channels to make their voices heard.[35] This included using the Joint Council of the National Indian Brotherhood (precursor to the Assembly of First Nations), comprised of twenty-one members of the interim Chiefs' Council and the Executive Council, with one representative from eleven provincial and territorial members, to articulate the substance of a section on Indigenous and Treaty Rights.[36] Of course, Indigenous constitutional deliberations were grounded in Indigenous Peoples' extensive and ongoing histories of exercising sovereignty[37] and in a constitutionalism that predates and contests the exclusion of Indigenous Peoples from Canadian federalism.[38] To a certain extent, Indigenous Peoples have always had to engage in "constitutional talks" to combat a Canadian revisionist political history. The clause itself was viewed by many Indigenous leaders at the time as an interim measure that did not go far enough in protecting inherent Indigenous Rights.[39] Despite initially being included, the proposed section regarding Indigenous and Treaty Rights was cut from the accord as talks went into their final round—much to the utter disbelief of Indigenous leaders.

Drawing primarily on an international law memo that questioned Canada's delegated authority from Westminster to amend Indigenous and Treaty Rights,[40] FSI leaders met with Blakeney to insist on the reinclusion of Section 35.[41] He gave them his word that, if negotiations reopened, he would push for the constitutional recognition of Indigenous and Treaty Rights, and he was ultimately successful in doing so.[42] Although the significance of including Section 35(1) in the *Constitution Act, 1982* could not have been foretold at the time, Blakeney identified his primary motive for pushing for its inclusion by saying, "We needed to give Aboriginal people some weapons against the political establishment, including us."[43] It would seem that Blakeney's pragmatic commitment to democratic principles and First Nations' commitment to treaty federal principles converged for a moment in the fundamental belief that *people* or *peoples* must be the ultimate guardians of their own rights and interests.

CONSULTATION AND ACCOMMODATION AS A DUTY

The concept of treaty federalism outlines how autonomy and jurisdiction must be shared between Indigenous and non-Indigenous governments. Similarly, the duty to consult is a legal measure intended to set out a sphere of shared decision making between First Nations and the crown in situations in which Indigenous and Treaty Rights are potentially affected. The duty was articulated as a means of both *minimizing* and *justifying* the infringement of constitutional Indigenous and Treaty Rights by the crown or provincial and federal governments.[44] The *Haida Nation* case of 2004 clarified that the duty applied to both proven and unproven rights, given the need to abide by the honour of the crown, and proceeded to set out a more defined process of consultation.[45] The *Taku River* case of 2004 and the *Mikisew Cree* case of 2005 rounded out the parameters of the duty, such as its application to crown authorizations of the taking up of Treaty Lands.[46] Following this seminal "trilogy" of cases, hundreds more have added to our understanding of what consultation now entails.

As I show in this section, legally mandated consultation, while purporting to include First Nations in shared decision making, falls short of the federal relationship envisioned by the historical treaties. Specifically, though the duty to consult envisions an intercultural dialogue between First Nations and the crown, it fails to recognize any autonomy for First Nations or to balance this autonomy with the interdependence of the parties based upon the principles of *mutual consent* and *mutual recognition of and respect for nationhood*. Its failure can be attributed to three key aspects: it devolves into a one-sided conversation, sidelines its own stated aim of reconciliation, and defers to crown sovereignty.

Initially, the procedural aspects of consultation seem to enable a genuine dialogue between culturally diverse and distinct nations. The process must begin as soon as governments know that their proposed action or plan might affect Indigenous or Treaty Rights.[47] To a large extent, the courts have also articulated a pre-consultation stage of negotiation. This means that it would be difficult for the crown to convince a court that consultation was adequate if it was designed *without* first consulting the potentially affected nation.[48] In addition, both First Nations and the crown have a *reciprocal* obligation to participate fully in consultation, and they must exchange all relevant information and generally exhibit mutual respect for each other. Broad public modes of consultation, even if open to First Nations, are not necessarily sufficient to address the duty owed to First Nations.[49] In effect, the court's low threshold for consultation mandates dialogue between non-Indigenous and Indigenous governments on virtually all matters that might affect Indigenous and Treaty Rights. Reciprocal duties and tailoring of the process to First Nations point to dialogue that recognizes their unique status as holders of specific constitutional rights.

But the additional detail provided by the "sliding scale of consultation" denotes a more one-sided conversation. At the lowest end, where the claim is supposedly weak or the right is limited or the potential infringement is minor, "the only duty on the Crown may be to give notice, disclose information, and discuss any issues raised in response to the notice."[50] In effect, one party, the crown, decides unilaterally what constitutes a weak right or limited infringement, because it determines what requires "notice," albeit with the guiding principles of when the duty is triggered. At this stage, notice should go beyond indicating that a decision has been made to providing notice that a decision will be made, with the invitation for discussion. But the very method of communication as notice implies that a determination has been made that would preclude further discussion. Granted, at the higher end of consultation, the court envisions "deep consultation" that might require more of a give-and-take discussion. The parties are to engage in "testing and being prepared to amend policy proposals in the light of information received, and providing feedback."[51] Although the crown has an obligation to substantially incorporate Indigenous concerns into its decision making where the crown has determined that the right and potential infringement are more serious, and to provide a written report on how these concerns were incorporated,[52] there is no requirement for further discussion beyond this single act of justification. Although they must aim to reach agreement, at the end of the day agreement is not necessary.[53] What if, upon receiving the written report, the other party is not convinced that its concerns were adequately taken into account or accommodated? At this point, it seems the only recourse would be to pursue litigation. Thus, the process offers only a weak attempt at truly shared decision making or meaningful dialogue.

On a more substantive level, the ultimate purpose of consultation—reconciliation—undermines the mutual recognition of and respect for nationhood. The court initially set out reconciliation as a compromise between "the pre-existence of aboriginal societies with the sovereignty of the Crown."[54] But the Supreme Court of Canada in *Haida Nation* revised this position, stating that treaties involve reconciling pre-existing Indigenous sovereignty with "assumed" crown sovereignty, and later, as part of the same decision, referred to crown control over Indigenous lands as being de facto rather than de jure.[55] However, for First Nations, their societies and sovereignty are not only pre-existing but also "still existing" since they are "unconquered peoples,"[56] so First Nations cannot reconcile with unilateral crown sovereignty, whether it is construed as assumed or not. The conception of sovereignty as absolute and vested in the crown is still the driving rationale for consultation and its range of potential outcomes. The initial impetus for consultation proceeds from the assumption that the crown has the power to infringe the constitutional rights of Indigenous Peoples. It is this risk of infringement, not the rights themselves, that triggers the question of reconciliation, which causes the actual rights to become a backdrop to discussing only the risk. The full range of rights and their implementation are rarely the focus of consultation.

With industry proponents allowed to participate in consultation, by carrying out some of its procedural aspects, it is somewhat unlikely that reconciliation will be their main priority. In effect, industry proponents have the least leeway to consider substantially Indigenous rights with the aim of reconciliation, because they have clearly defined positions and a much narrower focus on doing what makes economic sense. As a result, industry players in any decision-making setting are "not typically in the business of reconsidering and reflecting on their positions, and engaging in a process of mutual justification."[57] In addition, the "timelines for reconciliation are out of step with timelines for authorizing development."[58] Industry also comes to the process with vastly unequal resources for advancing its particular interests. For instance, it can provide the financial incentives of private business agreements with First Nations to sway a community to support a proposed project. The presence of industry also negates the nation-to-nation basis of the process. With the conflicting aims, the process is at risk of devolving into a type of interest group advocacy forum instead of an intercultural dialogue between nations.

In addition, though there is a substantive component to consultation, the duty to accommodate, the courts have stated explicitly that First Nations do not hold a veto over proposed crown action.[59] As well, the possibility of requiring the consent of First Nations to a proposed action, except perhaps in cases of established Indigenous Title, is not within the range of possibilities, in terms of outcomes.[60] In the absence of agreement, the court has assigned the power to the crown to "balance interests." Such bookending of crown power throughout the process of consultation clearly places the balance of power with the crown. The autonomy of First Nations is negated by this assertion of absolute crown sovereignty.

Arguably, to achieve the stated aims of the duty to consult and accommodate, especially the affirmation of rights and reconciliation, what is required is a sphere of intercultural dialogue that balances First Nations and crown autonomy and jurisdiction. But it must somehow rise above the current context of crown domination that impedes genuine discussion. It can do so only if it truly embodies all the principles of treaty federalism. At present, the immediacy of dealing with the potential risk to Indigenous Rights posed by a government or an authorized third-party action delays any sort of reconciliation if that is the correct aim of consultation. The duty has only served to bring the parties to the table, but the quality of the discussion at this table is sorely lacking.

CONSULTATION IN PRACTICE

In this section, I focus on describing the consultation process and evaluating the resulting Saskatchewan consultation policy with First Nations that came into force in June 2010. As of 2019, this consultation framework remains in place as the official policy of the Saskatchewan government but has not been endorsed by the Federation of Sovereign Indigenous Nations (FSIN, formerly the Federation of Saskatchewan Indian Nations).

In December 2007, a newly elected Saskatchewan government announced the dawn of a new relationship with First Nations based upon "mutual respect and trust" that would allow *all* citizens to "move forward together."[61] A key driver in this process was the duty to consult. To embolden this new relationship, the premier invited Chiefs from across the province to the first traditional feast held on the grounds of the legislature.[62] Later that year, the premier attended a Chiefs' Legislative Assembly and pledged his intention to hold within the next 180 days a "historic" roundtable with Indigenous people, industry, and government to discuss consultations on lands and resources.[63] This held the promise of truly bringing the parties together in a practical way. However, rather than furthering a new relationship, the negotiations illustrated the difficulty in translating the rhetoric of mutuality and cooperation into a workable process with designated roles and responsibilities. What began as a pragmatic process for tackling the duty to consult quickly became a question of what, exactly, the concept of the new relationship entailed. By early 2010, the provincial government and FSIN appeared to be at a block in the road.

In May 2008, Brad Wall, the new premier, made good on his promise and held a two-day roundtable with Indigenous leaders and industry representatives to discuss the creation of a new consultation process on lands and resources approximately 173 days after his swearing-in ceremony. A report of the proceedings was released on October 6, 2008,[64] and a draft consultation framework was issued on December 22, 2008,[65] for review by First Nations and industry stakeholders. In addition to the roundtable, meetings were held with smaller groups of First Nations, primarily regional tribal councils. The provincial government anticipated that a final policy would be in place by early 2009.[66] However, in February 2009, First Nations unanimously rejected the draft framework at a special FSIN Legislative Assembly and called for more time and meetings to discuss the duty to consult.[67] The policy was rejected for "seriously and negatively affecting the Inherent and Treaty rights of First Nations in Saskatchewan, and failing to meet the legal requirements set out by the Canadian courts for meaningful consultation and accommodation with First Nations."[68] The FSIN identified the need for a broader, more collaborative process that discussed how to consult about and how to share in resource revenues, because both issues affected collective inherent and Treaty Rights of First Nations. The extended deadline of June 1, 2009, for a final policy then passed.

In December 2009, a new deadline of March 31, 2010, for a final policy was set by the provincial government. In March 2010, the FSIN Chiefs-in-Assembly adopted Resolution #1684, entitled *Declaration and First Nations Model Procedure on Consultation and Accommodation*, in which a "Model Law Template on Consultation" was adopted, with accompanying documents, all of which were provided to First Nations to tailor potentially to their needs. The province then released a final policy on June 15, 2010, along with a supplementary document titled *Report on How Feedback Was Addressed in the Government of Saskatchewan First Nations and Métis Consultation Policy Framework.*[69] To date, this policy has not been endorsed by any individual First Nation, tribal council, or the FSIN.

No substantial differences exist in the content of the 2008 draft policy compared with that of the 2010 final policy except that industry proponents appear to have been elevated to equal stakeholders in the consultation process. The final policy sets out a single, overarching goal not present in the earlier draft: to "facilitate mutually beneficial relationships among the Government of Saskatchewan, First Nations, Métis and industry that contribute to a growing provincial economy."[70] This change is worth noting given its emphasis on industry as occupying a place in the consultation process on par with those of both the province and First Nations. This change does not seem to be in keeping with the court's enunciation of industry as a delegate with no constitutional duty to consult and accommodate. In addition, the explicit emphasis here is on reconciliation to build the provincial economy rather than on reconciling Indigenous Rights and asserted crown sovereignty, which seems to belie the court-sanctioned purpose of consultation.

However, respect and protection for Treaty and Indigenous Rights as well as reconciliation are two of three stated objectives of the final policy though not included in the overarching policy goal. A stable and secure investment climate is the third objective, also present in the draft policy. But in the draft the wording of the objective stated that First Nations and Métis would also be included as "full participants in the provincial economy,"[71] but this wording is omitted from the final policy objectives.

The emphasis in the 2008 draft policy on provincial control over decision making is reiterated in the 2010 final policy. The same five levels of consultation are set out, beginning with level 1, which requires no notice because no impact is determined. At level 2, short-term disturbance to land and/or change in resource availability with a potentially minor impact, the province is required to give notice but not to provide any opportunity for input from the First Nation. At level 3, short- and long-term disturbances to land and/or changes in resource availability and/or *permanent* uptake of land with a potentially minor impact, written notice is again required, but follow-up or discussion with the First Nation is not required at this stage either. At the final two stages, which involve potentially significant infringements on and permanent disturbances to lands and resources, actual discussions are mandated to take place. However, funding for "capacity needs" for First Nations is contemplated only at the fifth and final stage of consultation. The 2010 draft policy adds three criteria that the provincial government will use during its pre-consultation phase to determine if consultation is required, an improvement on the 2008 policy since it provides some basis for how the government plans to act unilaterally to determine the strength of an Indigenous Right or the impact of a potential action on it. With the final policy, the timelines for decisions on different levels of consultation remain the same. The relative sameness of the 2008 draft policy and the 2010 final policy makes one wonder what *was heard* during consultation.

Overall, the list of clarifications under the "What We Heard" subject heading in the report on feedback does not change the substance of the consultation process. Instead, the clarifications are simply restatements of the same position that the province has taken on the issues. Most notably, in the final policy of 2010, the province maintains its position on the Numbered Treaties that title to land was given up while acknowledging that "the oral histories of the First Nations offer a different view of the intent of the Treaties."[72] The initial draft framework[73] set out the same major stumbling block of consultation—differing interpretations of the treaties by provincial and First Nations governments. As previously mentioned, First Nations do not agree with the interpretation of treaties as blanket extinguishments of Indigenous Title to lands and resources. But the provincial government steadfastly maintains that the treaties do represent a cession of Indigenous Title and any Indigenous Right in the land, including resources, in exchange for certain Treaty Rights. Although recognizing these differing perspectives, the provincial government concludes that the perspective of First Nations is unsupportable and proceeds to outline a consultation process based upon its own interpretation of the treaties. The 2010 final policy reiterates this position and asserts that resolving such differences in the interpretation of Treaty Rights is explicitly excluded from the purpose of the policy. The stance of the provincial government appears to forgo the very purpose of consultation: to determine how potential Indigenous Rights might be balanced, at a minimum, with provincial objectives rather than disregarded outright. If collective inherent and Treaty Rights are to be "proven" and affirmed, then surely this involves the consideration rather than the denial of oral history and treaty federal history.

Although Saskatchewan recognizes some relational authority of First Nations, it continues to hold the Numbered Treaties at arm's length. The province recognized the inherent right of self-government for First Nations,[74] and tripartite negotiations at a "common table" focusing on a comprehensive final agreement on self-government led to a draft tripartite agreement in 2003 among the FSIN, Canada, and Saskatchewan. Meanwhile, negotiations at the "exploratory table" have resulted in a bilateral protocol between the FSIN and Saskatchewan to guide relations. But both agreements maintain that the primary relationship is between First Nations and Canada, with the relationship between Saskatchewan and First Nations simply a working one.[75]

Finally, the lack of a definitive dispute resolution process within the consultation process also speaks to the asserted power of the crown to act unilaterally. This means that, if First Nations believe a crown decision to be unjust, their only recourse is civil disobedience and/or litigation. As well, without a dispute resolution process in place, the risk that crown infringement of an Indigenous or Treaty Right will result in irreparable damage rises, which can leave only limited accommodation as the possible redress.

Overall, the final policy not only fails to take into account the commitment of First Nations to honour the *spirit* and *intent* of the Numbered Treaties but also becomes the antithesis of such a position. On the whole, the FSIN states that the initial draft policy maintains control over lands and resources in the hands of government and corporations,[76] and this is reiterated in the final policy. The FSIN calls for a more equal relationship with the crown, especially when it comes to lands and resources. This stance, again, is rooted in the First Nations understanding of a just treaty relationship. The crown as represented by the provincial and federal governments has a choice to go beyond minimal legal interpretations to foster a relationship that respects and recognizes First Nations; however, with respect to the current consultation policy, Saskatchewan has not exercised that choice. Its policy supports a weak dialogue with First Nations that panders to industry interests.

CONCLUSION

The potential infringement of constitutional rights should require, *at a minimum*, genuine discussion with the bearers of those rights. The duty to consult, both in theory and in practice, does not facilitate a dialogue that promotes understanding through a genuine give-and-take process. Instead, the process of consultation functions more like a meeting of interest groups, intent on expeditious project approval with little consideration of the larger aim of reconciliation or the affirmation of constitutional rights protection. The dominance of the crown throughout the process prevents discussion about broader issues of importance to First Nations, such as treaty interpretation and implementation. Indigenous law, customs, and traditions, including Indigenous understandings, must come to bear on the process. Another forum for expanding the conversation in a setting in which rights are not at risk and parties are on an equal footing is necessary, perhaps with a third party to facilitate meaningful discussion. The sad fact is that consultation as mandated by the courts is focused primarily on project approval, not on serious acknowledgement of or respect for First Nations and their collective and Treaty Rights.

A forum more conducive to affirming and implementing inherent collective and Treaty Rights in Saskatchewan might be provided by the OTC, the federally mandated body established in 1989 to review issues in the TLE process in Saskatchewan. The OTC has facilitated the exploratory table between Canada and First Nations in Saskatchewan, with the province as an observer, which has resulted in a number of political developments and documents, such as common understandings of fourteen treaty principles underlying the treaty relationship.[77] In addition, in 1996, the OTC co-established, with the province and First Nations, a common table to "facilitate effective processes for negotiating and implementing First Nations governance in Saskatchewan building on the treaty relationship, and for related jurisdictional and fiscal arrangements, in addition to discussions of treaty issues that affect all three parties."[78] One weakness of using the OTC to facilitate rights implementation is that it reports to the federal government, which undermines accountability to First Nations. One proposed solution is to have the OTC report to an international forum, such as the United Nations.[79]

However, with regard to Treaty Rights, the province has adopted a "position of non-participation," asserting that "it was not a Party to the treaties, since the province did not exist at the time all but one of the treaties were negotiated, and consequently has no policy framework to mandate participation by the crown in right of Saskatchewan in discussions to examine and implement the treaties and the treaty relationship."[80] This stance is incongruent with the Saskatchewan government's enjoyment and full implementation of its constitutional powers, even though the province did not exist during Confederation when the *Constitution Act, 1867* was negotiated. In addition, Canada is a federation founded on compound monarchies, whereby the crown has always been divided between federal and provincial authorities.[81] On the flip side, First Nations must also acknowledge that the crown with which they signed the Numbered Treaties now includes provincial governments, so they too ought to be willing to discuss the treaties with the province.

The OTC states that the province's position is unsustainable "if it becomes a barrier to treaty implementation."[82] In fact, the province's current position of non-participation is such a barrier. As a matter of basic practicality, Saskatchewan must participate in treaty implementation, whether modern or historical, because it must negotiate with First Nations on how jurisdictions currently under its authority will be shared under the terms of a treaty. If it refuses to do so, then any treaty will be impossible to implement.

The OTC has already proposed a role for Saskatchewan in treaty implementation. The Treaty Implementation Framework Agreement recommends that the province participate in negotiations to define and implement collective inherent and Treaty Rights; facilitate the orderly exercise of First Nations' rights to hunt, fish, trap, and gather renewable resources; and settle through negotiation First Nations' access to renewable resources and revenues from resource exploitation. All the elements included in this proposed agreement mirror the issues the province refuses to discuss within the scope of consultation. Participating in implementing this agreement represents but one possible option for establishing a more just and lasting relationship between First Nations and Saskatchewan. Through further intercultural dialogue among consenting parties, other avenues likely could be developed.

I speculate that a Blakeney-led government would have long recognized the need for provincial inclusion in the process of Indigenous Rights affirmation and the pragmatic necessity of meaningful consultation or intercultural dialogue. Ultimately, the political relationship between First Nations and the Blakeney government helped to lay the groundwork for a more equitable relationship that included many of the features of treaty federalism. This was done through both an adherence to principles and a pragmatic approach. His willingness to protect and affirm Indigenous and Treaty Rights against the opposition of the majority will of Saskatchewan citizens came both from a commitment to the self-determining wisdom of all people and from a willingness and openness to listen and learn that enabled Blakeney to hear and understand this wisdom. It is a truism that clear thinking often requires not only intelligence but also courage.

CHAPTER 12

TROUBLED MARRIAGE
LIBERAL PLURALIST DEMOCRACIES AND RELIGION

Reg Whitaker

I begin with two related questions. First, why does a secular/agnostic political scientist address religion? Second, why address religion in a book in honour of Allan Blakeney, a secular social democrat?

My answer to the first question is that it is precisely because of a historical tendency among secular social scientists to ignore, downplay, or misjudge the role of religion against the evidence of the continuous relevance of religion to understanding human behaviour, in particular political behaviour. The early twenty-first century, convulsing with renascent fundamentalist movements arising from multiple faiths that have often spilled over into overtly violent political expressions, is a terrain particularly resistant to those who would equate progress and modernization with secular advance and religious decline.

There are two answers to the second question. First, the New Democratic Party (NDP) government of Saskatchewan that Blakeney led in the 1970s might have evolved into a largely secular political organization, but its roots in the old Cooperative Commonwealth Federation (CCF) were firmly in the soil of the social gospel: one need only cite J.S. Woodsworth, Tommy Douglas, and Stanley Knowles to recall how intertwined the CCF project was with the social gospel and the intellectual currents of radical Christianity.[1] Second, a point to which I will return, the challenge today to secular social democratic parties and progressive movements is posed by the continuing power of religion to move people in ways that strictly political appeals do not.

Traditionally, political science has examined various "cleavages" in civil society that can be used as tools to analyze political behaviour. I would submit that it is a mistake to equate religion with other cleavages, perhaps not in voting studies in which it works as well as any other cleavage, but in the political theory of how liberal democracies should function. That is because religions promise or threaten to bring to the public space something that no other form of identity or association can bring to it: *transcendent metanarratives* that claim to situate their followers in relation to their fellow citizens not only with regard to their civic rights and obligations but also with regard to the deepest questions of human existence. Religions claim to situate people not just in relation to each other but also in relation to the universe, to time, to existence itself.

Political ideologies are pale creatures beside metanarratives that transcend the mundane. In the twentieth century, secular political ideologies purported to offer metanarratives that could compete with those offered by religions and even replace them in the hearts and minds of those under their power and influence. Communism and fascism once proved to be mighty engines of destruction and oppression. Yet one thing that they signally failed to destroy, despite their best efforts, was religion. Throughout much of the developing world, nationalist and anti-imperialist movements that once had strong left-wing secular orientations have now largely given way to movements driven by an ideology that, though still political, is infused with religious imagery and religious zeal.

Even the liberal democracies of North America and Europe have not been immune from political struggles infused with religious controversies. From the sexual politics of gay and lesbian rights and the abortion issue to the current controversy over an assisted dying law, not to speak of Islamophobic anti-immigrant and anti-refugee campaigns, religious metanarratives have become deeply entangled in the everyday politics of Western democracies.

The classic study of the profound conundrums that can result when secular law comes into direct conflict with moral standards based upon transcendent metanarratives is found in *Antigone* by Sophocles. Creon, King of Thebes, decreed that the body of Polynices, killed while attacking the city in a failed attempt to replace Creon on the throne, be left unburied in ignominy on the field where he fell, while that of his brother Eteocles, who defended

Thebes, be given all honours. Antigone, the sister of Polynices, cannot bear this insult to the natural law, defies the secular law, and buries the body with her own hands. Brought before the king, she acknowledges that the order forbidding her act was legal when Creon asks "and yet you dared to contravene it?" "Yes," Antigone replies,

> That order did not come from God. Justice,
> That dwells with the gods below, knows no such law.
> I did not think your edicts strong enough
> To overrule the unwritten unalterable laws
> Of God and heaven, you being only a man.[2]

Hegel, drawing on *Antigone*, famously defined the essence of tragedy as the conflict of right against right, in which one protagonist's right can be fully realized only by infringing on or denying the equally justified right of the other.[3] It is true that Creon is a king; however, transposing this truth to the situation of religious-based conscience confronting the laws of a democratic state, Antigone's resistance becomes if anything more tragic. Instead of opposing the will of a tyrannical king, in a democracy Antigone must confront "the will of the people" in their majority as well as the decisions of the courts in a country under the rule of law. But oppose she must if she is to remain true to her faith.

I turn now to some contemporary issues that echo, albeit in diluted form, the paradigm of Antigone versus Creon, religion versus politics. The cases of same-sex marriage, abortion rights, and assisted dying all illustrate the conflicts between differing conceptions of right in liberal pluralist democracies. In each case, opposition to the proposed extension of rights became passionate, on occasion—especially with the abortion issue—reaching the mobilization of mass movements of resistance. In each case, opposition was inspired largely, though never entirely, by claims that the proposed new rights would directly challenge religious standards of morality. However, just as passionate support was demonstrated by those who demanded the extension of rights as befitting the dignity and equality of citizens previously discriminated against; these arguments were sometimes cast, though less often than by opponents, in religious terms. Politicians and political parties in democracies are congenitally allergic to taking decisive positions on issues that bitterly divide the country and even their own supporters—even more so when the issue is cast in the alarming terms of right versus right.

SAME-SEX MARRIAGE: AN UNEXPECTED SUCCESS STORY FOR THE DEMOCRATIC PROCESS

This is really a two-step story of rights extension. The first step was the recognition of equal rights for gay and lesbian citizens, pointing to the end of harshly discriminatory treatment in the law, in the workplace, and in social practices. In Canada, this began with the 1967–69 legislative initiative by then Minister of Justice Pierre Elliott Trudeau, meeting fierce but ultimately futile resistance from religious-inspired hostility to homosexuality.[4]

The second step was the demand for legal recognition of the right of gays and lesbians to marry. This demand initially aroused intense religious-based opposition throughout the Western world. Perhaps this was because of the long association of marriage with churches and the concept of marriage as a "sacrament," reinforced by strong cultural aversion to homosexuality in some ethnic communities where religious affiliation remains high. But the level of rejection was high enough, and vehement enough, that politicians were reluctant to undertake any legislative initiative in this area. Instead, the courts became the preferred route. Armed since 1982 with the *Charter of Rights and Freedoms*, same-sex proponents won a series of victories in the courts, culminating in a landmark Ontario Court of Appeal decision in 2002 and a Supreme Court reference in 2004. With this clear legal direction, the Liberal government of Jean Chrétien prepared legislation to recognize same-sex marriage, enacted under his successor, Paul Martin, in 2005.[5] Canada thus became only the third country in the world at that time to recognize same-sex unions.

Although the Conservative Party in opposition had opposed recognizing same-sex marriage, the government of Stephen Harper made no effort over its nine years in office to reverse the legal status. In their first national convention after being defeated in 2015, the Tories voted overwhelmingly (1,036-462) to adopt a neutral definition of marriage, accepting the legitimacy of same-sex unions. Various party luminaries welcomed the change, characterizing it as "a message of modernization and moving on," "the right thing to do," and "just having the language catch up with reality."[6]

It might now be said with confidence that same-sex marriage is an accepted, virtually non-controversial, fact of Canadian life. Opposition is no longer seriously pursued by any mainstream religious organization and has no place in the platform of any mainstream political party. The situation in the United States presents an even more striking example of the reversal of public attitudes, since opposition to same-sex marriage was stronger in that country than in Canada. Again the courts were the initial route to reform as legislatures showed no appetite for challenging the moral status quo. Yet, as a string of state court decisions extended marriage rights, public opinion also shifted to greater liberality. Thus, in 2012, President Barack Obama, who had ducked the issue, came out fully in support and made same-sex marriage rights a plank in his re-election platform. Even with the victory of Donald Trump in 2016, with a host of social conservatives trailing in his wake, the reversal of same-sex marriage seems to be unlikely.

Any doubts about the assured future of same-sex marriage in the Western world were laid to rest by a remarkable referendum victory in Ireland in 2015, in which 63 percent of Irish voters voted yes to an amendment to the Irish Constitution legalizing same-sex marriage, carrying majorities in all but a single county across the country. Getting the amendment to a referendum had been opposed by the Catholic Church, which had also campaigned for a no vote. However, even in a country where Catholic influence had historically been higher than in most other European countries, religious-based opposition failed spectacularly.[7]

How do we account for the decisive result in this case? The key to understanding the failure of religious opposition is not to see it as a "defeat" in the sense that the religious view was crushed by *force majeure*. Rather, there was a debate in which "pro" arguments won on the merits of their case. This was signalled by the growing number of original opponents coming to agreement with the other side. The crucial part of the winning argument was that there is no demonstrable harm imposed on heterosexual marriage by the recognition of same-sex marriage. The Canadian federal law, for instance, carefully avoids imposing any obligation on any religious organization with regard to recognizing or "sanctifying" same-sex unions while extending equal rights to all. In the United States, conservative Republican support for same-sex marriage began to grow with the recognition that it might actually strengthen rather than weaken the institution of marriage, seen as the foundation of a stable conservative society.

The same-sex issue is thus a case study in democratic success. A major change has been brought about in advancing equality rights. Religious opposition, based upon transcendent metanarratives that under other circumstances might have left their adherents angry and alienated by their defeat, was largely reconciled peacefully with the result. This marked a triumph for the process of civil democratic deliberation in which the judicial and legislative branches of government work together and the public is informed and made more knowledgeable about the issue by the legal and political debate. Unfortunately, the next two case studies do not yield such positive results.

"PRO-LIFE" VERSUS "PRO-CHOICE": DIALOGUE OF THE DEAF?

Abortion was legalized in the United States in 1973 by the Supreme Court in *Roe v Wade*.[8] In Canada, amendments to the Criminal Code in 1969 permitted abortions only when the health of the woman was in danger, as determined by a three-doctor hospital committee. In practice, abortion services continued to be difficult if not impossible to access for Canadian women. Dr. Henry Morgentaler defied the law by opening a series of abortion clinics across the country that ignored the legal provisions for committee approval, and he paid the price by facing repeated criminal charges (and juries that refused to convict him). In 1988, his legal challenge resulted in the landmark *Morgentaler* decision in the Supreme Court.[9] The majority in *Morgentaler* held that the abortion provision in the Criminal Code violated a woman's right under Section 7 of the *Charter* to "security of the person." This did not establish the right to abortion, but it did establish the right of a woman to choose an abortion. Subsequent attempts by the government of Brian Mulroney to legislate on the issue failed. In effect, abortion had simply been removed from the Criminal Code, placing Canada in the same position as the United States after *Roe v Wade*.

In neither country, however, has judicial determination quieted the issue or silenced pro-life opposition. In the United States, abortion has remained a hot-button issue, with diehard opponents of *Roe v Wade* actively seeking to overturn that decision or to undermine it by various legislative devices at both state and federal levels. All Republican candidates for the 2016 presidential nomination pronounced themselves in opposition to *Roe v Wade*, some even proclaiming their support for the total recriminalization of abortion even in cases of rape or incest. The victory of Donald Trump has thrown the viability of *Roe v Wade* into question. The controversial confirmation of Trump's second Supreme Court appointment, Brett Kavanaugh, raised the imminent possibility of a pro-life majority on the highest court. Outside the political system, pro-life mobilization has continued unabated. Picketing and attempted shutdowns of abortion clinics are on the relatively peaceful end of a continuum of activism that has included bombings and murders by an extremist fringe of the movement. And many of the Christian churches, the Roman Catholics prominent among them, have maintained their unswerving opposition to abortion, whatever the law and the courts might have ruled.

On the other side, a 2018 referendum in Ireland to liberalize access to abortion was approved by two out of three voters, despite fierce opposition from Roman Catholic prelates in this once traditionally Catholic country.[10]

In Canada, violent pro-life protest has been less evident than in the United States, though it has not been entirely absent. The Canadian political sphere has been less accommodating of pro-life views than the American political sphere. In line with its general avoidance of "social conservative" issues, the Harper government suppressed the efforts of its pro-life backbenchers to place the issue back before Parliament. The Liberal government of Justin Trudeau is committed to the pro-choice position. But the improbability of reopening a major political debate over reversing abortion rights has not precluded resistance to abortion rights from taking another, less publicly visible, form.

Medical practitioners can refuse to provide abortion services on moral—most often religious—grounds. Conscientious objection to carrying out a procedure that the practitioner finds morally repugnant has been respected in law and practice. But there is a qualification: a woman who wishes to have an abortion should be referred to other medical practitioners or other institutions that will provide that service. Some conscientious objectors argue that referring a patient to another practitioner who will carry out what the objector believes is a morally repugnant procedure is just as unethical as carrying out the procedure oneself. If aborting an unborn child is considered murder, then referring a pregnant woman to someone who will carry out that act constitutes complicity in the murder. The conscientious objector can cite Section 2 of the *Charter* guaranteeing everyone the "fundamental...freedom of conscience and religion." But the woman who seeks termination of a pregnancy and is blocked from that procedure can equally cite, following *Morgentaler*, her Section 7 right to "security of the person and the right not to be deprived thereof except in accordance with the principles of fundamental justice."[11]

This problem is magnified when there is such a concentration in a region or province of medical practitioners and hospitals that refuse to provide abortion that the right to abortion is nullified in practice. This appears to be a leading cause of the situation in New Brunswick, which specified that abortions would be funded only if performed in hospitals, but abortions have almost never been available in hospitals.[12] Private clinics have had to charge the full cost to the patients, making the procedure too expensive for many women. As a result, the only private abortion clinic in the province closed. Women have been forced to travel out of the province to gain access to abortions. In short, in New Brunswick, abortion rights have been trumped in effect by some medical practitioners' rights to freedom of conscience and religion. A new provincial government elected in 2014 promised to change this situation and did make a start, but the results so far have been minimal.[13]

Prince Edward Island was even more resistant to abortions and became the target of a legal challenge in 2016. Not a single elective abortion had been performed in that province since the *Morgentaler* case in 1988, so pro-choice activists launched a lawsuit accusing the province of violating women's rights based upon a moral choice that they said the government has no right to make. The lawsuit threatened to take the courts into a new realm, "judicially required abortion services."[14] However, the province, after taking a quick look at its legal position, capitulated and agreed to make abortion services available to women on the island. Pro-life campaigners declared the decision "shameful," but the pro-choice campaign had prevailed in the last holdout province.[15]

Why has the abortion issue followed such a different and more troubled trajectory than the same-sex marriage issue? In the latter case, as we have seen, judicial intervention initiated a political and social debate that reached a resolution and a new civil consensus. This consensus became possible because the debate revealed that no demonstrable harm was caused to heterosexual marriage by the extension of marriage to same-sex couples. The abortion issue is different. Religious metanarratives teaching that life begins at conception must view abortion as murder, even admitting some reasonable safeguard for the life of the woman. In the eyes of the state, it can now be considered lawful as a routine practice, but in the eyes of the religiously inspired pro-life proponent "lawful" murder remains murder. Some simply turn their faces away, accepting abortion as one among many things done in the public sphere of which they disapprove but about which they are unable to do anything. Others continue to express their opposition publicly. The case of medical practitioners is more difficult in that they might be forced to make personal decisions that could implicate them directly; the invocation of their right to freedom of conscience and religion is the result.

On the other side is a different but no less compelling conception of right. That those who support abortion rights call their cause "pro-choice" is more than positive political spin. No one argues that abortion per se is a good thing. It is an uncomfortable choice for many. Some who support the right to choose would not consider it an option for themselves. The point is rather that the dignity of an adult woman as a mature moral agent requires that it should be her choice and her choice alone whether to continue or terminate a pregnancy. The putative right of the fetus to life that might trump the woman's right to choose termination has been explicitly rejected by the Supreme Court in a post-*Morgentaler* decision.[16]

These two conceptions of rights are simply incompatible, yet each is rooted in strong support from its adherents. The bipolar aspect of the abortion issue is reflected in public opinion surveys. When questioned in terms of a woman's "right to choose," the Canadian public generally responds favourably in the majority. When questioned in terms of "protecting life," approval of abortion tends to decline. Unsurprisingly, but unhelpfully, pro-life and pro-choice groups promote surveys structured to elicit outcomes favourable to their own side.

These are parallel but separate universes. The political conundrum arises when they come into direct conflict with one another. This happens when the exercise of freedom of conscience and religion clashes with the right of women to effective access to abortion services. Unlike the same-sex marriage case, it seems to be highly unlikely that any further amount of democratic debate and deliberation will serve to reconcile these two sharply conflictual concepts of right. Nor is either side in the least likely to relent and cede ground on the rights terrain to the other. The pro-life argument, rooted in a transcendent religious metanarrative, is relatively impervious to political challenge. The pro-choice argument is embedded at the centre of the contemporary feminist campaign for equality rights and the transformation of gender relations that surely is irreversible.

The conflict between these rights in effect has been adjudicated, in the courts, in the legislatures, and in public opinion. The decision has come down on the side of the right of women to choose. There is a point at which the debate must end and the state must enforce the effective exercise of the right that has been given legal precedence. Conscientious objections based upon religion must be respected but must not be allowed to undermine in practice the recognized right of women to abortion services. In the end, this is a problem that politicians have to confront, however much they might like to avoid it.

ASSISTED DYING: ABORTION REDUX?

The case of physician-assisted dying covers much of the same ground as the abortion debate but with some unique features. The story begins in 1993 with the case of Sue Rodriguez, who suffered from amyotrophic lateral sclerosis, also known as Lou Gehrig's disease. Finding her life unendurable, she went to court to challenge the provision of the Criminal Code prohibiting assisted dying. In a five-four decision, the Supreme Court affirmed the constitutionality of the provision.[17] The majority did recognize that her right to the security of her person under Section 7 of the *Charter* was being denied because Rodriguez was unable to exercise her personal choice to end her suffering. The principle of fundamental justice, however, precluded the deliberate taking of a human life, even with the consent of that individual, thus limiting Section 7 rights.

In the years since *Rodriguez*, a number of Canadian jurisdictions have legislated assisted dying. In 2014, Quebec enacted legislation legalizing physician-assisted dying for consenting adult patients who suffer from an incurable illness, an advanced state of irreversible decline in capability, and constant and unbearable suffering.[18] In 2011, the British Columbia Civil Liberties Association filed a lawsuit challenging the constitutionality of the law against assisted dying on behalf of two plaintiffs who suffered from debilitating and incurable conditions. In February 2015, the Supreme Court, in what has become known as the *Carter* decision after the plaintiff Kay Carter, unanimously overturned its earlier *Rodriguez* decision to allow physician-assisted dying for "a competent adult person who (1) clearly consents to the termination of life and (2) has a grievous and irremediable medical condition (including an illness, disease or disability) that causes enduring suffering that is intolerable to the individual in the circumstances of his or her condition."[19] The court ruled that the prohibition of assisted dying did indeed violate Section 7 of the *Charter*'s protection of "life, liberty and security of the person."

The court gave the federal government a deadline to draw up legislation that conformed to the principles enunciated in the decision. A debate ensued both inside and outside Parliament.[20] Those with religious or other forms of conscientious objection to assisted dying were vocal in their opposition. Significantly, Roman Catholic health boards, which operate many hospitals across the country, firmly refused on moral grounds to offer assisted dying in their institutions. In the words of the Catholic Health Sponsors of Ontario,

> physician assisted death is morally incompatible with the mission and values of our Catholic health providers and is soon regrettably to become a legal reality. Should a request for physician assisted death occur in our organizations we will not abandon the person in our care.... This is completely consistent with our moral and ethical tradition. We will not provide the medical service of physician assisted death in our institutions nor will we directly or explicitly refer a patient to receive this same medical procedure.[21]

The prospect that assisted dying services would be refused at all Catholic hospitals immediately roused apprehensions that the constitutional interpretation of the Supreme Court and the will of Parliament could be substantially undermined in practice by the resistance of conscientious objectors, not all of whom are Catholic.

A contentious issue is that Catholic hospitals are publicly funded institutions. An assisted dying advocacy official singled out the recommendation of the parliamentary committee that the service be available at all publicly funded medical facilities: "This is one of the pieces where the rubber is going to hit the road for access....These are institutions that receive public funds and they should honour patients' Charter rights to an assisted death."[22] The Canadian Medical Association (CMA) had argued before the committee that "doctors who oppose assisted dying on grounds of conscience should not be required to refer patients to a colleague willing to provide or administer drugs that would end their lives."[23] The CMA expressed its disappointment that this was not contained in the committee recommendations and warned that, if the referral requirement were enshrined in legislation, there might even be doctors who would quit the profession rather than submit to a requirement that they found morally repugnant.[24]

There is a serious potential problem here, not unlike the case of conscientious objection to abortion. One difference between the two cases is that, though both involve medical procedures that terminate life, assisted dying is limited to adult persons who voluntarily ask for their lives to be terminated. This is partially muddied by the question of patients in late stages of dementia who might not fully appreciate the nature of the decision, but this is marginal to the main focus of the proposed legislation that sees fully documented voluntary consent as the necessary, though not sufficient, condition for assisted dying. Nevertheless, the moral objections of medical practitioners to the deliberate taking of life stand apart from the question of the voluntary choice of the patient. These moral objections can arise in many cases not only from religious reasons but also from doctors' interpretation of the secular obligations imposed by the Hippocratic Oath.

When the Liberal government of Prime Minister Justin Trudeau finally brought in legislation to comply with the court order, it did not provide any mechanism to which objecting physicians could have recourse. Instead, Bill C-14, *An Act to Amend the Criminal Code (Medical Assistance in Dying)* includes exemptions for conscience.[25] Regulations on referral requirements are in effect left to the provinces to specify in detail. After a highly charged debate and some back and forth between House and Senate, C-14 became the law of the land.

Immediately, it was reported that "groups representing more than 4,700 Christian doctors across the country have launched a court challenge to

Ontario regulations that require them to refer patients to physicians willing to provide an assisted death, arguing the referrals are morally equivalent to participating in the procedure."[26] The Ontario regulations insist that doctors must perform an "effective referral." The Ontario College of Physicians and Surgeons explains that an effective referral means a "referral made in good faith, to a non-objecting, available, and accessible physician, nurse practitioner or agency. The referral must be made in a timely manner to allow the patient to access medical assistance in dying. Patients must not be exposed to adverse clinical outcomes due to delayed referral."[27] According to the lawyer for the faith groups mounting the court challenge, "our position is doctors who opposed assisted suicide or physician-assisted death are put in a position now where they either need to violate their conscience and their religious and moral belief or face being disciplined by the college."[28]

Various work-arounds have been suggested involving arm's-length referral committees, but attempts to settle conflicting rights claims have fallen short in practice. Late in 2016 André Picard, the *Globe and Mail*'s medical correspondent, reported that in some provinces hospitals were opting out of observance of the law to an alarming degree. In the Saskatoon region, for example, twelve institutions, including the area's only palliative care unit, had declared conscientious objection to the law. Any patient who requested assisted dying had to be transferred to a cooperating facility somewhere else in the province—imposing an appalling choice on people already suffering in the last stages of life. As Picard indignantly stated,

> institutions do not have a conscience. Institutions do not have rights. People do. Yet, as provinces fashion regulations to conform to Canada's new federal law on assisted death, they are consistently putting the concerns of hospitals (and other institutions) ahead of those of providers and patients....These approaches may well be outright unconstitutional; at best, they offend the spirit of the law and the principles of medicare.[29]

Assisted dying, like abortion, is about life and death and touches on the deepest and most sensitive moral and ethical conundrums. When these issues are reinforced by religious convictions, a feasible compromise can become elusive. As with abortion, it might eventually become necessary for the democratic state, reluctantly, to end the debate and impose a resolution that protects one set of legally recognized rights from being undermined and rendered ineffective in practice by the conscientious objections of others based upon other rights. In the tragic conflict between right and right, it is necessary for a liberal democracy to adjudicate and decide which right will finally prevail. Antigone will not be reconciled. But democracy does not become tyrannical when it makes a necessary adjudication between conflicting rights.

WHEN (SOME) RELIGIONS BECOME POLITICALLY SUSPECT

I have focused up to now on cases in which religion has been pitted against the legal and political systems. In liberal pluralist democracies, however, there is never *religion* as such but *religions*. Moreover, the political life of a democracy has often been riven by religious conflicts. Some states, such as Ireland, continue to be haunted by ancient communal conflicts in which a primary division is along sectarian lines. More states, including Canada, have had severe sectarian cleavages in the past that have gradually diminished over time to the vanishing point.

Until the mid-twentieth century, one non-Christian religion was a perpetual candidate for political suspicion throughout the predominantly Christian West: Judaism. Drawing on both religious and ethnic prejudice, anti-Semitism flourished in all Western countries to varying degrees, reaching a monstrous apogee in the Holocaust unleashed by the Nazi Third Reich. Anti-Semitism remains an ugly problem never eradicated, but Islam has replaced it as the most suspect "other" religion and ethnic identity, and Islamophobia has become highly politicized throughout Western Europe and North America. This has been driven in large part, of course, by the post-9/11 threat of terrorism in the name of violent extremist Islamist ideologies. But anti-immigrant sentiments focusing above all on Muslim groups were already evident in Europe well before 9/11. Neo-fascist anti-foreign political parties have risen in popularity and influence all across Europe. The ideologies of such parties in the past often had strong anti-Semitic overtones, but they have been largely replaced by overt hostility to Islam and Muslims, not only on political but also on cultural and religious grounds. The transition is symbolized by the action of French National Front leader Marine Le Pen in expelling from the party its former leader and her own father, Jean-Marie Le Pen, for his anti-Semitic and Holocaust-denying outbursts. Yet Marine Le Pen herself was recently acquitted on charges of hate speech brought against her for remarks likening Muslims in France to the Nazi occupation; her National Front is virulently Islamophobic.

In North America, the political and evangelical right has come to identify uncritically with the state of Israel and rising suspicion of and hostility to

Islam. In the American case, this can be clearly identified in the presidency of Trump, who has imposed a ban on the admission of immigrants and refugees from a number of Muslim countries, a ban upheld by a five-four majority in the US Supreme Court.[30]

In Canada, the Conservative government of Stephen Harper subordinated its entire Middle Eastern policy to one of unquestioning adherence to the positions of the Israeli government on Israeli-Palestinian relations and on the alleged existential threat to Israel posed by the Islamic state of Iran. Nor did it shrink from regularly accusing Canadian critics of Israeli actions of anti-Semitism. The other side of this coin was that the Harper government, in its last desperate attempts to hang on to office in the 2015 election, opted to play (unsuccessfully) the Islamophobia card. This came not out of the blue but out of growing restiveness about the rising number of Muslims in Canada that had been evident for some time.

In fact, Quebec was the first part of the country that began registering concern about Islam, especially the alleged threat of sharia law being imported into Canada. Concern in Quebec over the "reasonable accommodation" of religious and cultural differences resulted in a commission of inquiry in 2008 under the direction of sociologist Gérard Bouchard and philosopher Charles Taylor. The short-lived Parti Québécois (PQ) minority government led by Pauline Marois from 2012 to 2014 introduced a highly controversial "Quebec Charter of Values" that would have regulated and in some cases barred the wearing of distinctive religious symbols and dress among Quebec public servants and officials.[31] Although the objects of this regulation were not specific to any one religion, there was little doubt that the main target was the hijab worn by some Muslim women, a highly visible symbol of ethnocultural distinctiveness seen by many as threatening to the majority. This legislative project set off a firestorm of criticism from both outside and inside Quebec. Despite controversy, the Liberal government that succeeded the PQ brought in new restrictions on face and head coverings[32] suspended by the courts. An election in 2018 brought yet another party, the Coalition avenir Québec, to provincial office that not only promised to bring in legislation to ban religious wear but also threatened to invoke Section 33 of the Constitution, the notwithstanding clause, to override objections to the violation of the *Charter*.[33]

It is important to emphasize that this attack on religious symbolism was waged in the name of *laïcité* (or "secularity"), a leading idea in Quebec since the Quiet Revolution of the 1960s removed the Roman Catholic Church from its formerly dominant position in Quebec life. Yet it was also impossible to miss that the power of this movement rose not just from the popularity of *laïcité* but also from the reaction of the older Catholic Quebec against the appearance of a new and threatening religious competitor, Islam. These were strange bedfellows: a secularism established in reaction to a once-dominant Catholicism and a Catholicism still smarting from its removal from the centre of Quebec life by secularism. But they could unite in identifying Islam as an equal threat.

Another stage in the campaign to regulate or ban religious symbols came during the 2015 federal election. When a Muslim woman sought the right to attend the ceremony in which she would be awarded her Canadian citizenship wearing a face-covering *niqab*, the embattled Harper government in Ottawa sensed an issue on which it thought it could capitalize and challenged the woman in court. As an "issue," the *niqab* lives in the realm of symbolism alone. There was no substance to warnings about deception resulting from citizenship being given to a woman whose face was covered, for she had already established her identity visually in a setting in which she felt comfortable; in fact, she had already met all of the conditions to qualify for citizenship. The citizenship ceremony, as such, is purely symbolic. That presumably was the point both of the claim and of the opposition. It was recognition of the equal legitimacy of the Islamic faith within the ritual theatre of Canadian citizenship award that was at stake. Opposition to this recognition, coming from the Harper Conservatives and from the Bloc Québécois, was surely intended to send a political message that Muslims were to be denied the full legitimacy already enjoyed by other faiths, that citizenship for Muslims should be conditional on terms defined by the majority. This became clear when two prominent Conservative cabinet ministers raised the idea of a "snitch line" for Canadians to denounce their fellow citizens for their "barbaric cultural practices."

The NDP, as the leading party in Quebec, felt constrained to defend basic principles of liberal democracy and refused to join in the anti-*niqab* hubbub. The result was disastrous for the party, which immediately saw a precipitous fall in its support in Quebec, eventually losing over forty of the fifty-nine seats that it had won in 2011. Outside Quebec, the *niqab* not only failed to save the Harper government but also might well have been a factor that led many to turn away from the Conservatives. The snitch line in particular repelled even some long-time supporters of the Conservatives. The NDP was collateral damage.

The results of the *niqab* controversy are thus mixed, but on the whole it seems that Canada emerged from this experience with its liberal approach enhanced rather than weakened. This might be confirmed by the decision of the incoming Liberal government to admit up to 50,000 Syrian refugees despite security fears about the entry of potential terrorists expressed by the previous government. Only Germany, much more on the front line of the refugee wave than Canada, showed the same openness, while many other Western countries shut their doors altogether. In the German case, Islamophobic anti-refugee reaction has generated a powerful political backlash. In the United States, the projected inflow of Syrians would amount to about one-fiftieth of the Canadian total on a per capita basis; this paltry number has still been denounced by Republicans and many state governors as posing a severe threat to national security. In short, Canada might be an outrider with regard to an Islamophobic wave that, in conjunction with fears of jihadi terrorism, has swept across the Western world.

Unfortunately, though, Canada has hardly been immune from ugly manifestations of the same trend. On January 29, 2017, at a mosque in Quebec City, six worshippers were killed and nineteen others injured by a lone gunman who appeared to have been inspired by far-right Islamophobic racism. Nor has this horrific act restrained the continued expression of anti-Muslim views on Quebec media such as talk radio shows.

This experience tells us that liberal democracies remain vulnerable to cultural and political panic over the threat of religion when that religion is a suspect non-Christian/Judaic other and especially when it is associated, fairly or unfairly, with political violence. This experience again illustrates the special status of the religious identities of citizens of liberal democracies. The religious faithful follow metanarratives that transcend the secular sphere. In the first three case studies that I examined, this potentially placed some followers at odds with the law, in an uneasy relationship with the democratic political system. This might indicate a permanent tension that requires careful management, which all three cases show is possible in practice as well as desirable in theory.

The Islamophobia case, like anti-Semitism before it, raises darker, more unsettling, questions. Adherents of suspect religions, precisely because of their transcendent ideologies, can be seen potentially to hold a *higher loyalty* beyond that owed to the secular democratic state. Just as communists in the Cold War were seen to have a higher loyalty to the communist homeland than to their own countries, and thus posed permanent security risks to their states, so too Muslim immigrants and refugees can be seen to pose a permanent security risk by virtue of their beliefs. Indeed, since their beliefs are religious, they might seem to pose an even greater challenge than did adherents of communist ideology, a merely secular political set of ideas lacking the passionate force of religious zeal. Whether anti-Muslim reaction springs from secular or Christian sources, or some combination of them, the result is the same: liberal democracies face a challenge to the principle of religious pluralism.

With Trump in the White House, and a rising tide of Islamophobic far-right populism across Europe, it is no longer alarmist to fear that liberal democracy might be giving way to more authoritarian forms. If so, it is hard to escape the irony that religion will have been one of the triggers but in a way that no one would have anticipated from the long history of religion and democratic politics.

CULTURE WARS AND THE POLITICS OF RELIGION

There is one last variation that I would like to make on this theme of religion and politics, a last twist, as it were, in how we should understand this relationship. The recent controversies over same-sex marriage, abortion, and assisted dying tend to situate the ideological colour of religious intervention in politics as conservative rather than "progressive forces" seeking to extend or expand rights. In part, this identification of religion with the political right stems from the so-called culture wars that have animated American politics for the past few decades. The conservative reaction to the politics of the 1960s stressed the dangers to American society of the "permissiveness" of the decade. The rise of the evangelical Christian right indelibly associated politicized religion with right-wing politics. One wing of the Republican Party waged war on the culture front in close concert with evangelical activists who sought closer moral regulation of American society.

By the time of the Obama administration, earlier cultural issues had begun to fade, to be replaced by a new focus on immigration as the threat to American values, a "conflation"—in the words of one observer—"of race, religion, and national identity. This has helped transform immigration into a highly charged, highly polarized culture-war-style issue."[34] The demagogic rise of Trump is the political embodiment of this trend. Even though his own religious credentials, not to speak of his personal lifestyle, are highly suspect from a Christian point of view, many evangelical leaders cynically threw their weight behind his candidacy and have continued their uncritical support of his embattled presidency.

But focusing too much on this recent alliance of evangelicals and conservatives can miss a much bigger and more significant point about religion and politics. In the wider sweep of history, there is no reason to confine the political affinities of religion to conservatism. Religious metanarratives can serve well as searching critiques of the status quo of wealth and power, and often they have been the inspiration for radical and even revolutionary political movements. The resistance to the Vietnam War that convulsed late-1960s and early-1970s America drew a great deal of inspiration from Christian "witnesses against war." The great transformation of race relations in America was a struggle organized and led most often by religious figures such as Martin Luther King Jr. and inspired throughout by religious images of the liberation of the oppressed and the Promised Land that lay in reach.

In Canada as well, when religion has touched on politics in recent decades, it has tended to be associated with the political right. However, the alliance of the political and religious right has been less comfortable in Canada. Former Prime Minister Stephen Harper actively suppressed social conservatives in his caucus from raising the concerns of the religious right, such as abortion, in Parliament, even as his party made a quiet electoral appeal to "theo-cons." Canadian voters seem to be less inclined than their American counterparts to welcome extreme ideas into mainstream politics, and Canadian parties tend to downplay rather than feature association with aggressive assertions of divisive points of views, though Maxime Bernier's new People's Party of Canada might indicate a shift in this regard. Yet, however much Canadian progressives are rightly repelled by American-style evangelical reactions in this country, they should not forget that in many areas of social concern churches and religious groups have often contributed progressively. One thinks of issues such as refugee reception and integration, urban poverty and homelessness, and environmental protection. As for any "natural" affiliation of religion with political conservatism, it is precisely the social democratic tradition in Canada, with its deep roots in the social gospel movements of the nineteenth and twentieth centuries, that suggests that religion is open rather than closed with regard to its political implications.

We might conclude, then, that when religion interacts with politics it is not necessarily going to come from either right or left. At different times and in different places, religion has played both conservative and progressive roles, and often it has played both roles simultaneously. Religious doctrine is not political ideology. It stands apart from and above politics, but it informs politics and shapes it in unanticipated, often surprising, ways.

Contrary to the hopes of secularists, religion shows no sign of going away any time soon, if ever. There is a lesson here for social democracy, which has largely lost touch with its own religious roots in the social gospel. The left must recover a way of connecting with, associating with, and learning from religions as one way to construct a more effective, popular alternative to neoliberalism. Religion provides a language for many people to understand their world. Losing touch with that language means to some degree losing touch with potential supporters of progressive politics.

Religions and liberal pluralist democracies find themselves locked in a perpetually troubled marriage. But divorce is not an option. As with many marriages, it is a case of "can't live with them, can't live without them."

CHAPTER 13

FEDERAL ELECTORAL BOUNDARY COMMISSIONS
WHAT'S RIGHT, WHAT'S WRONG, AND WHAT CAN BE DONE ABOUT IT?

John C. Courtney

*Without the right to vote in free and fair elections,
all other rights would be in jeopardy.*
—Madam Justice Beverley McLachlin, 1989[1]

It is a privilege to be part of a volume celebrating Allan Blakeney's contributions to public life in Saskatchewan and Canada. Blakeney was a dedicated public servant, a committed social democrat, and a politician whose powerful intellect shone through on countless occasions. He, along with his beloved T.C. Douglas, was one of a handful of Canadian premiers in the last half of the twentieth century who made a profound difference to Canadian government and society. In so doing, Blakeney brought honour to public service—an all too rare gift of political leaders. It is no accident that he chose as the title of his published memoirs *An Honourable Calling*.[2]

Blakeney was interested in electoral reform, one aspect of which he acted on as premier of Saskatchewan. Early in his eleven years as premier, his government legislated an end to partisan gerrymandering of electoral districts. It replaced the age-old practice of electoral boundaries being crafted by the government of the day with legislation mandating the establishment every decade of non-partisan redistribution commissions operating at arm's length from elected politicians. In this chapter, I examine the institution upon which Saskatchewan, in 1972, based its own system: the then decade-old federal electoral boundary commission legislation. I ask what is right about the federal boundary delimitation process, what is not, and what can be done to improve it.

The institutional framework that we commonly label an "electoral system" is an essential part of any liberal democracy. In constructing a fair, open, and trusted electoral system, several questions must be answered. How inclusive is the franchise? Does the method of registering voters guarantee that the names of all eligible voters will be included on the voters' lists? Are the management and operation of an election entrusted to competent individuals committed to overseeing an election in an impartial and scrupulously fair manner? Will the regulations and laws respecting media coverage, party and candidate fundraising, and campaign expenditures be strictly applied so as to ensure a level playing field for all participants?

Additional questions arise when elections are waged on the first-past-the-post (FPTP) method of voting, in which the candidate with the largest share (either majority or plurality) of the valid votes cast wins the entire constituency. Geography and population are at the core of an FPTP system, and how those two elements are reconciled is critical to the provision of electoral legitimacy. Are the boundaries of the constituencies periodically redrawn to reflect population shifts? Is the process by which the redesign of the constituencies widely accepted as objective and legitimate? Is the redistribution process (the periodic redrawing of constituencies) designed to ensure a substantial measure of voter equality? Finally, is "effective representation," which the Supreme Court of Canada has ruled is at the heart of an electoral system, safeguarded by the system? These questions of fairness and transparency in electoral systems were central to Blakeney's commitment to democracy—none more so than his championing the case for independent electoral boundary commissions.

Near the conclusion of the classic Mel Brooks comedy *The Producers*, the two principal characters express surprise, alarm, and finally dismay at the instant success of their Broadway musical *Springtime for Hitler*. The show was designed to be a sure-fire flop so that they could pocket the money bilked from little old ladies who had put it up to produce the play in the first place. The mastermind behind the swindle, Max Bialystock, groans following the show's hugely successful opening "How could this happen? I was so careful. I picked the wrong play, the wrong director, the wrong cast. Where did I go right?"

My intention here is to do a 180 on the second of those two questions by asking "Where did we go wrong?" with electoral districting in Canada. In contrast to the stated goal of Bialystock, the legislative framework for conducting regular federal redistributions was carefully crafted to ensure the success of electoral districting by non-partisan commissions and to keep in some reasonable measure parliamentary constituencies in line with shifts in population. Yet as we will see, in some important respects the federal process has fallen short of its intended goals.

The federal *Electoral Boundaries Readjustment Act* (EBRA) was adopted with all-party support in a minority Parliament in the mid-1960s. It was a long-overdue institutional reform that anticipated by twenty-five years the judgment issued by then Madam Justice McLachlin in the 1989 *Dixon* case that signalled the court's acceptance of the need to guarantee "fair elections." McLachlin reasoned that such elections would be unthinkable without some measure of voter equity among electoral districts.[3] As well, the periodic redesign of those electoral districts should be entrusted to commissioners operating at arm's length from politicians.

The federal EBRA became an important part of the package of reforms that, by the early twenty-first century, had come to define Canadian electoral democracy. The Office of the Chief Electoral Officer (known popularly as Elections Canada) was established in 1920 to organize and supervise the conduct of elections with scrupulous independence. The right to vote, notably after acceptance of the *Canadian Charter of Rights and Freedoms* in 1982, was gradually extended to include all Canadian citizens eighteen years and older. Strict and comparatively small caps were placed on both fundraising and expenditures of parties and candidates for electoral purposes.

The EBRA became part of that overall reform package. It was the first of its kind at the federal level in Canada and was seen on both sides of the House of Commons as an appropriate solution to an age-old problem: partisan redrawing of constituency boundaries. Political activists, national media commentators, and members of the public who followed federal politics carefully agreed that the transfer of electoral boundary readjustments from politicians to independent commissions would enhance Canadian electoral democracy and eliminate partisan gerrymandering.[4]

However, as successful as the independent electoral boundary process has been over the past six decades, it has nonetheless exposed problems that cry out for changes to the *EBRA*. Where did things go wrong, and what can we do about it? And, in keeping with the theme of this volume, what does it all tell us about Canadian democracy?

Once we determine what went right and why, we can identify the problems with the process as it has operated over the decades. I conclude the chapter with four proposals to improve what is otherwise an established and respected process—the envy of electoral reformers in many countries, not least the United States, where persistently partisan battles over the design of electoral districts have become the norm.

It is important to note that Saskatchewan borrowed heavily from the federal *EBRA* in constructing its electoral boundary readjustment act. There are differences, of course, between the two statutes. They include a markedly smaller allowable population variance among the provincial constituencies than the federal constituencies (+/- 5 percent as opposed to 25 percent of the average constituency population) and the selection of two of the three-member commissions by the cabinet following consultation with the government and opposition sides of the legislature (provincial) rather than appointment by the speaker of the House of Commons (federal). But the two main principles to be adhered to by both federal and provincial commissions in the construction of constituencies are the same: (1) purposeful reliance on geographic and physical configurations and (2) respect for local communities of interest.

Blakeney's commitment to fairness in electoral institutions such as constituency boundary redistributions made the federal act a logical (and convenient) one from which to borrow. Although I devote the remainder of this chapter to an analysis of the federal process, disputes over the definition of electoral fairness, the appropriateness of one set of boundaries in contrast to another, and the competing communities of interest apply equally to provincial and federal commissions and to their respective boundary delimitation processes.

WHAT IS RIGHT?

Canada's *Electoral Boundaries Readjustment Act*, enacted in 1964, borrowed heavily from Australia's *Commonwealth Electoral Act*. In place for many decades, the Australian process of redistributing electoral district boundaries was considered the "gold standard" for non-partisan, extraparliamentary constituency readjustments by independent commissions. Canadian members of Parliament (MPs) saw the Australian system as appropriate to Canada, similar in many respects to Australia. Both are federal and parliamentary democracies whose relatively small populations are unevenly distributed over large land masses.

Also in advance of the federal move, in 1955 Manitoba changed how it redistributed the seats in the legislature. In so doing, it drew on the Australian model of non-partisan commissions. Manitoba's grounds for making the switch offered lessons to MPs as they debated in 1964 how best to ensure a fair and impartial process at the federal level.[5]

As it now stands, the *EBRA* includes a number of important features that, for the most part, have been in place since the legislation was first adopted over fifty years ago.

- A redistribution (boundary readjustment) of all federal electoral districts is to follow every decennial census.
- A separate three-member commission is named for each province.
- A judge, appointed by the chief justice of a province, chairs a commission, and the remaining two members are appointed by the speaker of the House of Commons from among the residents of that province.
- No senator, MP, or member of a Legislative Assembly is eligible for membership in a commission.
- No constituency's population can vary by more than 25 percent of a provincial electoral quota unless a commission can justify going either above or below that limit and then only in "extraordinary circumstances."
- A province's electoral quota is determined by dividing its population, as determined by the latest decennial census, by the number of seats assigned to the province according to a formula prescribed by Sections 51 and 51A of the *Constitution Act, 1867*.
- The population of each electoral district of a province is to correspond to the electoral quota for the province *as closely as reasonably possible*. In designing the electoral districts, a commission *shall consider* two other variables: a *community of interest, community of identity, or historical pattern* of an electoral district and a *manageable geographic size for districts in sparsely populated, rural, or northern regions* of the province.
- A commission has a limit of ten months within which to complete its set of maps, with the possibility of an extension of up to two months.
- Each commission prepares a preliminary report setting out its recommendations for the new set of maps, together with the reasons for the choices that it has made.

- Public hearings are then held in various centres across each province at which groups, political parties, MPs, former and prospective candidates, or any interested individual may present comments or briefs.
- In addition, members of the public are invited to forward written submissions to a commission with suggestions for changes.
- With the public hearings completed, a commission returns to the map-drawing exercise and prepares its final report and set of maps.
- Once the final report has been completed and forwarded through the Chief Electoral Office to the speaker of the House of Commons, MPs, via a House committee report, have up to thirty days to state their objections to the new maps as long as at least ten members agreed to the objections.
- With parliamentary objections in hand, a commission decides if alterations along the lines suggested by MPs are warranted or not. The maps that the commission then agrees on are the basis, in turn, for the "representation orders" prepared by the Chief Electoral Office and proclaimed by a cabinet order-in-council with the names and legal descriptions of the new constituencies.
- The new districts come into effect seven months after the representation orders have been proclaimed.

This step-by-step description of the process points to two fundamental characteristics of federal electoral boundary readjustments under the *EBRA*. Members of the public can be part of the exercise, and determination of the new district boundaries is firmly in the hands of the three-member, extraparliamentary commissions. Both were revolutionary changes in how federal ridings are designed.

The debate in the House of Commons in 1964 over the *EBRA* left no doubt about parliamentarians' expectations for commissioners: their task was to be carried out in a strictly non-partisan and independent manner. Elected officials and political parties were to have no part in the process, nor were commissioners expected to act in any way, or design their maps, or state reasons for their decisions that reflected partisan interests. Whether that expectation has always been met forms the basis for one of my proposed reforms of the *EBRA*.[6]

Finally, as is to be expected in a federal country such as Canada, a program introduced in one jurisdiction is often observed by other jurisdictions. With the Manitoba and federal electoral boundary readjustment models to point to, Saskatchewan's newly elected Blakeney government legislated in 1972 the change from politically directed redistributions to independent ones.[7] All other provinces have since followed suit, though with differences among them because of local political customs and histories.

SIX DECADES OF FEDERAL REDISTRIBUTIONS

We now have a database of sixty federal redistributions (six decades in ten provinces) upon which to base an evaluation of the process and upon which to propose improvements. On balance, the record to date, in my view, is strongly positive. I would rate it an eight out of ten. Two particularly encouraging aspects of the process stand out.

Public hearings and a commission's call for written submissions from individuals and groups have, as intended, opened the process to interested citizens and groups. The post-2011 redistributions in Ontario and British Columbia, for example, point to the level of interest that the exercise can generate. The Ontario commission held thirty-one public hearings in twenty-two centres around the province at which 509 presentations were made by individuals, groups, and municipalities.[8] Another 569 written submissions were made to the commission as well as "countless" emails, faxes, and petitions.[9] For its part, the BC commission held twenty-three public hearings at which 354 presentations were given.[10] In addition, the commission received over 600 written submissions.[11]

These might not be large numbers considering the population of several million in each province. But that should be only part of the measure of citizen interest. Public hearings and presenters' submissions typically generate a great deal of local (and occasionally national) media attention. That attention goes unreported in the reports filed by the various commissions.

In addition, the inevitable social media debates that have become so much a feature of public connection with politics over the past decade points to a far greater number of people sufficiently mobilized and (one hopes) informed to enter into discussions of the shape and size of the proposed electoral districts in the provinces. Again, the bare numbers of submissions to commissions or appearances at public hearings do not capture that side of citizen participation.

Moreover, there is no question that, when a set of proposals for redefined electoral boundaries is particularly contentious, members of the public are more likely to mobilize. The recent federal redistribution in Saskatchewan speaks to that point. In large measure because it proposed a major transformation of seven of the province's mixed urban-rural seats into five strictly urban and two largely rural ones, the commission's work generated interest, discussion, criticism, and support. The two previous federal redistributions (1991 and 2001) each received fewer than forty submissions and some public hearings were cancelled because of the lack of public interest. In contrast, the 2011 commission received 2,879 written submissions, held twelve public hearings, and had in-person presentations from 230 individuals.

The 2,879 submissions were made up of letters, emails, faxes, postcards, and petitions. Radio talk shows, newspaper editorials, opinion pieces, and talk on social media and coffee row made it abundantly clear that the seemingly mundane practice of redesigning electoral districts had hit a collective nerve in Saskatchewan. In the final stage of public consultation, the commission had no choice but to extend its proposed eight days of public hearings to twelve. All that in a province of 1.1 million people! Blakeney would have applauded the degree to which the people of Saskatchewan became engaged in this democratic exercise.

Judged by one empirical measure, an important representational standard has emerged over time in federal redistributions among the various commissions. Since the first federal redistribution of 1966, over 90 percent of all federal electoral districts have consistently been designed within +/- 15 percent of a province's population quota. Moreover, in the most recent redistribution, 80 percent of the 335 districts assigned to the provinces (the three territorial seats have been excluded from this exercise) were created within +/- 10 percent of their provincial quota, and 52 percent fell within +/- 5 percent of the quota. I have based my calculations upon statistics presented in all federal electoral boundary reports from 1966 to 2012.

These figures point to the fact that a substantial measure of voter equality has been achieved within the provinces irrespective of the wide allowances in district size (+/- 25 percent) that the EBRA allows and in spite of the fact that commissions are established anew every decade. Why such relatively small numbers of districts should have been created outside the +/- 15 percent margin is answered partly by institutional capacity building and partly by evolving cultural norms of a democratic electoral system that emphasizes citizen equality.

Public administration theory would lead us to expect that any process that requires decision-making bodies such as redistribution commissions to be newly established every ten years is doomed to fall short of ensuring a capacity-building, institutional framework. It could be reasonably assumed that the norms and practices would vary among ten commissions, from one commission to the next in the same province, and among the different commissions over time.[12]

Yet the previously cited record of districts that have consistently fallen within the 15 percent population range shows that, even in the absence of an institutional capacity-building imperative, the commissioners have tried to live up to their statutory obligation under the EBRA to create districts with populations "as close as reasonably possible" to the provincial quota.[13]

The tendency to create districts within a province that are reasonably close to one another in population is easily explained. Limited though it might be by its dearth of continuing membership and its absence of individual or collective institutional memory, every new commission is nonetheless obliged to start somewhere—and that, as it turns out, is not with a tabula rasa but with the status quo. When commissioners first meet, they have before them the existing district maps (those designed by a previous commission a decade earlier) and the population of each district as determined by the most recent decennial census. Understandably, with its task of designing seats of a manageable size, with a reasonable degree of population parity, and reflective of communities of interest, a commission starts with what was created in the previous redistribution and sees which changes, if any, are needed and, if so, how they can best be accomplished.

As has been demonstrated in studies of decision making in similar situations, those charged with making the decisions generally "exhibit a significant *status quo* bias."[14] The EBRA captures that fact in its instruction to commissions to consider, along with community of interest and community of identity, an electoral district's "historical pattern."[15] When little significant change or growth in a province's population has occurred from one decade to the next, it is entirely understandable why commissions have a demonstrated tendency to do little to alter the status quo apart from "tinkering at the margins" of districts to correct obvious population inequalities among the existing districts.

AN INTRACTABLE TENSION IN THE PROCESS

The default procedural option for commissions is to make little more than incremental changes to an existing map. However, we would expect exceptions when a commission finds that the existing map is so out of sync with the demographic reality of a province that significant changes must be made. Moreover, a province's population growth or decline, combined with intraprovincial population shifts, can prompt commissions to rework the existing maps in strikingly different ways.

That was the experience in Saskatchewan when the 2011–13 federal redistribution commission was presented with the existing maps and the most recent census population figures for the province. The commissioners noted that the 2001 commission had abandoned its original proposal to create a few strictly urban districts in light of the criticisms that it had received. The 2001 commission had reworked the maps that had been devised a decade earlier (in 1991) to take account of the population shifts over the intervening decade, but the changes had amounted to little more than tinkering at the edges. The population shifts of that decade had been minor compared with those of 2001–11. The status quo maps with which the 2011 commission dealt were by then, in effect, twenty years out of date.

Saskatchewan's demographics had changed markedly between 2001 and 2011. Changes—*dramatic* changes in the opinion of the majority of the commissioners—in the electoral district maps were needed to reflect the demographic reality of the province. The 2011 census showed that in the decade since the previous census rural to urban migration had dwindled to the lowest point since the 1930s and that there had been sizable net gains in both interprovincial and international migration. The growth was most pronounced in the two major cities, where, for the first time, 40 percent of the province's population lived. The 2011 census showed that the four fastest-growing electoral districts—all twenty-year-old hybrid districts—had grown by more than 15 percent in the previous decade, whereas the remaining ten districts in the province had grown by barely 1.5 percent.[16]

The overall population growth of the two biggest cities was accompanied by an impressive change in their demographic composition. More than ever, a pronounced "urban" culture had emerged in them that had been missing from Saskatchewan up to then. It was separate from and had less obvious attachment to the communities and familial linkages of the past and was more in tune with the urban cultures of the rest of Canada. It was palpable and easily observed by anyone who chose to look at or listen to the issues raised in submissions and public hearings by individuals who were part of the new and vastly more socially diverse population of Saskatchewan.

To redress the population inequities among the ridings and to reflect as best as possible the province's new urban character, a majority of the commissioners opted for substantial changes by designing five strictly urban districts (two in Regina and three in Saskatoon). The dissenting member, whose objections to the changes were echoed by the province's Conservative

MPs in their attacks on the proposals, would have preferred relatively minor alterations to the existing maps, leaving "the electoral boundaries as close as the commission can in their current form in Saskatchewan."[17]

The condemnation of the majority's proposal by Conservative parliamentarians and party activists points to an inherent tension in the redistribution process as it currently exists. Proposals for major changes in an electoral map can provoke widely different interpretations of what a commission should do. Whereas politicians view the redistribution exercise through a partisan lens, commissioners are obliged to exercise their judgment about district boundaries in accordance with the EBRA.

The conflict inherent in the exercise reflects the following reality. On the one side of the issue are MPs, local parties, candidates, and political organizers for whom the process is a way of protecting partisan self-interests. MPs in particular want to hold on to what they know and where they were elected. In a wonderfully frank admission—worthy of Yogi Berra—to his fellow MPs reviewing the Saskatchewan redistricting proposals in a House of Commons committee, one Saskatchewan Conservative MP captured the custodial sentiment common to many MPs about their particular ridings: "I'd like to maintain the status quo as it is."[18] On the other side of the issue are the commissioners, for whom the process is framed by an obligation to ensure that, to the best of their abilities, the electoral districts are constructed according to the requirements of the governing statute: communities of interest/identity, manageable geographic size, and populations as reasonably close to one another as possible.

MPs, their attention focused on preserving what they are most familiar with (their ridings), understandably pay little or no attention to the larger picture (their province as a whole). That job falls to the commissioners. When MPs or members of the public who present submissions to a commission make their cases for a certain configuration of the boundaries of an electoral district, they do so without acknowledging the implications of their proposals for neighbouring constituencies. In its 2012 final report, the Alberta commission captured this point of stress. MPs and others pressing for a particular map chose not to admit that "a perfect configuration for one electoral district often negatively impacts adjoining electoral districts and beyond. Redistribution [by arm's-length commissions] is directed at ensuring fair federal representation for all citizens, not at creating preferred electoral districts for some."[19]

In the final analysis, the process of redistribution all but guarantees disagreement when a commission proposes substantial changes to an existing set of maps. There likely is no way around this tension, best described as "intractable." That said, it is hard to escape the conclusion that MPs, particularly those whose ridings are likely to be substantially changed, willingly choose to ignore the real purpose of the adjustments or that some commissions fall short of presenting convincing reasons for alterations.

WHAT IS WRONG?

As electoral institutions go, the federal electoral boundary process should be judged an overall success, though that judgment must come with some qualifications. When approved by all parties in Parliament in 1964, the EBRA was a landmark and long-overdue piece of legislation. Since then, the record suggests that there have been no major problems with the institution that have cried out for immediate action. However, some changes should be made to improve what is already an accepted and legitimate institutional process.

As it now stands, the EBRA remains largely as it was in the mid-1960s. To improve and update the process of electoral redistribution, reforms should be agreed to by parliamentarians. Fortunately, immediate deadlines are not looming. Since the next redistribution starts following the release by Statistics Canada of the first population data from the 2021 census, there is sufficient time for parliamentary committees, scholars, and Elections Canada to study the following, and possibly other, proposals for improvements.

First, electronic communications and social media have opened new avenues for the public to express their views on the redistribution under way in their home provinces. In 2012, several commissions took advantage of that fact soon after they were established. Many of them put out calls via their websites and press conferences for public input before they drew up their sets of proposed maps and began to hold public hearings. At the conclusion of the process, they judged the experiment to be valuable and worthy of formal acknowledgement.[20] The statute does not expressly contemplate such a move, but neither does it disallow it.

To ensure clarity and standard practice across all provinces, the act should instruct commissions to call for public submissions about the redistribution soon after they first meet. If public submissions were allowed early in the exercise, the process would be brought in line with the new realities of communication and further enhance its legitimacy. In addition, commissions should be given the option of holding a preliminary set of public hearings when, in their opinion, the information gathered from the hearings would inform the commissioners of the principal issues to be addressed in the task before them. An initial set of public hearings is allowed in provincial redistributions in both British Columbia and Alberta, as well as in Australia, the country from which Canada copied the electoral boundary readjustment institutional framework. Commissioners in those jurisdictions attest to the value of that added stage.

The principal objection to adding a second set of hearings would focus on the added time that it would take a commission to complete its work. This need not be a concern. Adding a preliminary period of public consultations could go hand in hand with a reform that would eliminate a later stage—which now lasts several months—of the present process.

Second, as matters now stand, membership in the federal three-member commission in each province is an open question from one decade to the next. The chief justice of the province names the chair of the commission, but the speaker of the House of Commons is free to consult fellow parliamentarians, cabinet ministers, Elections Canada officials, and possibly others prior to choosing the two additional members of a commission. It is a fluid and subjective process that on occasion could lead to the appointment of individuals with little apparent understanding of the task at hand or with partisan leanings that might call into question their impartiality. To ensure the integrity of ten independent and non-partisan institutions, it is vital that the speaker exercise independence and non-partisanship in selecting commission members.

The model that commends itself on this issue lies, once again, in the Australian process of redistribution, in which professional public servants are named ex officio to every commission. Australia's redistribution committees consist of the federal election commissioner, the Australian electoral officer for the state or territory, the state surveyor general, and the state auditor general.[21]

The logic of naming commissioners from the ranks of the public service is obvious. Senior public servants such as a province's chief electoral officer, auditor general, census bureau chief, or a university president would rightly be expected to be knowledgeable about the topography, demographics, and population shifts of the province. And, more important, they are at some remove from partisan politics.

Manitoba's provincial redistribution process demonstrates that "professional" electoral districting can be done successfully in Canada. Since the province adopted its boundary commission legislation in 1955, it has guaranteed the independence of the commission by naming certain office-holders in the public sector to serve as commission members on an ex officio basis. In the province's most recent redistribution (2008), those named as commissioners were the chief justice of Manitoba; the presidents of the University of Manitoba, Brandon University, and the University College of the North; and the chief electoral officer of Manitoba.[22] A similar change could be introduced in Canada's EBRA to avoid any suggestion of partisanship among a commission's members.

Third, MPs occupy a privileged position in the redistribution exercise. They and their local party organizers are free to make written submissions to the commissions, to present briefs to and appear before the commissioners at public hearings, and, in the final stage of the exercise, to raise objections to the proposals in the Standing Committee on Procedure and House Affairs.[23] Unlike other Canadians, MPs have three opportunities to make their cases about the proposals. But there is no obvious argument to be made for this, and it adds considerably to the length of time before the representation orders establishing the new electoral districts can be prepared.

The final reports of the ten commissions charged with the redistribution in 2012 make it abundantly clear that, with the exception of Ontario and Quebec, the commissioners designed their first maps, read the submissions and petitions presented to them, held public hearings, revised the maps, and completed their final reports within the time stipulated in the EBRA, ten months from the date of appointment. Because of the larger number of districts that they were designing and the complexity of the issues that they faced, the Ontario and Quebec commissions of 2012 were granted an additional two months to complete their work. But MPs' objection stage and commissions' disposition of the objections added four to six months to what otherwise could have been a ten- to twelve-month process from date of appointment to completion of report (see Table 1 for the procedural timetables of four commissions).

Table 1. Time from Establishment of Four Commissions to Their Final Disposition of Objections

Province (# of Districts)	Date Established	Report Completed	MPs' Objections and Disposition
BC (42)	21 Feb 2012	18 Dec 2012	17 June 2013
SK (14)	21 Feb 2012	19 Dec 2012	28 June 2013
ON (121)	21 Feb 2012	14 Feb 2013	31 July 2013
QC (78)	21 Feb 2012	15 Feb 2013	28 June 2013

What about the objections that MPs filed with the parliamentary committee? The fact is that little of any substance is presented as MPs' objections to the districts designed by the commissions. But more important, it has been demonstrated over several decades that the MPs' objection stage has had little to no substantive impact on commissions' decisions.[24] An MP's greatest opportunity to influence a commission comes not at the end but at the start of the process, both through a written brief in advance of the initial proposals being drafted and through a submission to or an appearance at public hearings.[25] Overwhelmingly, the objections amount either to a request for a change in the name assigned by the commission to a particular riding or a call for a relatively insignificant boundary change.

The Alberta and Quebec redistribution commissions of 2012 illustrate how few in number and how strikingly minor are objections raised by MPs. Alberta MPs filed ten objections with that province's commission, which dismissed seven, allowed two (one for a name change and one concerning a boundary affecting five electors), and partially allowed one concerning a small geographic area.[26] The Quebec commission was little different.[27] MPs filed twenty-five objections, nine of which favoured the commission's maps. Of the remaining sixteen, five called for specific boundary changes, and eleven requested a change to a riding's name, and all were accepted. Requests for small changes to groupings of municipalities in three ridings were accepted, one was partially accepted, and one was denied.

There is no clear justification for scheduling a parliamentary objection stage for the purpose of changing the name of a constituency. A single Parliament typically passes, often en masse, several bills altering names of particular ridings. It is a simple procedure, and MPs of all parties engage in this practice. It amounts to little more than highlighting particular interests—a town that wants to be acknowledged, a historical association's interest in preserving a name, and the like. During the life of a Parliament, it seems that the name of a constituency is in the preserve of its current MP.

Australia has long accepted that objections can be filed with a commission by any citizen—including members of the House of Representatives—at any time during the life of a redistribution committee. Nothing exists in Australia equivalent to Canada's parliamentary "objection stage."[28]

Fourth, as noted earlier, boundary commissions have consistently designed the overwhelming majority of their electoral districts within +/- 15 percent of their provincial population quotas. In the 2012 redistribution, for example, only 24 of the 335 seats (7.2 percent) allocated to the provinces had populations outside the 15 percent range. In four provinces (Prince

Edward Island, Manitoba, Saskatchewan, and Alberta), all federal districts were designed within a 10 percent population variance. The *EBRA* should be amended to reflect the fact that the 15 percent variance has long been widely accepted by commissioners as the appropriate goal at which to aim.

MPs from geographically large and often sparsely populated parts of a province could be expected to object to a reduction in the variance. To allay their concerns, an amended act could permit commissions to design a small number of ridings in their respective provinces with populations outside the 15 percent limit. The logic behind such a move rests in the "*exceptional circumstances*" clause added to the *EBRA* in 1985. It allows commissions to create districts with populations above or below the 25 percent limit when they can be justified on grounds of small population, remoteness, and size. Currently, only 3 of the 335 provincial electoral districts exceed the 25 percent variance limit: one each in Newfoundland and Labrador, Quebec, and Ontario. With a 15 percent variance as the new base for districts with exceptional circumstances, the number of such ridings could be expected to rise to 20 to 25 of the 335 districts assigned to the provinces.

Support for a reduction in the population variance comes from a variety of sources, both federal and provincial. The Royal Commission on Electoral Reform and Party Financing, the Lortie Commission, started the debate when, in 1991, it recommended a 15 percent maximum deviation. The lower population limits were seen as reasonable in a federal country that tries to accommodate differences in population density among the provinces. At the same time, it was seen as a way of ensuring a measure of population equality within individual provinces.[29]

Moreover, to address the problem of "vote dilution" among Canada's increasingly visible minority and urban electorate, scholars of electoral districting in Canada have pushed for even tighter variance limits than the Lortie Commission. Arguing that 10 or possibly even 5 percent variances should replace the current 25 percent level, Michael Pal and Sujit Choudhry rest their case on grounds of voter equity and democratic legitimacy.[30] Michael Pal and Melissa Molson advance the case for a 5 percent variance in southern Ontario, the principal focus of their study.[31]

Once again, some provinces have taken the lead on this issue. Manitoba and Saskatchewan have legislated the tightest variance limits in Canada for their provincial boundary redistributions: 10 percent in Manitoba and 5 percent in Saskatchewan. Both provinces provide legislated protection for two northern seats of large geographic size. Relatively tight limits such as those in Manitoba and Saskatchewan have the advantage not only of being more egalitarian and, therefore, more in tune with democratic values but also of leaving little room for serious objections to the maps drawn by the commissioners.

CONCLUSION

Adoption of the *EBRA* in the 1960s, on which Allan Blakeney's government established Saskatchewan's independent boundary delimitation process a decade later, was a sensible, long-overdue move. The process has many strengths and is now an accepted institutional feature of Canadian government and politics. That much has "gone right." But six decades of federal electoral districting in Canada point to a mismatch between what the public expects of the decennial exercise and how commissioners perform the task with which they have been charged. Members of the public who take an interest in the redistribution exercise— together with MPs, candidates, and political activists—look for the protection of particular communities of interest or identity—often without due regard for population disparities among districts. Those communities are frequently seen through the lens of vested political interests. Nowhere was that more obvious than in the Conservatives' championing a continuation of hybrid electoral districts in Saskatchewan in 2012 in spite of the obvious fact that the province had undergone substantial population shifts in the previous decade.

The record suggests that commissioners have typically aimed for a substantial measure of population equality among their province's federal districts—much tighter than the allowable population variance of +/- 25 percent in the *EBRA*.[32] This reflects, at least implicitly, their acceptance of an important element of representation in a liberal democracy. Proximate voter equality within the provinces (what the act refers to as populations as "close as reasonably possible" to the electoral quota) has now emerged as the key representational pillar in Canada.

Four aspects of the current redistribution process should be addressed so as to enhance its standing among Canadians. The place of electronic communications and social media as a legitimate part of the procedure needs to be ensured; the speaker's appointments to the commissions should be replaced with a legislated list of appropriate ex officio provincial public servants; the MPs' objection stage ought to be eliminated; and the intraprovincial population variance limits should be reset at +/- 15 percent, with exceptions to that rule for possibly as many as two dozen remote and/or sparsely populated districts. If a "demonstration effect" is needed for the suitability or practicality of any or all of these reforms, the experiences of other jurisdictions with their unique models of independent electoral boundary commissions would serve as helpful reference points.

CHAPTER 14

MONEY MATTERS
A DEMOCRATIC ASSESSMENT OF CANADA'S POLITICAL FINANCE SYSTEM

David Coletto

We cannot ignore the role of money in a modern democratic system. Money funds the political activities of political parties and candidates. It pays for research, advertising, office space, and staff. Between elections, political entities furiously compete to raise it to help fund the next campaign but also to demonstrate their relevance, competitiveness, and credibility to voters, the media, and their supporters.

But the design and function of a political finance system are strongly linked to the health and quality of democracy. How money flows to and from political entities can influence their ability to communicate with voters, the level of competition in a political system, the ability of new political entities to enter that system, and the relative power of different interests in a society to influence public policy. Understanding how political entities fund their activities can tell us a lot about *why* a democracy functions the way it does. Political finance can explain why some groups have more influence on decision making than others, why some political entities do better than others in elections. It can tell us why new political entities have a hard time entering the system when others remain despite a loss of support. Political finance can explain why political entities act the way they do, why they highlight certain issues over others, and why they pursue policy options that might seem to be counterintuitive or simply bad choices.

Moreover, political finances are often at the centre of political scandals. We have seen it many times; for example, when campaign contributors pay for access to politicians and political favours. Perceptions of corrupt politicians who favour their campaign funders over members of the public go to the heart of the problem of political finance. In some systems, those with more money can have greater influence on political outcomes. The perception that this is happening is as powerful as if it actually is occurring.

Changes to systems of political finance often follow high-profile political scandals involving contributions, access to politicians, and policy changes. In the United States, reforms to the election finance system followed a series of scandals involving members of the House of Representatives and the Senate. In Canada, the Liberal government introduced major reforms to the country's political finance system in 2003 after several ethical issues challenged the reputation and legacy of Prime Minister Jean Chrétien. And more recently, in Ontario, the Liberal government of Kathleen Wynne introduced sweeping reforms following revelations that her government was providing special access to, and favouring the interests of, those who contributed to the Ontario Liberal Party.

No system of political finance is perfect. Designers make trade-offs between competing values that often consider the self-interest of political actors rather than the best interest of the democratic system. There is substantial variation among political finance systems across the democratic world influenced by the democratic values that each political system prioritizes.

Allan Blakeney recognized the link between the quality of democracy and political finance. In Saskatchewan, his government made major reforms to the political finance system. It enacted spending limits during elections and required full disclosure of the sources of contributions to the province's political parties. His government also banned government advertising during election campaigns.[1]

In this chapter, I assess the current political finance system in Canada through the lens of three democratic values. I conclude that the system in place as of September 2016 is effective at limiting the influence of outside interests and well-financed individuals, corporations, or unions, and its rules for transparency allow the public to know who funds politics in the country. But its strict contribution limits and lack of direct public funding constrain competition, discourage the entry of new political parties into the party system, and encourage political polarization and the consumerization of public policy development as political parties seek to mobilize large numbers of small contributions to fund the permanent campaign required for politics today.

The permanent campaign means that parties now have an insatiable thirst for money. This demand means that the pressure to raise money increases in a system with strict contribution limits and little direct public funding, forcing political entities to shift to a consumerist model. This model causes them to pursue many small donations and leads them to concentrate on niche issues that excite or anger potential donors. Examining ways to provide fair public subsidies to parties, such as having citizens check off on their tax returns which parties they would like their tax dollars to support, could alleviate this problem.

THEORETICAL FRAMEWORK

How well does Canada's political finance system work? Does it improve the quality of Canadian democracy or weaken it? To answer these questions, we must first explore what we mean by democratic quality.

There are many ways to judge the quality of a political finance system and its impact on democracy. In fact, the design of the system is often a function of the democratic values of a country or jurisdiction. For example, in the United States, political finance has been influenced by libertarian values in the political culture and judicial interpretation by the Supreme Court, which has ruled that money is speech, and the state cannot limit an individual's right to use his or her financial resources to advocate for or against causes or political candidates. The American system does have strict limits on political contributions to formal political entities but allows unlimited spending by those entities. There is no real system of state funding, election expenses are not reimbursed, and contributors receive no tax credits for contributions to parties or candidates. At the same time, as a result of the US Supreme Court ruling in *Citizens United v FEC*,[2] independent organizations can spend unlimited amounts of money to influence elections and public opinions as long as they do not coordinate with candidates or political parties.

In Canada, as well as in most continental European countries, the political finance system is more egalitarian. Regulations limit the sources and amounts of contributions that political entities can receive and how those funds can be spent. These systems, in an effort to level the playing field and remove undue influence from the political system, often also include generous state funding mechanisms such as direct subsidies, tax credits for political contributions, and spending rebates for eligible parties and candidates. Whereas the American political finance system seeks to defend everyone's right to speech and to encourage deliberation by not limiting the amount of money in the system, a European-style political finance system values political equality over deliberation and competition.

Is there really a better way to regulate political finance? One way to assess the impact of political finance on democracy is to explore how design choices affect three important democratic principles: electoral competitiveness, political equality, and deliberation.[3]

Electoral competition refers to the economic understanding of the concept. That is, for a system to be democratic, there must be "free competition for a free vote," and meaningful competition "requires [that] there be opposition parties waiting in the wings, criticizing the government and offering voters potential alternatives." In other words, a competitive system allows major opposition parties to compete while "easing the burden of entering competition for third parties."[4]

Since money is needed to compete between and during elections, a political finance system can strongly influence the extent to which opposing parties can mount effective campaigns. The design of the system can also prevent new parties from forming if the limits to raising money are too strict or if the criteria by which political entities receive state funding disadvantages or completely excludes new entrants into the party system.

Along with competition, political equality is fundamental to democracy. Political equality "requires that no citizen have more power over the political process than other citizens."[5] Wealth, class, rank, or position should not give one individual or a group more influence over the political process than others. As Keena Lipsitz notes, "the principle of one person—one vote is a natural extension of the belief in the intrinsic equality of citizens.[6] This principle can also be extended to political entities in a system. A democratic system that values political equality will also ensure that no one party, candidate, or group has a systematic advantage over others in being able to engage with citizens and contest elections.

The political finance system can greatly influence the level of political equity not only between political entities—by limiting the amount of money that one party can raise or spend—but also between citizens—by limiting the influence of those who have more money to contribute than other citizens. Ronald Dworkin's concept of political equality asserts that "if one candidate controls the flow of political communication, she will be able to manipulate the opinions of voters; as a consequence, her viewpoint will carry more weight than those of other candidates—not to mention the viewpoints of average citizens."[7]

A democratic system must strive to encourage competition and political equality, but it must also ensure that the level of deliberation, between political entities and citizens as well as among citizens themselves, is sufficient for citizens to make informed choices. It is not just that there is competition and equity but also that citizens have enough information about the choices before them. This means that political entities need resources to communicate with voters and engage them in the political process. A political system starved of financial resources, therefore, cannot produce a level of deliberation necessary to produce favoured outcomes in the best interests of its citizens.

And it is the political finance system itself that can allow for full deliberation among citizens and political entities or retard deliberation by preventing those entities from having the resources they need to engage with citizens, develop public policies, and communicate those policies during elections.

It is from these democratic values—competition, equality, and deliberation—that I assess political finance in Canada and its impact on Canadian democracy.

THE PURPOSE OF POLITICAL FINANCE

A political finance system has three primary functions. First, it determines to what extent money flows into and out of the political system by controlling the demand for and the supply of funding. The political finance system can dictate who can contribute to political parties, candidates, and third-party organizations and how much each contributor can donate. It can control the demand for funds by imposing spending limits. The control of income and expenditure affects the level of equity between political parties and candidates based upon the amount of money that they can raise and spend as well as the influence of contributors on political parties and candidates when it comes to political decision making.

Second, the level of disclosure required by a political finance regime can influence behaviour by allowing the public and political opponents to understand who is giving to political actors, how much they are giving, and whether those contributions are influencing the decisions of those receiving the funds. Spending disclosure also ensures that political actors are following spending limits that might exist and holds political parties and candidates accountable to their contributors, as well as the public, on how they use funds raised from public and non-public sources.

Third, a political finance regime outlines the role of the state in funding political activities. Direct public subsidies, spending rebates, and tax credits for contributors are mechanisms regularly used to support political parties and candidates. State intervention in political finance can increase equity between parties, replace funding prohibited by contribution limits, and ensure that political parties and candidates have the necessary resources to contest elections.

But these mechanisms can also limit competition, equality, and deliberation. A system heavily reliant on state funding can insulate political parties from the preferences of citizens, making them unresponsive to those preferences. Moreover, if state funding is determined by previous election results and other forms of funding are strictly limited, then existing parties can be protected at the expense of new entrants. Systems with few revenue or expenditure limits can encourage new entrants, but they can also give parties able to access unlimited resources an advantage over other parties, thereby weakening political equality and the level of effective competition among existing parties. Finally, if a political finance system severely limits both the source of funding and the expenditure-revenue, then the levels of deliberation, engagement, and communication can be lowered, thereby producing an ill-informed electorate. How, then, do these choices in design affect the operation of the electoral system and the broader political system?

The design of a political finance system has consequences beyond simply who can fund election campaigns and politics and what money can be spent on them. Depending on the design, some political entities benefit, whereas others are harmed, which is why political finance reform has become such a political topic. Although recent reforms in Canada were justified on ideological or policy grounds, their impacts were political and clearly to the benefit of the government that implemented the changes and to the detriment of its opponents. But this chapter is not about *why* political finance systems change but about the *impact* of system design on the functioning of democracy.

The impact of the design of a political finance system can be understood as follows. Those able to contribute more to political entities have greater access to and influence on those entities. Hence, their interests are more likely to be heard and therefore addressed. If one's interests are not heard and understood, then they cannot be addressed. Therefore, political parties and actors that represent the interests of those with greater financial resources should have more financial resources than political parties or actors that represent the interests of those without the financial means to contribute to entities that might represent their interests. This financial advantage can lead to an electoral advantage.[8] In a system with strict contribution limits, power and influence are dispersed because a political entity cannot count on a small number of contributors to fund its political activities.

But limits on financial contributions also affect the amount of money available to fund political activities. Political entities need money. Money funds a range of functions critical to communicate with, persuade, and mobilize voters. Entities without financial resources are at a severe disadvantage. Money might not win elections, but it does help. In this way, the competitiveness and deliberative nature of a political system are directly influenced by the levels of resources of competing political entities. If the amount of overall resources available is low—because the limits on fundraising are strict—then political entities will be unable to communicate with and motivate voters. Political information drops, interest falls, and voters might become unaware of their options. If the political finance regime creates a situation in which the amount of financial resources is severely unequal—one or more parties have more financial resources than their support in the electorate would reasonably dictate—then full competition and deliberation will be limited.

In these ways, a political finance system is strongly related to the democratic quality of a political system. When money is fundamental to the ability of a political entity to compete electorally and fulfill functions such as policy development, opposing governing parties, and engaging with citizens between elections, how and whether political entities can raise and spend money are of great importance to the function and quality of a democracy. In the case of Canada, the political finance system has evolved substantially over the past four decades. In the next section, I summarize this evolution and assess the democratic value of the regulatory framework currently in place.

THE EVOLUTION OF POLITICAL FINANCE IN CANADA

Prior to 1974, Canada had no legal framework to regulate political finance at the federal level. Political parties and candidates could raise unlimited amounts of money from any contributor (individual, corporation, or union) and spend unlimited amounts between and during elections. There was no disclosure or transparency on who gave what to political entities and no disclosure on how they spent the money. I describe this era as the *premodern* period of political finance in Canada.

In 1974, amendments to the *Canada Elections Act* established the foundation of the current political finance regime and transitioned Canada into the *modern* period of political finance. The reforms introduced spending limits for both political parties and candidates, required that parties and candidates disclose the sources of all donations over $100 as well as total amounts spent during campaigns, reimbursed a portion of election expenditures by political entities that met certain thresholds, and created tax credits for individuals who made small contributions to political parties and candidates.[9] Apart from some minor changes to the reimbursements for election spending, the thresholds for disclosure, and the value of the tax credit for political contributions, most of the 1974 reforms remained intact until 2003, when fundamental reforms were introduced in the final months of the Chrétien Liberal government.

In 2004, the Liberal government passed Bill C-24, which radically reformed the political finance system in Canada and transitioned it into the *syndicate* period of political finance.[10] The reforms instituted strict contribution limits for the first time. Individuals could contribute a maximum of $5,000 per year to a political party, a candidate, or an electoral district association (EDA), the new legal term used to describe local party organizations. Limits were also placed on corporations, associations, and trade unions, which could now contribute to local candidates or EDAs but not national political parties. The legislation also, for the first time, instituted direct funding from the state in the form of a quarterly allowance paid directly to eligible political parties based upon the number of votes that a party received in the previous election. Two years later, following the election of Stephen Harper and the Conservative Party, the *Accountability Act* was the first piece of legislation passed that banned all contributions except those from individuals and limited the amount that a person could give in a single year to a political entity to $1,000.

Soon after the 2008 federal election, the Conservative government announced in a fiscal update that it was going to eliminate the per-vote subsidy. Partly in response to this announcement, the opposition parties, which held most of the seats in the House of Commons, announced that they would form a coalition and ask the governor general to give them an opportunity to govern after a vote of non-confidence was passed in Parliament. Instead of facing that vote, the Conservative government prorogued Parliament, preventing the opposition parties from implementing their plan. When Parliament was recalled, the Conservative government did not follow through on its plan to eliminate the per-vote subsidy. Harold Jansen and Lisa Young argue that the behaviour of the Liberal, New Democratic, and Green Parties was like that of a syndicate, working to protect the state subsidy because they had become dependent on it.[11]

After they won a majority government in 2011, the Conservatives moved ahead with their long-held policy position to eliminate the per-vote subsidy or quarterly allowance. The government announced in its 2011 budget that it would phase out the quarterly allowance over five years, ending it in 2015. There would be no replacement for this money to parties or changes to contribution limits. To put the value of the quarterly allowances in context, almost $30 million was distributed to the five eligible political parties throughout 2011. The Conservative Party received $11.7 million, the NDP $7.5 million, and the Liberal Party $6.8 million, while the Bloc Québécois and Green Party split the remaining $4 million. In comparison, using Elections Canada data, those five parties raised $31.3 million from individual contributions in 2011, which means that 50 percent of the total revenue for Canada's major political parties came from per-vote direct state funding. That funding was being phased out. What did not change from 2003 to 2011 was the amount of money that a political party or candidate could spend. The election spending limits enacted in 1974 have remained largely unchanged.

In 2014, the Conservative government introduced the *Fair Elections Act*, which included a number of amendments to the political finance system in Canada. It tightened rules for loans to political parties, candidates, and party leadership candidates. It increased the annual contribution limit to $1,500, increased the amount that a candidate or leadership candidate could give to his or her own campaign, increased the overall spending limits for national and local campaigns by 5 percent each, and permitted higher campaign spending for registered political parties and candidates if the election period is longer than the thirty-seven-day minimum.

Overall, these reforms changed little in the design of the system, but they did complete the transition of Canada's political finance system from a *syndicate system*—in which parties relied heavily on direct state funding—to a *consumerist system*. Individual contribution limits were increased slightly, as was the amount that parties and candidates could spend during the formal campaign period. The amendments did not replace the lapsed per-vote subsidy with any new mechanism of state funding. So political entities have become more reliant on mass funding—small contributions from more donors without any direct financial support from the state. Indirect public funding remains in place only in the form of spending rebates for parties and candidates who meet a certain threshold of support and generous tax credits for those who do contribute to political parties.

ASSESSING THE CURRENT SYSTEM

The current political finance system in Canada evolved over four decades in which stricter limits were placed on the sources of revenues for political entities and how those funds could be spent during elections. Moreover, throughout this period, the role of the state in funding political activities increased to the degree that the state provided more than 50 percent of revenue to political parties. At the same time, spending restrictions were not tightened. Political parties can still spend as much as they wish outside the formal campaign period, and the law was changed in 2014 to allow higher spending limits for longer campaigns.

So what have been the impacts of these changes on the amounts of money in the political system? Thanks to disclosure laws, data are available to understand how the evolution from the modern system to the consumerist system has affected the resources available to parties.

The reforms enacted by the Liberal government in 2003 took a significant source of funding for political entities out of the system. Unlimited contributions from individuals, corporations, and unions were eliminated, and only individuals could contribute to political parties. These changes and those enacted by the Conservative government in 2006 did not reduce the overall amount of money in the system. According to Elections Canada data, income to the five major national parties increased soon after the reforms took effect, going from under $40 million in 2001 and 2002 (in 2014 dollars) to almost $60 million in 2004 and 2005. In fact, despite the stricter contribution limits, the introduction of the per-vote subsidy increased the amount of total revenue that parties collected annually throughout the entire syndicate period (from 2004 to 2011) compared with data available prior to that period.

At the same time, the system concentrated revenue among the national political parties at the expense of electoral district associations and local candidates.[12] This was partly because of the per-vote subsidy and partly because raising small contributions from more donors was prohibitive for local party organizations and done more easily by the central parties. From 2004 to 2012, using Elections Canada data, the percent of total party revenue raised by the national parties increased from 60 percent to 85 percent, concentrating revenue at the national level at the expense of local parties and candidates.

Starting in 2012, the amount that each party would receive from the per-vote subsidy declined by 25 percent each year. Despite this loss of stable revenue, most of the major parties in the system were able to replace most of this lost revenue by increasing the amounts raised from individual contributions.

However, the net effect has been a reduction in total revenue to all major parties in the system.

The removal of direct state funding has meant that political parties are entirely reliant on revenue raised from individual contributions. This has important consequences for the functioning of these political organizations.

First, parties need capital to raise money from small donors. Although advances in digital fundraising might change this in the future, parties need to invest significant resources in fundraising, and between elections much is spent on building a campaign war chest for the next election. Elections Canada data indicate that in 2014 the Conservative, Liberal, and New Democratic Parties raised approximately $45 million from individual contributions but spent almost $11 million to raise it. In other words, it takes about a quarter of a dollar to raise a dollar. This is a significant barrier to entry for smaller or newer parties that do not have the resources to invest in fundraising infrastructure.

Second, strict contribution limits not only force political parties to invest in a substantial fundraising infrastructure to harvest small donations from a larger group of people, these strict limits encourage divisive political rhetoric and policy proposals to mobilize donations. We know from research that political contributors are at least partly motivated to give money because of a desire to influence political outcomes.[13] They hope that the money they contribute helps to elect political parties and candidates that support positions they support. Political fundraisers thus know that they need to generate enthusiasm for a cause to initiate giving. As such, issues that excite or anger potential donors are more likely to lead to donations.

But there are upsides to a decrease in reliance on state funding, as seen during the syndicate period of political finance in Canada. Generous direct state funding, like the per-vote subsidy, can lead to political parties less reliant on membership dues and voluntary contributions from supporters. Parties too reliant on direct state funding can become isolated and disconnected from both their members and the electorate. This could decrease competition and deliberation within the political system as a whole.

Third, banning corporate and union contributions to political parties encourages the formation of extraparliamentary political organizations. Instead of large contributions flowing from corporations, unions, or individuals to registered political parties, they now flow to organizations that are not required to disclose their activities and operate outside the formal, regulated political system. Organizations such as the Manning Centre for Building Democracy, founded by former Reform Party leader and Member of

Parliament Preston Manning, or the Broadbent Institute, founded by former NDP leader Ed Broadbent, now perform many of the functions that political parties used to perform. They offer candidate-training programs, conduct policy research, and engage the public in debate on policy issues of concern. In effect, political finance reforms have had the unintended consequence of shifting some of the traditional roles of political parties from the public sphere to the private sphere because they banned corporate and union contributions. Instead of stopping the flow of money into political life, these reforms diverted it to external, unregulated organizations not required to disclose their contributors.

Fourth, the current political finance system in Canada makes it difficult for new political parties to form and compete. To compete effectively with established parties, new parties require funding. But the strict contribution limits, restrictive political loan rules, and reimbursement-based public funding mean that new political parties will have a difficult time finding the required "seed" money to launch new political movements.

So the current political finance system has its strengths. It limits the sizes and sources of contributions, thereby limiting the influence of big money on political and policy decision making. Spending limits prevent one party or candidate from gaining too great an advantage during an official election campaign. The disclosure rules ensure transparency of where funds come from and how they are spent. Indirect state funding through tax credits and reimbursements provides a significant source of funds to help political entities manage the costs of running elections and encouraging contributions.

But there are weaknesses that can affect the quality of democracy in Canada. Eliminating the per-vote subsidy and not replacing it with a new revenue source have made fundraising from small donors a top priority for political parties. Instead of developing policy or seeking to unite the electorate, parties are incentivized to divide and conquer and compete aggressively to raise money. At the same time, political entities have less money, meaning that they spend less time engaging with the public, developing policy, and building social capital and more time stocking the campaign war chest for the next election.

Moreover, the lack of spending restrictions between formal election periods means that parties can spend unlimited amounts of money on advertising prior to an election. This is especially troublesome given that fixed election dates are now in practice in most jurisdictions, including at the federal level.

CONCLUSION

The political finance system in Canada has evolved over the past forty years from one in which there were no limits on fundraising or spending to one in which there are strict contribution and spending limits, generous donation tax credits and spending reimbursements, and limited direct public funding. To fund their activities, parties must constantly raise small amounts of money from many contributors. Yet, as the political finance system has changed, so has the way in which politics is conducted.

Canadian political parties are now in a permanent campaign mode. They are constantly communicating with Canadians, developing campaign infrastructure, and conducting research. To fund the activities of the permanent campaign, political parties need money. The demand created by the permanent campaign, along with the nature of Canada's political finance system, has meant a shift toward a consumerist model of party finance. As built, the system encourages political parties to focus on ideologically polarizing issues that anger or inspire donors and push them to give more (e.g., the Conservatives and the gun registry). So relying on relatively small donations from thousands of individuals has entrenched and encouraged ideological polarization while closing Canada's political system to new entrants. Choking off the sources of funds, as the current Canadian political finance system does, in an environment in which the demand for money has never been greater is a serious threat to democracy. Instead of focusing on developing good public policy or engaging with the public, political leaders become focused on raising money.

Given the realities of the permanent campaign and how Canada's current political finance regime operates, reform is needed. Here are five suggestions for reforming political finance in Canada.

1. The system must prevent the actual or perceived influence of big money on politics by placing strict contribution limits on who can give and how much can be given.
2. The system must ensure that political entities have adequate funds to engage and mobilize voters between and during formal election periods. Democracy is stronger when voters have adequate information to make informed decisions and when all political actors can communicate with the electorate. The elimination of public subsidies to political parties between elections should be reconsidered.

3. The system should encourage political parties to perform functions other than simply selecting candidates and raising money. Ways should be found to ensure that public funds given to political parties are tied to policy development and public consultation.
4. The formula to distribute direct public funding should be a function of a party's current support rather than its past performance. Basing generous public funding on previous election results—as the Canadian system did between 2004 and 2015—can freeze a political system and artificially sustain political parties that have lost public support. One possibility is to allow Canadians to check off a box on their annual income tax forms that gives a certain amount of their tax liability (e.g., five or ten dollars) to the political party of their choice.
5. The system long needs to ensure that new political entities can be formed and allowed to enter the political system. Political finance rules can make a party system inaccessible by choking start-up funding needed to get a new political movement off the ground. Public subsidies could be structured to encourage political "start-ups" and prevent cartelization.

Allan Blakeney recognized that just as a political system changes so too must its political finance rules. He believed that, if Saskatchewan was going to be a modern, strong, and progressive democracy, then its political finance system had to change. His government's political finance reforms limited campaign spending, prevented governments from advertising during elections, and introduced new transparency and disclosure requirements for contributions. Like Blakeney in his day, it is time for today's political leaders to put aside their self-interest and rebuild Canada's political finance system. In doing so, they will help to protect and enhance Canadian democracy.

CONCLUSION

BLAKENEY'S RELEVANCE TO THE ROAD AHEAD

At the heart of great political leadership is understanding the dynamics, needs, and challenges of the times. That virtue would certainly characterize Allan Blakeney's tenure as premier of Saskatchewan. Blakeney was an active political leader, responding in timely and prudent ways to the demands that arose during the more than a decade that he was in power—leading his government's engagement with the challenges to Saskatchewan's resource-based economy; managing service demands that arose from demographic shifts; developing outstanding public policy processes supported by a skilful public service; actively and constructively responding to Canada's constitutional reform process; constantly staying alert to the need for new, or improved, public goods; and striving to act in ways that reflected democracy's ideals of openness, civility, and acceptance of the legitimacy of criticism.

But great political leaders also set templates for future governance. Although substantive issues change, the habits of political engagement and of conduct in holding power can set the stage for future sound democratic practice. In face of the rise of right-wing populism in both Canada and around the world that threatens to undermine democratic institutions, do Blakeney's values and commitments instruct us about revitalizing democracy in the twenty-first century? How can we strengthen the democratic state to be a bulwark against extreme ideologies that disregard the importance of democratic deliberation and threaten the rights of minorities?

The chapters in the first part of this book show that Blakeney was strongly committed to both state activism and democracy. Indeed, for him, an activist state dedicated to achieving equality also had to be a democratic state. In this way, he brought the "social" and the "democracy" parts of the ideology of social democracy together.

The chapters in Part 1 show Blakeney's commitment to the modern activist state. The chapters by Marchildon and McGrane illustrate that Blakeney strongly believed the state was a positive force for society that should be harnessed to solve the problems of everyday people, protect their rights, and improve their quality of life. Marchildon's chapter depicts how Blakeney believed that, under the guidance of expert public administrators and earnest politicians, an activist, intelligent, efficient state would emerge. When the government enacts effective and competent programs leading to more just outcomes for all citizens, the public would identify the intrinsic value of government and appreciate the role it plays in society. Activism and effectiveness go hand in hand for a government to maintain its legitimacy. McGrane's chapter portrays how Blakeney held that an activist state was necessary in achieving growing economic, social, legal, and regional equality within society. Indeed, the expansion of the government's realm of activities was the key to achieving his vision of a good society in which all citizens enjoy a high standard of living and are free from discrimination based on their identity or their residence within a certain region of the country. For Blakeney, there was no way to achieve essential equality in society without extensive state activism.

At the same time, the chapters in Part 1 show that there was something profoundly democratic about Blakeney's statism. The chapters by Romanow and Chambers describe Blakeney's views on elections and statecraft. Romanow's discussion of provincial elections in Saskatchewan during the 1970s illustrates how Blakeney conceived of elections as opportunities in which voters—presented with competing visions of the polity contained in parties' platforms—chose one vision over another. In the case of Saskatchewan's "resource wars" that Romanow examines, voters chose public development over private development of Saskatchewan's natural resources. For Blakeney (and Romanow, his attorney general at the time), the platform on which a party campaigns is a solemn promise to voters that must be fulfilled. But democracy is about more than just elections that happen once every four years. Once elected as the government, politicians work alongside public servants to implement the specific policy objectives of their party's platform. Both Romanow and Chambers point out that Blakeney thought that, as politicians govern over the course of their mandate, they must inform and interact with the voters whom they have been chosen to serve. Through such interaction, they are able to stay abreast of what the public deems acceptable as solutions to problems that might not have been foreseen or fully understood at the time of the election. Through a two-way dialogue, politicians and the public can find achievable solutions within the political, economic, and legal environment of their society at that time in history. Politicians come to reconcile their ideals with what is achievable given the circumstances they face. For Chambers and Romanow, Blakeney's statecraft entailed a combination of following one's electoral platform and continuing the dialogue with voters to understand how to solve problems that arise, thereby making the government responsive and legitimate.

In Part 2, the role "the people" played in Blakeney's view of democracy is made clear as Newman and Whyte examine the relationship between the judicial and legislative branches of the democratic state. Although Newman and Whyte hold opposing views on the "notwithstanding clause" of the *Canadian Charter of Rights and Freedoms*, they agree that Blakeney saw the representatives of the people sitting in Parliament and legislatures as the appropriate protectors and arbitrators of human rights within a society. For him, the forms that rights take ought to be determined by the people's elected representatives as opposed to judicial elites. In this sense, Blakeney held that a democratic state requires a healthy respect for representative democracy, and as the instrument of that principle it needs to possess the ability to place limits on the activism of unelected judges and lawyers.

However, his populism was much different from the type of right-wing populism of strongman politicians of today such as Turkey's Erdogan, Canada's Ford, or America's Trump. They regard political power as the unbounded right to exercise control over political opponents with no regard for their points of view and with disdain for the exercise of their opponents' political responsibilities. For Blakeney, the political power of the executive was exercised in dialogue with voters between elections and with political opponents inside and outside the legislature. He believed that political power needed to be accountable to the public and political opponents so that genuine debates preceded government decisions. Being an elected representative of the people did not mean that a politician could act without regard for long-established democratic norms and without following appropriate deliberative processes in which differences of opinion are expressed and mediated. Contrary to what right-wing populists appear to think, a democratic mandate from the people through an election does not confer on the head of government the ability to do whatever he or she wants with disregard for the political responsibility to dialogue with opponents and citizens before acting.

The major theme that emerges from the chapters in Parts 1 and 2 is that Blakeney's positive vision of the good things the government can do dovetailed with his positive vision of the good things democracy could accomplish. The emergence of an activist state needs to be paired with a well-functioning representative democracy and an efficient government. *In short, the activist state has to be a democratic one.* For a government to be active in the lives of citizens, they must believe that they have ultimate democratic control over the government. They need to have trust in democratic processes ensuring that activist governments are alert, accountable, and transparent to their citizens. They must have confidence that their government is running as efficiently as possible and is protecting their rights.

For Blakeney, a democratic state that does not build the bonds of trust between those who govern and those who are governed cannot create the conditions for government activism. When citizens believe that their democratic will is not respected, and when they believe that their government does not listen to them, they naturally want less government. If citizens do not trust that their government can deliver publicly funded programs in an efficient manner respectful of the democratic will of the polity, then they will not want the government to be expanded. If citizens do not think that their representatives are protecting their fundamental rights, then they become wary of politicians who talk about the need for a larger government. For Blakeney, an unresponsive democracy, a wasteful government, and disrespect for rights are the recipe for a smaller, less active government.

Part 3 of this volume demonstrates why Blakeney's concept of a democratic state and his advocacy of an activist state are still relevant today. Whether it be the challenge of engaging citizens in governance, increased political cynicism, lack of progress on economic inequality, or tension over diversity in society, Blakeney's values and commitments can act as important anchors for how we think about such challenges. His commitments and values allow us to identify problems of the democratic state in Canada and to start to think about solutions. Even if Blakeney's norms for the holding of democratic power do not always provide the answer, they can point us in the right direction.

As Atkinson's chapter reminds us, the art of governance involves balancing popular demands with technocratic expertise. With a media and communications environment moving ever faster and becoming more varied (including recent phenomena such as social media and fake news), Blakeney's commitment to governance by bureaucratic experts that maintains a dialogue between citizens and their political leaders is as important now as in the 1970s. A healthy democracy in the twenty-first century might depend on finding ways to connect citizens to their elected representatives and unelected public servants to build trust in the legitimacy of government activism. The chapters by Courtney and Coletto point out that the perception that democratic elections are unfair can feed increased cynicism about politics. Blakeney's attention to ensuring that the machinery of elections reflected the principles of fair democratic competition remains pertinent to Canadian politics. Following his example, continually improving the administration of elections—key moments in the life of a democracy—should be a top priority of Canadian governments.

The chapters by Wiseman and Himelfarb argue that Canada has yet to achieve the level of economic equality envisioned by Blakeney when he was premier. Governments in Canada need to continue to build up and expand the welfare state if progress on fighting economic inequality is to be made. However, enlarging the welfare state cannot take place in the absence of a progressive taxation regime similar to the one that Blakeney enacted when he was in government. If we are to realize the type of economic equality that Blakeney envisioned, then reforming how Canadian governments think and talk about taxes and realizing the intimate connection between good social programs and fair taxation are necessary prerequisites to making real progress.

The chapters by Thomas, Walker, and Whitaker show how Canada has become even more diverse since Blakeney was premier of Saskatchewan, and they illustrate the importance of valuing and accommodating that diversity. Yet these three chapters also demonstrate how the language of rights has become more pronounced, and this situation has led to problems with conflicting views of rights resulting in backlash against the extension of rights of marginalized groups. Blakeney's commitment to an activist state that values diversity can act as a guide for Canadian governments as they grapple with competing rights claims. Indeed, diversity cannot really be valued and accommodated by a passive state. Recognizing and valuing diversity as a strength in society require a government ready to act when it sees discrimination and unfairness. Following Blakeney's example during his time as premier, governments need to be leaders as society struggles with conflicting rights claims and seeks to combat racism, patriarchy, homophobia, and other forms of social exclusion.

The world, including the world of political practice, has, of course, changed since Blakeney was premier of Saskatchewan in the 1970s. It is not in spite of, but because of, these changes that his normative positions on governing and on democracy deserve to be revived. The leitmotif of his political life was respect for others—other people and other views—and for the established processes for the political mediation of competing ideas about social need and social good. His legacy can serve as a guide to revitalize Canadian democracy and remove from it the harsh irreconcilabilities that result from pitting one faction against another and from right-wing populisms that threaten our democratic values and traditions. As we enter the third decade of the twenty-first century, we need an active state and a democratic state to achieve economic and social justice in a society in which too many are left behind. Blakeney's idea of an intelligent and efficient state supported by a vibrant and well-functioning democracy is needed now more than ever. As this book shows, Blakeney is not just a historical figure, the study of whom simply explains what happened in the past, but also a historically significant figure whose life offers a contemporary guide to realizing a just state based on government activism exercised within democratic principles.

ENDNOTES

INTRODUCTION

1 Ian Bremmer, "The 'Strongmen Era' Is Here: Here's What It Means for You," *Time*, May 3, 2018, http://time.com/5264170/the-strongmen-era-is-here-heres-what-it-means-for-you/.
2 Jeff Grey, "As Ontario Government Plans Rare Weekend Session, Charter Architects Condemn Premier's Action," *Globe and Mail*, September 14, 2018, A8.
3 Ibid.
4 Quoted in John Paul Tasker, "Maxime Bernier Criticizes Liberals for 'Extreme Multiculturalism,'" CBC News, August 13, 2018, https://www.cbc.ca/news/politics/maxime-bernier-extreme-multiculturalism-1.4783325.
5 Allan Blakeney and Sandford Borins, *Political Management in Canada* (Toronto: University of Toronto Press, 1989).

CHAPTER 1

1 Data 360, "Spot Oil Price: West Texas Intermediate," n.d., http://www.data360.org/dataset.aspx?Data_Set_Id=428.
2 "Saskatchewan Doubles Fee for Potash," *Globe and Mail*, October 3, 1973, B11.
3 Ibid.
4 "REPORT ON CANADA: Potash Prorationing Is Suspended by Saskatchewan to Meet Demand," *Globe and Mail*, April 23, 1974, B3; "Saskatchewan Boosts Potash Output Quota to 68% of Its Capacity," *Wall Street Journal*, November 7, 1973, 32.
5 "Saskatchewan Boosts Potash Output," 32.
6 Allan Blakeney, letter to the Right Honourable Pierre Elliott Trudeau, October 10, 1978, personal archives of Roy Romanow.
7 "REPORT ON CANADA," B3.
8 Ibid.

9 "Tax on Potash Quadrupled, Saskatchewan Seeks Equity," *Globe and Mail*, October 24, 1974, B1.
10 Lawrence Welsh, "Potash Producers Defer Expansions Worth $200 Million," *Globe and Mail*, January 11, 1975, B1.
11 Lawrence Welsh, "Saskatchewan to Study Failure of Firms to Pay Potash Taxes," *Globe and Mail*, August 19, 1975, B1.
12 Ibid.
13 Arne Paus-Jenssen, "Resource Taxation and the Supreme Court of Canada: The Cigol Case," *Canadian Public Policy/Analyse de politiques* 5, no. 1 (1979): 45–58.
14 Thomas Kennedy, "NEB Told $6.50 Price for Crude Rests on Continued Sales to U.S.," *Globe and Mail*, February 4, 1974, B2.
15 Parliament of Canada, *November 1974 Federal Budget Speech by John Turner* (Ottawa: Ministry of Finance, 1974), 13.
16 Ibid.
17 Saskatchewan NDP, *NDP…Keeping Saskatchewan Ahead* (Regina: Service Printers, 1975), 2.
18 Quoted in William Borders, "Tax Dispute Halts Canada's Potash Growth: Tax Dispute Is Hobbling Canada's Potash Growth," *New York Times*, February 3, 1975, 47.
19 *Constitution Act, 1982*, being Schedule B to the Canada Act 1982 (UK), 1982, c 11.
20 *Debates of the Saskatchewan Legislature*, November 12, 1975, 9.
21 "Industry Finds Timing of Potash Proposals Surprising," *Globe and Mail*, November 13, 1975, B5.
22 *Debates of the Saskatchewan Legislature*, November 18, 1975, 74.
23 John H. Allan, "Move Follows Province's Potash Takeover Step: Saskatchewan Is Selling Issue of $125 Million," *New York Times*, November 17, 1976, 91.
24 Ibid.

CHAPTER 2

1 Government of Saskatchewan, *1974 Budget Speech, Delivered by Wes Robbins* (Regina: Department of Finance, 1974), 38.
2 A.M. McBriar, *Fabian Socialism and English Politics, 1884–1918* (Cambridge, UK: Cambridge University Press, 1962).
3 Quoted in Ed Wallis, ed., *From the Workhouse to Welfare: What Beatrice Webb's 1909 Minority Report Can Teach Us Today* (London: Fabian Society, 2009), 14.
4 Sidney Webb, "Historic," in *Fabian Essays in Socialism*, ed. George Bernard Shaw (Garden City, NY: Dolphin Books, 1889), 79.
5 Ibid.
6 Government of Saskatchewan, *1982 Budget Speech, Delivered by Ed Tchorzewski* (Regina: Department of Finance, 1982), 3.

7   Government of Saskatchewan, *1972 Budget Speech, Delivered by Allan Blakeney* (Regina: Department of Finance, 1972), 32.
8   Ibid.
9   Government of Saskatchewan, "The Public Sector, Statement by Premier Allan Blakeney," in *Federal-Provincial Conference of First Ministers, Ottawa, February 13–15, 1978* (Ottawa: Government of Canada, 1978), 3.
10 Allan Blakeney, "Taxes, Speech from 1971 Provincial Election," Saskatchewan Archives Board (hereafter SAB), Blakeney Papers, R800.LIX.1a, 9.
11 Saskatchewan NDP, *NDP...Keeping Saskatchewan Ahead* (Regina: Service Printers, 1975), 6.
12 Pierre Bourdieu and Loic Wacquant, *An Invitation to Reflexive Sociology* (Chicago: University of Chicago Press, 1992); Robert D. Putnam, *Bowling Alone: The Collapse and Revival of American Community* (New York: Simon and Schuster, 2000).
13 David McGrane, *Remaining Loyal: Social Democracy in Quebec and Saskatchewan* (Montreal and Kingston: McGill-Queen's University Press, 2014), 116–19.
14 Allan Blakeney, "The Crisis of Inequality in Canada," *Globe and Mail*, January 23, 1974, 6–7.
15 Allan Blakeney, "Notes for Remarks by Premier Allan Blakeney to the National Farmers' Union," 1977, SAB, Blakeney Papers, R800.LIX.10ss.
16 Saskatchewan Department of Intergovernmental Affairs, *Brief Presented to the Task Force on Canadian Unity by Premier Allan Blakeney, October 20, 1977* (Ottawa: Government of Canada, 1977).
17 John Burton, *Potash: An Inside Account of Saskatchewan's Pink Gold* (Regina: University of Regina Press, 2014); John Richards and Larry Pratt, *Prairie Capitalism: Power and Influence in the New West* (Toronto: McClelland and Stewart, 1979); Roy J. Romanow, John D. Whyte, and Howard A. Leeson, *Canada—Notwithstanding: The Making of the Constitution, 1976–1982* (Toronto: Carswell Publishing, 1984).
18 Richards and Pratt, 53.
19 Blakeney, "The Crisis of Inequality in Canada," 6.
20 Government of Saskatchewan, *Why Just Oil? The Case for Extending the Equalization Principle to Other Commodities* (Regina: Queen's Printer, 1974).
21 Mary Janigan, *Let the Eastern Bastards Freeze in the Dark: The West versus the Rest since Confederation* (Toronto: Knopf Canada, 2012).
22 Allan Blakeney, *Energy Policy and National Economic Development, Opening Statement of the Province of Saskatchewan to the First Ministers Conference on Energy, January 22–23, 1974* (Ottawa: Government of Canada, 1974).
23 Government of Saskatchewan, "Press Release: Oil Companies Could Reap Huge Profits," November 28, 1973, SAB, Blakeney Papers, R574.IX.7.
24 Saskatchewan NDP, *NDP...Keeping Saskatchewan Ahead*.

25 Allan Blakeney, *An Honourable Calling: Political Memoirs* (Toronto: University of Toronto Press, 2008).
26 McGrane, *Remaining Loyal*.
27 Blakeney, *Energy Policy and National Economic Development*.
28 Allan Blakeney, "Notes for Remarks by Premier Allan Blakeney to the Saskatchewan Wheat Pool Annual Meeting, Regina, Saskatchewan—November 16, 1976," SAB, Blakeney Papers, R800.LIX.8xx.
29 Saskatchewan Department of Agriculture, "Saskatchewan Challenges 'The Pepin Plan,'" 1982, SAB, Blakeney Papers, R-1106.III.1.f.
30 Government of Saskatchewan, *1979 Budget Speech, Delivered by Walter Smishek* (Regina: Department of Finance, 1979), 15; Government of Saskatchewan, "Speech from the Throne," in *Saskatchewan Legislative Debates and Proceedings, Second Session—Nineteenth Legislature*, November 29, 1979, 3.
31 Government of Saskatchewan, *1973 Budget Speech, Delivered by Elmwood Cowley* (Regina: Department of Finance, 1973), 8.
32 Blakeney, *Energy Policy and National Economic Development*.
33 Government of Saskatchewan, "The Public Sector."
34 Government of Saskatchewan, *1976 Budget Speech, Delivered by Walter Smishek* (Regina: Department of Finance, 1976).
35 Government of Saskatchewan, "Speech from the Throne," in *Saskatchewan Legislative Debates and Proceedings, Fourth Session—Nineteenth Legislature*, November 26, 1981, 2.
36 Government of Saskatchewan, "Statement by the Honourable Allan Blakeney, Premier of Saskatchewan, on Fiscal Arrangements and Cost-Shared Programs," *Federal-Provincial Conference of First Ministers, Ottawa, June 14, 1976* (Ottawa: Government of Canada, 1976).
37 David McGrane, "Western Alienation or Mere Critique of Federal Government Policies? Saskatchewan Social Democrats' View of Federalism from 1900 to Present," *International Journal of Canadian Studies* 32 (2005): 205–35.
38 Allan Blakeney, "CBC Program—National Unity," 1977, SAB, Blakeney Papers, R565.VI.60.
39 David McGrane, "A Mixed Record: Gender and Saskatchewan Social Democracy," *Journal of Canadian Studies* 42, no. 1 (2008): 179–203.
40 Valerie Bryson, *Feminist Political Theory: An Introduction, 2nd Edition* (New York: Palgrave Macmillan, 2003), 139.
41 Rosemarie Tong, *Feminist Thought: A More Comprehensive Introduction, 2nd Edition* (Boulder, CO: Westview Press, 1998).
42 Allan Blakeney, "Status of Women, Speech from 1971 Provincial Election," SAB, Blakeney Papers, R800.LIX.1a.
43 Ibid.
44 Jill Vickers, *Reinventing Political Science: A Feminist Approach* (Halifax: Fernwood Books, 1997).

45 David McGrane, "From Liberal Multiculturalism to Civic Republicanism: An Historical Perspective on Multiculturalism in Manitoba and Saskatchewan," *Canadian Ethnic Studies* 43 (2011): 81–108.
46 Pierre Trudeau, "Statement on Multiculturalism Policy," in *Debates of the House of Commons*, Twenty-Eighth Parliament, Third Session, October 8, 1971, 8545–46.
47 Hugh D. Forbes, "Trudeau as the First Theorist of Canadian Multiculturalism," in *Multiculturalism and the Canadian Constitution*, ed. Stephen Tierney (Vancouver: UBC Press, 2007), 27–42.
48 Government of Saskatchewan, *Brief Presented to the Task Force on Canadian Unity by Premier Allan Blakeney, October 20, 1977* (Ottawa: Government of Canada, 1977).
49 Government of Saskatchewan, *Report on the Proceedings of the Seminar '73: Multiculturalism in Saskatchewan...an Opportunity for Action, a Challenge* (Regina: Queen's Printer, 1973).
50 Ibid.
51 *An Act Establishing the Saskatchewan Multicultural Advisory Council and the Providing for Assistance to Individuals and Groups*, RSS 1974, c S-2, s 2 (d).
52 Government of Saskatchewan, *Report on the Proceedings of the Seminar '73*, 53.
53 Government of Saskatchewan, "Speech from the Throne," in *Saskatchewan Legislative Debates and Proceedings, Third Session—Nineteenth Legislature*, November 27, 1980, 1.
54 Allan Blakeney, "CBC Program—National Unity."
55 Allan Blakeney, "Indian and Métis, Speech from 1971 Provincial Election," SAB, Blakeney Papers, R800.LIX.1a.
56 Ibid.
57 National Indian Brotherhood, *Indian Control of Indian Education, Policy Paper Presented to the Minister of Indian Affairs and Northern Development* (Ottawa: National Indian Brotherhood, 1972).
58 Allan Blakeney, "An Address Delivered by the Honourable Allan E. Blakeney, Premier, Province of Saskatchewan, November 24, 1981," in *Proceedings of Omamawi-Atoskewin: Working Together* (Regina: University of Regina Library, 1981), 15.
59 See Allyson Stevenson, "Intimate Integration: A Study of Aboriginal Transracial Adoption in Saskatchewan, 1944–1984" (PhD diss., University of Saskatchewan, 2015).
60 Elections Saskatchewan, "Voter Turnout Figures for 28th Saskatchewan Election Released," 2016, http://www.elections.sk.ca/media/news-releases/final-voter-turnout/.
61 Paul Gingrich, *Boom and Bust: The Growing Income Gap in Saskatchewan* (Regina: Canadian Centre for Policy Alternatives, 2009).
62 Randall Akee, William Copeland, E. Jane Costello, John B. Holbein, and Emilia Simeonova, "Family Income and the Intergenerational Transmission of Voting

Behavior: Evidence from an Income Intervention," 2018, National Bureau of Economic Research Working Paper 24770, http://www.nber.org/papers/w24770.
63 Allan Blakeney, "Political Ideas and the Reality of Political Power," 1983, SAB, Blakeney Papers, R-1106.I.3.ii.

CHAPTER 3

1 Edward Broadbent, "Social Democracy or Liberalism in the New Millennium?," in *The Future of Social Democracy: Views of Leaders from around the World*, ed. Peter Russell (Toronto: University of Toronto Press, 1999), 76.
2 Eleanor Glor, *Policy Innovation in the Saskatchewan Public Service, 1971–82* (Toronto: Captus Press, 1997).
3 Robert I. McLaren, *The Saskatchewan Practice of Public Administration in Historical Perspective* (Lewiston, NY: Edwin Mellen Press, 1998).
4 Allan Blakeney, *An Honourable Calling: Political Memoirs* (Toronto: University of Toronto Press, 2008).
5 Gregory P. Marchildon, "Foreword," in *Dream No Little Dreams: A Biography of the Douglas Government of Saskatchewan, 1944–1961*, ed. Al W. Johnson (Toronto: University of Toronto Press, 2004), xv–xxxi.
6 Allan E. Blakeney and Sandford Borins, *Political Management in Canada, 2nd Edition* (Toronto: University of Toronto Press, 1998); M.A. MacPherson, "The Relationship between the Senior Public Servant and the Minister of the Crown," in *Proceedings of the Fifth Annual Conference of the Institute of Public Administration of Canada*, ed. Philip Clark (Toronto: Institute of Public Administration of Canada, 1953), 143–51.
7 McLaren, *The Saskatchewan Practice of Public Administration*.
8 A.W. Johnson, "Administrative Systems and Methods," in *Proceedings of the Fourth Annual Conference of the Institute of Public Administration of Canada*, ed. Philip Clark (Toronto: Institute of Public Administration of Canada, 1952), 34–44; A.W. Johnson, "The Treasury Board in Saskatchewan," in *Proceedings of the Seventh Annual Conference of the Institute of Public Administration of Canada*, ed. Philip Clark (Toronto: Institute of Public Administration of Canada, 1955), 99–112; David Levin, "Measuring the Effectiveness of Programs," in *Proceedings of the Fifth Annual Conference of the Institute of Public Administration of Canada*, ed. Philip Clark (Toronto: Institute of Public Administration of Canada, 1953), 119–25; Thomas H. McLeod, "Budgeting Provincial Expenditure," in *Proceedings of the Fifth Annual Conference of the Institute of Public Administration of Canada*, ed. Philip Clark (Toronto: Institute of Public Administration of Canada, 1953), 11–19; Thomas H. McLeod, "Administrative and Constitutional Problems Peculiar to Crown Corporations," in *Proceedings of the Eighth Annual Conference of the Institute of Public Administration of Canada*, ed. Philip Clark and Frank McGilly (Toronto: Institute of Public Administration of Canada, 1956), 153–61; Tommy K.

Shoyama, "Advisory Committees in Administration," in *Proceedings of the Ninth Annual Conference of the Institute of Public Administration of Canada*, ed. Philip Clark and Frank McGilly (Toronto: University of Toronto Press, 1957), 145–53.
9 Allan Blakeney, "Saskatchewan's Crown Corporations: A Case Study," in *Proceedings of the Fifth Annual Conference of the Institute of Public Administration of Canada*, ed. Philip Clark (Toronto: Institute of Public Administration of Canada, 1954), 413–20.
10 Douglas F. Stevens, *Corporate Autonomy and Institutional Control: The Crown Corporation as a Problem in Organizational Design* (Montreal and Kingston: McGill-Queen's University Press, 1993); Tom Waller, "Framework for Economic Development: The Role of Crown Corporations and the Crown Investments Corporation of Saskatchewan," in *Policy Innovation in the Saskatchewan Public Sector, 1971–82*, ed. Eleanor Glor (Toronto: Captus Press, 1997), 29–48.
11 Robin F. Badgley and Samuel Wolfe, *Doctor's Strike: Medical Care and Conflict in Saskatchewan* (New York: Atherton Press, 1967); Allan Briens, "The 1960 Saskatchewan Provincial Election," (MA thesis, University of Regina, 2004); Gregory P. Marchildon and Klaartje Schrijvers, "Physician Resistance and the Forging of Public Health Care: A Comparative Analysis of Doctors' Strikes in Canada and Belgium in the 1960s," *Medical History* 55, no. 2 (2011): 203–22.
12 Dennis Gruending, "Allan Blakeney," in *Saskatchewan Premiers of the Twentieth Century*, ed. Gordon L. Barnhart (Regina: Canadian Plains Research Center, 2004), 271–316.
13 Blakeney, *An Honourable Calling*.
14 Allan Blakeney, "The Struggle to Implement Medicare," in *Making Medicare: New Perspectives on the History of Medicare in Canada*, ed. Gregory P. Marchildon (Toronto: University of Toronto Press, 2012), 277–81.
15 Gruending, "Allan Blakeney."
16 Blakeney, *An Honourable Calling*; Blakeney, "The Struggle to Implement Medicare."
17 Blakeney, *An Honourable Calling*.
18 Ibid.; Marchildon and Schrijvers, "Physician Resistance and the Forging of Public Health Care."
19 Stan Rands, *Privilege and Policy: A History of Community Clinics in Canada*, ed. Gregory P. Marchildon and Catherine Levington-Reid (Regina: Canadian Plains Research Center, 2012).
20 James Dosman, "The Medical Care Issue as a Factor in the Electoral Defeat of the Saskatchewan Government" (MA thesis, University of Saskatchewan, 1969).
21 Dale Eisler, *Rumours of Glory: Saskatchewan and the Thatcher Years* (Edmonton: Hurtig Publishers, 1987); Gruending, "Allan Blakeney."
22 Blakeney, *An Honourable Calling*; Dennis Gruending, *Promises to Keep: A Political Biography of Allan Blakeney* (Saskatoon: Western Producer Prairie Books, 1990).

23 Gruending, "Allan Blakeney."
24 Ibid.; Roy Romanow, interview with Gregory P. Marchildon, Saskatoon, March 19, 2003.
25 Gruending, "Allan Blakeney."
26 Gregory P. Marchildon, "The Secretary to the Cabinet in Saskatchewan: Evolution of the Role, 1944–2006," in *Searching for Leadership: Secretaries to the Cabinet in Canada*, ed. Patrice Dutil (Toronto: University of Toronto Press, 2008), 161–84; Romanow, interview with Marchildon.
27 Quoted in Gruending, "Allan Blakeney," 286.
28 Ken Rasmussen and Gregory P. Marchildon, "Saskatchewan's Executive Decision-Making Style: The Centrality of Planning," in *Executive Styles in Canada: Cabinet Structures and Leadership Practices in Canadian Government*, ed. Luc Bernier, Keith Brownsey, and Michael Howlett (Toronto: University of Toronto Press, 2005), 184–207.
29 Marchildon, "The Secretary to the Cabinet in Saskatchewan."
30 Blakeney and Borins, *Political Management in Canada, 2nd Edition*.
31 Ibid.
32 Ibid., 5–6.
33 Ibid., 6.
34 Rasmussen and Marchildon, "Saskatchewan's Executive Decision-Making Style."
35 Ibid.
36 Stevens, *Corporate Autonomy and Institutional Control*; Waller, "Framework for Economic Development."
37 Rasmussen and Marchildon, "Saskatchewan's Executive Decision-Making Style."
38 Gruending, "Allan Blakeney," 281.
39 Gregory P. Marchildon, "The Great Divide," in *The Heavy Hand of History: Interpreting Saskatchewan's Past*, ed. Gregory P. Marchildon (Regina: Canadian Plains Research Center, 2005), 51–66.
40 Blakeney, *An Honourable Calling*.
41 A.W. Johnson, *Dream No Little Dreams: A Biography of the Douglas Government of Saskatchewan, 1944–1961* (Toronto: University of Toronto Press, 2004).
42 Blakeney, *An Honourable Calling*, 143.
43 Ibid., 160.
44 Gruending, "Allan Blakeney."
45 Ibid.
46 Gruending, *Promises to Keep*; Gruending, "Allan Blakeney."
47 Gruending, *Promises to Keep*; Gruending, "Allan Blakeney."
48 Gruending, *Promises to Keep*, 181–82.
49 Ibid.
50 Paul F. Barker, "The Formulation and Implementation of the Saskatchewan Dental Plan" (PhD diss., University of Toronto, 1985).
51 Glor, *Policy Innovation in the Saskatchewan Public Service*, v.

52 Blakeney and Borins, *Political Management in Canada, 2nd Edition*, vii.
53 Blakeney, *An Honourable Calling*; Johnson, *Dream No Little Dreams*.
54 Glor, *Policy Innovation in the Saskatchewan Public Service*.
55 John Burton, "Resource Rent and Taxation—Application of New Principles and Approaches in Saskatchewan," in *Policy Innovation in the Saskatchewan Public Sector, 1971–1982*, ed. Eleanor Glor (Toronto: Captus Press, 1997), 59–78; Waller, "Framework for Economic Development."
56 Stevens, *Corporate Autonomy and Institutional Control*; Waller, "Framework for Economic Development."
57 Blakeney and Borins, *Political Management in Canada, 2nd Edition*, vii.
58 Blakeney, *An Honourable Calling*.
59 Kent Roach, *The Supreme Court on Trial: Judicial Activism or Democratic Dialogue* (Toronto: Irwin Law, 2001).

CHAPTER 4

1 André Bächtiger, John Dryzek, Jane Mansbridge, and Mark Warren, eds., *Oxford Handbook of Deliberative Democracy* (Oxford: Oxford University Press, 2018).
2 Kimmo Grönlund, André Bächtiger, and Maija Setälä, *Deliberative Mini-Publics: Involving Citizens in the Democratic Process* (Colchester, UK: ECPR Press, 2014).
3 Simone Chambers, "Balancing Epistemic Quality and Equal Participation in a Systems Approach to Deliberative Democracy," *Social Epistemology* 31, no. 3 (2017): 266–76; Simone Chambers, "The Epistemic Ideal of Reason-Giving in Deliberative Democracy," *Social Epistemology Review and Reply Collective* 6, no. 10 (2017): 59–64; Jürgen Habermas, *Between Facts and Norms: Contributions to a Discourse Theory of Law and Democracy*, trans. William Rheg (Malden, MA: MIT Press, 1996).
4 Simone Chambers, "Deliberative Democratic Theory," *Annual Review of Political Science* 6 (2003): 307–26.
5 Max Weber, *Economy and Society: An Outline of Interpretive Sociology* (Berkeley: University of California Press, 1968), 991.
6 Allan Blakeney, "Goal-Setting: Politicians' Expectations of Public Administration," *Canadian Public Administration* 24 (1981): 3.
7 Allan Blakeney, "The Relationship between Provincial Ministers and Their Deputy Ministers," *Canadian Public Administration* 15 (1972): 43.
8 Ibid.
9 Blakeney, "Goal-Setting," 3.
10 Blakeney, "Relationship," 44.
11 Blakeney, "Goal-Setting," 3.
12 Blakeney, "Relationship," 43.
13 Blakeney and Borins, *Political Management in Canada*.
14 Ibid., 193.

15 Robert Goodin, *Innovating Democracy: Democratic Theory and Practice after the Deliberative Turn* (Oxford: Oxford University Press, 2008).
16 Robert A. Dahl, *Polyarchy: Participation and Opposition* (New Haven, CT: Yale University Press, 1973), 1.
17 Andrew Sabl, "The Two Cultures of Democratic Theory: Responsiveness, Democratic Quality, and the Empirical-Normative Divide," *Perspectives on Politics* 13, no. 2 (2015): 346.
18 G. Bingham Powell Jr., "Representation in Context: Election Laws and Ideological Congruence between Citizens and Governments," *Perspectives on Politics* 11, no. 1 (2013): 9–10.
19 Lawrence Jacobs and Robert Shapiro, *Politicians Don't Pander: Political Manipulation and the Loss of Democratic Responsiveness* (Chicago: University of Chicago Press, 2000); Benjamin Page, "Democratic Responsiveness? Untangling the Links between Public Opinion and Policy," *PS: Political Science and Politics* 27 (1994): 25–29.
20 Lawrence Jacobs and Benjamin Page, "Who Influences us Foreign Policy?," *American Political Science Review* 99, no. 1 (2005): 107–23.
21 Larry M. Bartels, *Unequal Democracy: The Political Economy of the New Gilded Age* (Princeton, NJ: Princeton University Press, 2008).
22 Sabl, "The Two Cultures of Democratic Theory."
23 James Druckman, "Pathologies of Studying Public Opinion, Political Communication, and Democratic Responsiveness," *Political Communication* 31 (2014): 467–92.
24 Larry M. Bartels, "Is Popular Rule Possible? Polls, Political Psychology, and Democracy," *Brookings Review* 21 (2003): 12–15.
25 Christopher H. Achen and Larry M. Bartels, *Democracy for Realists: Why Elections Do Not Produce Responsive Government* (Princeton, NJ: Princeton University Press, 2016).
26 James Druckman and Lawrence Jacobs, *Who Governs? Presidents, Public Opinion, and Manipulation* (Chicago: University of Chicago Press, 2015).
27 John Zaller, "What Nature and Origins Leaves Out," *Critical Review* 24 (2012): 569–642.
28 Joseph Schumpeter, *Capitalism, Socialism, and Democracy* (New York: Harper and Row, 1950), 262.
29 Achen and Bartels, *Democracy for Realists*, 12.
30 Ibid., 21–51.
31 Ibid., 3.
32 Hanna Pitkin, *The Concept of Representation* (Berkeley: University of California Press, 1967).
33 Edmund Burke, "Speech at Mr. Burke's Arrival in Bristol," in *The Portable Edmund Burke*, ed. Isaac Kramnick (New York: Penguin Classics, 1999), 155.
34 Schumpeter, *Capitalism*, 284–85.

35 John Richards and Larry Pratt, *Prairie Capitalism: Power and Influence in the New West* (Toronto: McClelland and Stewart, 1979).
36 Sidney Verba, "The Citizen as Respondent: Sample Surveys and American Democracy," *American Political Science Review* 90, no. 1 (1996): 2.
37 Habermas, *Between Facts and Norms*; Jürgen Habermas, "Political Communication in Media Society: Does Democracy Still Enjoy an Epistemic Dimension? The Impact of Normative Theory on Empirical Research," *Communication Theory* 16 (2006): 411–26.
38 Habermas, "Political Communication in Media Society," 412.
39 James Fishkin, *When the People Speak: Deliberative Democracy and Public Consultation* (Oxford: Oxford University Press, 2009).
40 Pew Research Center, "Changing Attitudes on Gay Marriage: Public Opinion on Same-Sex Marriage," June 26, 2017, http://www.pewforum.org/2016/05/12/changing-attitudes-on-gay-marriage/.
41 Simone Chambers, "Deliberation and Mass Democracy," in *Deliberative Systems*, ed. Jane Mansbridge and John Parkinson (Cambridge, UK: Cambridge University Press, 2012), 52–71.
42 Habermas, "Political Communication in Media Society."
43 Ibid., 412.
44 Blakeney and Borins, *Political Management in Canada*, 188.
45 Ibid.
46 Ibid.

CHAPTER 5

1 Dwight Newman, *Natural Resource Jurisdiction in Canada* (Toronto: LexisNexis, 2013).
2 *Canadian Charter of Rights and Freedoms*, Part I of the *Constitution Act, 1982*, being Schedule B to the *Canada Act 1982* (UK), 1982, c 11.
3 *Chaoulli v Quebec (Attorney General)*, [2005a] 1 SCR 791.
4 Respectively, *Canada (Attorney General) v PHS Community Services Society*, [2011] 3 SCR 134; *Canada (Attorney General) v Bedford*, [2013] 3 SCR 1101; *Carter v Canada*, [2015] 1 SCR 331.
5 Allan Blakeney, *An Honourable Calling: Political Memoirs* (Toronto: University of Toronto Press, 2008).
6 Ibid., 201–02.
7 Dwight Newman, "The PHS Case and Federalism-Based Alternatives to Charter Activism," *Constitutional Forum* 22, no. 1 (2013): 85–91; Dwight Newman, "Judicial Method and Three Gaps in the Supreme Court of Canada's Assisted Suicide Judgment in Carter," *Saskatchewan Law Review* 78 (2015): 1–6.
8 Guy Régimbald and Dwight Newman, *The Law of the Canadian Constitution* (Toronto: LexisNexis, 2013).

9 Allan Blakeney, "The Notwithstanding Clause, the *Charter*, and Canada's Patriated Constitution: What I Thought We Were Doing," *Constitutional Forum* 19, no. 1 (2010): 1–9.
10 Various sources cite the remark as having been made on CBC Radio on December 19, 2003.
11 Marjorie Nichols, "Trudeau Promise Comes Back to Haunt Liberals," *Ottawa Citizen*, April 15, 1989, A3.
12 Tsvi Kahana, "The Notwithstanding Mechanism and Public Discussion: Lessons from the Ignored Practice of Section 33 of the Charter," *Canadian Public Administration* 44 (2001): 255–91; Tsvi Kahana, "Understanding the Notwithstanding Mechanism," *University of Toronto Law Journal* 52 (2002): 221–74.
13 Guillaume Rousseau, "Théorie québécoise de la disposition dérogatoire: Quand la langue, l'identité, ou le social prime l'individuel," in *Un regard québécois sur le droit constitutionnel: Mélanges en l'honneur d'Henri Brun et de Guy Tremblay*, ed. Patrick Taillon, Eugénie Brouillet, and Amélie Binette (Montréal: Éditions Yvon Blais, 2016), 703–18.
14 Donna Greschner and Ken Norman, "The Courts and Section 33," *Queen's Law Journal* 12 (1987): 155–98.
15 John D. Whyte, "Sometimes Constitutions Are Made in the Streets: The Future of the Charter's Notwithstanding Clause," *Constitutional Forum* 16 (2007): 79–87.
16 Blakeney, "The Notwithstanding Clause."
17 Barry L. Strayer, "The Evolution of the Charter," in *Patriation and Its Consequences: Constitution Making in Canada*, ed. Lois Harder and Steve Patten (Vancouver: UBC Press, 2015), 90.
18 Ibid.
19 Respectively, Peter Lougheed, *Why a Notwithstanding Clause?* (Edmonton: University of Alberta Centre for Constitutional Studies, 1998); Rousseau, "Théorie québécoise de la disposition dérogatoire."
20 Blakeney, "The Notwithstanding Clause."
21 Ibid.
22 Blakeney, *An Honourable Calling*.
23 Blakeney, "The Notwithstanding Clause."
24 Dwight Newman, *Community and Collective Rights: A Theoretical Framework for Rights Held by Groups* (London: Bloomsbury Academic, 2011).
25 Blakeney, "The Notwithstanding Clause."
26 Ibid.
27 Lougheed, *Why a Notwithstanding Clause?*
28 Blakeney, *An Honourable Calling*.
29 Ibid.
30 See, for example, Seymour Lipset, *Agrarian Socialism: The Cooperative Commonwealth Federation in Saskatchewan: A Study in Political Sociology* (New York: Doubleday, 1968).

31 Whyte, "Sometimes Constitutions Are Made in the Streets."
32 Blakeney, "The Notwithstanding Clause."
33 Jeremy Waldron, "Some Models of Dialogue between Judges and Legislators," in *Constitutionalism in the Charter Era*, ed. Grant Huscroft and Ian Brodie (Markham, ON: LexisNexis, 2004), 7–47.
34 Jeremy Waldron, "A Rights-Based Critique of Constitutional Rights," *Oxford Journal of Legal Studies* 13, no. 1 (1993): 18–51.
35 Jeffrey Goldsworthy, *Parliamentary Sovereignty: Contemporary Debates* (Cambridge, UK: Cambridge University Press, 2010), 205.
36 Jeremy Waldron, *Law and Disagreement* (Oxford: Oxford University Press, 1999), 254.
37 See, for example, Janet Ajzenstat, *The Canadian Founding: John Locke and Parliament* (Montreal and Kingston: McGill-Queen's University Press, 2007); Michel Ducharme, *The Age of Liberty in Canada during the Age of Atlantic Revolution, 1776–1838*, trans. Peter Feldstein (Montreal and Kingston: McGill-Queen's University Press, 2014).
38 Whyte, "Sometimes Constitutions Are Made in the Streets."
39 See, for example, Francis Fukuyama, *Trust: The Social Virtues and the Creation of Prosperity* (New York: Free Press, 1996); Robert D. Putnam, *Bowling Alone: The Collapse and Revival of American Community* (New York: Simon and Schuster, 2000).
40 Blakeney, *An Honourable Calling*, 179.
41 See Adrian Vermeule, "The Atrophy of Constitutional Powers," *Oxford Journal of Legal Studies* 32, no. 3 (2012): 421–44.
42 Kahana, "The Notwithstanding Mechanism and Public Discussion."
43 Vermeule, "The Atrophy of Constitutional Powers."
44 Sarah Burningham, "Use the Notwithstanding Clause, if You Must," *National Post*, December 21, 2015, http://news.nationalpost.com/full-comment/sarah-burningham-use-the-notwithstanding-clause-if-you-must; Tonda MacCharles, "Ottawa Surprises Top Court Judges by Allowing Assisted Suicide to Proceed in Quebec," *Toronto Star*, January 11, 2016, https://www.thestar.com/news/canada/2016/01/11/ottawa-surprises-top-court-judges-by-asking-for-more-time-on-assisted-suicide.html.

CHAPTER 6

1 Alexander Hamilton and James Madison, "The Federalist No. 51, 1788," in *The Federalist: A Commentary on the Constitution of the United States*, ed. Edward Meade Earle (New York: Modern Library, 1937), 337.
2 John D. Whyte, "Federalism Dreams," *Queen's Law Journal* 34 (2008): 1–24.
3 Roy J. Romanow, John D. Whyte, and Howard A. Leeson, *Canada—Notwithstanding: The Making of the Constitution, 1976–1982* (Toronto: Carswell-Methuen, 1984).

4 *Re: Resolution to Amend the Constitution*, [1981], SCR 753.
5 Ibid.
6 Allan Blakeney, "The Notwithstanding Clause, the *Charter*, and Canada's Patriated Constitution: What I Thought We Were Doing," *Constitutional Forum* 19, no. 1 (2010): 1–9.
7 Allan Blakeney, *An Honourable Calling: Political Memoirs* (Toronto: University of Toronto Press, 2008).
8 John D. Whyte, "Sometimes Constitutions Are Made in the Streets: The Future of the Charter's Notwithstanding Clause," *Constitutional Forum* 16 (2007): 79–87.
9 James Madison, "The Federalist No. 10," in *The Federalist: A Commentary on the Constitution of the United States*, ed. Edward Meade Earle (New York: Modern Library, 1937), 51.
10 Ibid.
11 Ibid.
12 Alina Mungiu-Pippidi, "The Evolution of Political Order," *Journal of Democracy* 26, no. 4 (2015): 169–77.
13 J.R. Miller, *Lethal Legacies: Current Native Controversies in Canada* (Toronto: McClelland and Stewart, 2004).
14 Bruce Ackerman, "The Storrs Lectures: Discovering the Constitution," *Yale Law Journal* 93, no. 6 (1984): 1013–72.

CHAPTER 7

1 Joseph S. Nye, Philip D. Zelikow, and David C. King, *Why People Don't Trust Government* (Cambridge, MA: Harvard University Press, 1997); Robert D. Putnam and Susan J. Pharr, *Disaffected Democracies: What's Troubling the Trilateral Countries?* (Princeton, NJ: Princeton University Press, 2000).
2 Pippa Norris, *Critical Citizens: Global Support for Democratic Governance* (New York: Oxford University Press, 1999).
3 Russell J. Dalton, *Democratic Challenges, Democratic Choices: The Erosion of Political Support in Advanced Industrial Democracies* (New York: Oxford University Press, 2004).
4 Michael M. Atkinson, Loleen Berdahl, Stephen White, and David McGrane, "Are Canadians Stealth Democrats? An American Idea Comes North," *American Review of Canadian Studies* 46, no. 1 (2016): 59.
5 John R. Hibbing and Elizabeth Theiss-Morse, *Stealth Democracy: Americans' Beliefs about How Government Should Work* (Cambridge, UK: Cambridge University Press, 2002).
6 Amartya Sen, "Democracy as a Universal Value," *Journal of Democracy* 10, no. 3 (1999): 4.
7 Stephen Levitsky and Daniel Ziblatt, *How Democracies Die* (New York: Crown Publishing, 2018).

8 David Runciman, *The Confidence Trap: A History of Democracy in Crisis from World War I to the Present* (Princeton, NJ: Princeton University Press, 2013), 294.
9 Jason Brennan, *Against Democracy* (Princeton, NJ: Princeton University Press, 2016).
10 Ilya Somin, *Democracy and Political Ignorance: Why Smaller Government Is Smarter* (Stanford, CA: Stanford University Press, 2013).
11 Robert D. Tollison, "Rent-Seeking: A Survey," *Kyklos* 35, no. 4 (1982): 575–602.
12 Henry B. Mayo, "Justifying Democracy," *American Political Science Review* 56, no. 3 (1962): 555–66.
13 Adam Przeworski, "Minimalist Theory of Democracy: A Defense," in *Democracy's Value*, ed. Ian Shapior and Casiano Hacker-Cordon (Cambridge, UK: Cambridge University Press, 1999), 23–55.
14 Alina Mungiu-Pippidi, *The Quest for Good Governance: How Societies Develop Control of Corruption* (Cambridge, UK: Cambridge University Press, 2015).
15 Nicolas Charron and Victor LaPuente, "Does Democracy Produce Quality of Government?" *European Journal of Political Research* 49 (2010): 443–70; Hung-En Sung, "Democracy and Political Corruption: A Cross-National Comparison," *Crime, Law, and Social Change* 41 (2004): 179–94.
16 Phillip Keefer, "Clientelism, Credibility, and the Political Choices of Young Democracies," *American Journal of Political Science* 51, no. 4 (2007): 804–21.
17 Soren Holmberg and Bo Rothstein, "Correlates of Democracy," working paper 10, Quality of Government Institute, University of Gothenberg, 2011.
18 Bo Rothstein, "The Three Worlds of Governance: Arguments for a Parsimonious Theory of Quality of Government," working paper 12, Quality of Government Institute, University of Gothenberg, 2013.
19 Adam Przeworski, Michael E. Alvarez, José Antonio Cheibub, and Fernando Limongi, *Democracy and Development: Political Institutions and Well-Being in the World, 1950–1990* (Cambridge, UK: Cambridge University Press, 2000).
20 Francis Fukuyama, *State Building: Governance and World Order in the 21st Century* (Ithaca, NY: Cornell University Press, 2004).
21 Bo Rothstein, "Creating Political Legitimacy: Electoral Democracy versus Quality of Government," *American Behavioral Scientist* 53, no. 3 (2009): 311–30; Bo Rothstein, *The Quality of Government* (Chicago: University of Chicago Press, 2011).
22 Matt Andrews, "The Good Governance Agenda: Beyond Indicators without Theory," *Oxford Development Studies* 36, no. 4 (2008): 379–407.
23 Bo Rothstein and Jan Teorell, "What Is Quality of Government? A Theory of Impartial Government Institutions," *Governance* 21, no. 2 (2008): 165–90.
24 Douglas C. North, *Structure and Change in Economic History* (New York: W.W. Norton and Company, 1982).
25 Alasdair Roberts, *The Logic of Discipline: Global Capitalism and the Architecture of Government* (New York: Oxford University Press, 2011).
26 Michael Barber, *How to Run a Government So that Citizens Benefit and Taxpayers Don't Go Crazy* (Milton Keynes, UK: Alan Lane, 2015); Peter H. Schuck, *Why*

Government Fails So Often: And How It Can Do Better (Princeton, NJ: Princeton University Press, 2015).

27 Friedrich A. Hayek, "The Use of Knowledge in Society," *The American Economic Review* 35, no. 4 (1945): 519–30.

28 Amihai Glazer and Lawrence S. Rothenberg, *Why Government Succeeds and Why It Fails* (Cambridge, MA: Harvard University Press, 2001).

29 David Estlund, "Beyond Fairness and Deliberation," in *Deliberative Democracy: Essays on Reason and Politics*, ed. James Bohman and William Rehg (Cambridge, MA: MIT University Press, 1997); Hélène Landemore, *Democratic Reason: Politics, Collective Intelligence, and the Rule of the Many* (Princeton, NJ: Princeton University Press, 2013).

30 Christian List and Robert E. Goodin, "Epistemic Democracy: Generalizing the Condorcet Theorem," *The Journal of Political Philosophy* 9, no. 3 (2001): 277–306.

31 Albert Weale, *Democracy* (New York: St. Martin's Press, 1999), 14.

32 Kenneth J. Arrow, *Social Choice and Individual Values, 2nd ed.* (New York: Wiley, 1963). See also Eric Maskin and Amartya Sen, *The Arrow Impossibility Theorem* (New York: Columbia University Press, 2014).

33 Christian List, "Collective Wisdom: Lessons from the Theory of Judgment Aggregation," in *Collective Wisdom: Principles and Mechanisms*, ed. Hélène Landemore and Jon Elster (Cambridge, UK: Cambridge University Press, 2012), 203–29.

34 Christopher H. Achen and Larry M. Bartels, *Democracy for Realists: Why Elections Do Not Produce Responsive Government* (Princeton, NJ: Princeton University Press, 2016), 27.

35 Gerry Mackie, *Democracy Defended* (Cambridge, UK: Cambridge University Press, 2003).

36 Achen and Bartels, *Democracy for Realists*, 28–29.

37 Bryan Caplan, *The Myth of the Rational Voter: Why Democracies Choose Bad Policies* (Princeton, NJ: Princeton University Press, 2007); Somin, *Democracy and Political Ignorance*.

38 Henry Milner, *The Internet Generation: Engaged Citizens or Political Dropouts?* (Medford, MA: Tufts University Press, 2010), 97–114.

39 Patrick Fournier, "The Uninformed Canadian Voter," in *Citizen Politics: Research and Theory in Canadian Political Behaviour*, ed. Joanna Everitt and Brenda O'Neill (Toronto: Oxford University Press, 2002), 92–109.

40 Arthur W. Lupia and Mathew D. McCubbins, *The Democratic Dilemma* (Cambridge, UK: Cambridge University Press, 1998).

41 Paul Goren, *On Voter Competence* (New York: Oxford University Press, 2013).

42 Arthur W. Lupia, *Uninformed: Why People Know So Little about Politics and What We Can Do about It* (New York: Oxford University Press, 2016).

43 Donald Wittman, *The Myth of Democratic Failure* (Chicago: University of Chicago Press, 1995).

44 Scott L. Althaus, "Information Effects in Collective Preferences," *American Political Science Review* 92, no. 3 (1998): 548–55.
45 Achen and Bartels, *Democracy for Realists*.
46 Jennifer Hochschild and Katherine Levine Einstein, "Do Facts Matter? Information and Misinformation in American Politics," *Political Science Quarterly* 130, no. 4 (2015–16): 122.
47 Richard Johnson, André Blais, Elisabeth Gidengil, and Neil Nevitte, *The Challenge of Direct Democracy: The 1992 Canadian Referendum* (Montreal and Kingston: McGill-Queen's University Press, 1996).
48 Scott L. Althaus, *Collective Preferences in Democratic Politics: Opinion Surveys and the Will of the People* (Cambridge, UK: Cambridge University Press, 2003).
49 Brennan, *Against Democracy*.
50 Caplan, *The Myth of the Rational Voter*.
51 Bryan Caplan, "From Friedman to Wittman: The Transformation of Chicago Political Economy," *Econ Journal Watch* 2, no. 1 (2005): 1–21.
52 Ibid., 17.
53 Paul Quirk, "Putting Experts in Their Place," *Critical Review* 20, no. 3 (2008): 351.
54 Toke S. Aidt and Jayasri Dutta, "Policy Myopia and Economic Growth," *European Journal of Political Economy* 23 (2007): 734–53.
55 Donald Wittman, *The Myth of Democratic Failure* (Chicago: University of Chicago Press, 1995).
56 Terry M. Moe, "Vested Interests and Political Institutions," *Political Science Quarterly* 130, no. 2 (2015): 284.
57 James A. Robinson, "Theories of 'Bad Policy,'" *Journal of Economic Policy Reform* 2, no. 1 (1998): 1–46.
58 Martin Gilens, "Inequality and Democratic Responsiveness," *Public Opinion Quarterly* 69, no. 5 (2005): 778–896.
59 Martin Gilens and Benjamin Page, "Testing Theories of American Politics: Elites, Interest Groups, and Average Citizens," *Perspectives on Politics* 12, no. 3 (2014): 575.
60 Robert A. Dahl, *Democracy and Its Critics* (New Haven, CT: Yale University Press, 1999).
61 Bernard Grofman and Scott L. Feld, "Rousseau's General Will: A Condorcetian Perspective," *American Political Science Review* 82, no. 2 (1988): 567–76.
62 Lu Hong and Scott E. Page, "Some Microfoundations of Collective Wisdom," in *Collective Wisdom: Principles and Mechanisms*, ed. Hélène Landemore and Jon Elster (Cambridge, UK: Cambridge University Press, 2012), 56–71; Scott E. Page, *The Difference: How the Power of Diversity Creates Better Firms, Schools, Groups, and Societies* (Princeton, NJ: Princeton University Press, 2007).
63 Landemore, *Democratic Reason*.
64 Page, *The Difference*, 163.
65 Hélène Landemore, "Yes, We Can (Make It Up on Volume): Answers to Critics," *Critical Review* 26, nos. 1–2 (2014): 188.

66 Landemore, *Democratic Reason*.
67 Brennan, *Against Democracy*.
68 Philip Kitcher, "Public Knowledge and the Difficulties of Democracy," *Social Research* 73, no. 4 (2006): 1217.
69 Jon Elster, "Conclusion," in *Collective Wisdom: Principles and Mechanisms*, ed. Hélène Landemore and Jon Elster (Cambridge, UK: Cambridge University Press, 2012), 402.
70 Ruth W. Grant, "Ethics and Incentives: A Political Approach," *American Political Science Review* 100, no. 1 (2006): 29–39.
71 Charles Lindblom, *The Intelligence of Democracy* (New York: Free Press, 1965), 9.
72 Ibid., 143–51.
73 Landemore, *Democratic Reason*, 215.
74 Daniel A. Bell, *China Model: Political Meritocracy and the Limits of Democracy* (Princeton, NJ: Princeton University Press, 2015), 179.
75 Somin, *Democracy and Political Ignorance*.
76 See Adrian Vermeule, *Law and the Limits of Reason* (Oxford: Oxford University Press, 2009), 50–53.
77 Robert Goodin and Kai Spiekermann, "Epistemic Aspects of Representative Government," *European Political Science Review* 4 (2012): 303–25.
78 William A. Niskanen, *Bureaucracy and Representative Government* (Chicago: Aldine Atherton, 1971).
79 Jack Knight and James Johnson, *The Priority of Democracy: Political Consequences of Pragmatism* (Princeton, NJ: Princeton University Press, 2011).
80 Elizabeth Anderson, "The Epistemology of Democracy," *Episteme: A Journal of Social Epistemology* 3, nos. 1–2 (2006): 13.
81 Donald Savoie, *What Is Government Good At?* (Montreal and Kingston: McGill-Queen's University Press, 2015).
82 See also Bell, *China Model*.
83 Timothy J. Besley, Jose G. Montalvo, and Marta Reynal-Querol, "Do Educated Leaders Matter?," *The Economic Journal* 121 (2011): F207–27.

CHAPTER 8

1 Allan Blakeney, "Reaffirming Our Principles," *The Commonwealth* 59, no. 7 (1999): 31.
2 John Weidlich, "'Bland Sells': Former Saskatchewan Premier Allan Blakeney," CBC News, November 28, 2008, https://www.cbc.ca/news/canada/saskatchewan/bland-sells-former-saskatchewan-premier-allan-blakeney-1.741887.
3 Roberto Foa and Yascha Mounk, "The Danger of Deconsolidation," *Journal of Democracy* 27, no. 3 (2016): 5–17.
4 Ibid., 7.

5 Wolfgang Streeck and Armin Schäfer, eds., *Politics in the Age of Austerity* (London: Polity Press, 2013).
6 Conference Board of Canada, "Confidence in Parliament," 2016, http://www.conferenceboard.ca/hcp/details/society/trust-in-parliament.aspx; Marc J. Hetherington, *Why Trust Matters* (Princeton, NJ: Princeton University Press, 2006).
7 Jean Crete, Réjean Pelletier, and Jérome Couture, "Political Trust in Canada: What Matters: Politics or Economics?," paper prepared for the annual meeting of the Canadian Political Science Association, Toronto, 2006; Frank Graves, "Canadian Public Opinion on Taxes," in *Tax Is Not a Four-Letter Word*, ed. Alex Himelfarb and Jordan Himelfarb (Waterloo, ON: Wilfrid Laurier University Press, 2013), 83–100.
8 Bo Rothstein, *The Quality of Government* (Chicago: University of Chicago Press, 2011).
9 Graves, "Canadian Public Opinion on Taxes."
10 Hetherington, *Why Trust Matters*.
11 Jon Pammet and Lawrence LeDuc, "Explaining the Turnout Decline in Canadian Federal Elections: A New Survey of Non-Voters," Elections Canada, Ottawa, 2003.
12 Jesse Ferreras, "Canada's Voter Turnout in the Election Was the Highest in Decades," *Huffington Post*, October 21, 2015, 1.
13 John Ibbitson, *Stephen Harper* (Toronto: Signal, 2015).
14 Ibid.
15 Liberal Party of Canada, "Moving Canada Forward: The Paul Martin Plan for Getting Things Done," 2004, http://www.collectionscanada.gc.ca/eppp-archive/100/205/300/liberal-ef/05-05-24/www.liberal.ca/documents/platform_en.pdf.
16 Tax Policy Centre, "OECD Taxes as Share of GDP, 1965–2015," 2017, http://www.taxpolicycenter.org/statistics/oecd-taxes-share-gdp.
17 See Graves, "Canadian Public Opinion on Taxes"; Rebecca Medel, "Falling Flat on Taxes," *Public Interest Alberta*, August 8, 2014, 3–4.
18 Ibid.
19 Niccolo Machiavelli, *The Prince* (Boston: Dante University Press, 1903).
20 Alex Himelfarb and Jordan Himelfarb, *Tax Is Not a Four-Letter Word* (Waterloo, ON: Wilfrid Laurier University Press, 2013).
21 Bryan Caplan, "The Myth of the Rational Voter," *Cato Unbound*, November 6, 2006, 7–9.
22 Michel Crozier, Samuel P. Huntington, and Joji Watanuki, *The Crisis of Democracy: On the Governability of Democracies* (New York: New York University Press, 1975), 113.
23 Andrew Gamble, *Can the Welfare State Survive?* (Cambridge: Polity Press, 2016), 45.
24 Robert Reich, "The Government Problem," *Huffington Post*, December 24, 2014, 3.

25 CBC News, "Canada's Deficits and Surpluses 1963–2015," 2015, http://www.cbc.ca/news/multimedia/canada-s-deficits-and-surpluses-1963-to-2015-1.3042571.
26 Bruce Bartlett, "Tax Cuts and 'Starve the Beast,'" *Forbes*, May 6, 2010, https://www.forbes.com/forbes/welcome/?toURL=https://www.forbes.com/2010/05/06/tax-cuts-republicans-starve-the-beast-columnists-bruce-bartlett.html&refURL=https://www.google.ca/&referrer=https://www.google.ca/.
27 Mariana Mazzucato, *The Entrepreneurial State* (London: Anthem Press, 2013).
28 Rothstein, *The Quality of Government*.
29 Adam Kahane, "Alex Himelfarb on Austerity, Inequality, and 'Trickle-Down Meanness,'" *Globe and Mail*, December 19, 2014, 9.
30 Herbert Gans, *The War against the Poor* (New York: Basic Books, 1995).
31 David J. Hulchanski, "The Three Cities within Toronto: Income Polarization among Toronto's Neighbourhoods, 1970–2005," Cities Centre, University of Toronto, 2010.
32 Miles Corak, "Inequality, Life Chances, and Public Policy," paper presented to the European Investment Bank, Luxembourg, 2016.
33 Tony Judt, *Ill Fares the Land* (New York: Penguin, 2010).
34 Ibbitson, *Stephen Harper*.
35 Antonio Gramsci, *Prison Notebooks* (New York: Columbia University Press, 2011).
36 Joseph E. Stiglitz, "Globalization and Its New Discontents," *Project Syndicate*, August 5, 2016, 1–4.
37 Chris Hedges, *Wages of Rebellion* (New York: Nation Books, 2016).
38 Andrew Potter, "Canadian Elections for Naifs and Cynics," in *In Due Course: A Canadian Public Affairs Blog*, June 24, 2015, http://www. http://induecourse.ca/canadian-electons-for-naifs-and-cynics/.
39 Blakeney, "Reaffirming Our Principles," 31.

CHAPTER 9

1 Allan Blakeney, *An Honourable Calling: Political Memoirs* (Toronto: University of Toronto Press, 2008), 66.
2 Lynn McDonald, *The Party that Changed Canada: The New Democratic Party, Then and Now* (Toronto: Macmillan, 1987).
3 Edward Broadbent, "Social Democracy or Liberalism in the New Millennium?," in *The Future of Social Democracy: Views of Leaders from Around the World*, ed. Peter Russell (Toronto: University of Toronto Press, 1999), 73–93; Lewis Thomas, ed., *The Making of a Socialist: The Recollections of T.C. Douglas* (Edmonton: University of Alberta Press, 1982).
4 Robert T. Kudrle and Theodore R. Marmor, "The Development of Welfare States in North America," in *The Development of Welfare States in Europe and North America*, ed. Peter Flora and Arnold J. Heidenheimer (London: Transaction Books, 1981), 81–122.

5   Dennis Bueckert, "Medicare Tops the Flag, Anthem, and Hockey as National Icon; Queen Last," Canadian Press, April 3, 2003, http://www.freedominion.com.pa/phpBB2/viewtopic.php?t=10436&view=previous#p84113.
6   CBC News, "And the Greatest Canadian of All Time Is," CBC Digital Archives, 2004, http://www.cbc.ca/archives/categories/arts-entertainment/media/media-general/and-the-greatest-canadian-of-all-time-is.html.
7   Rod Preece, "The Political Wisdom of John A. Macdonald," *Canadian Journal of Political Science* 17, no. 2 (1984): 459–86.
8   Donald G. Creighton, "George Brown, Sir John A. Macdonald, and the 'Workingman,'" *Canadian Historical Review* 24, no. 4 (1943): 362–76.
9   Wilfrid Laurier, *Lecture on Political Liberalism* (Quebec City: Morning Chronicle, 1877).
10 William Lyon Mackenzie King, *Industry and Humanity: A Study in the Principles Under-Lying Industrial Reconstruction* (Toronto: Houghton Mifflin, 1918).
11 Keith Archer and Alan Whitehorn, *Political Activists: The NDP in Convention* (Toronto: Oxford University Press, 1997).
12 William M. Chandler, "Canadian Socialism and Policy Impact: Contagion from the Left?," *Canadian Journal of Political Science* 10, no. 4 (1977): 755.
13 Lynda Erickson and Maria Zakharova, "Members, Activists, and Party Opinion," in *Reviving Social Democracy: The Near Death and Surprising Rise of the Federal NDP*, ed. David Laycock and Lynda Erickson (Vancouver: UBC Press, 2015), 170.
14 Canadian Election Study, 2015, https://ces-eec.arts.ubc.ca/english-section/home/.
15 Gad Horowitz, "Conservatism, Liberalism, and Socialism in Canada: An Interpretation," *Canadian Journal of Economics and Political Science* 32, no. 2 (1966): 168.
16 Frank Feigert, *Canada Votes, 1935–1988* (Durham, NC: Duke University Press, 1989), 13.
17 Colin D. Howell, "Medical Science and Social Criticism: Alexander Peter Reid and the Ideological Origins of the Welfare State," in *Canadian Health Care and the State: A Century of Evolution*, ed. C. David Naylor (Montreal and Kingston: McGill-Queen's University Press, 1992), 16–37.
18 Robert H. Babcock, "Blood on the Factory Floor: The Workers' Compensation Movement in Canada and the United States," in *Social Welfare Policy in Canada: Historical Readings*, ed. Raymond B. Blake and Jeff Keshen (Toronto: Copp Clark, 1995), 105–203.
19 Quoted in Elisabeth Wallace, "The Origin of the Welfare State in Canada, 1867–1900," *Canadian Journal of Economics and Political Science* 16, no. 3 (1950): 392.
20 John Hay, "A General View of Socialistic Schemes," *Queen's Quarterly* 3, no. 4 (1896): 291–94.
21 Stewart Crysdale, *The Industrial Struggle and Protestant Ethics in Canada: A Survey of Changing Power Structures and Christian Social Ethics* (Toronto: Ryerson Press, 1961).

22 James S. Woodsworth, "Unemployment," in *Forum: Canadian Life and Letters, 1920–70*, ed. J.L. Granatstein and Peter Stevens (Toronto: University of Toronto Press, 1972), 5.
23 Grace MacInnis, *J.S. Woodsworth, a Man to Remember* (Toronto: Macmillan, 1953).
24 Quoted in J. Castell Hopkins, *Canadian Annual Review of Public Affairs, 1926–27* (Toronto: Canadian Review, 1927), 297.
25 Doug Owram, "Economic Thought in the 1930s: The Prelude to Keynesianism," *Canadian Historical Review* 66, no. 3 (1985): 344–77.
26 Nelson Wiseman and Benjamin Isitt, "Social Democracy in Twentieth Century Canada: An Interpretive Framework," *Canadian Journal of Political Science* 40, no. 3 (2007): 567–89.
27 Bernard L. Vigod, "The Quebec Government and Social Legislation during the 1930s: A Study in Political Self-Destruction," *Journal of Canadian Studies* 14, no. 1 (1979): 59–69.
28 Kenneth Bryden, *Old Age Pensions and Policy-Making in Canada* (Montreal and Kingston: McGill-Queen's University Press, 1974).
29 Research Committee of the League for Social Reconstruction (hereafter RCLSR), *Social Planning for Canada* (Toronto: University of Toronto Press, 1935); RCLSR, *Democracy Needs Socialism* (Toronto: Thomas Nelson and Sons, 1938).
30 Norman MacKenzie and Jeanne MacKenzie, *The Fabians* (New York: Simon and Schuster, 1977), 380.
31 RCLSR, *Social Planning for Canada* (Toronto: University of Toronto Press, 1975), ix–x.
32 Michiel Horn, *The League for Social Reconstruction: Intellectual Origins of the Democratic Left in Canada, 1930–1942* (Toronto: University of Toronto Press, 1980), 15–16.
33 Parliament of Canada, *House of Commons Debates*, 17th Parliament, 2nd Session, April 29, 1931, 1095 ff.
34 Harry M. Cassidy, *Social Security and Reconstruction in Canada* (Toronto: Ryerson Press, 1943); Leonard Marsh, *Report on Social Security for Canada* (Ottawa: King's Printer, 1943).
35 Michael Bliss, "Preface," in Leonard Marsh, *Report on Social Security for Canada* (Toronto: University of Toronto Press, 1975), ix.
36 Sir William Beveridge, *Social Insurance and Allied Services* (New York: Macmillan, 1942).
37 Cooperative Commonwealth Federation, *The Regina Manifesto*, 1933, http://www.socialisthistory.ca/Docs/ccf/ReginaManifesto.htm.
38 Allan Irving, "Canadian Fabians: The Work and Thought of Harry Cassidy and Leonard Marsh, 1930–1945," *Canadian Journal of Social Work Education* 7, no. 1 (1981): 7–28.
39 Gunnar Adler-Karlson, *Reclaiming the Canadian Economy: A Swedish Approach through Functional Socialism* (Toronto: Anansi, 1970).

40 Parliament of Canada, *House of Commons Debates*, 16th Parliament, 3rd Session, May 27, 1929, 2783.
41 Dorothy Stepler, "Family Allowances for Canada?," *Behind the Headlines* 3, no. 2 (1945): 1–32.
42 Dennis Guest, *The Emergence of Social Security in Canada*, 3rd ed. (Vancouver: UBC Press, 1999).
43 Parliament of Canada, *House of Commons Debates*, 19th Parliament, 5th Session, July 26, 1944, 5406 ff.
44 Raymond B. Blake, *From Rights to Needs: A History of Family Allowances in Canada, 1929–92* (Vancouver: UBC Press, 2009).
45 David Lewis and Frank Scott, *Make This Your Canada: A Review of CCF History and Policy* (Toronto: Central Canada Publishing, 1943).
46 Rand Dyck, *Provincial Politics in Canada: Towards the Turn of the Century* (Scarborough, ON: Prentice-Hall, 1996), 338.
47 Lawrence LeDuc, Judith I. McKenzie, Jon H. Pammett, and André Turcotte, *Dynasties and Interludes: Past and Present in Canadian Electoral Politics* (Toronto: Dundurn, 2010), 143–44.
48 Susan Prentice, "Workers, Mothers, Reds: Toronto's Postwar Daycare Fight," *Studies in Political Economy* 30 (1989): 115–41.
49 Montague A. Sanderson, "Sugar-Coating the Arsenic," *Globe and Mail*, July 29, 1943, 2.
50 John Boyko, *Into the Hurricane: Attacking Socialism and the CCF* (Winnipeg: J. Gordon Shillingford, 2006), 112.
51 "Some Changes Have Been Made," *Globe and Mail*, September 19, 1959, 6.
52 Meyer Brownstone, "The Douglas-Lloyd Governments: Innovation and Bureaucratic Adaptation," in *Essays on the Left: Essays in Honour of T.C. Douglas*, ed. Laurier LaPierre et al. (Toronto: McClelland and Stewart, 1971), 65–80; George Cadbury, "Planning in Saskatchewan," in *Essays on the Left*, 51–64.
53 Rand Dyck, "The Canada Assistance Plan: The Ultimate in Cooperative Federalism," *Canadian Public Administration* 19, no. 4 (1976): 590.
54 Patrice Dutil, *The Guardian: Perspectives on the Ministry of Finance of Ontario* (Toronto: University of Toronto Press, 2011), 326–27.
55 Parliament of Canada, *House of Commons Debates*, 26th Parliament, 2nd Session, December 21, 1964, 70.
56 John Saywell, ed., *Canada Annual Review for 1966* (Toronto: University of Toronto Press, 1967).
57 Paul Stevens and John Saywell, "Parliament and Politics," in *Canadian Annual Review of Politics and Public Affairs, 1972*, ed. John Saywell (Toronto: University of Toronto Press, 1974), 11–14.
58 John Morgan, "Social Welfare Services in Canada," in *Social Purpose for Canada*, ed. Michael Oliver (Toronto: University of Toronto Press, 1961), 83–114.

59 Lewis Thomas, ed., *The Making of a Socialist: The Recollections of T.C. Douglas* (Edmonton: University of Alberta Press, 1982).
60 Quoted in Duane Mombourquette, "'An Inalienable Right': The CCF and Rapid Health Care Reform, 1944–1948," *Saskatchewan History* 43, no. 3 (1991): 102.
61 Guest, *The Emergence of Social Security in Canada*, 140.
62 Blakeney, *An Honourable Calling*, 3.
63 Jared J. Wesley, *Code Politics: Campaigns and Cultures on the Canadian Prairies* (Vancouver: UBC Press, 2011), 127.
64 Blakeney, *An Honourable Calling*, 87–91.
65 Nelson Wiseman, *Social Democracy in Manitoba* (Winnipeg: University of Manitoba Press, 1985).
66 Susan Prentice, "Manitoba's Childcare Regime: Social Liberalism in Flux," *Canadian Journal of Sociology* 29, no. 2 (2004): 193.
67 Martha Friendly, Jane Beach, Carolyn Ferns, and Michelle Turiano, *Early Childhood Education and Care in Canada 2006* (Toronto: Childcare Resource and Research Unit, University of Toronto, 2007).
68 Michael Prince, "At the Edge of Canada's Welfare State: Social Policy-Making in British Columbia," in *Politics, Policy, and Government in British Columbia*, ed. R. Kenneth Carty (Vancouver: UBC Press, 1996), 251.
69 Denis C. Bracken and Peter Hudson, "Manitoba," in *Privatization and Provincial Public Social Services in Canada*, ed. Jacqueline S. Ismael and Yves Vaillancourt (Edmonton: University of Alberta Press, 1988), 95–117.
70 Quoted in "Schreyer Calls for Review of Welfare Programs for the Able-Bodied," *Globe and Mail*, December 18, 1972, 8.
71 Stevens and Saywell, "Parliament and Politics."
72 "Welfare Crackdown," *Maclean's*, April 11, 1994, 21.
73 Robert Drummond, "Ontario," in *Canadian Annual Review of Politics and Public Affairs, 1995*, ed. David Leyton-Brown (Toronto: University of Toronto Press, 2002), 103–17.
74 Government of Ontario, *Ministry of Community and Social Services*, "Social Assistance Reform: Proposed Program Model," 1992.
75 Lesley Byrne, "Feminists in Power: Women Cabinet Ministers in the New Democratic Party (NDP) Government of Ontario, 1990–1995," *Policy Studies Journal* 25, no. 4 (1997): 601–12.
76 Saywell, *Canada Annual Review for 1966*, 25.
77 Parliament of Canada, *House of Commons Debates*, 30th Parliament, 4th Session, October 13, 1978, 83 ff.
78 Parliament of Canada, *House of Commons Debates*, 34th Parliament, 2nd Session, November 20, 1989, 5860 ff.
79 Keith C. Banting, "The Welfare State and Inequality in the 1980s," *Canadian Review of Sociology and Anthropology* 24, no. 3 (1987): 309–38.

80 Marilyn Callahan and Chris McNiven, "British Columbia," in *Privatization and Provincial Public Social Services in Canada*, ed. Jacqueline S. Ismael and Yves Vaillancourt (Edmonton: University of Alberta Press, 1988), 13–39.
81 Michael O'Sullivan and Sandra Sorensen, "Saskatchewan," in *Privatization and Provincial Public Social Services in Canada*, ed. Jacqueline S. Ismael and Yves Vaillancourt (Edmonton: University of Alberta Press, 1988), 77.
82 Judith Martin, "The Continuing Struggle for Universal Daycare," in *Social Policy and Social Justice: The NDP Government in Saskatchewan during the Blakeney Years*, ed. Jim Harding (Waterloo, ON: Wilfrid Laurier University Press, 1995), 17–52.
83 David McGrane, "Explaining the Saskatchewan NDP's Shift to Third Way Social Democracy," paper presented at the Annual Conference of the Canadian Political Science Association, Toronto, 2006, 5.
84 Bracken and Hudson, "Manitoba."
85 Robert Everett, "Parliament and Politics," in *Canadian Annual Review of Politics and Public Affairs, 1992*, ed. David Leyton-Brown (Toronto: University of Toronto Press, 1998), 15.
86 "PM Shells Out $4.6B for NDP's Support," CBC News, 2005, http://www.cbc.ca/news/canada/pm-shells-out-4-6b-for-ndp-s-support-1.541632.
87 New Democratic Party, "Giving Families a Break," 2011, http://xfer.ndp.ca/2011/2011-Platform/ndp-2011-Platform-En.pdf; New Democratic Party, "Building the Country of Our Dreams," 2015, http://xfer.ndp.ca/2015/2015-Full-Platform-EN.pdf.
88 EKOS, "From the End of History to the End of Progress: The Shifting Meaning of Middle Class," 2014, http://www.ekospolitics.com/index.php/category/inequality/.
89 Quoted in Daniel Cohen, "The Political Legacy of Neoconservative Rhetoric and Governance: A Comparative Study of the Impact of Political Leadership on Consumer Sentiment in Canada and the United States" (PhD diss., Carleton University, 1998), 334.
90 Sylvia B. Bashevkin, *Welfare Hot Buttons: Women, Work, and Social Policy Reform* (Toronto: University of Toronto Press, 2002), 28.
91 Janice MacKinnon, "'Agrarian Socialism' and Saskatchewan's Distinctiveness: A Perspective from the 1990s," in *Lipset's Agrarian Socialism: A Re-Examination*, ed. David E. Smith (Regina: Saskatchewan Institute of Public Policy, 2007), 51–62.
92 Broadbent, "Social Democracy or Liberalism in the New Millennium?," 84–85.
93 Mowat Centre, "Renewing Canada's Social Architecture," 2015, http://social-architecture.ca/.
94 Arthur Gould, "The Salaried Middle Class in the Corporatist Welfare State," *Policy and Politics* 9, no. 4 (1981): 401–18.
95 Elim Papadakis, "Class Interests, Class Politics, and Welfare State Regime," *British Journal of Sociology* 44, no. 2 (1993): 267.

96 Adam Przeworski, "Material Interests, Class Compromise, and the Transition to Socialism," *Politics and Society* 10, no. 2 (1980): 125.

CHAPTER 10

1 David McGrane, "A Mixed Record: Gender and Saskatchewan Social Democracy," *Journal of Canadian Studies* 42, no. 1 (2008): 179–203.
2 Ibid., 191.
3 Hanna Pitkin, *The Concept of Representation* (Berkeley: University of California Press, 1967).
4 Jane Mansbridge, "Should Blacks Represent Blacks and Women Represent Women? A Contingent 'Yes,'" *The Journal of Politics* 61, no. 3 (1999): 628–57.
5 Ibid.
6 See, for example, Elisabeth Gidengil, "Beyond the Gender Gap: Presidential Address to the Canadian Political Science Association, Saskatoon, 2007," *Canadian Journal of Political Science* 40, no. 4 (2007): 815–31; Elisabeth Gidengil, Allison Harell, and Bonnie Erickson, "Network Diversity and Vote Choice: Women's Social Ties and Left Voting in Canada," *Politics and Gender* 3, no. 2 (2007): 151–77; and Pei-Te Lien, "Does the Gender Gap in Political Attitudes and Behavior Vary across Racial Groups?," *Political Research Quarterly* 51, no. 4 (1998): 869–94.
7 Manon Tremblay, "Do Female MPs Substantively Represent Women? A Study of Legislative Behaviour in Canada's 35th Parliament," *Canadian Political Science Review* 31, no. 3 (1998): 435–65.
8 Lyn Kathlene, "Power and Influence in State Legislative Policymaking: The Interaction of Gender and Position in Committee Hearing Debates," *The American Political Science Review* 88, no. 3 (1994): 560–76.
9 Rebecca J. Hannagan and Christopher W. Larimer, "Does Gender Composition Affect Group Decision Outcomes? Evidence from a Laboratory Experiment," *Political Behavior* 32, no. 1 (2010): 51–68.
10 Tali Mendelberg, Christopher F. Karpowitz, and J. Baxter Oliphant, "Gender Inequality in Deliberation: Unpacking the Black Box of Interaction," *Perspectives on Politics* 12, no. 1 (2014): 18–44.
11 Andrew Coyne, "Trudeau Cabinet Should Be Based on Merit, Not Gender," *National Post*, November 2, 2015, http://news.nationalpost.com/full-comment/andrew-coyne-trudeau-cabinet-should-be-built-on-merit-not-gender; Susan Franceschet, Karen Beckwith, and Claire Annesley, "Why Are We Still Debating Diversity versus Merit in 2015?," Federation for the Humanities and Social Sciences, 2015, http://www.ideas-idees.ca/blog/why-are-we-still-debating-diversity-versus-merit-2015.
12 *Canadian Charter of Rights and Freedoms*, s 3, Part I of the *Constitution Act*, 1982, being Schedule B to the *Canada Act 1982* (UK), 1981, c 11.

13 Canadian Human Rights Commission, "Voting Rights," n.d., http://www.chrc-ccdp.ca/historical-perspective/en/browseSubjects/humanRights1975-1999.asp.
14 Parliament of Canada, "Women Candidates in General Elections—1921 to Date," 2015, http://www.parl.gc.ca/About/Parliament/FederalRidingsHistory/hfer.asp?Search=WomenElection&Language=E; Terri Coles, "Women and Visible Minorities Make Election Gains," *Yahoo News*, October 20, 2015, https://ca.news.yahoo.com/blogs/canada-politics/women-and-visible-minorities-make-election-gains-154729934.html.
15 Statistics Canada, "National Household Survey (NHS) Profile, Canada, 2011," 2013, http://www12.statcan.gc.ca/nhs-enm/2011/dp-pd/prof/index.cfm?Lang=E.
16 Parliament of Canada, "Top 10 Occupations," 2012, http://www.parl.gc.ca/parlinfo/Lists/Top10Occupations.aspx?Menu=PARL-hoc.
17 Kathryn Kopniak, "Women in Canadian Municipal Politics: Two Steps Forward, One Step Back," *Canadian Review of Sociology and Anthropology* 22, no. 3 (1985): 394–410; Melanee Thomas, "Barriers to Women's Political Participation in Canada," *University of New Brunswick Law Journal* 64, no. 1 (2013): 218–32.
18 Parliament of Canada, "Women Candidates in General Elections."
19 Gabriel Almond and Sidney Verba, *The Civic Culture: Political Attitudes and Democracy in Five Nations* (Newbury Park, CA: SAGE Publications, 1963); Angus Campbell, Philip E. Converse, Warren E. Miller, and Donald E. Stokes, *The American Voter* (Chicago: University of Chicago Press, 1960); Paul Lazarsfeld, Bernard Berelson, and Hazel Gaudet, *The People's Choice: How the Voter Makes Up His Mind in a Presidential Election* (New York: Columbia University Press, 1948).
20 Sarah Jane Ferguson, "Women and Education: Qualifications, Skills, and Technology," in *Women in Canada: A Gender-Based Statistical Report* (Ottawa: Statistics Canada, 2016), catalogue no. 89-503-X.
21 Vincent Ferraro, "Paid Work," Statistics Canada, Social and Aboriginal Statistics Division, 2010.
22 Marie Drolet, "Why Has the Gender Wage Gap Narrowed?," Statistics Canada, 2010.
23 Mary Beach, "Gender Pay Gap in Canada More than Twice Global Average, Study Shows," *Globe and Mail*, May 5, 2015, https://www.theglobeandmail.com/news/british-columbia/gender-pay-gap-in-canada-more-than-twice-global-average-study-shows/article24274586/.
24 André Blais, *To Vote or Not to Vote? The Merits and Limits of Rational Choice Theory* (Pittsburgh: University of Pittsburgh Press, 2000); Elisabeth Gidengil, André Blais, Neil Nevitte, and Richard Nadeau, *Citizens* (Vancouver: UBC Press, 2004).
25 William P. Cross, *Political Parties* (Vancouver: UBC Press, 2004); Gidengil et al., *Citizens*.
26 See Elections Canada, "Limit for Nomination Campaign Expenses (CES, Paragraph 476.67(b))," 2013, http://www.elections.ca/content.aspx?section=pol&document=index&dir=limits/limitnom42&lang=e.

27 Cross, *Political Parties*.
28 Ibid.
29 Stephen E. Bennett, "Knowledge of Politics and Sense of Subjective Political Competence: The Ambiguous Connection," *American Politics Research* 25, no. 2 (1997): 230–40; Linda L. Bennett and Stephen E. Bennett, "Enduring Gender Differences in Political Interest: The Impact of Socialization and Political Dispositions," *American Politics Research* 17, no. 1 (1989): 105–22; Nancy Burns, Kay Schlozman, and Sidney Verba, *The Private Roots of Public Action* (Cambridge, MA: Harvard University Press, 2001); Gidengil et al., *Citizens*; Dietlind Stolle and Elisabeth Gidengil, "What Do Women Really Know? A Gendered Analysis of Varieties of Political Knowledge," *PS: Perspectives on Politics* 8, no. 1 (2010): 93–109.
30 Elisabeth Gidengil, Janine Giles, and Melanee Thomas, "The Gender Gap in Self-Perceived Understanding of Politics in Canada and the United States," *Politics and Gender* 4, no. 4 (2008): 535–61; Melanee Thomas, "The Complexity Conundrum: Why Hasn't the Gender Gap in Subjective Political Competence Closed?," *Canadian Journal of Political Science* 45, no. 2 (2012): 337–58.
31 Jennifer Lawless and Richard Fox, *It Still Takes a Candidate: Why Women Don't Run for Office* (Cambridge, UK: Cambridge University Press, 2010).
32 Melanee Thomas, "Gender and Psychological Orientations to Politics" (PhD diss., McGill University, 2012).
33 Thomas, "The Complexity Conundrum."
34 Christina Wolbrecht and David E. Campbell, "Leading by Example: Female Members of Parliament as Political Role Models," *American Journal of Political Science* 51, no. 4 (2007): 921–39.
35 Thomas, "Gender and Psychological Orientations to Politics."
36 Lawless and Fox, *It Still Takes a Candidate*; Thomas, "The Complexity Conundrum."
37 Lawless and Fox, *It Still Takes a Candidate*, 172–73; Alberta Urban Municipalities Association, "Women in Municipal Government," 2012, http://www.auma.ca/live/AUMA/Toolkits+%26+Initiatives/Women_in_Municipal_Government.
38 Anne Milan, Leslie-Anne Keown, and Covadonga Robles Urquijo, "Families, Living Arrangements, and Unpaid Work," in *Women in Canada: A Gender-Based Statistical Report* (Ottawa: Statistics Canada, 2011), catalogue 89-503-X.
39 Lawless and Fox, *It Still Takes a Candidate*, 71; Thomas, "Barriers to Women's Political Participation in Canada."
40 Lawless and Fox, *It Still Takes a Candidate*.
41 Ibid., 82.
42 Melanee Thomas and Lisa Lambert, "Private Moms vs. Political Dads? Communications of Parental Status in the 41st Canadian Parliament," in *Mothers and Others: The Impact of Family Life on Politics*, ed. Melanee Thomas and Amanda Bittner (Vancouver: UBC Press, 2017), 135–54.
43 Ibid., 9.
44 Ibid., 10.

45 Monica C. Schneider and Angela L. Bos, "Measuring Stereotypes of Female Politicians," *Political Psychology* 35, no. 2 (2014): 245–66.
46 Jill Greenlee, Mirya Holman, and Rachel VanSickle-Ward, "Why Women's Representation May Suffer When Hillary Clinton Is Attacked as 'Ambitious' and 'Unqualified,'" *Washington Post*, April 10, 2016, https://www.washingtonpost.com/news/monkey-cage/wp/2016/04/10/why-womens-representation-may-suffer-when-hillary-clinton-is-attacked-as-ambitious-and-unqualified/?utm_term=.e2259fa97603.
47 Elizabeth Goodyear-Grant, "Who Votes for Women and Why? Evidence from Recent Canadian Elections," in *Voting Behaviour in Canada*, ed. Cameron D. Anderson and Laura B. Stephenson (Vancouver: UBC Press, 2010), 43–64.
48 Tessa M. Ditonto, Allison J. Hamilton, and David P. Redlawsk, "Gender Stereotypes, Information Search, and Voting Behavior in Political Campaigns," *Political Behavior* 36, no. 2 (2014): 335–58.
49 Goodyear-Grant, "Who Votes for Women and Why?"; Melissa Miller, Jeffrey Peake, and Brittany Boulton, "Testing the Saturday Night Live Hypothesis: Fairness and Bias in Newspaper Coverage of Hillary Clinton's Presidential Campaign," *Politics and Gender* 6, no. 2 (2010): 169–98.
50 Miller et al., "Testing the Saturday Night Live Hypothesis."
51 Amanda Bittner, "Personality Matters: The Evaluation of Party Leaders in Canadian Elections," in *Voting Behaviour in Canada*, ed. Cameron D. Anderson and Laura B. Stephenson (Vancouver: UBC Press, 2010), 183–210; Richard Johnston, "Prime Ministerial Contenders in Canada," in *Leaders' Personalities and the Outcomes of Democratic Elections*, ed. Anthony King (Oxford: Oxford University Press, 2002), 158–83.
52 Cross, *Political Parties*.
53 Ibid.
54 Lisa Young and William Cross, "Women's Involvement in Canadian Political Parties," in *Women and Electoral Politics in Canada*, ed. Manon Tremblay and Linda Trimble (Oxford: Oxford University Press, 2003), 92–109.
55 Christine Cheng and Margit Tavits, "Informal Influences in Selecting Female Political Candidates," *Political Research Quarterly* 64, no. 2 (2011): 460–71.
56 Melanee Thomas and Marc André Bodet, "Sacrificial Lambs, Women Candidates, and District Competitiveness in Canada," *Electoral Studies* 32, no. 1 (2013): 153–66.
57 Brenda O'Neill and Melanee Thomas, "'Because It's 2015': Gender and the 2015 Federal Election," in *The Canadian Federal Election of 2015*, ed. Jon H. Pammett and Christopher Dornan (Toronto: Dundurn Press, 2016), 275–304.
58 Jeanette Ashe and Kennedy Stewart, "Legislative Recruitment: Using Diagnostic Testing to Explain Underrepresentation," *Party Politics* 18 (2012): 687–707.
59 Federation of Canadian Municipalities (hereafter FCM), "About Women in Local Government," 2015, http://www.fcm.ca/home/programs/women-in-local-government/about-women-in-local-government.htm.

60 FCM, "Women in Local Government: Regional Champions," 2016, http://www.fcm.ca/home/programs/women-in-local-government/diverse-voices-for-change/regional-champions.htm; FCM, "Women in Local Government: Diverse Voices for Change," 2016, http://www.fcm.ca/home/programs/women-in-local-government/diverse-voices-for-change.htm.
61 Kathlene, "Power and Influence in State Legislative Policymaking"; Tali Mendelberg, Christopher F. Karpowitz, and J. Baxter Oliphant, "Gender Inequality in Deliberation: Unpacking the Black Box of Interaction," *Perspectives on Politics* 12, no. 1 (2014): 18–44; Tremblay, "Do Female MPs Substantively Represent Women?"
62 Goodyear-Grant, "Who Votes for Women and Why?"
63 Ibid.; Caroline Heldman, Susan J. Carroll, and Stephanie Olson, "She Brought Only a Skirt: Print Media Coverage of Elizabeth Dole's Bid for the Republican Presidential Nomination," *Political Communication* 22, no. 3 (2005): 315–35; Miller et al., "Testing the Saturday Night Live Hypothesis"; Linda Trimble, "Gender, Political Leadership, and Media Visibility: *Globe and Mail* Coverage of Conservative Party of Canada Leadership Contests," *Canadian Journal of Political Science* 40, no. 4 (2007): 969–93; Linda Trimble, Angelia Wagner, Shannon Sampert, Daisy Raphael, and Bailey Gerrits, "Is It Personal? Gendered Mediation in Newspaper Coverage of Canadian National Party Leadership Contests, 1975–2012," *The International Journal of Press/Politics* 18, no. 4 (2013): 462–81.
64 Miller et al., "Testing the Saturday Night Live Hypothesis."
65 Johnston, "Prime Ministerial Contenders in Canada"; Bittner, "Personality Matters."
66 Thomas and Lambert, "Private Moms vs. Political Dads?"
67 Scott Dippel, "Calgary MLA Stephanie McLean Makes History as Alberta's First Pregnant MLA," CBC News, November 3, 2015, https://www.cbc.ca/news/canada/calgary/mla-stephanie-mclean-is-pregnant-in-a-first-for-alberta-1.3302148. In contrast, Kathleen Ganley, the third minister in Notley's cabinet to give birth while in office, took a three-month maternity leave from December 2017 to February 2018. See Melanee Thomas, "Governing as if Women Mattered: Rachel Notley as Alberta Premier," in *Doing Politics Differently: Women Premiers in Canada's Provinces and Territories*, ed. Sylvia Bashevkin (Vancouver: UBC Press, forthcoming).
68 Joanna Smith, "MP and Her Baby Welcome Back in Commons after 'Misunderstanding,'" Toronto Star, February 8, 2012, https://www.thestar.com/news/canada/2012/02/08/mp_and_her_baby_welcome_back_in_commons_after_misunderstanding.html.
69 Thomas and Lambert, "Private Moms vs. Political Dads?"
70 Ibid.
71 Ibid.

72 "Here's Why Being a Woman in Politics Can Suck," Press Progress, 2015, http://www.pressprogress.ca/here_s_why_being_a_woman_in_politics_can_suck.
73 Reid Southwick, "NDP Government Will 'Build Feminism in Alberta,' Status of Women Minister Says," Calgary Herald, September 9, 2015, http://calgaryherald.com/news/local-news/ndp-government-will-build-feminism-in-alberta-status-of-women-minister-says.
74 Laura Payton, "Justin Trudeau's Feminism 'Lights the Fire' Globally: UN Official," CTV News, June 6, 2016, https://www.ctvnews.ca/politics/justin-trudeau-s-feminism-lights-the-fire-globally-un-official-1.2933520.
75 See Melanee Thomas, "Ready for Rachel: The 2015 Alberta NDP Campaign," in *The Orange Chinook: Politics in the New Alberta*, ed. Duane Bratt, Keith Brownsey, Richard Sutherland, and David Taras (Calgary: University of Calgary Press, 2019).
76 Mona Lena Krook, *Quotas for Women in Politics: Gender and Candidate Selection Reform Worldwide* (Oxford: Oxford University Press, 2009).
77 Lisa Young, "Party, State, and Political Competition in Canada: The Cartel Model Reconsidered," *Canadian Journal of Political Science* 31, no. 2 (1998): 339–58.
78 James McCarten, ed., *The Canadian Press Stylebook: A Guide for Writers and Editors* (Toronto: Canadian Press, 2013), 22.
79 Becky Gardiner, Mahana Mansfield, Ian Anderson, Josh Holder, Daan Louter, and Monica Ulmanu, "The Dark Side of Guardian Comments," *The Guardian*, April 12, 2016, https://www.theguardian.com/technology/2016/apr/12/the-dark-side-of-guardian-comments.
80 Bill Kaufmann, "Province Rejects Reappointment of U of C Governors," *Calgary Herald*, April 22, 2016, https://calgaryherald.com/news/local-news/province-rejects-reappointment-of-u-of-c-governors.

CHAPTER 11

1 David Newhouse and Yale Belanger, "The Canada Problem in Aboriginal Politics," in *Visions of the Heart: Canadian Aboriginal Issues, 3rd Edition*, ed. Olive Patricia Dickason and David Long (Toronto: Oxford University Press, 2011), 353.
2 Priscilla Kennedy, "The Duty to Consult: Constitutional Recognition of Treaty and Aboriginal Rights," no. 33, *Legal Resource Centre of Alberta*, 2008, 1–5.
3 Martin Papillon, "Canadian Federalism and the Emerging Mosaic of Aboriginal Multilevel Governance," in *Canadian Federalism: Performance, Effectiveness, and Legitimacy*, ed. Herman Bakvis and Grace Skogstad (Don Mills, ON: Oxford University Press, 2008), 291–313.
4 John Borrows, "Ground-Rules: Indigenous Treaties in Canada and New Zealand," *New Zealand Universities Law Review* 22, no. 2 (2006): 188–212; Kiera L. Ladner, "Treaty Federalism: An Indigenous Vision of Canadian Federalisms," in *New Trends in Canadian Federalism, 2nd ed.*, ed. M. Smith

and F. Rocher (Peterborough, ON: Broadview, 2003), 167–96; Thomas O. Hueglin, "Exploring Concepts of Treaty Federalism," in *For Seven Generations: An Information Legacy of the Royal Commission on Aboriginal Peoples* (Ottawa: Royal Commission on Aboriginal Peoples, 1997), 1–88; James Tully, *Strange Multiplicity: Constitutionalism in an Age of Diversity* (Cambridge, UK: Cambridge University Press, 1995); James (Sakej) Youngblood Henderson, "Empowering Treaty Federalism," *Saskatchewan Law Review* 58, no. 2 (1994): 241–329.

5 Tully, *Strange Multiplicity*.
6 John Borrows, "Domesticating Doctrines: Aboriginal Peoples after the Royal Commission," *McGill Law Journal* 46, no. 3 (2001): 615–61.
7 Borrows, "Ground-Rules"; Henderson, "Empowering Treaty Federalism"; Hueglin, "Exploring Concepts of Treaty Federalism."
8 Frances Abele and Michael J. Prince, "Four Pathways to Aboriginal Self-Government in Canada," *The American Review of Canadian Studies* 36, no. 4 (2006): 568–71.
9 Gina Consentino, "Treaty Federalism: Bridging Praxis, Theory, Research, and Pedagogy," in *Racism Eh? A Critical Inter-Disciplinary Anthology of Race and Racism in Canada*, ed. Camille A. Nelson and Charmaine A. Nelson (Concord, ON: Captus Press, 2004), 136–52.
10 Frances Abele and Michael J. Prince, "Aboriginal Governance and Canadian Federalism: A To-Do List for Canada," in *New Trends in Canadian Federalism, 2nd edition*, ed. François Rocher and Miriam Smith (Toronto: Broadview Press, 2003), 139.
11 D.N. Sprague, "Canada's Treaties with Aboriginal Peoples," *Manitoba Law Journal* 23 (1995): 341–51.
12 Hueglin, "Exploring Concepts of Treaty Federalism"; Sheldon Krasowski, *No Surrender: The Land Remains Indigenous* (Regina: University of Regina Press, 2019).
13 Henderson, "Empowering Treaty Federalism," 263.
14 Ibid., 296.
15 Abele and Prince, "Aboriginal Governance and Canadian Federalism."
16 Consentino, "Treaty Federalism."
17 Maria Morellato, "The Crown's Constitutional Duty to Consult and Accommodate Aboriginal and Treaty Rights," research paper for the National Centre for First Nations Governance, 2008.
18 Ibid., 14.
19 Office of the Treaty Commissioner (hereafter OTC), "Treaty Implementation: Fulfilling the Covenant," 2007, http://www.otc.ca/ABOUT_TREATIES/Treaty_Implementation_Report/, viii.
20 Howard Adams, *Prison of Grass: Canada from the Native Point of View* (Toronto: General, 1975).

21 Bonita Beatty, "Saskatchewan First Nations Politics: Organization, Institutions, and Governance," in *Saskatchewan Politics: Crowding the Centre*, ed. Howard Leeson (Regina: Canadian Plains Research Center, 2008), 199–222.
22 See the chapter by Roy Romanow in this volume.
23 Allan Blakeney, *An Honourable Calling: Political Memoirs* (Toronto: University of Toronto Press, 2008), 198; see Marchildon (this volume) for more on technocracy.
24 Blakeney, *An Honourable Calling*, 114–15.
25 Ibid.
26 Ibid., 107.
27 Ibid.
28 Ibid.
29 Dennis Gruending, *Promises to Keep: A Political Biography of Allan Blakeney* (Saskatoon: Western Producer Prairie Books, 1990).
30 James M. Pitsula, "The Blakeney Government and the Settlement of Treaty Indian Land Entitlements in Saskatchewan, 1975–1982," *Historical Papers/Communications historiques* 24, no. 1 (1989): 190–209.
31 Keith Howell, "Public Relations Enhanced by Program," *Saskatchewan Indian* 9, nos. 11–12 (1979): 14.
32 Pitsula, "Blakeney Government"; Gruending, *Promises to Keep*.
33 Gruending, *Promises to Keep*, 218.
34 Federation of Sovereign Indigenous Nations (hereafter FSIN), FSIN Annual Report 2015–2016, 2016, http://www.fsin.com/2016/10/27/fsin-annual-report-2015-2016/.
35 Michael Woodward and Bruce George, "The Canadian Indian Lobby of Westminster, 1979–1982," *Journal of Canadian Studies* 18, no. 3 (1983): 119–43.
36 Beth Cuthand, "The Constitution: 'Existing' Rights Recognized But...," *Saskatchewan Indian* 11, no. 11 (1981): 1–2.
37 Madeline R. Knickerbocker and Sarah Nickel, "Negotiating Sovereignty: Indigenous Perspectives on the Patriation of a Settler Colonial Constitution, 1975–83," *BC Studies* 190 (2016): 67.
38 Ladner, "Treaty Federalism."
39 Cuthand, "The Constitution."
40 Union of BC Indian Chiefs, "The Indian Nations and the Federal Government's View on the Constitution," 1980, http://constitution.ubcic.bc.ca/sites/constitution.ubcic.bc.ca/files/OCRIndianNations&FederalGovView.pdf, 1–33.
41 Cuthand, "The Constitution."
42 Blakeney, *An Honourable Calling*; Doug Cuthand, "Allan Blakeney Showed Politics a Noble Calling," *StarPhoenix* [Saskatoon], April 21, 2011, A15; Roy J. Romanow, John D. Whyte, and Howard A. Leeson, *Canada—Notwithstanding: The Making of the Constitution, 1976–1982* (Toronto: Thomson Carswell, 1984).
43 Gareth Morley, "Judges: Canada's New Aristocracy," *Inroads* 18 (2006): 43.
44 *R v Sparrow*, [1990] 1 SCR 1075.

45 *Haida Nation v British Columbia (Minister of Forests)*, [2004] 3 SCR 511.
46 *Taku River Tlingit First Nation v British Columbia (Project Assessment Director)*, [2004] SCC 74; *Mikisew Cree First Nation v Canada* (Minister of Canadian Heritage), [2005] SCC 69.
47 *Haida Nation v British Columbia (Minister of Forests)*, [2004] 3 SCR 511.
48 *Dene Tha' First Nation v Canada (Minister of Environment)*, [2006] FC 1354.
49 *Mikisew Cree First Nation v Canada (Minister of Canadian Heritage)*, [2005] SCC 69.
50 *Haida Nation v British Columbia (Minister of Forests)*, [2004] 3 SCR 511 at para 43.
51 Ibid.
52 *Mikisew Cree First Nation v Canada (Minister of Canadian Heritage)*, [2005] SCC 69.
53 *Haida Nation v British Columbia (Minister of Forests)*, [2004] 3 SCR 511.
54 *R v Van der Peet*, [1996] CanLII 216 at para 31.
55 *Haida Nation v British Columbia (Minister of Forests)*, [2004] 3 SCR 511 at para 20 and para 32.
56 Kaitlin Ritchie, "Issues Associated with the Implementation of the Duty to Consult and Accommodate Aboriginal Peoples: Threatening the Goals of Reconciliation and Meaningful Consultation," *University of British Columbia Law Review* 46 (2013): 406.
57 Carolyn M. Hendriks, *The Politics of Public Deliberation: Citizen Engagement and Interest Advocacy* (New York: Palgrave Macmillan, 2011), 5.
58 Ria E. Tzimas, "Haida Nation and Taku River: A Commentary on Aboriginal Consultation and Reconciliation," *Supreme Court Law Review* 29, no. 2 (2005): 482.
59 *Haida Nation v British Columbia (Minister of Forests)*, [2004] 3 SCR 511.
60 Ibid.
61 Saskatchewan Party, "Securing the Future: New Ideas for Saskatchewan," 2007, http://www.saskparty.com/assets/pdf/New%20Ideas/SecuringTheFuturePlatform.pdf.
62 Government of Saskatchewan, "First Ever Chiefs' Feast at the Legislature Marks a New Relationship," 2007, http://www.gov.sk.ca/news?newsId=47281237-3862-44bf-8f01-9b87e3d1f2f6.
63 FSIN, *Portfolio Report: Lands and Resources Secretariat*, 2008, http://www.FSIN.com/landsandresources/downloads/Lands%20Resources%20Commission%20Portfolio%20Report%20Nov%202008.pdf.
64 Government of Saskatchewan, Ministry of First Nations and Métis Relations, *Seeking Common Ground: Roundtable Conference Report*, October 6, 2008, http://www.fnmr.gov.sk.ca/Consultation-Roundtable/.
65 Government of Saskatchewan, Ministry of First Nations and Métis Relations, *Draft Government of Saskatchewan First Nation and Métis Consultation Policy Framework*, December 2008, http://www.fnmr.gov.sk.ca/Consultation-Framework/.

66 Government of Saskatchewan, Ministry of First Nations and Métis Relations, *Ministry of First Nations and Métis Relations. 2008–2009 Annual Plan*, 2009, http://www.fnmr.gov.sk.ca/annual-report/.
67 L. Simcoe, "FSIN Rejects Proposal," *Leader-Post* [Regina], February 20, 2009, A7.
68 FSIN, *FSIN Annual Report 2015–2016*, 2016, http://www.fsin.com/2016/10/27/fsin-annual-report-2015-2016/.
69 Government of Saskatchewan, *Report on How Feedback Was Addressed in the Government of Saskatchewan First Nations and Métis Consultation Policy Framework*, June 15, 2010.
70 Ibid., 3.
71 Ibid., 1.
72 Ibid., 14.
73 Government of Saskatchewan, Ministry of First Nations and Métis Relations, *Draft Government of Saskatchewan First Nation and Métis Consultation Policy Framework*, December 2008, http://www.fnmr.gov.sk.ca/Consultation-Framework/
74 Government of Saskatchewan, Ministry of First Nations and Métis Relations, *Government of Saskatchewan Guidelines for Consultation with First Nations and Métis People: A Guide for Decision Makers*, 2006, http://www.nafaforestry.org/forest_home/documents/Sask-Guidelines_for_Consultation.pdf.
75 Government of Saskatchewan, Ministry of Government Relations and Aboriginal Affairs, *Ministry of Government Relations and Aboriginal Affairs Annual Report 2003–2004*, 2004, http://www.publications.gov.sk.ca/details.cfm?p=10177.
76 Simcoe, "FSIN Rejects Proposal."
77 OTC, *Statement of Treaty Issues: Treaties as a Bridge to the Future*, 1998, http://www.otc.ca/pdfs/otc_sti.pdf.
78 Ibid., 5.
79 Sharon Venne, "Treaties Made in Good Faith," in *Natives and Settlers, Now and Then: Historical Issues and Current Perspectives on Treaties and Land Claims in Canada*, ed. Paul W. DePasquale (Edmonton: University of Alberta Press, 2007), 1–16.
80 OTC, "Treaty Implementation," 160.
81 David E. Smith, *The Invisible Crown: The First Principle of Canadian Government* (Toronto: University of Toronto Press, 1995).
82 OTC, "Treaty Implementation," 160.

CHAPTER 12

1 R.B.Y. Scott and Gregory Vlastos, eds., *Towards the Christian Revolution* (Chicago: Willett, Clark, and Company, 1936).
2 Sophocles *Antigone*, in *The Theban Plays*, trans. E.F. Watling (London: Penguin Books, 1947), 138.
3 Charles Taylor, *Hegel* (Cambridge, UK: Cambridge University Press, 1975).

4 *Criminal Law Amendment Act, 1968–69*, SC 1968–69, c 38.
5 *Civil Marriage Act*, SC 2005, c 33.
6 Jason Fekete, "'Government Does Not Have a Place in Your Bedroom': Conservatives Vote to Accept Same Sex Marriages," *Ottawa Citizen*, May 28, 2016.
7 Henry McDonald, "Ireland Becomes First Country to Legalise Gay Marriage by Popular Vote," *The Guardian*, May 23, 2015.
8 *Roe v Wade*, 410 US 113 (1973).
9 *R v Morgentaler*, [1988] 1 SCR 30.
10 Henry McDonald, Emma Graham-Harrison, and Sinead Baker, "Ireland Votes by Landslide to Legalise Abortion," *The Guardian*, May 26, 2018.
11 *Canadian Charter of Rights and Freedoms*, Part 1 of the *Constitution Act, 1982*, being Schedule B to the *Canada Act 1982* (UK), c 11.
12 Rachael Johnstone, "The Politics of Abortion in New Brunswick," *Atlantis* 36, no. 2 (2014): 73–87.
13 Kelly Grant, "Second Moncton Hospital Only New Site to Offer Abortions in N.B.," *Globe and Mail*, February 24, 2015.
14 Sean Fine, "Pro-Choice Group to Take PEI to Court over Abortion Access," *Globe and Mail*, January 5, 2016.
15 Sean Fine, "PEI Drops Opposition to Abortion Plans to Provide Access by Year's End," *Globe and Mail*, March 31, 2016.
16 *Tremblay v Daigle*, [1989] 2 SCR 530.
17 *Rodriguez v British Columbia (Attorney General)*, [1993] 3 SCR 519.
18 Bill 60, Quebec National Assembly, 40th Legislature, 1st Session, 2014.
19 *Carter v Canada*, [2015] 1 SCR 331.
20 Special Joint Committee on Physician-Assisted Dying, Kelvin Kenneth Ogilvie and Robert Oliphant, Joint Chairs, *Medical Assistance in Dying: A Patient-Centred Approach*, 42nd Parliament, 1st Session, 2016.
21 Catholic Health Sponsors of Ontario, "Catholic Health Sponsors of Ontario Response to Physician Assisted Dying," 2015, http://www.chac.ca/ethics/docs/PAD/CHSO%20Response%20to%20Physician%20Assisted%20Death%20-%20December%2017,%202015.pdf.
22 Geordon Omand, "Catholic Health Provider Cautious about Assisted Dying Ahead of New Law," *Canadian Press*, February 25, 2016.
23 Sheryl Ubelacker, "Recommendation to Require Referrals for Assisted Death Disappointing: CMA," *Canadian Press*, February 26, 2016.
24 Ibid.
25 *An Act to Amend the Criminal Code (Medical Assistance in Dying)*, SC 2016, c. 3.
26 Sean Fine, "Christian Doctors Challenge Ontario's Assisted Death Referral Requirement," *Globe and Mail*, June 22, 2016.
27 Ontario College of Physicians and Surgeons, "Medical Assistance in Dying," 2016, http://www.cpso.on.ca/Policies-Publications/Policy/Physician-Assisted-Death.
28 Ibid.

29 André Picard, "Hospitals Have No Right to Opt Out of Assisted Dying," *Globe and Mail*, December 13, 2016.
30 *Trump v Hawaii*, US No 17-965 (2018).
31 Bill 52, Quebec National Assembly, 40th Legislature, 1st Session, 2014.
32 *Recueil annuel des lois du Québec*, 2017, c 19.
33 Les Perreaux, "Legault to Use Notwithstanding Clause to Ban Religious Symbols for Civil Servants," *Globe and Mail*, October 2, 2018.
34 Rhys H. Williams, "Immigration and National Identity in Obama's America: The Expansion of Culture-War Politics," *Canadian Review of American Studies* 42, no. 3 (2012): 322.

CHAPTER 13

1 *Dixon v British Columbia (Attorney General)*, [1989] 59 DLR (4th) 247.
2 Allan Blakeney, *An Honourable Calling: Political Memoirs* (Toronto: University of Toronto Press, 2008).
3 *Dixon v British Columbia*.
4 John C. Courtney, *Commissioned Ridings: Designing Canada's Electoral Districts* (Montreal and Kingston: McGill-Queen's University Press, 2000).
5 On the Manitoba model, see ibid.
6 Courtney, *Commissioned Ridings*.
7 *The Constituency Boundaries Act*, RSS 1973.
8 Redistribution Federal Electoral Districts (hereafter RFED), *Report of the Federal Electoral Boundaries Commission for the Province of Ontario* (Ottawa: Elections Canada, 2012).
9 Ibid., 7.
10 RFED, *Report of the Federal Electoral Boundaries Commission for the Province of British Columbia* (Ottawa: Elections Canada, 2012).
11 Ibid., 7–8.
12 Christopher Potter and Richard Brough, "Systematic Capacity Building: A Hierarchy of Needs," *Health Policy and Planning* 19, no. 2 (2000): 336–45.
13 *Electoral Boundaries Readjustment Act*, RSC, s 15(1a).
14 William Samuelson and Richard Zeckhauser, "Status Quo Bias in Decision Making," *Journal of Risk and Uncertainty* 1 (1988): 8.
15 *Electoral Boundaries Readjustment Act*, RSC, s 15(1b).
16 RFED, *Report of the Federal Electoral Boundaries Commission for the Province of Saskatchewan* (Ottawa: Elections Canada, 2012).
17 Ibid., 18.
18 Parliament of Canada, Standing Committee on Procedure and House Affairs, "Minutes of Proceedings," 2013, 13.
19 RFED, *Report of the Federal Electoral Boundaries Commission for the Province of Alberta* (Ottawa: Elections Canada, 2012), 56.

20 See, for example, RFED, *Report of the Federal Electoral Boundaries Commission for the Province of Nova Scotia* (Ottawa: Elections Canada, 2012); RFED, *Report of the Federal Electoral Boundaries Commission for the Province of Ontario.*
21 *Commonwealth Electoral Amendment Bill,* 2016.
22 *The Electoral Divisions Act,* 2014.
23 *Electoral Boundaries Readjustment Act.*
24 Courtney, *Commissioned Ridings.*
25 Ibid.
26 RFED, *Report of the Federal Electoral Boundaries Commission for the Province of Alberta.*
27 RFED, *Report of the Federal Electoral Boundaries Commission for the Province of Quebec* (Ottawa: Elections Canada, 2012).
28 John C. Courtney, "Electoral Boundary Redistributions: Contrasting Approaches to Parliamentary Representation," in *Comparative Political Studies: Australia and Canada,* ed. Malcolm Alexander and Brian Galligan (Melbourne: Longmans Cheshire, 1992); John C. Courtney, "Naming Canada's Constituencies," *Canadian Parliamentary Review* 23 (2000): 27–29.
29 Royal Commission on Electoral Reform and Party Financing, *Final Report: Reforming Electoral Democracy* (Ottawa: Minister of Supply and Services Canada, 1991).
30 Michael Pal and Sujit Choudhry, "Is Every Ballot Equal? Visible-Minority Vote Dilution in Canada," *IRPP Choices* 13, no. 1 (2007): 1–30.
31 Michael Pal and Melissa Molson, *Moving toward Voter Equality* (Toronto: Mowat Centre, 2012).
32 Lisa Handley and Bernard Grofman, eds., *Redistricting in Comparative Perspective* (Oxford: Oxford University Press, 2008), 272–75.

CHAPTER 14

1 Gordon Barnhart, "'Efficiency, Not Speed': Parliamentary Reform in the Saskatchewan Legislature, 1969–1981," *The Table: The Journal of the Society of Clerks-at-the-Table in Commonwealth Parliaments* 50 (1982): 80–86.
2 The US Supreme Court held (five to four) on January 21, 2010, that the First Amendment to the US Constitution forbid governments from restricting independent campaign expenditures by non-profits, labour unions, and other associations.
3 Keena Lipsitz, "Democratic Theory and Political Campaigns," *Journal of Political Philosophy* 12, no. 2 (2004): 163–89.
4 Ibid., 166.
5 Ibid.
6 Ibid.

7   Ibid., 168.
8   See Kenneth Carty and Munroe Eagles, "Do Local Campaigns Matter? Campaign Spending, the Local Canvass, and Party Support in Canada," *Electoral Studies* 18, no. 1 (1999): 69–87; Gary Jacobson, "Measuring Campaign Spending Effects in U.S. House Elections," in *Capturing Campaign Effects*, ed. Henry E. Brady and Richard Johnston (Ann Arbor: University of Michigan Press, 2009), 199–220; Marie Rekkas, "The Impact of Campaign Spending on Votes in Multiparty Elections," *The Review of Economics and Statistics* 89, no. 3 (2007): 573–85.
9   For details, see Lisa Young, "Regulating Campaign Finance in Canada: Strengths and Weaknesses," *Election Law Journal* 3, no. 3 (2004): 444–62.
10 Harold Jansen and Lisa Young, "Cartels, Syndicates, and Coalitions: Canada's Political Parties after the 2004 Reforms," in *Money, Politics, and Democracy: Canada's Party Finance Reforms*, ed. Lisa Young and Harold Jansen (Vancouver: UBC Press, 2011), 82–103.
11 Ibid.
12 David Coletto, Lisa Young, and Harold Jansen, "Stratarchical Party Organization and Party Finance in Canada," *Canadian Journal of Political Science* 44, no. 1 (2011): 111–36; Conference Board of Canada, "Confidence in Parliament," 2016, http://www.conferenceboard.ca/hcp/details/society/trust-in-parliament.aspx.
13 Sandford Gordon, Catherine Hafer, and Dimitri Landa, "Consumption or Investment? On Motivations for Political Giving," *Journal of Politics* 69, no. 4 (2007): 1057–72.

REFERENCES

GOVERNMENT AND LEGAL DOCUMENTS

An Act to Amend the Criminal Code (Medical Assistance in Dying), SC 2016, c 3.
An Act Establishing the Saskatchewan Multicultural Advisory Council and the Providing for Assistance to Individuals and Groups, RSS 1973–74, c 101.
Bill 52. Quebec National Assembly, 40th Leg, 1st Sess (2014).
Bill 60. Quebec National Assembly, 40th Leg, 1st Sess (2014).
Canada (Attorney General) v Bedford, [2013] 3 SCR 1101.
Canada (Attorney General) v PHS Community Services Society, [2011] 3 SCR 134.
Canadian Charter of Rights and Freedoms, Part 1 of the *Constitution Act, 1982*, being Schedule B to the *Canada Act 1982* (UK), c 11.
Carter v Canada, [2015] 1 SCR 331.
Chaoulli v Quebec (Attorney General), [2005] 1 SCR 791.
Civil Marriage Act, SC 2005, c 33.
Commonwealth Electoral Amendment Bill. House of Representatives, Parliament of Australia, 2016.
The Constituency Boundaries Act, RSS 1973, c 18.
Constitution Act, 1982, being Schedule B to the *Canada Act 1982* (UK), 1982, c 11.
Criminal Law Amendment Act, 1968–69, SC 1968–69, c 38.
Dene Tha' First Nation v Canada (Minister of Environment), [2006] FC 1354.
Dixon v British Columbia (Attorney General), [1989] 59 DLR (4th) 247.
Elections Canada. "Limit for Nomination Campaign Expenses (CES, Paragraph 476.67(*b*))." 2013. http://www.elections.ca/content.aspx?section=pol&document=index&dir=limits/limitnom42&lang=e.
Elections Saskatchewan. "Voter Turnout Figures for 28th Saskatchewan Election Released." 2016. http://www.elections.sk.ca/media/news-releases/final-voter-turnout/.
Electoral Boundaries Readjustment Act, RSC 1985, c E-3.

The Electoral Divisions Act, CCSM 2014, c E40.

Government of Ontario. Ministry of Community and Social Services. "Social Assistance Reform: Proposed Program Model." 1992.

Government of Saskatchewan. "Brief Presented to the Task Force on Canadian Unity by Premier Allan Blakeney." Ottawa, October 20, 1977.

———. *1972 Budget Speech, Delivered by Allan Blakeney*. Regina: Department of Finance, 1972.

———. *1973 Budget Speech, Delivered by Elmwood Cowley*. Regina: Department of Finance,1973.

———. *1974 Budget Speech, Delivered by Wes Robbins*. Regina: Department of Finance, 1974.

———. *1976 Budget Speech, Delivered by Walter Smishek*. Regina: Department of Finance, 1976.

———. *1979 Budget Speech, Delivered by Walter Smishek*. Regina: Department of Finance, 1979.

———. *1982 Budget Speech, Delivered by Ed Tchorzewski*. Regina: Department of Finance, 1982.

———. "First Ever Chiefs' Feast at the Legislature Marks a New Relationship." 2007. http://www.gov.sk.ca/news?newsId=47281237-3862-44bf-8f01-9b87e3d1f2f6.

———. "The Public Sector, Statement by Premier Allan Blakeney." In *Federal-Provincial Conference of First Ministers, Ottawa, February 13–15, 1978*. Ottawa: Government of Canada, 1978.

———. "Press Release: Oil Companies Could Reap Huge Profits." November 28, 1973.

———. "Report on How Feedback Was Addressed in the Government of Saskatchewan First Nations and Métis Consultation Policy Framework." June 15, 2010

———. *Report on the Proceedings of the Seminar '73: Multiculturalism in Saskatchewan...an Opportunity for Action, a Challenge*. Regina: Queen's Printer, 1973.

———. "Speech from the Throne." In *Debates and Proceedings (Hansard)*, 18th Leg, 1st Sess (November 12, 1975), 1–12.

———. "Speech from the Throne." In *Debates and Proceedings (Hansard)*, 19th Leg, 2nd Sess (November 29, 1979), 1–10.

———. "Speech from the Throne." In *Debates and Proceedings (Hansard)*, 19th Leg, 3rd Sess (November 27, 1980), 1–7.

———. "Speech from the Throne." In *Debates and Proceedings (Hansard)*, 19th Leg, 4th Sess (November 26, 1981), 1–9.

———. "Statement by the Honourable Allan Blakeney, Premier of Saskatchewan, on Fiscal Arrangements and Cost-Shared Programs." In *Federal-Provincial Conference of First Ministers, Ottawa, June 14, 1976*. Ottawa: Government of Canada, 1976.

———. *Why Just Oil? The Case for Extending the Equalization Principle to Other Commodities*. Regina: Queen's Printer, 1974.

———. Ministry of First Nations and Métis Relations. "Draft Government of Saskatchewan First Nation and Métis Consultation Policy Framework." 2008. http://www.fnmr.gov.sk.ca/Consultation-Framework/.

———. ———. "Government of Saskatchewan Guidelines for Consultation with First Nations and Métis People: A Guide for Decision Makers." 2006. http://www.nafaforestry.org/forest_home/documents/Sask-Guidelines_for_Consultation.pdf.

———. ———. "Ministry of First Nations and Métis Relations 2008–2009 Annual Plan." 2009. http://www.fnmr.gov.sk.ca/annual-report/.

———. ———. "Seeking Common Ground: Roundtable Conference Report." October 6, 2008. http://www.fnmr.gov.sk.ca/Consultation-Roundtable/.

———. Ministry of Government Relations and Aboriginal Affairs. "Ministry of Government Relations and Aboriginal Affairs Annual Report 2003–2004." 2004. http://www.publications.gov.sk.ca/details.cfm?p=10177.

Haida Nation v British Columbia (Minister of Forests), [2004] 3 SCR 511.

House of Commons Debates, 16th Parl, 3rd Sess (1929).

House of Commons Debates, 17th Parl, 2nd Sess (1931).

House of Commons Debates, 19th Parl, 5th Sess (1944).

House of Commons Debates, 26th Parl, 2nd Sess (1964).

House of Commons Debates, 30th Parl, 4th Sess (1978).

House of Commons Debates, 34th Parl, 2nd Sess (1989).

Hupacasath First Nation v British Columbia (Minister of Forests), [2005] BCSC 1712.

Mikisew Cree First Nation v Canada (Minister of Canadian Heritage), [2005] SCC 69.

Parliament of Canada. "Medical Assistance in Dying: A Patient-Centred Approach." Report of the Special Joint Committee on Physician-Assisted Dying, 42nd Parl, 1st Sess (2016).

———. "Members of the House of Commons Average Age: Current List." 2015. http://www.parl.gc.ca/parlinfo/lists/ParliamentarianAge.aspx?Menu=HOC-Bio&Parliament=&Chamber=03d93c58-f843-49b3-9653-84275c23f3fb&Section=Default&Gender=F&Name=&Province=&Party.

———. *November 1974 Federal Budget Speech by John Turner*. Ottawa: Ministry of Finance, 1974.

———. "Top 10 Occupations." 2012. http://www.parl.gc.ca/parlinfo/Lists/Top10Occupations.aspx?Menu=PARL-HOC.

———. "Women Candidates in General Elections—1921 to Date." 2015. http://www.parl.gc.ca/About/Parliament/FederalRidingsHistory/hfer.asp?Search=WomenElection&Language=E.

———. Standing Committee on Procedure and House Affairs. Minutes of Proceedings, 2013.

R v Morgentaler, [1988] 1 SCR 30.

R v Sparrow, [1990] 1 SCR 1075.

R v Van der Peet, [1996] CanLII 216.

Recueil annuel des lois du Québec, 2017, c 19.

Redistribution Federal Electoral Districts (RFED). *Report of the Federal Electoral Boundaries Commission for the Province of Alberta*. Ottawa: Elections Canada, 2012.
——. *Report of the Federal Electoral Boundaries Commission for the Province of British Columbia*. Ottawa: Elections Canada, 2012.
——. *Report of the Federal Electoral Boundaries Commission for the Province of Nova Scotia*. Ottawa: Elections Canada, 2012.
——. *Report of the Federal Electoral Boundaries Commission for the Province of Ontario*. Ottawa: Elections Canada, 2012.
——. *Report of the Federal Electoral Boundaries Commission for the Province of Quebec*. Ottawa: Elections Canada, 2012.
——. *Report of the Federal Electoral Boundaries Commission for the Province of Saskatchewan*. Ottawa: Elections Canada, 2012.
Re: Resolution to Amend the Constitution, [1981] SCR 753.
Rodriguez v British Columbia (Attorney General), [1993] 3 SCR 519.
Roe v Wade, 410 US 113 (1973).
Royal Commission on Electoral Reform and Party Financing. *Final Report: Reforming Electoral Democracy*. Ottawa: Minister of Supply and Services Canada, 1991.
Saskatchewan Department of Agriculture. "Saskatchewan Challenges 'The Pepin Plan.'" 1982. Saskatchewan Archives Board, Blakeney Papers, R-1106.III.1.f.
Saskatchewan Department of Intergovernmental Affairs. "Brief Presented to the Task Force on Canadian Unity by Premier Allan Blakeney." October 20, 1977.
Taku River Tlingit First Nation v British Columbia (Project Assessment Director), [2004b] SCC 74.
Tremblay v Daigle, [1989] 2 SCR 530.
Trudeau, Pierre. "Statement on Multiculturalism Policy." In *House of Commons Debates*, 28th Parl, 3rd Sess (October 8, 1971), 8545–46.
Trump v Hawaii, US No 17-965 (2018).

ARTICLES AND BOOKS

Abele, Frances, and Michael J. Prince. "Aboriginal Governance and Canadian Federalism: A To-Do List for Canada." In *New Trends in Canadian Federalism, 2nd edition*, edited by François Rocher and Miriam Smith, 135–65. Toronto: Broadview Press, 2003.
——. "Four Pathways to Aboriginal Self-Government in Canada," *The American Review of Canadian Studies* 36, no. 4 (2006): 568–71.
Achen, Christopher H., and Larry M. Bartels. *Democracy for Realists: Why Elections Do Not Produce Responsive Government*. Princeton, NJ: Princeton University Press, 2016.
Ackerman, Bruce. "The Storrs Lectures: Discovering the Constitution." *Yale Law Journal* 93, no. 6 (1984): 1013–72.

Adams, Howard. *Prison of Grass: Canada from the Native Point of View*. Toronto: General, 1975.
Adler-Karlson, Gunnar. *Reclaiming the Canadian Economy: A Swedish Approach through Functional Socialism*. Toronto: Anansi, 1970.
Aidt, Toke S., and Jayasri Dutta. "Policy Myopia and Economic Growth." *European Journal of Political Economy* 23 (2007): 734–53.
Ajzenstat, Janet. *The Canadian Founding: John Locke and Parliament*. Montreal and Kingston: McGill-Queen's University Press, 2007.
Akee, Randall, William Copeland, E. Jane Costello, John B. Holbein, and Emilia Simeonova. "Family Income and the Intergenerational Transmission of Voting Behavior: Evidence from an Income Intervention." National Bureau of Economic Research Working Paper 24770, 2018. http://www.nber.org/papers/w24770.
Alberta Urban Municipalities Association. "Women in Municipal Government." 2012. http://www.auma.ca/live/AUMA/Toolkits+%26+Initiatives/Women_in_Municipal_Government.
Allan, John H. "Move Follows Province's Potash Takeover Step: Saskatchewan Is Selling Issue of $125 Million." *New York Times*, November 17, 1976, 91.
Almond, Gabriel, and Sidney Verba. *The Civic Culture: Political Attitudes and Democracy in Five Nations*. Newbury Park, CA: SAGE Publications, 1963.
Althaus, Scott L. *Collective Preferences in Democratic Politics: Opinion Surveys and the Will of the People*. Cambridge, UK: Cambridge University Press, 2003.
———. "Information Effects in Collective Preferences." *American Political Science Review* 92, no. 3 (1998): 548–55.
Anderson, Elizabeth. "The Epistemology of Democracy." *Episteme: A Journal of Social Epistemology* 3, nos. 1–2 (2006): 8–26.
Andrews, Matt. "The Good Governance Agenda: Beyond Indicators without Theory." *Oxford Development Studies* 36, no. 4 (2008): 379–407.
Archer, Keith, and Alan Whitehorn. *Political Activists: The NDP in Convention*. Toronto: Oxford University Press, 1997.
Arrow, Kenneth J. *Social Choice and Individual Values*. 2nd ed. New York: Wiley, 1963.
Ashe, Jeanette, and Kennedy Stewart. "Legislative Recruitment: Using Diagnostic Testing to Explain Underrepresentation." *Party Politics* 18 (2012): 687–707.
Atkinson, Michael M., Loleen Berdahl, Stephen White, and David McGrane. "Are Canadians Stealth Democrats? An American Idea Comes North." *American Review of Canadian Studies* 46, no. 1 (2016): 55–73.
Babcock, Robert H. "Blood on the Factory Floor: The Workers' Compensation Movement in Canada and the United States." In *Social Welfare Policy in Canada: Historical Readings*, edited by Raymond B. Blake and Jeff Keshen, 105–203. Toronto: Copp Clark, 1995.
Bächtiger, André, John Dryzek, Jane Mansbridge, and Mark Warren, eds. *Oxford Handbook of Deliberative Democracy*. Oxford: Oxford University Press, 2018.

Badgley, Robin F., and Samuel Wolfe. *Doctor's Strike: Medical Care and Conflict in Saskatchewan*. New York: Atherton Press, 1967.

Banting, Keith C. "The Welfare State and Inequality in the 1980s." *Canadian Review of Sociology and Anthropology* 24, no. 3 (1987): 309–38.

Barber, Michael. *How to Run a Government So that Citizens Benefit and Taxpayers Don't Go Crazy*. Milton Keynes, UK: Alan Lane, 2015.

Barker, Paul F. "The Formulation and Implementation of the Saskatchewan Dental Plan." PhD diss., University of Toronto, 1985.

Barnhart, Gordon. "'Efficiency, Not Speed': Parliamentary Reform in the Saskatchewan Legislature, 1969–1981." *The Table: The Journal of the Society of Clerks-at-the-Table in Commonwealth Parliaments* 50 (1982): 80–86.

Bartels, Larry M. "Is Popular Rule Possible? Polls, Political Psychology, and Democracy." *Brookings Review* 21 (2003): 12–15.

———. *Unequal Democracy: The Political Economy of the New Gilded Age*. Princeton, NJ: Princeton University Press, 2008.

Bartlett, Bruce. "Tax Cuts and 'Starve the Beast.'" *Forbes*, May 6, 2010. https://www.forbes.com/forbes/welcome/?toURL=https://www.forbes.com/2010/05/06/tax-cuts-republicans-starve-the-beast-columnists-bruce-bartlett.html&refURL=https://www.google.ca/&referrer=https://www.google.ca/.

Bashevkin, Sylvia B. *Welfare Hot Buttons: Women, Work, and Social Policy Reform*. Toronto: University of Toronto Press, 2002.

Baunach, Dawn M. "Changing Same-Sex Marriage Attitudes in America from 1988 through 2010." *Public Opinion Quarterly* 76 (2012): 364–78.

Beach, Mary. "Gender Pay Gap in Canada More than Twice Global Average, Study Shows." *Globe and Mail*, May 5, 2015.

Beatty, Bonita. "Saskatchewan First Nations Politics: Organization, Institutions, and Governance." In *Saskatchewan Politics: Crowding the Centre*, edited by Howard Leeson, 199–222. Regina: Canadian Plains Research Center, 2008.

Bell, Daniel A. *China Model: Political Meritocracy and the Limits of Democracy*. Princeton, NJ: Princeton University Press, 2015.

Bennett, Linda L., and Stephen E. Bennett. "Enduring Gender Differences in Political Interest: The Impact of Socialization and Political Dispositions." *American Politics Research* 17, no. 1 (1989): 105–22.

Bennett, Stephen E. "Knowledge of Politics and Sense of Subjective Political Competence: The Ambiguous Connection." *American Politics Research* 25, no. 2 (1997): 230–40.

Berman, Mark. "Oklahoma Governor Vetoes Bill that Would Make It a Felony to Perform Abortions." *Washington Post*, May 20, 2016. https://www.washingtonpost.com/news/post-nation/wp/2016/05/20/oklahoma-governor-vetoes-bill-that-would-make-it-a-felony-to-perform-abortions.

Besley, Timothy J., Jose G. Montalvo, and Marta Reynal-Querol. "Do Educated Leaders Matter?" *The Economic Journal* 121 (2011): F207–27.

Beveridge, Sir William. *Social Insurance and Allied Services*. New York: Macmillan, 1942.
Bittner, Amanda. "Personality Matters: The Evaluation of Party Leaders in Canadian Elections." In *Voting Behaviour in Canada*, edited by Cameron D. Anderson and Laura B. Stephenson, 183–210. Vancouver: UBC Press, 2010.
Blais, André. *To Vote or Not to Vote? The Merits and Limits of Rational Choice Theory*. Pittsburgh: University of Pittsburgh Press, 2000.
Blais, André, Elisabeth Gidengil, Neil Nevitte, Patrick Fournier, and Joanna Everitt. *The 2004 Canadian Election Study* (data set).
Blake, Raymond B. *From Rights to Needs: A History of Family Allowances in Canada, 1929–92*. Vancouver: UBC Press, 2009.
Blakeney, Allan. "An Address Delivered by the Honourable Allan E. Blakeney, Premier, Province of Saskatchewan, November 24, 1981." In *Proceedings of Omāmawi-Atoskēwin: Working Together*, 55–65. Regina: University of Regina Library Collection, 1981. CA6F18I058.
——. "CBC Program: National Unity." 1977. Saskatchewan Archives Board (hereafter SAB), Blakeney Papers, R565.VI.60.
——. "The Crisis of Inequality in Canada." *Globe and Mail*, January 23, 1974, 6–7.
——. *Energy Policy and National Economic Development, Opening Statement of the Province of Saskatchewan to the First Ministers Conference on Energy, January 22–23, 1974*. Ottawa: Government of Canada, 1974.
——. "Goal-Setting: Politicians' Expectations of Public Administration." *Canadian Public Administration* 24 (1981): 1–7.
——. *An Honourable Calling: Political Memoirs*. Toronto: University of Toronto Press, 2008.
——. "Indian and Métis, Speech from 1971 Provincial Election." SAB, Blakeney Papers, R800.LIX.1a.
——. Letter to the Right Honourable Pierre Elliott Trudeau. October 10, 1978.
——. "Notes for Remarks by Premier Allan Blakeney to the National Farmers' Union." 1977. SAB, Blakeney Papers, R800.LIX.10ss.
——. "Notes for Remarks by Premier Allan Blakeney to the Saskatchewan Wheat Pool Annual Meeting, Regina, Saskatchewan—November 16, 1976." SAB, Blakeney Papers, R800.LIX.8xx.
——. "The Notwithstanding Clause, the *Charter*, and Canada's Patriated Constitution: What I Thought We Were Doing." *Constitutional Forum* 19, no. 1 (2010): 1–9.
——. "Political Ideas and the Reality of Political Power." 1983. SAB, Blakeney Papers, R-1106.I.3.ii.
——. "Reaffirming Our Principles." *The Commonwealth* 59, no. 7 (1999): 31.
——. "The Relationship between Provincial Ministers and Their Deputy Ministers." *Canadian Public Administration* 15 (1972): 42–45.
——. "Saskatchewan's Crown Corporations: A Case Study." In *Proceedings of the Fifth Annual Conference of the Institute of Public Administration of Canada*,

edited by Philip Clark, 413–20. Toronto: Institute of Public Administration of Canada, 1954.
———. "Status of Women, Speech from 1971 Provincial Election." SAB, Blakeney Papers, R800.LIX.1a.
———. "The Struggle to Implement Medicare." In *Making Medicare: New Perspectives on the History of Medicare in Canada*, edited by Gregory P. Marchildon, 277–81. Toronto: University of Toronto Press, 2012.
———. "Taxes, Speech from 1971 Provincial Election." SAB, Blakeney Papers, R800.LIX.1a.
Blakeney, Allan, and Sandford Borins. *Political Management in Canada*. Toronto: University of Toronto Press, 1989.
———. *Political Management in Canada, 2nd Edition*. Toronto: University of Toronto Press, 1998.
Bliss, Michael. "Preface." In *Report on Social Security for Canada*, edited by Leonard Marsh, iii–v. Toronto: University of Toronto Press, 1975.
Borders, William. "Tax Dispute Halts Canada's Potash Growth: Tax Dispute Is Hobbling Canada's Potash Growth." *New York Times*, February 3, 1975, 47.
Borrows, John. "Domesticating Doctrines: Aboriginal Peoples after the Royal Commission." *McGill Law Journal* 46, no. 3 (2001): 615–62.
———. "Ground-Rules: Indigenous Treaties in Canada and New Zealand." *New Zealand Universities Law Review* 22, no. 2 (2006): 188–212.
Bouchard, Gérard, and Charles Taylor. *Building the Future: A Time for Reconciliation*. Quebec: Government of Quebec, 2008.
Bourdieu, Pierre, and Loic Wacquant. *An Invitation to Reflexive Sociology*. Chicago: University of Chicago Press, 1992.
Boyko, John. *Into the Hurricane: Attacking Socialism and the CCF*. Winnipeg: J. Gordon Shillingford, 2006.
Bracken, Denis C., and Peter Hudson. "Manitoba." In *Privatization and Provincial Social Services in Canada: Policy, Administration and Service Delivery*, edited by Jacqueline S. Ismael and Yves Vaillancourt, 95–117. Edmonton: University of Alberta Press, 1988.
Bremmer, Ian. "The 'Strongmen Era' Is Here: Here's What It Means for You." *Time*, May 3, 2018. http://time.com/5264170/the-strongmen-era-is-here-heres-what-it-means-for-you/.
Brennan, Jason. *Against Democracy*. Princeton, NJ: Princeton University Press, 2016.
Briens, Allan. "The 1960 Saskatchewan Provincial Election." MA thesis, University of Regina, 2004.
Broadbent, Edward. "Social Democracy or Liberalism in the New Millennium?" In *The Future of Social Democracy: Views of Leaders from around the World*, edited by Peter Russell, 73–93. Toronto: University of Toronto Press, 1999.
Brooks, Stephen. *Canadian Democracy*. Don Mills, ON: Oxford University Press, 2012.

Brownstone, Meyer. "The Douglas-Lloyd Governments: Innovation and Bureaucratic Adaptation." In *Essays on the Left: Essays in Honour of T.C. Douglas*, edited by Laurier LaPierre et al., 65–80. Toronto: McClelland and Stewart, 1971.

Bryden, Kenneth. *Old Age Pensions and Policy-Making in Canada*. Montreal and Kingston: McGill-Queen's University Press, 1974.

Bryson, Valerie. *Feminist Political Theory: An Introduction, 2nd Edition*. New York: Palgrave Macmillan, 2003.

Bueckert, Dennis. "Medicare Tops the Flag, Anthem, and Hockey as National Icon; Queen Last." Canadian Press, April 3, 2003. http://www.freedominion.com.pa/phpBB2/viewtopic.php?t=10436&view=previous#p84113.

Burke, Edmund. "Speech at Mr. Burke's Arrival in Bristol." In *The Portable Edmund Burke*, edited by Isaac Kramnick, 155–57. New York: Penguin Classics, 1999.

Burningham, Sarah. "Use the Notwithstanding Clause, if You Must." *National Post*, December 21, 2015. http://news.nationalpost.com/full-comment/sarah-burningham-use-the-notwithstanding-clause-if-you-must.

Burns, Nancy, Kay Schlozman, and Sidney Verba. *The Private Roots of Public Action*. Cambridge, MA: Harvard University Press, 2001.

Burton, John. *Potash: An Inside Account of Saskatchewan's Pink Gold*. Regina: University of Regina Press, 2014.

——. "Resource Rent and Taxation—Application of New Principles and Approaches in Saskatchewan." In *Policy Innovation in the Saskatchewan Public Sector, 1971–1982*, edited by Eleanor Glor, 59–78. North York: Captus Press, 1997.

Byrne, Lesley. "Feminists in Power: Women Cabinet Ministers in the New Democratic Party (NDP) Government of Ontario, 1990–1995." *Policy Studies Journal* 25, no. 4 (1997): 601–12.

Cadbury, George. "Planning in Saskatchewan." In *Essays on the Left: Essays in Honour of T.C. Douglas*, edited by Laurier LaPierre et al., 51–64. Toronto: McClelland and Stewart, 1971.

Callahan, Marilyn, and Chris McNiven. "British Columbia." In *Privatization and Provincial Public Social Services in Canada*, edited by Jacqueline S. Ismael and Yves Vaillancourt, 13–39. Edmonton: University of Alberta Press, 1988.

Campbell, Angus, Philip E. Converse, Warren E. Miller, and Donald E. Stokes. *The American Voter*. Chicago: University of Chicago Press, 1960.

"Canadian Election Study." 2015. https://ces-eec.arts.ubc.ca/english-section/home.

Canadian Human Rights Commission. *Voting Rights*. n.d. http://www.chrc-ccdp.ca/historical-perspective/en/browseSubjects/humanRights1975-1999.asp.

Caplan, Bryan. "From Friedman to Wittman: The Transformation of Chicago Political Economy." *Econ Journal Watch* 2, no. 1 (2005): 1–21.

——. "The Myth of the Rational Voter." *Cato Unbound*, November 6, 2006, 7–9.

——. *The Myth of the Rational Voter: Why Democracies Choose Bad Policies*. Princeton, NJ: Princeton University Press, 2007.

Carty, Kenneth, and Munroe Eagles. "Do Local Campaigns Matter? Campaign Spending, the Local Canvass, and Party Support in Canada." *Electoral Studies* 18, no. 1 (1999): 69–87.

Cassidy, Harry M. *Social Security and Reconstruction in Canada*. Toronto: Ryerson Press, 1943.

Catholic Health Sponsors of Ontario. "Catholic Health Sponsors of Ontario Response to Physician Assisted Dying." 2015. http://www.chac.ca/ethics/docs/PAD/CHSO%20Response%20to%20Physician%20Assisted%20Death%20-%20December%2017,%202015.pdf.

CBC News. "And the Greatest Canadian of All Time Is." 2004. http://www.cbc.ca/archives/categories/arts-entertainment/media/media-general/and-the-greatest-canadian-of-all-time-is.html.

———. "Canada's Deficits and Surpluses 1963–2015." 2015. http://www.cbc.ca/news/multimedia/canada-s-deficits-and-surpluses-1963-to-2015-1.3042571.

———. "PM Shells Out $4.6B for NDP's Support." 2005. http://www.cbc.ca/news/canada/pm-shells-out-4-6b-for-ndp-s-support-1.541632.

Chambers, Simone. "Balancing Epistemic Quality and Equal Participation in a Systems Approach to Deliberative Democracy." *Social Epistemology* 31, no. 3 (2017): 266–76.

———. "Deliberation and Mass Democracy." In *Deliberative Systems*, edited by Jane Mansbridge and John Parkinson, 52–71. Cambridge, UK: Cambridge University Press, 2012.

———. "Deliberative Democratic Theory." *Annual Review of Political Science* 6 (2003): 307–26.

———. "The Epistemic Ideal of Reason-Giving in Deliberative Democracy." *Social Epistemology Review and Reply Collective* 6, no. 10 (2017): 59–64.

Chandler, William M. "Canadian Socialism and Policy Impact: Contagion from the Left?" *Canadian Journal of Political Science* 10, no. 4 (1977): 755–80.

Charron, Nicolas, and Victor LaPuente. "Does Democracy Produce Quality of Government?" *European Journal of Political Research* 49 (2010): 443–70.

Cheng, Christine, and Margit Tavits. "Informal Influences in Selecting Female Political Candidates." *Political Research Quarterly* 64, no. 2 (2011): 460–71.

Cohen, Daniel. "The Political Legacy of Neoconservative Rhetoric and Governance: A Comparative Study of the Impact of Political Leadership on Consumer Sentiment in Canada and the United States." PhD diss., Carleton University, 1998.

Coles, Terri. "Women and Visible Minorities Make Election Gains." *Yahoo News*, 2015. https://ca.news.yahoo.com/blogs/canada-politics/women-and-visible-minorities-make-election-gains-154729934.html.

Coletto, David, Lisa Young, and Harold Jansen. "Stratarchical Party Organization and Party Finance in Canada." *Canadian Journal of Political Science* 44, no. 1 (2011): 111–36.

Conference Board of Canada. "Confidence in Parliament." 2016. http://www.conferenceboard.ca/hcp/details/society/trust-in-parliament.aspx.

Consentino, Gina. "Treaty Federalism: Bridging Praxis, Theory, Research, and Pedagogy." In *Racism Eh? A Critical Inter-Disciplinary Anthology of Race and Racism in Canada*, edited by Camille A. Nelson and Charmaine A. Nelson, 136–52. Concord, ON: Captus Press, 2004.

Cooperative Commonwealth Federation. "The Regina Manifesto." 1933. http://www.socialisthistory.ca/Docs/CCF/ReginaManifesto.htm.

Corak, Miles. "Inequality, Life Chances, and Public Policy." Paper presented to the European Investment Bank, Luxembourg, 2016.

Courtney, John C. *Commissioned Ridings: Designing Canada's Electoral Districts*. Montreal and Kingston: McGill-Queen's University Press, 2000.

———. "Electoral Boundary Redistributions: Contrasting Approaches to Parliamentary Representation." In *Comparative Political Studies: Australia and Canada*, edited by Malcolm Alexander and Brian Galligan, 45–58. Melbourne: Longmans Cheshire, 1992.

———. "Naming Canada's Constituencies." *Canadian Parliamentary Review* 23 (2000): 27–29.

Coyne, Andrew. "Trudeau Cabinet Should Be Based on Merit, Not Gender." *National Post*, November 2, 2015. http://news.nationalpost.com/full-comment/andrew-coyne-trudeau-cabinet-should-be-built-on-merit-not-gender.

Creighton, Donald G. "George Brown, Sir John A. Macdonald, and the 'Workingman.'" *Canadian Historical Review* 24, no. 4 (1943): 362–76.

Crete, Jean, Réjean Pelletier, and Jérome Couture. "Political Trust in Canada: What Matters: Politics or Economics?" Paper prepared for the annual meeting of the Canadian Political Science Association, Toronto, 2006.

Cross, William P. *Political Parties*. Vancouver: UBC Press, 2004.

Crysdale, Stewart. *The Industrial Struggle and Protestant Ethics in Canada: A Survey of Changing Power Structures and Christian Social Ethics*. Toronto: Ryerson Press, 1961.

Cuthand, Beth. "The Constitution: 'Existing' Rights Recognized But…" *Saskatchewan Indian* 11, no. 11 (1981): 1–2.

Cuthand, Doug. "Allan Blakeney Showed Politics a Noble Calling." *StarPhoenix* [Saskatoon], April 21, 2011, A15.

Dahl, Robert A. *Democracy and Its Critics*. New Haven, CT: Yale University Press, 1999.

———. *Polyarchy: Participation and Opposition*. New Haven, CT: Yale University Press, 1973.

Dalton, Russell J. *Democratic Challenges, Democratic Choices: The Erosion of Political Support in Advanced Industrial Democracies*. New York: Oxford University Press, 2004.

Data 360. "Spot Oil Price: West Texas Intermediate." N.d. http://www.data360.org/dataset.aspx?Data_Set_Id=428.

Dippel, Scott. "Calgary MLA Stephanie McLean Makes History as Alberta's First Pregnant MLA." CBC News, November 3, 2015. https://www.cbc.ca/news/canada/calgary/mla-stephanie-mclean-is-pregnant-in-a-first-for-alberta-1.3302148.

Ditonto, Tessa M., Allison J. Hamilton, and David P. Redlawsk. "Gender Stereotypes, Information Search, and Voting Behavior in Political Campaigns." *Political Behavior* 36, no. 2 (2014): 335–58.

Dosman, James. "The Medical Care Issue as a Factor in the Electoral Defeat of the Saskatchewan Government." MA thesis, University of Saskatchewan, 1969.

Drolet, Marie. "Why Has the Gender Wage Gap Narrowed?" Statistics Canada, 2010.

Druckman, James. "Pathologies of Studying Public Opinion, Political Communication, and Democratic Responsiveness." *Political Communication* 31 (2014): 467–92.

Druckman, James, and Lawrence Jacobs. *Who Governs? Presidents, Public Opinion, and Manipulation*. Chicago: University of Chicago Press, 2015.

Drummond, Robert. "Ontario." In *Canadian Annual Review of Politics and Public Affairs, 1995*, ed. David Leyton-Brown, 103–17. Toronto: University of Toronto Press, 2002.

Ducharme, Michel. *The Age of Liberty in Canada during the Age of Atlantic Revolution, 1776–1838*. Translated by Peter Feldstein. Montreal and Kingston: McGill-Queen's University Press, 2014.

Dutil, Patrice. *The Guardian: Perspectives on the Ministry of Finance of Ontario*. Toronto: University of Toronto Press, 2011.

Dyck, Rand. "The Canada Assistance Plan: The Ultimate in Cooperative Federalism." *Canadian Public Administration* 19, no. 4 (1976): 587–602.

———. *Provincial Politics in Canada: Towards the Turn of the Century*. Scarborough, ON: Prentice-Hall, 1996.

Eisler, Dale. *Rumours of Glory: Saskatchewan and the Thatcher Years*. Edmonton: Hurtig Publishers, 1987.

EKOS. "From the End of History to the End of Progress: The Shifting Meaning of Middle Class." 2014. http://www.ekospolitics.com/index.php/category/inequality.

Elster, Jon. "Conclusion." In *Collective Wisdom: Principles and Mechanisms*, edited by Hélène Landemore and Jon Elster, 393–404. Cambridge, UK: Cambridge University Press, 2012.

Erickson, Lynda, and Maria Zakharova. "Members, Activists, and Party Opinion." In *Reviving Social Democracy: The Near Death and Surprising Rise of the Federal NDP*, edited by David Laycock and Lynda Erickson, 156–96. Vancouver: UBC Press, 2015.

Erikson, Robert S., Michael B. Mackuen, and James A. Stimson. *The Macro Polity*. Cambridge, UK: Cambridge University Press, 2002.

Estlund, David. "Beyond Fairness and Deliberation: The Epistemic Dimension of Democratic Authority." In *Deliberative Democracy: Essays on Reason and Politics*, edited by James Bohman and William Rehg, 173–204. Cambridge, MA: MIT Press, 1997.

Everett, Robert. "Parliament and Politics." In *Canadian Annual Review of Politics and Public Affairs, 1992,* edited by David Leyton-Brown, 13–58. Toronto: University of Toronto Press, 1998.

Federation of Canadian Municipalities. "About Women in Local Government." 2015. http://www.fcm.ca/home/programs/women-in-local-government/about-women-in-local-government.htm.

———. "Women in Local Government: Diverse Voices for Change." 2016. http://www.fcm.ca/home/programs/women-in-local-government/diverse-voices-for-change.htm.

———. "Women in Local Government: Regional Champions." 2016. http://www.fcm.ca/home/programs/women-in-local-government/diverse-voices-for-change/regional-champions.htm.

Federation of Sovereign Indigenous Nations (FSIN). "FSIN Annual Report 2015–2016." 2016. http://www.fsin.com/2016/10/27/fsin-annual-report-2015-2016/.

———. "Portfolio Report: Lands and Resources Secretariat." 2008. http://www.fsin.com/landsandresources/downloads/Lands%20Resources%20Commission%20Portfolio%20Report%20Nov%202008.pdf.

Feigert, Frank. *Canada Votes, 1935–1988.* Durham, NC: Duke University Press, 1989.

Fekete, Jason. "'Government Does Not Have a Place in Your Bedroom': Conservatives Vote to Accept Same Sex Marriages." *Ottawa Citizen,* May 28, 2016. https://nationalpost.com/news/canada/government-does-not-have-a-place-in-your-bedroom-conservatives-vote-to-accept-same-sex-marriages.

Ferguson, Sarah Jane. "Women and Education: Qualifications, Skills, and Technology." In *Women in Canada: A Gender-Based Statistical Report,* 1–31. Ottawa: Statistics Canada, 2016. Catalogue No. 89-503-X. https://www150.statcan.gc.ca/n1/pub/89-503-x/2015001/article/14640-eng.htm.

Ferraro, Vincent. "Paid Work." Statistics Canada, Social and Aboriginal Statistics Division, 2010.

Ferreras, Jesse. "Canada's Voter Turnout in the Election Was the Highest in 2 Decades." *Huffington Post,* October 21, 2015. https://www.huffingtonpost.ca/2015/10/20/canada-voter-turnout_n_8335662.html.

Fine, Sean. "Christian Doctors Challenge Ontario's Assisted Death Referral Requirement." *Globe and Mail,* June 22, 2016. https://www.theglobeandmail.com/news/national/christian-doctors-challenge-ontarios-assisted-death-referral-policy/article30552327.

———. "PEI Drops Opposition to Abortion, Plans to Provide Access by Year's End." *Globe and Mail,* March 31, 2016. https://www.theglobeandmail.com/news/national/pei-to-allow-abortions/article29474278.

———. "Pro-Choice Group to Take PEI to Court over Abortion Access." *Globe and Mail,* January 5, 2016. https://www.theglobeandmail.com/news/national/abortion-rights-group-plans-to-take-pei-to-court-over-access-issues/article28018169.

Fishkin, James. *When the People Speak: Deliberative Democracy and Public Consultation.* Oxford: Oxford University Press, 2009.

Foa, Roberto, and Yascha Mounk. "The Danger of Deconsolidation." *Journal of Democracy* 27, no. 3 (2016): 5–17.

Forbes, Hugh D. "Trudeau as the First Theorist of Canadian Multiculturalism." In *Multiculturalism and the Canadian Constitution*, edited by Stephen Tierney, 27–42. Vancouver: UBC Press, 2007.

Fournier, Patrick. "The Uninformed Canadian Voter." In *Citizen Politics: Research and Theory in Canadian Political Behaviour*, edited by Joanna Everitt and Brenda O'Neill, 92–109. Toronto: Oxford University Press, 2002.

Fournier, Patrick, Fred Cutler, Stuart Soroka, and Dietlind Stolle. *The 2011 Canadian Election Study* (data set).

Franceschet, Susan, Karen Beckwith, and Claire Annesley. "Why Are We Still Debating Diversity versus Merit in 2015?" *Federation for the Humanities and Social Sciences*, 2015. http://www.ideas-idees.ca/blog/why-are-we-still-debating-diversity-versus-merit-2015.

Friendly, Martha, Jane Beach, Carolyn Ferns, and Michelle Turiano. *Early Childhood Education and Care in Canada 2006*. Toronto: Childcare Resource and Research Unit, University of Toronto, 2007.

Fukuyama, Francis. *State Building: Governance and World Order in the 21st Century*. Ithaca, NY: Cornell University Press, 2004.

———. *Trust: The Social Virtues and the Creation of Prosperity*. New York: Free Press, 1996.

Gans, Herbert. *The War against the Poor*. New York: Basic Books, 1995.

Gardiner, Becky, Mahana Mansfield, Ian Anderson, Josh Holder, Daan Louter, and Monica Ulmanu. "The Dark Side of *Guardian* Comments." *The Guardian*, April 12, 2016. https://www.theguardian.com/technology/2016/apr/12/the-dark-side-of-guardian-comments.

Gidengil, Elisabeth. "Beyond the Gender Gap: Presidential Address to the Canadian Political Science Association, Saskatoon, 2007." *Canadian Journal of Political Science* 40, 4 (2007): 815–31.

Gidengil, Elisabeth, André Blais, Neil Nevitte, and Richard Nadeau. *Citizens*. Vancouver: UBC Press, 2004.

Gidengil, Elisabeth, Janine Giles, and Melanee Thomas. "The Gender Gap in Self-Perceived Understanding of Politics in Canada and the United States." *Politics and Gender* 4, no. 4 (2008): 535–61.

Gidengil, Elisabeth, Allison Harell, and Bonnie Erickson. "Network Diversity and Vote Choice: Women's Social Ties and Left Voting in Canada." *Politics and Gender* 3, no. 2 (2007): 151–77.

Gilens, Martin. "Inequality and Democratic Responsiveness." *Public Opinion Quarterly* 69, no. 5 (2005): 778–96.

Gilens, Martin, and Benjamin Page. "Testing Theories of American Politics: Elites, Interest Groups, and Average Citizens." *Perspectives on Politics* 12, no. 3 (2014): 564–81.

Gingrich, Paul. *Boom and Bust: The Growing Income Gap in Saskatchewan*. Regina: Canadian Centre for Policy Alternatives, 2009.

Glazer, Amihai, and Lawrence S. Rothenberg. *Why Government Succeeds and Why It Fails*. Cambridge, MA: Harvard University Press, 2001.

Globe and Mail. "Industry Finds Timing of Potash Proposals Surprising." *Globe and Mail*, November 13, 1975, B5.

———. "REPORT ON CANADA: Potash Prorationing Is Suspended by Saskatchewan to Meet Demand." *Globe and Mail*, April 23, 1974, B3.

———. "Saskatchewan Doubles Fee for Potash." *Globe and Mail*, October 3, 1973, B11.

———. "Schreyer Calls for Review of Welfare Programs for the Able-Bodied." *Globe and Mail*, December 18, 1972, A4.

———. "Some Changes Have Been Made." September 19, 1959, A10.

———. "Tax on Potash Quadrupled, Saskatchewan Seeks Equity." *Globe and Mail*, October 24, 1974, B1.

Glor, Eleanor. *Policy Innovation in the Saskatchewan Public Service, 1971–82*. Toronto: Captus Press, 1997.

Goldsworthy, Jeffrey. *Parliamentary Sovereignty: Contemporary Debates*. Cambridge, UK: Cambridge University Press, 2010.

Goodin, Robert. *Innovating Democracy: Democratic Theory and Practice after the Deliberative Turn*. Oxford: Oxford University Press, 2008.

Goodin, Robert, and Kai Spiekermann. "Epistemic Aspects of Representative Government." *European Political Science Review* 4 (2012): 303–25.

Goodyear-Grant, Elizabeth. "Who Votes for Women and Why? Evidence from Recent Canadian Elections." In *Voting Behaviour in Canada*, edited by Cameron D. Anderson and Laura B. Stephenson, 43–64. Vancouver: UBC Press, 2010.

Gordon, Sandford, Catherine Hafer, and Dimitri Landa. "Consumption or Investment? On Motivations for Political Giving." *Journal of Politics* 69, no. 4 (2007): 1057–72.

Goren, Paul. *On Voter Competence*. New York: Oxford University Press, 2013.

Gould, Arthur. "The Salaried Middle Class in the Corporatist Welfare State." *Policy and Politics* 9, no. 4 (1981): 401–18.

Gramsci, Antonio. *Prison Notebooks*. New York: Columbia University Press, 2011.

Grant, Kelly. "Second Moncton Hospital Only New Site to Offer Abortions in N.B." *Globe and Mail*, February 24, 2015. https://www.theglobeandmail.com/news/national/second-moncton-hospital-only-new-site-to-offer-abortions-in-nb/article23193068.

Grant, Ruth W. "Ethics and Incentives: A Political Approach." *American Political Science Review* 100, no. 1 (2006): 29–39.

Graves, Frank. "Canadian Public Opinion on Taxes." In *Tax Is Not a Four-Letter Word*, edited by Alex Himelfarb and Jordan Himelfarb, 83–100. Waterloo, ON: Wilfrid Laurier University Press, 2013.

Greenlee, Jill, Mirya Holman, and Rachel VanSickle-Ward. "Why Women's Representation May Suffer When Hillary Clinton Is Attacked as 'Ambitious' and 'Unqualified.'" *Washington Post*, April 10, 2016. https://www.washingtonpost.com/news/monkey-cage/wp/2016/04/10/why-womens-representation-may-suffer-when-hillary-clinton-is-attacked-as-ambitious-and-unqualified/?utm_term=.e2259fa97603.

Greschner, Donna, and Ken Norman. "The Courts and Section 33." *Queen's Law Journal* 12 (1987): 155–98.

Grey, Jeff. "As Ontario Government Plans Rare Weekend Session, Charter Architects Condemn Premier's Action." *Globe and Mail*, September 14, 2018, A8.

Grofman, Bernard, and Scott L. Feld. "Rousseau's General Will: A Condorcetian Perspective." *American Political Science Review* 82, no. 2 (1988): 567–76.

Grönlund, Kimmo, André Bächtiger, and Maija Setälä. *Deliberative Mini-Publics: Involving Citizens in the Democratic Process*. Colchester, UK: ECPR Press, 2014.

Gruending, Dennis. "Allan Blakeney." In *Saskatchewan Premiers of the Twentieth Century*, edited by Gordon L. Barnhart, 271–316. Regina: Canadian Plains Research Center, 2004.

——. *Promises to Keep: A Political Biography of Allan Blakeney*. Saskatoon: Western Producer Prairie Books, 1990.

Guest, Dennis. *The Emergence of Social Security in Canada, 3rd Edition*. Vancouver: UBC Press, 1999.

Habermas, Jürgen. *Between Facts and Norms: Contributions to a Discourse Theory of Law and Democracy*. Translated by William Rheg. Malden, MA: MIT Press, 1996.

——. "Political Communication in Media Society: Does Democracy Still Enjoy an Epistemic Dimension? The Impact of Normative Theory on Empirical Research." *Communication Theory* 16 (2006): 411–26.

Hamilton, Alexander, and James Madison. "The Federalist No. 51: The Structure of the Government must Furnish the Proper Checks and Balances Between the Different Departments (1788)." In *The Federalist: A Commentary on the Constitution of the United States, Being a Collection of Essays written in Support of the Constitution agreed upon September 17, 1787, by the Federal Convention*, from the original text of Alexander Hamilton, John Jay, and James Madison, 335–41. New York: The Modern Library, 1941.

Handley, Lisa, and Bernard Grofman, eds. *Redistricting in Comparative Perspective*. Oxford: Oxford University Press, 2008.

Hannagan, Rebecca J., and Christopher W. Larimer. "Does Gender Composition Affect Group Decision Outcomes? Evidence from a Laboratory Experiment." *Political Behavior* 32, no. 1 (2010): 51–68.

Harding, Jim. *Social Policy and Social Justice: The NDP Government in Saskatchewan during the Blakeney Years*. Waterloo, ON: Wilfrid Laurier University Press, 1995.

Hay, John. "A General View of Socialistic Schemes." *Queen's Quarterly* 3, no. 4 (1896): 281–95.

Hayek, Friedrich A. "The Use of Knowledge in Society." *The American Economic Review* 35, no. 4 (1945): 519–30.
Hedges, Chris. *Wages of Rebellion*. New York: Nation Books, 2016.
Heldman, Caroline, Susan J. Carroll, and Stephanie Olson. "She Brought Only a Skirt: Print Media Coverage of Elizabeth Dole's Bid for the Republican Presidential Nomination." *Political Communication* 22, no. 3 (2005): 315–35.
Henderson, James (Sakej) Youngblood. "Empowering Treaty Federalism." *Saskatchewan Law Review* 58, no. 2 (1994): 241–329.
Hendriks, Carolyn M. *The Politics of Public Deliberation: Citizen Engagement and Interest Advocacy*. New York: Palgrave Macmillan, 2011.
Hetherington, Marc J. *Why Trust Matters*. Princeton, NJ: Princeton University Press, 2006.
Hibbing, John R., and Elizabeth Theiss-Morse. *Stealth Democracy: Americans' Beliefs about How Government Should Work*. Cambridge, UK: Cambridge University Press, 2002.
Himelfarb, Alex, and Jordan Himelfarb, eds. *Tax Is Not a Four-Letter Word*. Waterloo, ON: Wilfrid Laurier University Press, 2013.
Hochschild, Jennifer, and Katherine Levine Einstein. "Do Facts Matter? Information and Misinformation in American Politics." *Political Science Quarterly* 130, no. 4 (2015–16): 585–624.
Holmberg, Soren, and Bo Rothstein. "Correlates of Democracy." Working Paper Series 10. Quality of Government Institute, University of Gothenberg, 2011.
Hong, Lu, and Scott E. Page. "Some Microfoundations of Collective Wisdom." In *Collective Wisdom: Principles and Mechanisms*, edited by Hélène Landemore and Jon Elster, 56–71. Cambridge, UK: Cambridge University Press, 2012.
Horn, Michiel. *The League for Social Reconstruction: Intellectual Origins of the Democratic Left in Canada, 1930–1942*. Toronto: University of Toronto Press, 1980.
Horowitz, Gad. "Conservatism, Liberalism, and Socialism in Canada: An Interpretation." *Canadian Journal of Economics and Political Science* 32, no. 2 (1966): 143–71.
Howell, Colin D. "Medical Science and Social Criticism: Alexander Peter Reid and the Ideological Origins of the Welfare State." In *Canadian Health Care and the State: A Century of Evolution*, edited by C. David Naylor, 16–37. Montreal and Kingston: McGill-Queen's University Press, 1992.
Howell, Keith. "Public Relations Enhanced by Program." *Saskatchewan Indian* 9, nos. 11–12 (1979): 14.
Hueglin, Thomas O. "Exploring Concepts of Treaty Federalism." In *For Seven Generations: An Information Legacy of the Royal Commission on Aboriginal Peoples*, 1–88. Ottawa: Royal Commission on Aboriginal Peoples, 1997.
Hulchanski, David J. "The Three Cities within Toronto: Income Polarization among Toronto's Neighbourhoods, 1970–2005." Cities Centre, University of Toronto, 2010.
Ibbitson, John. *Stephen Harper*. Toronto: Signal, 2015.

Irving, Allan. "Canadian Fabians: The Work and Thought of Harry Cassidy and Leonard Marsh, 1930–1945." *Canadian Journal of Social Work Education* 7, no. 1 (1981): 7–28.

Jacobs, Lawrence, and Benjamin Page. "Who Influences US Foreign Policy?" *American Political Science Review* 99, no. 1 (2005): 107–23.

Jacobs, Lawrence, and Robert Shapiro. *Politicians Don't Pander: Political Manipulation and the Loss of Democratic Responsiveness*. Chicago: University of Chicago Press, 2000.

Jacobson, Gary. "Measuring Campaign Spending Effects in U.S. House Elections." In *Capturing Campaign Effects*, edited by Henry E. Brady and Richard Johnston, 199–220. Ann Arbor: University of Michigan Press, 2009.

Janigan, Mary. *Let the Eastern Bastards Freeze in the Dark: The West versus the Rest since Confederation*. Toronto: Knopf Canada, 2012.

Jansen, Harold, and Lisa Young. "Cartels, Syndicates, and Coalitions: Canada's Political Parties after the 2004 Reforms." In *Money, Politics, and Democracy: Canada's Party Finance Reforms*, edited by Lisa Young and Harold Jansen, 82–103. Vancouver: UBC Press, 2011.

Johnson, Al W. "Administrative Systems and Methods." In *Proceedings of the Fourth Annual Conference of the Institute of Public Administration of Canada*, edited by Philip Clark, 34–44. Toronto: Institute of Public Administration of Canada, 1952.

———. *Dream No Little Dreams: A Biography of the Douglas Government of Saskatchewan, 1944–1961*. Toronto: University of Toronto Press, 2004.

———. "The Treasury Board in Saskatchewan." In *Proceedings of the Seventh Annual Conference of the Institute of Public Administration of Canada*, edited by Philip Clark, 99–112. Toronto: Institute of Public Administration of Canada, 1955.

Johnston, Richard. "Prime Ministerial Contenders in Canada." In *Leaders' Personalities and the Outcomes of Democratic Elections*, edited by Anthony King, 158–83. Oxford: Oxford University Press, 2002.

Johnston, Richard, André Blais, Elisabeth Gidengil, and Neil Nevitte. *The Challenge of Direct Democracy: The 1992 Canadian Referendum*. Montreal and Kingston: McGill-Queen's University Press, 1996.

Johnstone, Rachael. "The Politics of Abortion in New Brunswick." *Atlantis* 36, no. 2 (2014): 73–87.

Judt, Tony. *Ill Fares the Land*. New York: Penguin, 2010.

Kahana, Tsvi. "The Notwithstanding Mechanism and Public Discussion: Lessons from the Ignored Practice of Section 33 of the Charter." *Canadian Public Administration* 44 (2001): 255–91.

———. "Understanding the Notwithstanding Mechanism." *University of Toronto Law Journal* 52 (2002): 221–74.

Kahane, Adam. "Alex Himelfarb on Austerity, Inequality, and 'Trickle-Down Meanness.'" *Globe and Mail*, December 19, 2014. https://www.theglobeandmail.

com/opinion/alex-himelfarb-on-austerity-inequality-and-trickle-down-meanness/article22151886/.

Kathlene, Lyn. "Power and Influence in State Legislative Policymaking: The Interaction of Gender and Position in Committee Hearing Debates." *American Political Science Review* 88, no. 3 (1994): 560–76.

Kaufmann, Bill. "Province Rejects Reappointment of U of C Governors." *Calgary Herald*, April 22, 2016. https://calgaryherald.com/news/local-news/province-rejects-reappointment-of-u-of-c-governors.

Keefer, Phillip. "Clientelism, Credibility, and the Political Choices of Young Democracies." *American Journal of Political Science* 51, no. 4 (2007): 804–21.

Kennedy, Priscilla. "The Duty to Consult: Constitutional Recognition of Treaty and Aboriginal Rights." Paper No. 33, Legal Resource Centre of Alberta, 2008.

Kennedy, Thomas. "NEB Told $6.50 Price for Crude Rests on Continued Sales to U.S." *Globe and Mail*, February 4, 1974, B2.

King, William Lyon Mackenzie. *Industry and Humanity: A Study in the Principles Under-Lying Industrial Reconstruction*. Toronto: Houghton Mifflin, 1918.

Kitcher, Philip. "Public Knowledge and the Difficulties of Democracy." *Social Research* 73, no. 4 (2006): 1205–24.

Knickerbocker, Madeline R., and Sarah Nickel. "Negotiating Sovereignty: Indigenous Perspectives on the Patriation of a Settler Colonial Constitution, 1975–83." BC *Studies* 190 (2016): 67–87, 180.

Knight, Jack, and James Johnson. *The Priority of Democracy: Political Consequences of Pragmatism*. Princeton, NJ: Princeton University Press, 2011.

Kopniak, Kathryn. "Women in Canadian Municipal Politics: Two Steps Forward, One Step Back." *Canadian Review of Sociology and Anthropology* 22, no. 3 (1985): 394–410.

Krasowski, Sheldon. *No Surrender: The Land Remains Indigenous*. Regina: University of Regina Press, 2019.

Krook, Mona Lena. *Quotas for Women in Politics: Gender and Candidate Selection Reform Worldwide*. Oxford: Oxford University Press, 2009.

Kudrle, Robert T., and Theodore R. Marmor. "The Development of Welfare States in North America." In *The Development of Welfare States in Europe and North America*, edited by Peter Flora and Arnold J. Heidenheimer, 81–122. London: Transaction Books, 1981.

Ladner, Kiera L. "Treaty Federalism: An Indigenous Vision of Canadian Federalisms." In *New Trends in Canadian Federalism*, 2nd ed., edited by M. Smith and F. Rocher, 167–96. Peterborough, ON: Broadview, 2003.

Landemore, Hélène. *Democratic Reason: Politics, Collective Intelligence, and the Rule of the Many*. Princeton, NJ: Princeton University Press, 2013.

———. "Yes, We Can (Make It Up on Volume): Answers to Critics." *Critical Review* 26, nos. 1–2 (2014): 184–237.

Laurier, Wilfrid. *Lecture on Political Liberalism*. Quebec: Morning Chronicle, 1877.

Lawless, Jennifer, and Richard Fox. *It Still Takes a Candidate: Why Women Don't Run for Office*. Cambridge, UK: Cambridge University Press, 2010.

Lazarsfeld, Paul, Bernard Berelson, and Hazel Gaudet. *The People's Choice: How the Voter Makes Up His Mind in a Presidential Election*. New York: Columbia University Press, 1948.

LeDuc, Lawrence, Judith I. McKenzie, Jon H. Pammett, and André Turcotte. *Dynasties and Interludes: Past and Present in Canadian Electoral Politics*. Toronto: Dundurn, 2010.

Lemieux, Rodolphe, et al., eds. *Canadian Annual Review of Public Affairs, 1926–27*. Toronto: Canadian Review Company, 1927.

Levin, David. "Measuring the Effectiveness of Programs." In *Proceedings of the Fifth Annual Conference of the Institute of Public Administration of Canada*, edited by Philip Clark, 119–25. Toronto: Institute of Public Administration of Canada, 1953.

Levitsky, Stephen, and Daniel Ziblatt. *How Democracies Die*. New York: Crown Publishing, 2018.

Lewis, David. *The Good Fight*. Toronto: Macmillan, 1981.

Lewis, David, and Frank Scott. *Make This Your Canada: A Review of CCF History and Policy*. Toronto: Central Canada Publishing, 1943.

Lewis, Thomas, ed. *The Making of a Socialist: The Recollections of T.C. Douglas*. Edmonton: University of Alberta Press, 1982.

Liberal Party of Canada. *Moving Canada Forward: The Paul Martin Plan for Getting Things Done*. 2004. http://www.collectionscanada.gc.ca/eppp-archive/100/205/300/liberal-ef/05-05-24/www.liberal.ca/documents/platform_en.pdf.

Lien, Pei-Te. "Does the Gender Gap in Political Attitudes and Behavior Vary across Racial Groups?" *Political Research Quarterly* 51, no. 4 (1998): 869–94.

Lindblom, Charles. *The Intelligence of Democracy*. New York: Free Press, 1965.

Lipset, Seymour. *Agrarian Socialism: The Cooperative Commonwealth Federation in Saskatchewan: A Study in Political Sociology*. New York: Doubleday, 1968.

Lipsitz, Keena. "Democratic Theory and Political Campaigns." *Journal of Political Philosophy* 12, no. 2 (2004): 163–89.

List, Christian. "Collective Wisdom: Lessons from the Theory of Judgment Aggregation." In *Collective Wisdom: Principles and Mechanisms*, edited by Hélène Landemore and Jon Elster, 203–29. Cambridge, UK: Cambridge University Press, 2012.

List, Christian, and Robert E. Goodin. "Epistemic Democracy: Generalizing the Condorcet Theorem." *The Journal of Political Philosophy* 9, no. 3 (2001): 277–306.

Lougheed, Peter. *Why a Notwithstanding Clause?* Edmonton: University of Alberta Centre for Constitutional Studies, 1998.

Lupia, Arthur W. *Uninformed: Why People Know So Little about Politics and What We Can Do about It*. New York: Oxford University Press, 2016.

Lupia, Arthur W., and Mathew D. McCubbins. *The Democratic Dilemma*. Cambridge, UK: Cambridge University Press, 1998.

MacCharles, Tonda. "Ottawa Surprises Top Court Judges by Allowing Assisted Suicide to Proceed in Quebec." *Toronto Star*, January 11, 2016. https://www.thestar.com/news/canada/2016/01/11/ottawa-surprises-top-court-judges-by-asking-for-more-time-on-assisted-suicide.html.

Machiavelli, Niccolò. *The Prince*. 1532; reprinted, Boston: Dante University Press, 1903.

MacInnis, Grace. *J.S. Woodsworth, a Man to Remember*. Toronto: Macmillan, 1953.

MacKenzie, Norman, and Jeanne MacKenzie. *The Fabians*. New York: Simon and Schuster, 1977.

Mackie, Gerry. *Democracy Defended*. Cambridge, UK: Cambridge University Press, 2003.

MacKinnon, Janice. "'Agrarian Socialism' and Saskatchewan's Distinctiveness: A Perspective from the 1990s." In *Lipset's Agrarian Socialism: A Re-Examination*, edited by David E. Smith, 51–62. Regina: Saskatchewan Institute of Public Policy, 2007.

Maclean's. "Welfare Crackdown." *Maclean's*, April 11, 1994, 21.

MacPherson, Marion. "The Relationship between the Senior Public Servant and the Minister of the Crown." In *Proceedings of the Fifth Annual Conference of the Institute of Public Administration of Canada*, edited by Philip Clark, 143–51. Toronto: Institute of Public Administration of Canada, 1953.

Madison, James. "The Federalist No. 10: The Same Subject Continued (1787)." In *The Federalist: A Commentary on the Constitution of the United States, Being a Collection of Essays written in Support of the Constitution agreed upon September 17, 1787, by the Federal Convention*, from the original text of Alexander Hamilton, John Jay, and James Madison, 53–62. New York: The Modern Library, 1941.

Mansbridge, Jane. "Should Blacks Represent Blacks and Women Represent Women? A Contingent 'Yes.'" *The Journal of Politics* 61, no. 3 (1999): 628–57.

Marchildon, Gregory P. "Foreword." In *Dream No Little Dreams: A Biography of the Douglas Government of Saskatchewan, 1944–1961*, by Al W. Johnson, xv–xxxi. Toronto: University of Toronto Press, 2004.

———. "The Great Divide." In *The Heavy Hand of History: Interpreting Saskatchewan's Past*, edited by Gregory P. Marchildon, 51–66. Regina: Canadian Plains Research Center, 2005.

———. "The Secretary to the Cabinet in Saskatchewan: Evolution of the Role, 1944–2006." In *Searching for Leadership: Secretaries to the Cabinet in Canada*, edited by Patrice Dutil, 161–84. Toronto: University of Toronto Press, 2008.

Marchildon, Gregory P., and Catherine Leviten-Reid, eds. *Privilege and Policy: A History of Community Clinics in Saskatchewan*. Regina: Canadian Plains Research Center, 2012.

Marchildon, Gregory P., and Klaartje Schrijvers. "Physician Resistance and the Forging of Public Health Care: A Comparative Analysis of Doctors' Strikes in Canada and Belgium in the 1960s." *Medical History* 55, no. 2 (2011): 203–22.

Marsh, Leonard. *Report on Social Security for Canada*. Ottawa: King's Printer, 1943.
Martin, Judith. "The Continuing Struggle for Universal Daycare." In *Social Policy and Social Justice: The NDP Government in Saskatchewan during the Blakeney Years*, edited by Jim Harding, 17–52. Waterloo, ON: Wilfrid Laurier University Press, 1995.
Maskin, Eric, and Amartya Sen. *The Arrow Impossibility Theorem*. New York: Columbia University Press, 2014.
Mayo, Henry B. "Justifying Democracy." *American Political Science Review* 56, no. 3 (1962): 555–66.
Mazzucato, Mariana. *The Entrepreneurial State*. London: Anthem Press, 2013.
McBriar, A.M. *Fabian Socialism and English Politics, 1884–1918*. Cambridge, UK: Cambridge University Press, 1962.
McCarten, James, ed. *The Canadian Press Stylebook: A Guide for Writers and Editors*. Toronto: Canadian Press, 2013.
McDonald, Henry. "Ireland Becomes First Country to Legalise Gay Marriage by Popular Vote." *The Guardian*, May 23, 2015. https://www.theguardian.com/world/2015/may/23/gay-marriage-ireland-yes-vote.
McDonald, Henry, Emma Graham-Harrison, and Sinead Baker. "Ireland Votes by Landslide to Legalise Abortion." *The Guardian*, May 26, 2018. https://www.theguardian.com/world/2018/may/26/ireland-votes-by-landslide-to-legalise-abortion.
McDonald, Lynn. *The Party that Changed Canada: The New Democratic Party, Then and Now*. Toronto: Macmillan, 1987.
McGrane, David. "Explaining the Saskatchewan NDP's Shift to Third Way Social Democracy." Paper presented at the Annual Conference of the Canadian Political Science Association, Toronto, 2006.
———. "From Liberal Multiculturalism to Civic Republicanism: An Historical Perspective on Multiculturalism in Manitoba and Saskatchewan." *Canadian Ethnic Studies* 43 (2011): 81–108.
———. "A Mixed Record: Gender and Saskatchewan Social Democracy." *Journal of Canadian Studies* 42, no. 1 (2008): 179–203.
———. *Remaining Loyal: Social Democracy in Quebec and Saskatchewan*. Montreal and Kingston: McGill-Queen's University Press, 2014.
———. "Western Alienation or Mere Critique of Federal Government Policies? Saskatchewan Social Democrats' View of Federalism from 1900 to Present." *International Journal of Canadian Studies* 32 (2005): 205–35.
McLaren, Robert I. *The Saskatchewan Practice of Public Administration in Historical Perspective*. Lewiston, NY: Edwin Mellen Press, 1998.
McLeod, Thomas H. "Administrative and Constitutional Problems Peculiar to Crown Corporations." In *Proceedings of the Eighth Annual Conference of the Institute of Public Administration of Canada*, edited by Philip Clark and Frank McGilly, 153–61. Toronto: Institute of Public Administration of Canada, 1956.

———. "Budgeting Provincial Expenditure." In *Proceedings of the Fifth Annual Conference of the Institute of Public Administration of Canada*, edited by Philip Clark, 11–19. Toronto: Institute of Public Administration of Canada, 1953.
Medel, Rebecca. "Falling Flat on Taxes." *Public Interest Alberta*, August 8, 2014, 3–4.
Mendelberg, Tali, Christopher F. Karpowitz, and J. Baxter Oliphant. "Gender Inequality in Deliberation: Unpacking the Black Box of Interaction." *Perspectives on Politics* 12, no. 1 (2014): 18–44.
Milan, Anne, Leslie-Anne Keown, and Covadonga Robles Urquijo. "Families, Living Arrangements, and Unpaid Work." In *Women in Canada: A Gender-Based Statistical Report*, 1–25. Ottawa: Statistics Canada, 2011. Catalogue No. 89-503-X. https://www150.statcan.gc.ca/n1/pub/89-503-x/2010001/article/11546-eng.pdf.
Miller, J.R. *Lethal Legacies: Current Native Controversies in Canada*. Toronto: McClelland and Stewart, 2004.
Miller, Melissa, Jeffrey Peake, and Brittany Boulton. "Testing the *Saturday Night Live* Hypothesis: Fairness and Bias in Newspaper Coverage of Hillary Clinton's Presidential Campaign." *Politics and Gender* 6, no. 2 (2010): 169–98.
Milner, Henry. *The Internet Generation: Engaged Citizens or Political Dropouts?* Medford, MA: Tufts University Press, 2010.
Moe, Terry M. "Vested Interests and Political Institutions." *Political Science Quarterly* 130, no. 2 (2015): 277–318.
Mombourquette, Duane. "'An Inalienable Right': The CCF and Rapid Health Care Reform, 1944–1948." *Saskatchewan History* 43, no. 3 (1991): 101–16.
Morellato, Maria. "The Crown's Constitutional Duty to Consult and Accommodate Aboriginal and Treaty Rights." Research paper for the National Centre for First Nations Governance, 2008.
Morgan, John. "Social Welfare Services in Canada." In *Social Purpose for Canada*, edited by Michael Oliver, 83–114. Toronto: University of Toronto Press, 1961.
Morley, Gareth. "Judges: Canada's New Aristocracy." *Inroads* 18 (2006): 30–47.
Mowat Centre. "Renewing Canada's Social Architecture." 2015. http://social-architecture.ca/.
Mungiu-Pippidi, Alina. "The Evolution of Political Order." *Journal of Democracy* 26, no. 4 (2015): 169–77.
———. *The Quest for Good Governance: How Societies Develop Control of Corruption*. Cambridge, UK: Cambridge University Press, 2015.
National Indian Brotherhood. *Indian Control of Indian Education: Policy Paper Presented to the Minister of Indian Affairs and Northern Development*. Ottawa: National Indian Brotherhood, 1972.
New Democratic Party (NDP). *Building the Country of Our Dreams*. 2015. http://xfer.ndp.ca/2015/2015-Full-Platform-EN.pdf.
———. *Giving Families a Break*. 2011. http://xfer.ndp.ca/2011/2011-Platform/NDP-2011-Platform-En.pdf.

Newhouse, David, and Yale Belanger. "The Canada Problem in Aboriginal Politics." In *Visions of the Heart: Canadian Aboriginal Issues*, 3rd Edition, edited by Olive Patricia Dickason and David Long, 51–79. Toronto: Oxford University Press, 2011.
Newman, Dwight. *Community and Collective Rights: A Theoretical Framework for Rights Held by Groups*. London: Bloomsbury Academic, 2011.
———. "Judicial Method and Three Gaps in the Supreme Court of Canada's Assisted Suicide Judgment in *Carter*." *Saskatchewan Law Review* 78 (2015): 1–6.
———. *Natural Resource Jurisdiction in Canada*. Toronto: LexisNexis, 2013.
———. "The PHS Case and Federalism-Based Alternatives to Charter Activism." *Constitutional Forum* 22, no. 1 (2013): 85–91.
Nichols, Marjorie. "Trudeau Promise Comes Back to Haunt Liberals." *Ottawa Citizen*, April 15, 1989, A3.
Niskanen, William A. *Bureaucracy and Representative Government*. Chicago: Aldine Atherton, 1971.
Norris, Pippa. *Critical Citizens: Global Support for Democratic Governance*. New York: Oxford University Press, 1999.
North, Douglas C. *Structure and Change in Economic History*. New York: W.W. Norton, 1982.
Nye, Joseph S., Philip D. Zelikow, and David C. King. *Why People Don't Trust Government*. Cambridge, MA: Harvard University Press, 1997.
Office of the Treaty Commissioner (OTC). "Statement of Treaty Issues: Treaties as a Bridge to the Future." 1998. http://www.otc.ca/pdfs/OTC_STI.pdf.
———. "Treaty Implementation: Fulfilling the Covenant." 2007. http://www.otc.ca/ABOUT_TREATIES/Treaty_Implementation_Report/.
Omand, Geordon. "Catholic Health Provider Cautious about Assisted Dying Ahead of New Law." National Newswatch, February 25, 2016. https://www.nationalnewswatch.com/2016/02/25/assisted-death-should-be-available-in-all-publicly-funded-hospitals-report/#.XFtgMFVKipo.
O'Neill, Brenda, and Melanee Thomas. "'Because It's 2015': Gender and the 2015 Federal Election." In *The Canadian Federal Election of 2015*, edited by Jon H. Pammett and Christopher Dornan, 275–304. Toronto: Dundurn Press, 2016.
Ontario College of Physicians and Surgeons. "Medical Assistance in Dying." 2016. http://www.cpso.on.ca/Policies-Publications/Policy/Physician-Assisted-Death.
O'Sullivan, Michael, and Sandra Sorensen. "Saskatchewan." In *Privatization and Provincial Social Services in Canada: Policy, Administration and Service Delivery*, edited by Jacqueline S. Ismael and Yves Vaillancourt, 75–93. Edmonton: University of Alberta Press, 1988.
Owram, Doug. "Economic Thought in the 1930s: The Prelude to Keynesianism." *Canadian Historical Review* 66, no. 3 (1985): 344–77.
Page, Benjamin. "Democratic Responsiveness? Untangling the Links between Public Opinion and Policy." *PS: Political Science and Politics* 27 (1994): 25–29.

Page, Scott E. *The Difference: How the Power of Diversity Creates Better Firms, Schools, Groups, and Societies*. Princeton, NJ: Princeton University Press, 2007.

Pal, Michael, and Sujit Choudhry. "Is Every Ballot Equal? Visible-Minority Vote Dilution in Canada." *IRPP Choices* 13, no. 1 (2007): 1–30.

Pal, Michael, and Melissa Molson. *Moving toward Voter Equality*. Toronto: Mowat Centre, 2012.

Pammet, Jon, and Lawrence LeDuc. "Explaining the Turnout Decline in Canadian Federal Elections: A New Survey of Non-Voters." Elections Canada, 2003.

Papadakis, Elim. "Class Interests, Class Politics, and Welfare State Regime." *British Journal of Sociology* 44, no. 2 (1993): 249–70.

Papillon, Martin. "Canadian Federalism and the Emerging Mosaic of Aboriginal Multilevel Governance." In *Canadian Federalism: Performance, Effectiveness, and Legitimacy*, edited by Herman Bakvis and Grace Skogstad, 291–313. Don Mills, ON: Oxford University Press, 2008.

Paus-Jenssen, Arne. "Resource Taxation and the Supreme Court of Canada: The *Cigol* Case." *Canadian Public Policy/Analyse de politiques* 5, no. 1 (1979): 45–58.

Payton, Laura. "Justin Trudeau's Feminism 'Lights the Fire' Globally: UN Official." CTV News, June 6, 2016.

Perreaux, Les. "Legault to Use Notwithstanding Clause to Ban Religious Symbols for Civil Servants." *Globe and Mail*, October 2, 2018. https://www.theglobeandmail.com/canada/article-francois-legault-to-invoke-notwithstanding-clause-to-ban-quebec-public.

Pew Research Center. "Changing Attitudes on Gay Marriage." May 12, 2016. http://www.pewforum.org/2016/05/12/changing-attitudes-on-gay-marriage/.

Picard, André. "Hospitals Have No Right to Opt Out of Assisted Dying." *Globe and Mail*, December 13, 2016. https://www.theglobeandmail.com/opinion/hospitals-have-no-right-to-opt-out-of-assisted-dying/article33303680.

Pitkin, Hanna. *The Concept of Representation*. Berkeley: University of California Press, 1967.

Pitsula, James M. "The Blakeney Government and the Settlement of Treaty Indian Land Entitlements in Saskatchewan, 1975–1982." *Historical Papers/Communications historiques* 24, no. 1 (1989): 190–209.

Potter, Andrew. "Canadian Elections for Naifs and Cynics." *In Due Course: A Canadian Public Affairs Blog*, June 24, 2015. http://www. http://induecourse.ca/canadian-elections-for-naifs-and-cynics/.

Potter, Christopher, and Richard Brough. "Systematic Capacity Building: A Hierarchy of Needs." *Health Policy and Planning* 19, no. 2 (2000): 336–45.

Powell, G. Bingham Jr. "Representation in Context: Election Laws and Ideological Congruence between Citizens and Governments." *Perspectives on Politics* 11, no. 1 (2013): 9–21.

Preece, Rod. "The Political Wisdom of John A. Macdonald." *Canadian Journal of Political Science* 17, no. 2 (1984): 459–86.

Prentice, Susan. "Manitoba's Childcare Regime: Social Liberalism in Flux." *Canadian Journal of Sociology* 29, no. 2 (2004): 193–207.
——. "Workers, Mothers, Reds: Toronto's Postwar Daycare Fight." *Studies in Political Economy* 30 (1989): 115–41.
Press Progress. "Here's Why Being a Woman in Politics Can Suck." *Press Progress*, 2015. http://www.pressprogress.ca/here_s_why_being_a_woman_in_politics_can_suck.
Prince, Michael. "At the Edge of Canada's Welfare State: Social Policy-Making in British Columbia." In *Politics, Policy, and Government in British Columbia*, edited by R. Kenneth Carty, 236–71. Vancouver: UBC Press, 1996.
Przeworski, Adam. "Material Interests, Class Compromise, and the Transition to Socialism." *Politics and Society* 10, no. 2 (1980): 125–53.
——. "Minimalist Theory of Democracy: A Defense." In *Democracy's Value*, edited by Ian Shapiro and Casiano Hacker-Cordon, 23–55. Cambridge, UK: Cambridge University Press, 1999.
Przeworski, Adam, Michael E. Alvarez, José Antonio Cheibub, and Fernando Limongi. *Democracy and Development: Political Institutions and Well-Being in the World, 1950–1990*. Cambridge, UK: Cambridge University Press, 2000.
Putnam, Robert D. *Bowling Alone: The Collapse and Revival of American Community*. New York: Simon and Schuster, 2000.
Putnam, Robert D., and Susan J. Pharr. *Disaffected Democracies: What's Troubling the Trilateral Countries?* Princeton, NJ: Princeton University Press, 2000.
Quirk, Paul. "Putting Experts in Their Place." *Critical Review* 20, no. 3 (2008): 333–57.
Rasmussen, Ken, and Gregory P. Marchildon. "Saskatchewan's Executive Decision-Making Style: The Centrality of Planning." In *Executive Styles in Canada: Cabinet Structures and Leadership Practices in Canadian Government*, edited by Luc Bernier, Keith Brownsey, and Michael Howlett, 184–207. Toronto: University of Toronto Press, 2005.
Régimbald, Guy, and Dwight Newman. *The Law of the Canadian Constitution*. Toronto: LexisNexis, 2013.
Reich, Robert. "The Government Problem." *Huffington Post*, December 24, 2014. https://www.huffingtonpost.com/robert-reich/the-government-problem_b_6376972.html.
Rekkas, Marie. "The Impact of Campaign Spending on Votes in Multiparty Elections." *The Review of Economics and Statistics* 89, no. 3 (2007): 573–85.
Research Committee of the League for Social Reconstruction (RCLSR). *Democracy Needs Socialism*. Toronto: Thomas Nelson and Sons, 1938.
——. *Social Planning for Canada*. Toronto: University of Toronto Press, 1935.
——. *Social Planning for Canada*. Toronto: University of Toronto Press, 1975.
Richards, John, and Larry Pratt. *Prairie Capitalism: Power and Influence in the New West*. Toronto: McClelland and Stewart, 1979.

Ritchie, Kaitlin. "Issues Associated with the Implementation of the Duty to Consult and Accommodate Aboriginal Peoples: Threatening the Goals of Reconciliation and Meaningful Consultation." *University of British Columbia Law Review* 46 (2013): 297–438.

Roach, Kent. *The Supreme Court on Trial: Judicial Activism or Democratic Dialogue.* Toronto: Irwin Law, 2001.

Roberts, Alasdair. *The Logic of Discipline: Global Capitalism and the Architecture of Government.* New York: Oxford University Press, 2011.

Robinson, James A. "Theories of 'Bad Policy.'" *Journal of Economic Policy Reform* 2, no. 1 (1998): 1–46.

Romanow, Roy. Interview conducted with Gregory P. Marchildon, Saskatoon, March 19, 2003.

Romanow, Roy J., John D. Whyte, and Howard A. Leeson. *Canada–Notwithstanding: The Making of the Constitution, 1976–1982.* Toronto: Carswell-Methuen, 1984.

Rothstein, Bo. "Creating Political Legitimacy: Electoral Democracy versus Quality of Government." *American Behavioral Scientist* 53, no. 3 (2009): 311–30.

———. *The Quality of Government.* Chicago: University of Chicago Press, 2011.

———. "The Three Worlds of Governance: Arguments for a Parsimonious Theory of Quality of Government." Working Paper Series 12, Quality of Government Institute, University of Gothenberg, 2013.

Rothstein, Bo, and Jan Teorell. "What Is Quality of Government? A Theory of Impartial Government Institutions." *Governance* 21, no. 2 (2008): 165–90.

Rousseau, Guillaume. "Théorie québécoise de la disposition dérogatoire: Quand la langue, l'identité, ou le social prime l'individuel." In *Un regard québécois sur le droit constitutionnel: Mélanges en l'honneur d'Henri Brun et de Guy Tremblay*, edited by Patrick Taillon, Eugénie Brouillet, and Amélie Binette, 703–18. Montréal: Éditions Yvon Blais, 2016.

Runciman, David. *The Confidence Trap: A History of Democracy in Crisis from World War I to the Present.* Princeton, NJ: Princeton University Press, 2013.

Sabl, Andrew. "The Two Cultures of Democratic Theory: Responsiveness, Democratic Quality, and the Empirical-Normative Divide." *Perspectives on Politics* 13, no. 2 (2015): 345–65.

Samuelson, William, and Richard Zeckhauser. "Status Quo Bias in Decision Making." *Journal of Risk and Uncertainty* 1, no. 1 (1988): 7–59.

Sanderson, Montague A. "Sugar-Coating the Arsenic." *Globe and Mail*, July 29, 1943, A6.

Saskatchewan NDP. *NDP...Keeping Saskatchewan Ahead.* Regina: Service Printers, 1975.

Saskatchewan Party. "Securing the Future: New Ideas for Saskatchewan." 2007. http://www.saskparty.com/assets/pdf/New%20Ideas/SecuringTheFuturePlatform.pdf.

Savoie, Donald. *What Is Government Good At?* Montreal and Kingston: McGill-Queen's University Press, 2015.

Saywell, John, ed. *Canada Annual Review for 1966.* Toronto: University of Toronto Press, 1967.
Schneider, Monica C., and Angela L. Bos. "Measuring Stereotypes of Female Politicians." *Political Psychology* 35, no. 2 (2014): 245–66.
Schuck, Peter H. *Why Government Fails So Often: And How It Can Do Better.* Princeton, NJ: Princeton University Press, 2015.
Schultz, Gudrun. "PM Martin Threatens Notwithstanding Clause, Ignores Promise to Protect Church Rights." 2006. http://www.lifesite.net/ldo/2006/jan/06011008.html.
Schumpeter, Joseph. *Capitalism, Socialism, and Democracy.* New York: Harper and Row, 1950.
Scott, R.B.Y., and Gregory Vlastos, eds. *Towards the Christian Revolution.* Chicago: Willett, Clark, 1936.
Sen, Amartya. "Democracy as a Universal Value." *Journal of Democracy* 10, no. 3 (1999): 3–17.
Shoyama, Tommy K. "Advisory Committees in Administration." In *Proceedings of the Ninth Annual Conference of the Institute of Public Administration of Canada*, edited by Philip Clark and Frank McGilly, 145–53. Toronto: University of Toronto Press, 1957.
Simcoe, L. "FSIN Rejects Proposal." *Leader-Post* [Regina], February 20, 2009, A7.
Smith, David E. *The Invisible Crown: The First Principle of Canadian Government.* Toronto: University of Toronto Press, 2013.
Smith, Joanna. "MP and Her Baby Welcome Back in Commons after 'Misunderstanding.'" *Toronto Star*, February 8, 2012. https://www.thestar.com/news/canada/2012/02/08/mp_and_her_baby_welcome_back_in_commons_after_misunderstanding.html.
Somin, Ilya. *Democracy and Political Ignorance: Why Smaller Government Is Smarter.* Stanford, CA: Stanford University Press, 2013.
Sophocles. *Antigone.* In *The Theban Plays*, translated by E.F. Watling, 126–62. London: Penguin Books, 1947.
Southwick, Reid. "NDP Government Will 'Build Feminism in Alberta,' Status of Women Minister Says." *Calgary Herald*, September 9, 2015. http://calgaryherald.com/news/local-news/ndp-government-will-build-feminism-in-alberta-status-of-women-minister-says.
Sprague, D.N. "Canada's Treaties with Aboriginal Peoples." *Manitoba Law Journal* 23 (1995): 341–51.
Statistics Canada. *Annual Demographic Estimates: Canada, Provinces, and Territories.* 2012. http://www.statcan.gc.ca/pub/91-215-x/91-215-x2012000-eng.pdf. Catalogue No. 91-215-X.
–––. NHS [National Household Survey] *Profile, 2011.* http://www12.statcan.gc.ca/nhs-enm/2011/dp-pd/prof/index.cfm?Lang=E.
Stepler, Dorothy. "Family Allowances for Canada?" *Behind the Headlines* 3, no. 2 (1945): 1–32.

Stevens, Douglas F. *Corporate Autonomy and Institutional Control: The Crown Corporation as a Problem in Organizational Design*. Montreal and Kingston: McGill-Queen's University Press, 1993.

Stevens, Paul, and John Saywell. "Parliament and Politics." In *Canadian Annual Review of Politics and Public Affairs, 1972*, edited by John Saywell, 11–14. Toronto: University of Toronto Press, 1974.

Stevenson, Allyson. "Intimate Integration: A Study of Aboriginal Transracial Adoption in Saskatchewan, 1944–1984." PhD diss., University of Saskatchewan, 2015.

Stiglitz, Joseph E. "Globalization and Its New Discontents." *Project Syndicate*, August 5, 2016, 1–4.

Stolle, Dietlind, and Elisabeth Gidengil. "What Do Women Really Know? A Gendered Analysis of Varieties of Political Knowledge." *PS: Perspectives on Politics* 8, no. 1 (2010): 93–109.

Strayer, Barry L. "The Evolution of the *Charter*." In *Patriation and Its Consequences: Constitution Making in Canada*, edited by Lois Harder and Steve Patten, 72–92. Vancouver: UBC Press, 2015.

Streeck, Wolfgang, and Armin Schäfer, eds. *Politics in the Age of Austerity*. London: Polity Press, 2013.

Sung, Hung-En. "Democracy and Political Corruption: A Cross-National Comparison." *Crime, Law, and Social Change* 41 (2004): 179–94.

Tasker, John Paul. "Maxime Bernier Criticizes Liberals for 'Extreme Multiculturalism.'" CBC News, August 13, 2018. https://www.cbc.ca/news/politics/maxime-bernier-extreme-multiculturalism-1.4783325.

Tax Policy Centre. "OECD Taxes as Share of GDP, 1965–2015." 2017. http://www.taxpolicycenter.org/statistics/oecd-taxes-share-gdp.

Taylor, Charles. *Hegel*. Cambridge, UK: Cambridge University Press, 1975.

Thomas, Melanee. "Barriers to Women's Political Participation in Canada." *University of New Brunswick Law Journal* 64, no. 1 (2013): 218–32.

———. "The Complexity Conundrum: Why Hasn't the Gender Gap in Subjective Political Competence Closed?" *Canadian Journal of Political Science* 45, no. 2 (2012): 337–58.

———. "Gender and Psychological Orientations to Politics." PhD diss., McGill University, 2012.

———. "Governing as if Women Mattered: Rachel Notley as Alberta Premier." In *Doing Politics Differently: Women Premiers in Canada's Provinces and Territories*, edited by Sylvia Bashevkin. Vancouver: UBC Press, forthcoming.

———. "Ready for Rachel: The 2015 Alberta NDP Campaign." In *The Orange Chinook: Politics in the New Alberta*, edited by Duane Bratt, Keith Brownsey, Richard Sutherland, and David Taras, 57–77. Calgary: University of Calgary Press, 2019.

Thomas, Melanee, and Marc André Bodet. "Sacrificial Lambs, Women Candidates, and District Competitiveness in Canada." *Electoral Studies* 32, no. 1 (2013): 153–66.

Thomas, Melanee, and Lisa Lambert. "Private Moms vs. Political Dads? Communications of Parental Status in the 41st Canadian Parliament." In *Mothers and Others: The Impact of Family Life on Politics*, edited by Melanee Thomas and Amanda Bittner, 135–54. Vancouver: UBC Press, 2017.

Tolley, Erin. "Visible Minority and Indigenous Members of Parliament." *The Samara Blog*, November 26, 2015. http://www.samaracanada.com/samarablog/blog-post/samara-main-blog/2015/11/26/visible-minority-and-indigenous-members-of-parliament.

Tollison, Robert D. "Rent-Seeking: A Survey." *Kyklos* 35, no. 4 (1982): 575–602.

Tong, Rosemarie. *Feminist Thought: A More Comprehensive Introduction*, 2nd Edition. Boulder, CO: Westview Press, 1998.

Tremblay, Manon. "Do Female MPs Substantively Represent Women? A Study of Legislative Behaviour in Canada's 35th Parliament." *Canadian Political Science Review* 31, no. 3 (1998): 435–65.

Trimble, Linda. "Gender, Political Leadership, and Media Visibility: *Globe and Mail* Coverage of Conservative Party of Canada Leadership Contests." *Canadian Journal of Political Science* 40, no. 4 (2007): 969–93.

Trimble, Linda, Angelia Wagner, Shannon Sampert, Daisy Raphael, and Bailey Gerrits. "Is It Personal? Gendered Mediation in Newspaper Coverage of Canadian National Party Leadership Contests, 1975–2012." *The International Journal of Press/Politics* 18, no. 4 (2013): 462–81.

Tully, James. *Strange Multiplicity: Constitutionalism in an Age of Diversity*. Cambridge, UK: Cambridge University Press, 1995.

Tzimas, Ria E. "*Haida Nation* and *Taku River*: A Commentary on Aboriginal Consultation and Reconciliation." *Supreme Court Law Review* 29, no. 2 (2005): 461–85.

Ubelacker, Sheryl. "Recommendation to Require Referrals for Assisted Death Disappointing: CMA." Canadian Press, February 26, 2016.

Union of BC Indian Chiefs. "The Indian Nations and the Federal Government's View on the Constitution." 1980. http://constitution.ubcic.bc.ca/sites/constitution.ubcic.bc.ca/files/OCRIndianNations&FederalGovView.pdf.

Venne, Sharon. "Treaties Made in Good Faith." In *Natives and Settlers, Now and Then: Historical Issues and Current Perspectives on Treaties and Land Claims in Canada*, edited by Paul W. DePasquale, 1–16. Edmonton: University of Alberta Press, 2007.

Verba, Sidney. "The Citizen as Respondent: Sample Surveys and American Democracy." *American Political Science Review* 90, no. 1 (1996): 1–7.

Vermeule, Adrian. "The Atrophy of Constitutional Powers." *Oxford Journal of Legal Studies* 32, no. 3 (2012): 421–44.

——. *Law and the Limits of Reason*. Oxford: Oxford University Press, 2009.

Vickers, Jill. *Reinventing Political Science: A Feminist Approach*. Halifax: Fernwood Books, 1997.

Vigod, Bernard L. "The Quebec Government and Social Legislation during the 1930s: A Study in Political Self-Destruction." *Journal of Canadian Studies* 14, no. 1 (1979): 59–69.
Waldron, Jeremy. *Law and Disagreement*. Oxford: Oxford University Press, 1999.
———. "A Right-Based Critique of Constitutional Rights." *Oxford Journal of Legal Studies* 13, no. 1 (1993): 18–51.
———. "Some Models of Dialogue between Judges and Legislators." In *Constitutionalism in the Charter Era*, edited by Grant Huscroft and Ian Brodie, 7–47. Markham, ON: LexisNexis Canada, 2004.
Wall Street Journal. "Saskatchewan Boosts Potash Output Quota to 68% of Its Capacity." *Wall Street Journal*, November 7, 1973, 32.
Wallace, Elisabeth. "The Origin of the Welfare State in Canada, 1867–1900." *Canadian Journal of Economics and Political Science* 16, no. 3 (1950): 383–93.
Waller, Tom. "Framework for Economic Development: The Role of Crown Corporations and the Crown Investments Corporation of Saskatchewan." In *Policy Innovation in the Saskatchewan Public Sector, 1971–82*, edited by Eleanor Glor, 29–48. Toronto: Captus Press, 1997.
Wallis, Ed, ed. *From the Workhouse to Welfare: What Beatrice Webb's 1909 Minority Report Can Teach Us Today*. London: Fabian Society, 2009.
Weale, Albert. *Democracy*. New York: St. Martin's Press, 1999.
Webb, Sidney. "Historic." In *Fabian Essays in Socialism*, edited by George Bernard Shaw, 30–61. Garden City, NY: Dolphin Books, 1889.
Weber, Max. *Economy and Society: An Outline of Interpretive Sociology*. Berkeley: University of California Press, 1968.
Weidlich, John. "'Bland Sells': Former Saskatchewan Premier Allan Blakeney." CBC News, November 28, 2008. https://www.cbc.ca/news/canada/saskatchewan/bland-sells-former-saskatchewan-premier-allan-blakeney-1.741887.
Welsh, Lawrence. "Potash Producers Defer Expansions Worth $200 Million." *Globe and Mail*, January 11, 1975, B1.
———. "Saskatchewan to Study Failure of Firms to Pay Potash Taxes." *Globe and Mail*, August 19, 1975, B1.
Wesley, Jared J. *Code Politics: Campaigns and Cultures on the Canadian Prairies*. Vancouver: UBC Press, 2011.
Whyte, John D. "Federalism Dreams." *Queen's Law Journal* 34 (2008): 1–24.
———. "Sometimes Constitutions Are Made in the Streets: The Future of the Charter's Notwithstanding Clause." *Constitutional Forum* 16 (2007): 79–87.
Williams, Rhys H. "Immigration and National Identity in Obama's America: The Expansion of Culture-War Politics." *Canadian Review of American Studies/Revue canadienne d'études américaines* 42, no. 3 (2012): 322–46.
Wiseman, Nelson. *Social Democracy in Manitoba*. Winnipeg: University of Manitoba Press, 1985.

Wiseman, Nelson, and Benjamin Isitt. "Social Democracy in Twentieth Century Canada: An Interpretative Framework." *Canadian Journal of Political Science* 40, no. 3 (2007): 567–89.

Wittman, Donald. *The Myth of Democratic Failure*. Chicago: University of Chicago Press, 1995.

Wolbrecht, Christina, and David E. Campbell. "Leading by Example: Female Members of Parliament as Political Role Models." *American Journal of Political Science* 51, no. 4 (2007): 921–39.

Woodsworth, James S. "Unemployment." In *Forum: Canadian Life and Letters, 1920–70*, edited by J.L. Granatstein and Peter Stevens, 5–7. Toronto: University of Toronto Press, 1972.

Woodward, Michael, and Bruce George. "The Canadian Indian Lobby of Westminster, 1979–1982." *Journal of Canadian Studies* 18, no. 3 (1983): 119–43.

Young, Lisa. "Party, State, and Political Competition in Canada: The Cartel Model Reconsidered." *Canadian Journal of Political Science* 31, no. 2 (1998): 339–58.

———. "Regulating Campaign Finance in Canada: Strengths and Weaknesses." *Election Law Journal* 3, no. 3 (2004): 444–62.

Young, Lisa, and William Cross. "Women's Involvement in Canadian Political Parties." In *Women and Electoral Politics in Canada*, edited by Manon Tremblay and Linda Trimble, 92–109. Oxford: Oxford University Press, 2003.

Zaller, John. "What *Nature and Origins* Leaves Out." *Critical Review* 24 (2012): 569–64.

ABOUT THE CONTRIBUTORS

Michael M. Atkinson was the founding executive director of the Johnson-Shoyama Graduate School of Public Policy at the University of Saskatchewan and the University of Regina, and he is currently a professor emeritus at the school's Saskatoon campus. He has held a number of academic administrative appointments, including associate vice-president academic at McMaster University and provost and vice-president academic at the University of Saskatchewan. Atkinson has also held visiting appointments at Duke University, Western University, and Université de Strasbourg. His academic background is in political science, and he has published extensively in that field and in public administration and public policy. His research interests include public sector compensation, political ethics, and the broad topic of good governance. He is a past president of the Canadian Political Science Association and in 2012 was awarded the lieutenant governor's gold medal for achievement in public administration.

Simone Chambers is a professor of political science at the University of California Irvine. She has written and published on topics such as deliberative democracy, Canadian constitutional politics, public reason, the public sphere, secularism, rhetoric, civility, and the work of Jürgen Habermas and John Rawls. She recently published an edited volume (with Peter Nosco) on navigating pluralism, *Dissent on Core Beliefs: Religious and Secular Perspectives*, and she is currently working on a book entitled *An Ethics of Public Discourse*.

David Coletto is the CEO and a founding partner of Abacus Data, a public opinion firm based in Ottawa. He is also an adjunct professor at the Arthur Kroeger College of Public Affairs at Carleton University, where he teaches in the

Program in Political Management. He completed his PhD in political science in 2010 from the University of Calgary, where his research focused on the intersection of political finance laws, party organization, and electoral behaviour.

John C. Courtney is a professor emeritus of political studies and a senior policy fellow of the Johnson-Shoyama Graduate School of Public Policy at the Saskatoon campus. A former president of the Canadian Political Science Association, he is the author or editor of ten books and over sixty articles, chapters in books, and encyclopedia entries on Canadian and comparative elections, redistricting, leadership selection, and representational and electoral systems. His two most recent books are *Elections* (one of ten volumes in the Canadian Democratic Audit project) and *The Oxford Handbook of Canadian Politics* (co-edited with David E. Smith). Courtney has served as a consultant to the United Nations on electoral districting in Kenya and to the Canadian International Development Agency on voter registration in Bolivia. In addition to serving on two federal electoral boundary readjustment commissions in Saskatchewan, he has advised the chief electoral officers of British Columbia and Canada on boundary delimitation processes.

Alex Himelfarb is a former senior public servant who held a number of senior positions, including ambassador to Italy, San Marino, Malta, and Albania and clerk of the Privy Council and secretary to the cabinet, the most senior public service position, for three prime ministers. He received his PhD in sociology from the University of Toronto and had a decade-long career as an academic at the University of New Brunswick. Upon retirement from the public service, Himelfarb served for five years as the director of the Glendon School of Public and International Affairs, and now chairs or serves on numerous not-for-profit boards. He is also a fellow of the Broadbent Institute and the Parkland Institute. He has published numerous books and articles on Canadian society and public policy, including *Tax Is Not a Four-Letter Word* with his son, Jordan Himelfarb.

Russell Isinger is the university registrar at the University of Saskatchewan and a professional affiliate with the Department of Political Studies, University of Saskatchewan. His research interests lie in the area of Canadian and international defence policy. He is the author (with Donald C. Story) of "The Origins of the Cancellation of Canada's Avro CF-105 Arrow Fighter Program: A Failure of Strategy," published in the *Journal of Strategic Studies*, and other publications on the Avro Arrow program.

Gregory P. Marchildon is the Ontario research chair in health policy and system design at the Institute of Health, Policy, and Evaluation at the University of Toronto and a founding director of the North American Observatory on Health Systems and Policies. He is a fellow of the Canadian Academy of Health Sciences and a member of the editorial board of the European Observatory on Health Systems and Policies. After completing his PhD at the London School of Economics, he taught for five years at the School of Advanced International Studies at Johns Hopkins University. He then served as the deputy minister of intergovernmental affairs and as the cabinet secretary and deputy minister to the premier in the government of Saskatchewan. After serving as the executive director of the Royal Commission on the Future of Health Care in Canada, he returned to academic life, helping to establish the Johnson-Shoyama Graduate School of Public Policy at the University of Saskatchewan and the University of Regina. He is the author of numerous academic articles on Canadian federalism and comparative health systems as well as a number of books, including two editions of *Health Systems in Transition: Canada*.

David McGrane was born and raised in Moose Jaw and completed his PhD in political science at Carleton University in Ottawa. For the past decade, he has been an associate professor of political studies at St. Thomas More College and the University of Saskatchewan. His research interests include social democracy, Canadian political theory, political marketing, elections, and voter behaviour. He has published over twenty-five academic journal articles and book chapters and has written two books: *Remaining Loyal: Social Democracy in Quebec and Saskatchewan* (McGill-Queen's University Press, 2014) and *The New NDP: Moderation, Modernization, and Political Marketing* (UBC Press, 2019). He is active in his community as a member of the City of Saskatoon's Environmental Advisory Committee, the chair of the Political Action Committee of the Saskatoon and District Labour Council, and the former president of the Saskatchewan NDP. He also sits on the Board of Directors of the Douglas-Coldwell Foundation and is a fellow of the Broadbent Institute.

Dwight Newman is a professor of law and the Canada research chair in Indigenous Rights in constitutional and international law at the College of Law, University of Saskatchewan. He previously served a three-year term as the University of Saskatchewan's associate dean of law. He clerked for Chief Justice Lamer and Justice LeBel at the Supreme Court of Canada, worked for human rights NGOs in South Africa and Hong Kong and for the Canadian Department of Justice, and completed his graduate studies at Oxford University, where he studied as a Rhodes scholar and taught in the later years of his doctoral studies. Newman also taught as a visitor at the law faculties at the University of Alberta and McGill University. He has been a recent visiting fellow at Cambridge University, Princeton University, and the Université de Montréal. He is a member of the Ontario and Saskatchewan bars. He has published a hundred articles and a dozen books, including *Community and Collective Rights: A Theoretical Framework for Rights Held by Groups*, *Revisiting the Duty to Consult Aboriginal Peoples*, and *The Law of the Canadian Constitution* (co-authored).

The Honourable Roy Romanow is chancellor of the University of Saskatchewan and a senior fellow in public policy with the Department of Political Studies, University of Saskatchewan. During his more than thirty years in public office, he served as deputy premier and attorney general, leader of the opposition, and premier of Saskatchewan. After his tenure as premier, Romanow was appointed to head the Royal Commission on the Future of Health Care in Canada. He is an officer of the Order of Canada, a recipient of the Saskatchewan Order of Merit, and a recipient of the Pan American Health Organization's Administration Award. He is a member of the federal Privy Council through service on Canada's Security Intelligence Review Committee. Romanow is a former co-chair of the Advisory Board for the Canadian Index of Wellbeing, and he currently serves as a member of the Elections Canada Advisory Board and as the co-chair of the Canadian Alliance to End Homelessness. He is recognized as one of the University of Saskatchewan's 100 Alumni of Influence and is the recipient of numerous honorary degrees from Canadian universities.

Melanee Thomas is an associate professor of political science at the University of Calgary. Her research focuses on the causes and consequences of gender-based political inequality in Canada and other post-industrial democracies, with a particular focus on political attitudes, behaviour, and engagement. She is the co-editor of *Mothers and Others: The Role of Parenthood in Politics*, and her research has appeared in *Politics and Gender*, *Electoral Studies*, and the *Canadian Journal of Political Science*.

Katherine Walker is nehiyaw from the Okanese First Nation in Treaty 4 territory. She is a PhD student in political science at the University of British

Columbia, where she was granted a SSHRC doctoral fellowship, and she works on community and policy development with her First Nation. Having worked for the federal government, Indigenous political organizations, as well as a brief stint for a corporation, she has broad work experience and expertise in the area of policy development and Indigenous and Treaty Rights affirmation. Her research focuses on Indigenous Knowledge and political theory, land- and place-based worldviews, and treaty relations. She has presented her scholarly work at conferences of the Western Political Science Association and Native American and Indigenous Scholars Association.

Reg Whitaker is a distinguished research professor emeritus at York University and an adjunct professor of political science at the University of Victoria. He has authored or co-authored numerous books and articles on aspects of Canadian politics and political history, among them *The Government Party: Organizing and Financing the Liberal Party of Canada, 1930–1958*; *Double Standard: The Secret History of Canadian Immigration*; *A Sovereign Idea: Essays on Canada as a Democratic Community*; *Cold War Canada: The Making of a National Insecurity State, 1945–1957*; *The End of Privacy: How Total Surveillance Is Becoming a Reality*; *Canada and the Cold War*; and *Secret Service: Political Policing in Canada from the Fenians to Fortress America*.

John D. Whyte is a policy fellow at the Johnson-Shoyama Graduate School of Public Policy at the University of Regina campus. He was a member of the Queen's University Faculty of Law for twenty-eight years and served as its dean. He has held visiting appointments at York University, the University of Toronto, Niigata University, Tilburg University, and the University of Melbourne. Whyte was the Douglas McK. Brown professor of law at the University of British Columbia, a senior policy fellow at the Saskatchewan Institute of Public Policy, a Law Foundation of Saskatchewan professor at the University of Saskatchewan, and a professor of political science at the University of Regina. He holds an honorary degree from York University. Whyte's public service career includes serving as the director of constitutional law for the government of Saskatchewan and as Saskatchewan's deputy minister of justice and deputy attorney general. He has published extensively in the field of constitutional law.

Nelson Wiseman is a professor of political science at the University of Toronto. His books include *In Search of Canadian Political Culture*, *The Public Intellectual in Canada*, and *Social Democracy in Manitoba: A History of the*

CCF-NDP. Among his many journal publications are "The Socialist Imprint on Saskatchewan Politics," *Saskatchewan History*; "Reading Prairie Politics: Morton, Lipset, Macpherson," *International Journal of Canadian Studies*; "Ethnicity, Religion, and Socialism in Canada: The Twenties through the War," *Canadian Ethnic Studies*; "Early Socialism in Canada: International and Regional Impulses," *American Review of Canadian Studies*; and (with Benjamin Isitt) "Social Democracy in Twentieth Century Canada," *Canadian Journal of Political Science*.

INDEX

Aboriginal peoples, terminology, 167. *See also* Indigenous peoples
abortion rights issue: about, 190–93; notwithstanding clause, 74; religion vs. politics, 186–87, 192–93, 196–97, 200–201. *See also* religion and democracy
accountability: about, 51–52, 67–68, 238–39; Blakeney's views, 54, 89–93; goals of truth and efficiency, 51–52, 55; Habermas on, xiii, 52, 55–56, 64–68; minority vs. majoritarian democracy, 79, 93–100; parliamentary vs. judicial supremacy, xv–xvi, 89–93; to public vs. truth, 51–52; relationship of ministers and experts, 54–55. *See also* democratic input; elites; members of Parliament (MPs); ministers; public opinion
Accountability Act, 230
Achen, Christopher, 111
activism: activist state and social justice, 46, 118, 238, 240, 241; democracy as citizen activation, 31–32, 35. *See also* social democracy
Adams, Howard, 171
Advisory Council on the Status of Women, 151

agriculture: about, 22–23, 28; Confederation bargain, 20; government loans, 18; regional equality, 22–23; wheat and grain prices, 23, 42
Ahenakew, David, 172
Alberta: electoral boundaries, 219–20; NDP government, 148; OPEC crisis, 42; resources wars, 20–21; sexism, 164
Alberta Bill of Rights, 75
Antigone (Sophocles), 186–87
anti-Semitism, 197–98, 200. *See also* religion and democracy
Archambault, Joseph-Papin, 139–40
Arrow, Kenneth, 109
Assembly of First Nations, 174
assisted dying issue: about, 193–97; access to services, 194–95; *Charter* rights (s.7), 193–94; religion vs. politics, 186–87, 195–97, 200–201. *See also* religion and democracy
Atkinson, Michael M.: contributor, 317; on democracy and good government, xvi, xix, 105–20, 240–41
austerity and democracy: economic inequality, 130–32; impact on trust in democracy, 122–24, 240; policies (1990s), 128–30

Australia: electoral boundaries, 208–9, 217, 219
authoritarianism and totalitarianism: about, 84, 98, 239; democracy as response to, 84, 133; government distrust, 133; strongman rulers and democratic failures, 98, 119; as threat to democracy, 122, 133

Barrett, Dave, 145
Bartels, Larry, 60, 111
Bayda Commission, 44
Bell, Daniel, 116
Bennett, R.B., 139
Bernier, Maxime, x, 202
Beveridge, William, 141
Blakeney, Allan: conference on his legacy, vii–viii, 82; death (2011), xiii; early life, xii–xiii, 35; education, xii–xiii, 35, 77; political influence of, xi–xi, xvi; social democrat, 34, 238; socialist influences on, xii–xiii
Blakeney, Allan, career: lawyer, xiii, 35, 36; minister (Lloyd government), xiii, 36–38; MLA (1960–1988), xiii, 36; opposition leader (1970-1971), xiii, 38; public administration, 33–38; retirement (1988) and later career, xiii, 35, 71; senior civil servant, xiii, 34–36; technocrat, 33, 40, 46, 51, 56, 61–62, 172, 240–41. *See also* Blakeney, Allan, principled pragmatism
Blakeney, Allan, career as premier (1971-1982): about, xiii, 39–46; crown corporations, xiii, 35–36; economic development, 42–44; election campaign (1975), 8, 12–13, 41–42; equality innovations, 44–46; *New Deal for the People*, 8, 41–42; organizational innovations, 39–42; public ownership, 42–44; tax policy, 126. *See also* Blakeney, Allan, principled pragmatism; cabinet government; crown corporations; resource wars (1970s and 1980s); social democracy
Blakeney, Allan, principled pragmatism: about, xiv, 3, 12–14; achievable policies, xiv; alignment of policy with ideals, xiv; courage, 14; crown corporation decision, 10; faith in all peoples, 172, 175; as good government, 119–20; Indigenous relations, 171–75; informed decision making, 13, 172; negotiated compromises, 13, 172; overview of six principles, 12–14; revitalization of democracy, xviii–xx; rule of law, 12–13, 172; social democracy, 13–14, 120; treaty federalism, 171–72
Blakeney, Allan, views: about, 242; accountability, 54, 89–93; activist state, 34, 46, 118, 238, 240, 241; *Charter*, 72, 75–76, 89–93; courts and judges, xv–xvi, 78–79, 89–93; crown corporations, 35–36; democratic input, xiii, xvi, 59–61, 239, 241; diversity, 90, 241; economic equality, 15–20, 30–32; elections, 205–6, 238; electoral boundaries, xviii, 205–6, 211, 221; equality, xvi; federalism and western alienation, xi, 15, 20–21, 24–25; human rights, xv, 89–93, 241; Indigenous peoples, 16, 25, 28–30, 44, 168–69, 171–75, 184; liberal feminism, 25–26, 45; Medicare, 36; ministers, 54–57, 59–60; multiculturalism, 26–28; northern Saskatchewan, 172; notwithstanding clause, xv, 73, 75–82, 89–93, 239; parliamentary vs. judicial supremacy, xv–xvi, 89–93; political finance systems, 224, 236;

populism, xi, xx, 62, 239–40; potash industry, 4–6, 9–11; principled pragmatism, xiv, xvi, 3, 12–14; public administration, 48, 54; resource wars, 10–14; social democracy, 34, 105, 135, 238; tax policy, 126, 133–34, 241; welfare state, 146–47, 241; women and feminism, 25–26, 45, 151

Blakeney, Allan, works: *An Honourable Calling: Political Memoirs*, 72, 75, 77, 172, 205; keynote addresses to IPAC conferences (1970, 1980), 52, 54; "The Notwithstanding Clause, the *Charter*, and Canada's Patriated Constitution," 75–77; *Political Management in Canada* (with Borins), xiv, 48, 54, 57; "The Relationship between Provincial Ministers and Their Deputy Ministers," 52

Bliss, Michael, 140

Bloc Québécois, 199

Borins, Sandford, xiv, 48, 54, 57

Bouchard, Gérard, 198

Bouchard-Taylor Commission, 67

Britain. *See* United Kingdom

British Columbia: citizen forum, 116; electoral boundaries, 211, 218(t); social democracy, 144–48

British North America Act, 1867, 4, 93

Broadbent, Ed, 33–34, 234

Burke, Edmund, 60–62

cabinet government: about, xiv, 39–41, 46–49, 238; Blakeney's principled pragmatism, 13; Cabinet Planning Committee, 41, 45; centralized cabinet secretary, 39–40; Douglas-Lloyd governments, xiv, 39, 40, 47; Government Finance Office Board, 41; ministers and deputy ministers, 39–40; potash crown corporation, 10–11, 13, 43; systematic approach, 35–36, 39; Treasury Board, 40–41. *See also* ministers

Cadbury, George, 35

Canada Elections Act, 229–30

Canadian Bill of Rights (1960), 75

Canadian Charter of Rights and Freedoms. *See* Charter of Rights and Freedoms

Canadian Industrial Gas and Oil Ltd. (CIGOL) v Saskatchewan (1978), 11–12

The Canadian Press Stylebook, 166

Caplan, Bryan, 112, 126

Carter v Canada (2015), 194

Casgrain, Thérèse, 141

Cassidy, Harry, 140–41, 142

Catholic Church: abortion issue, 74, 190; assisted dying issue, 194–95; same-sex marriage, 189; secularism in Quebec, 198–99; social doctrine, 139–40. *See also* religion and democracy

CCF (Cooperative Commonwealth Federation): about, 147–48; change to NDP, 143; family allowances, 141; historical background, 139–49; influence on Blakeney, 34–35; Lloyd's government, xiv, 34, 36, 38, 47; Medicare, 144; Regina Manifesto, 38, 139, 140, 141; social gospel, 139, 142, 185–86, 202; welfare state, 139, 144–49. *See also* Douglas, Tommy; NDP (New Democratic Party)

Central Canada Potash (CCP), 5–6, 11–12, 43

Central Canada Potash v Saskatchewan (1979), 5–7, 12, 43

Chambers, Simone: contributor, 317; on democratic accountability, xix, 51–70, 238–39

Chaoulli v Quebec (2005), 72
Charter of Rights and Freedoms: about, 86–88; abortion issue, 191; assisted dying, 72, 193–94; Blakeney's views, 72, 75–76, 89–93; constitutional negotiations, 86–88; drug injection sites, 72; freedom of conscience and religion (s.2), 191, 192; health care, access to private, 72; life, liberty and security of person (s.7), 72, 191, 193–94; limitation of rights (s.1), 76; notwithstanding clause (s.33), x, 87–88; parliamentary vs. judicial supremacy, xv–xvi, 73, 74, 78–82, 89–93; prostitution legalization, 72; same-sex marriage, 188; textual vs. moral rights, 75–77; voting and political representation (s.3), 155, 207. *See also* notwithstanding clause (s.33 of *Charter*)
children and youth: child care, xix, 135–36, 142, 145–46; dental programs, 45, 46, 47–48; family allowances and child benefits, 131, 135, 141, 143, 146. *See also* education; welfare state
Choudhry, Sujit, 220
Chrétien, Jean: political finance system, 224, 230, 232; social democracy, 147; tax policy, 125, 128
Christianity: abortion rights issue, 190; assisted dying services, 194–95; religion and secularism in Quebec, 67, 92, 198–99; social gospel, 139, 142, 185–86, 202–3. *See also* Catholic Church; religion and democracy
CIGOL *(Canadian Industrial Gas and Oil Ltd.) v Saskatchewan* (1978), 11–12
citizens and citizenship: consent in democracies, 93–94; consumerist model, xviii, 225, 231, 235; economic inequality, 131–32; informed vs. uninformed, 59–60; public acceptance of policy, 57; state order vs. personal freedom, 93–94; tax policy and public trust, xvi, 122–30, 133–34, 240; unstable preferences, 60. *See also* democratic input; populism; public opinion; voters
climate change, 51
Coalition avenir Québec, 198
Coletto, David: contributor, 317–18; on political finances, xviii, xx, 223–36, 241
communications. *See* democratic input; media and communications; social media
Confederation: minority protections, 84–85, 99–100
conscientious objection, 191, 193, 194–97. *See also* religion and democracy
conservative ideology and welfare state, 136–37
Conservative Party (federal): influence of CCF on, 142; political ideology, 136–37; women candidates, 161, 165. *See also* Harper, Stephen, government
constitutions and democracy: about, xv, 84–85, 99; amending processes, 85–86; human rights, 86, 100–101; independent courts, 99; minority protections, 79, 84–85, 99–100; political consumerism vs. democratic discourse, 80; restraints on power, 84–85, 99–100; separation of powers, 99–100
Constitution Act, 1867: formula for number of MPs, 209
Constitution Act, 1982: amending processes, 85–86, 87–88; equalization payments, 66;

Indigenous peoples, xvii, 85, 174–75; natural resources, resource wars, 8–9, 11–12; patriation of, xv, 12, 74–75, 86–88, 174–75; Quebec's lack of support, 88; two founding peoples, 85. *See also* Charter of Rights and Freedoms; notwithstanding clause (s.33 of Charter)
consult, duty to. *See* Indigenous peoples, duty to consult
Converse, Philip, 60
Cooperative Commonwealth Federation. *See* CCF (Cooperative Commonwealth Federation)
Corak, Miles, 131
Courtney, John C.: contributor, 318; on federal electoral boundary commissions, xviii, xx, 205–22, 241
courts and judges: Blakeney's views, xv–xvi, 78–79, 89–93; elite values, 90–91, 93; parliamentary vs. judicial supremacy, xv–xvi, 73, 74, 78–79, 89–93; as protectors of rights, xv. *See also* Supreme Court of Canada
Cowley, Elwood, 8, 10
crown corporations: about, 17–18, 19–20, 21–22, 42–44, 47; Blakeney's views, 35–36; Douglas government, 5, 19; for economic equality, 17; Government Finance Office Board, 41; oil and gas (SaskOil), 42–43, 47; oversight of, 36, 41; potash, 6, 10–11, 13, 43; uranium industry, 8, 17, 43–44; for wealth redistribution, 6, 17. *See also* oil and gas industry; potash industry; uranium industry
Crown Investments Corporation (CIC), 41
culture wars, 201–3. *See also* religion and democracy

Dahl, Robert, 57
death, assisted. *See* assisted dying issue
deficiencies in democracies. *See* democratic deficiencies
democracy: about, x–xii, 83–85, 93–94; attributes of good states, 98; benefits of, 107–8, 113–20; as citizen activation, 31–32, 34; citizens, representatives, and experts, 54–55; collective competence, 114, 119; conditions for, 83–85; consent by citizens, 83, 93–95; decision making, 53, 109–10, 114–16, 119; deliberative democracy, 52–54; democratic revitalization, xviii–xx; elected representatives, 62, 110; entrenched rights, 100–101; Jury Theorem, 114; Madisonian democracy, 96; minority vs. majoritarian democracy, 79, 93–100; normative ideals, 54, 83; participation as "right of rights," 78; personal freedom vs. state order, 93–94; public opinion on, 122; public trust issues, 123–28, 240; response to citizens' needs, 57–58; as response to totalitarianism, 84; restraints on power, 84–85; risks of strong factions, 96; socioeconomic conditions, 107–8; talk-centric vs. vote-centric, 53–54; unity vs. diversity, 94–95, 100–101; universality of values, 106. *See also* constitutions and democracy; democracy and good government; democratic deficiencies; democratic input; parliamentary system
democracy and good government: about, 105–9, 118–20; Blakeney's principled pragmatism, 119–20; bureaucracies, 108, 117–18;

competition in policy choices, 119; democratic revitalization, xviii–xx; elected leaders, 119–20; epistemic value of democracy, 114–20; equality of treatment, 108; policy experimentation, 119; regulations, 108–9; rule of law, 84, 108. *See also* democratic deficiencies; democratic input

democratic deficiencies: about, xvi, 109–14, 118–20; bureaucrats, 117–18; corruption, 107–8; decision making, 109–10, 114–17, 119; epistemic bottlenecks, 116–17; epistemic value of democracy, 119–20; gender issues, 151–52, 155–57, 164–66; good and bad governments, 107–9; Impossibility Theorem, 109–10; incompetence of politicians, 110, 118; instability of voter preferences, 110; national vs. local communities, 116; political exploitation of anxieties, xvi; poverty and deprivation, 107; public opinion on, 106–7; size of government, 107; voters' ignorance, xvi, 118. *See also* democracy and good government; women and politics

democratic input: about, 57–58; Blakeney's views, 59–61; Burke's trustee model, 60–62; communicative responsiveness, 62–67; consultation vs. survey data, 59–60, 62–63; correlation between policies and public opinion, 58; diversity in decision making, 114–15, 119; electoral boundaries, 210, 211–12, 214, 215, 216–17, 218–19, 218(t); elite model, 60–62; feedback loops, 65–67, 120; good government and legitimate outcomes, 62, 109; Habermas on, xiii, 52, 55–56, 64–68; Impossibility Theorem, 109–10; instability of voter preferences, 110; by minorities, 63, 98; preference clarification, 63; research issues, 58–60, 63–64; responsiveness, 57–60, 63–65; royal commissions, xix, 66–68; vote aggregation, 109–11, 118–19. *See also* citizens and citizenship; populism; public opinion; voters

demographics: members of parliament, 155–56; migration, 214; rural to urban migration, 23, 214

dental programs, 45, 46, 47–48

deputy ministers: Blakeney's views, 52; cabinet government, 39–40; relationships of public, minister, and deputy minister, 54–55

Dewey, John, 118

Diefenbaker, John, 75

disabled people, 19

diversity: about, xvii, 25–26, 100–101, 241; aim of peaceful coexistence, 101; Blakeney's views, 90, 241; decision making, 114–15, 119; entrenched rights, 100–101; representatives on agencies, boards, and commissions, 166; underrepresentation in legislatures, 153–57, 165–66. *See also* human rights; LGBTQ people; marginalized people; multiculturalism; race and ethnicity; social equality

Dixon v British Columbia (1989), 207

Dombowsky, David, 10

Douglas, Tommy: about, 143–44; cabinet government, xiv, 34; crown corporations, 5, 19; federal NDP leader, 143; influence on Blakeney, xiv, 34, 47, 77; Medicare, 144; potash royalties, 5; Regina Manifesto's

influence, 140; social democracy, 143–44; social gospel, 185–86
duty to consult. *See* Indigenous peoples, duty to consult
Duval Potash Company, 11
Dworkin, Ronald, 226–27

Eastern European ethnic minorities, 25, 27–28
economy: 2008 financial crisis, 128–29. *See also* economy, government intervention; economic equality; economic inequality; neoliberalism; regional equality; tax policy
economy, government intervention: about, 15–16, 42–44; activist state and social justice, 46, 118, 238, 240, 241; infrastructure, 17–18; northern communities, 44–45; small businesses, 18. *See also* crown corporations; social democracy; tax policy; welfare state
economic equality: about, xvi–xvii, 15–20, 30–32; basic level of material well-being, 30; Blakeney's views, 15–20, 30–32; of conditions vs. opportunities, 141; crown corporations, 17–18, 19–20; Fabian socialism, 16–17, 140; historical background, 147–48; Keynesian demand stimulation, 17–18; labour policy, 20; national identity, 147–48; revitalization of democracy, xix–xx; self-development, 19, 30; tax policy, 17–18; values, 16–19; welfare state, 18–19, 147–48. *See also* crown corporations; social democracy; welfare state
economic inequality: about, 18–19, 130–32; austerity's impact, 130–32; impact on democratic participation, 31–32; neoliberalism and increase in, 130–32; payment of "fair share" of taxes, 125, 133–34. *See also* neoliberalism; tax policy
education: about, 45; Blakeney's views, 45; ethnic minorities, 27–28; federal funding, 24; Indigenous-controlled education, 28–30, 45; inner-city schools, 45; kindergarten programs, 18; notwithstanding clause and religious schools, 81; political literacy, 30–31; post-secondary education, 18–19, 30, 45; self-development, 19
Einstein, Katherine Levine, 111
elections: Blakeney's views, 205–6, 238; campaign finances, 158; in elite theories of democracy, 60; first-past-the-post system, 206; key questions, 206; by party vs. non-party system, 161–62; platform promises, 37, 41–42, 238–39. *See also* electoral boundaries; political finance systems; voters; women and politics
Elections Canada, 207
electoral boundaries: about, 205–8, 216–22; Australian model, 208–9, 217, 219; Blakeney's views, xviii, 205–6, 211, 221; census data, 209; commissions, independent, xviii, 206, 209–10, 217–18, 221; communities of interest/identity, 208, 209, 213, 215, 221; demographic changes, 214; *Dixon* case, 207; EBRA provisions, 206–13, 215–16, 218, 220–21; equality norms, 212–13, 215–16, 219–22; geographic aspects, 208, 209, 215, 220–21; gerrymandering, 206, 207; key questions, 206; legislation on, 208–10; Manitoba model, 209, 217–18; MP's input, 210, 215, 218–19, 218(t), 221; population

variations (+/- % of quota), 209, 212–13, 219–21; proposals for improving processes, 216–22; public input, 210, 211–12, 214, 215, 216–17; redistributions (1991, 2001, 2011, 2021), 211–12, 214–15, 216, 218(t); revitalization of democracy, 216–22; social media, xviii, 211, 216–17, 221; tensions in processes, 213–16; timeline, 218–19, 218(t); urban districts, 214–15, 221
Electoral Boundaries Readjustment Act (EBRA), 206–13, 215–16, 218, 220–21
electronic communications. *See* democratic input; media and communications; social media
elites: about, 60–62; civil service experts, 39, 54–55; communicative responsiveness, 62–68; deficiencies in, 112–13; as elected representatives, 65; interpreting and mediating roles, 60–61, 67–68; judges as legal elites, 78–79; media role in communication between citizens and elites, 65
Elster, Jon, 115
England. *See* United Kingdom
environmental issues: climate change, 51; government funding, 130; uranium mining, 43
equality: about, xiv–xv, 15–16, 30–32; Canadianism, 22–23; citizen activation, 31–32; cooperation vs. competition, xv; democracy and, 30–32, 107–8; economic, xiv–xv, 16–20; electoral boundaries, 212–13, 215–16, 219–22; gender equality, 152–53; legal, xiv–xv, 25–30; regional, xiv–xv, 20–25, 31–32; social, xiv–xv, 25–30. *See also* economic equality; economic inequality; human rights; legal equality; regional equality; same-sex marriage
equalization payments, 32, 66–67. *See also* regional equality
ethnic diversity. *See* diversity; race and ethnicity
experts in civil service, 39, 54–55

Fabian Society, 16–17, 140
farms and farmers. *See* agriculture
Federation of Saskatchewan Indians (FSI), 29, 172–73, 175
Federation of Sovereign Indigenous Nations (FSIN), 178–79, 182
feminism: about, 15–16, 25–26; abortion rights issue, 193; Blakeney's views, 25–26, 45; discrimination, 25–26, 31; gender differences in media coverage, 160, 164. *See also* equality; women; women and politics
finance, political. *See* political finance systems
finance, public. *See* economy, government intervention; tax policy
Fines, Clarence, 35
First Nations, terminology, 167. *See also* Indigenous peoples
First Nations University of Canada, 173
Fishkin, James, 64
Foa, Roberto, 122
Ford, Doug, x, 81, 239
French Canadians: constitutional rights, 99–100
FSI (Federation of Saskatchewan Indians), 29, 172–73, 175
FSIN (Federation of Sovereign Indigenous Nations), 178–79, 182
Fullerton, Doug, 10

Gans, Herbert, 131
gay people. *See* LGBTQ people

gender: about, 151–53; gendered media coverage, 160, 163–64, 166; political processes, 154–55, 160–61, 165–66; public opinion on gender roles, 152. *See also* LGBTQ people; marginalized people; women; women and politics
Gilens, Martin, 113
good government and democracy. *See* democracy; democracy and good government; democratic deficiencies
Governance Finance Office Board (GFO), 41
Gramsci, Antonio, 132

Habermas, Jürgen, xiii, 52, 55–56, 64–68
Haida Nation v British Columbia (2004), 175, 177
Hamilton, Alexander, 84
Harcourt, Mike, 145
Harper, Stephen, government: abortion rights issue, 191, 202; budget surplus (2006), 128; defeat (2015), 96, 199; Islamophobia, 198, 199; political finance system, 230–32; same-sex marriage, 188; tax cuts, 124–25, 128, 132
Hayek, Friedrich, 109
health care. *See* Medicare
Heaps, A.A., 140
Hedges, Chris, 132
Henderson, James, 170
Himelfarb, Alex: contributor, 318; on taxes and economic inequality, xvi–xvii, xix, 121–34, 241
Hochschild, Jennifer, 111
Holmberg, Soren, 108
homosexuality. *See* LGBTQ people
An Honourable Calling: Political Memoirs (Blakeney), 72, 77, 172, 205

Horgan, John, 162
Horwath, Andrea, 162
Hulchanski, David, 131
human rights: about, xv, 100–101, 241; Blakeney's views, xv, 89–93, 241; conflict of rights, 76; deep values, 100–101; democratic dialogue on, 78–79; democratic participation as "right of rights," 78; entrenched rights, 100–101; equal justice, 95; legal protections, 98–99; minority vs. majoritarian democracy, 79, 93–100; moral vs. *Charter* rights, 75–76; parliamentary vs. judicial supremacy, xv–xvi, 73, 74, 78–79, 89–93; personal freedom vs. state order, 94; vulnerable citizens, xv. See also *Charter of Rights and Freedoms*
Human Rights Commission, 26, 45, 47–48
Huntington, Samuel, 126

Ibbitson, John, 124, 132
ideology and welfare state, 136–37. *See also* welfare state
immigration: anti-immigrant campaigns, 186; populist political parties, x; Syrian refugees, 199–200. *See also* race and ethnicity
Impossibility Theorem, 109–10
incompetency in democracies. *See* democratic deficiencies
Indigenous peoples: about, 28–30, 167–68; affirmative action programs, 173; Blakeney's views, 16, 25, 28–30, 44, 168–69, 171–75, 184; colonialism, 172–73; *Constitution Act* rights (s.35), 85, 168, 169–70, 174–75; Constitutional debates, 85, 174–75; criminalization, 173; democratic participation, 31–32;

discrimination and racism, 25, 31, 44, 174; education, 28–30, 45, 172–73; federal/provincial relationship with, 182–84; historical injustices, 99–100; Idle No More, 168; Indigenous-controlled institutions, 28–29, 173; intercultural dialogue, xvii; interdependence, xvii; land claims, xvii, 29; northern Saskatchewan, 43–44; representation in House of Commons, 155–56; revitalization of democracy, xix; Saskatchewan Formula for land claims, xvii, 29; self-determination, 16, 28–30, 44, 100, 182; "Sixties Scoop," 30; sovereignty, 169, 171, 176–77; terminology, 167; uranium industry employment, 173; voter rights under *Charter* (s.3), 155. *See also* Indigenous peoples, duty to consult; Indigenous peoples, treaties

Indigenous peoples, duty to consult: about, xvii, 168, 175–78, 182–84; Blakeney's views, 168–69, 171–72, 184; consent, 169, 171, 176, 178; crown dominance, 170, 176–78, 180, 182–83; dispute resolution, 182; industry proponents, 177–78, 180, 182; intercultural dialogue, 169, 175–78, 182–83; processes, 176–82; reconciliation, 177–78, 180; Saskatchewan draft framework (2010), 178–82; scc cases, 175, 177, 180, 183; third-party facilitation, xix, 183

Indigenous peoples, treaties: land claims, 29; Numbered Treaties, 29, 170, 171, 181–84; OTC (Office of the Treaty Commissioner), 168, 170–71, 183–84; TLE (Treaty Land Entitlement Agreement), 173–74, 183; treaty federalism, xvii, 168–71, 175, 183–84; Treaty Implementation Framework Agreement, 184; Treaty Rights, xvii, 29, 169–70, 181–84, 182–84. *See also* Indigenous peoples

Institute of Public Administration of Canada (IPAC), 36
International Monetary Fund, 130
Irvine, William, 138
Isinger, Russell: contributor, 318; introduction by, ix–xx
Islam: Islamophobia, 197–201; Muslim ban in US, 198; religious symbols in Quebec's public sector, 67, 92, 198–99. *See also* religion and democracy

Jansen, Harold, 230
Johnson, A.W. (Al), 35, 44, 118, 143
Judaism: anti-Semitism, 197–98, 200. *See also* religion and democracy
judges. *See* courts and judges
Judt, Tony, 131
Jury Theorem, 114

King, William Lyon Mackenzie, 138–39, 140, 141, 142, 149
Knowles, Stanley, 141, 146, 185–86

La Ronge, 44–45
Landemore, Hélène, 116
languages, heritage, 28
Layton, Jack, 147
Le Pen, Jean-Marie and Marine, 197
League for Social Reconstruction (LSR), 140–41
Lee, Tim, 39
Leeson, Howard, 74
legal equality: about, 25–32; legal aid programs, 45–46, 47–48; liberal feminism, 25–26; liberal multiculturalism, 26–28; relation

to social equality, 25–26. *See also* equality; social equality
lesbians. *See* LGBTQ people
Lewis, David, 142, 145
LGBTQ people: *Charter* rights, 188; democratic participation, 31–32; discrimination against, 31, 188; public opinion in US, 64–65; religious-inspired hostility to homosexuality, 188–89. *See also* same-sex marriage
liberal ideology and welfare state, 136–37. *See also* welfare state
Liberal Party (federal): influence of CCF-NDP on, 137, 138–39, 141–43, 147, 149; political ideology, 136–37; tax policy, 125; welfare state, xvii; women candidates, 161. *See also* Chrétien, Jean; King, William Lyon Mackenzie; Trudeau, Justin; Trudeau, Pierre
library system, 19
Lindblom, Charles, 115
Lipsitz, Keena, 226
Lloyd, Woodrow, xiv, 34, 36, 38, 47
local governments: diversity in agencies, boards, and commissions, 166; elections by party vs. non-party system, 161–62; women and politics, 162–63
Longley, J.W., 138
Lortie Commission, 220
Lougheed, Peter, 42, 76
LSR (League for Social Reconstruction), 140–41
Lysyk, Ken, 10

Madison, James, 84, 96
Make This Your Canada (Lewis), 142
Manitoba: electoral boundaries, 209, 217–18, 219–20; social democracy, 144–45, 147–48

Manning, Preston, 233–34
Marchildon, Gregory P.: contributor, 319; on cabinet government, xiv, xix, 33–49, 238
marginalized people: about, 98–101; democratic input by, 63, 98; entrenched rights, 100–101; harm from failure to protect, 98–99; intersocietal conflict, 97; minority vs. majoritarian democracy, 79, 93–100; oppression in democracies, 97–98; recognition and accommodation, 97; totalitarian governments, 98; underrepresentation of, 63, 153–57, 165–66; vulnerable citizens, xv, 131–32
Marois, Pauline, 198
Marsh, Leonard, 140–41, 142
Martin, Paul, 73–74, 147, 188
Mazzucato, Mariana, 130
McGrane, David: contributor, 319; on equality in political thought, xiv–xv, xix, 15–32, 238; introduction by, ix–xx
McLaughlin, Audrey, 145
media and communications: about, 240–41; anti-Muslim views, 200; assisted dying issue, 196; *The Canadian Press Stylebook*, 166; election advertising, 224, 234; electoral boundary public input, 210, 211–12, 214, 215, 216–17, 221; fake news and misinformation, 111–12; gender and democratic deficit, xx; gender differences in political coverage, 160, 163–64, 166; Medicare controversies, 36–37; for political fundraising, 233; public opinion, 58–59; revitalization of democracy, xx; social media, 164, 166; stereotypes of women

politicians, xx, 154, 159–61, 163–64, 166. *See also* democratic input

Medicare: about, 144; access based on need, 37; Blakeney as health minister, 36–37, 143; Blakeney's views, 36; *Charter* cases (s.7), 71–72; drug injection sites, 72; election promises (1960), 37; expanded programs, 19; financing of, 37–38, 144; Hall Royal Commission, 66–67; historical background, 136, 144–45; legal challenges on access to private care, 72; moral right to health care, 76; opposition to, 37–38; out-of-pocket costs, 130; palliative care, 196; provincial/federal jurisdiction, 144–45; removal from market, 37; Saskatchewan as model, 144; user fees, 18, 45; wait times, 72. *See also* abortion rights issue; assisted dying issue

members of Parliament (MPs): Burke's trustee model, 60–62; demographics, 155–56; electoral boundaries input, 210, 215, 218–19, 218(t); occupational backgrounds, 145, 156; socio-economic resources, 157–58; underrepresentation of women, 155–57, 165–66

men: gendered political processes, 154–55, 163; overrepresentation in politics, 166; socio-economic resources, 158; treatment of women leaders, 154, 163. *See also* gender

Methodist Church, 138. *See also* religion and democracy

Métis. *See* Indigenous peoples

Mikisew Cree v Canada (2005), 175

ministers: about, 54–58; Blakeney's views, 54–57, 59–60; Burke's trustee model, 60–62; cabinet government, xiv, 39–40; civil servants and, 39, 54–55; division of labour, 55; independence of, 56; interpreting and mediating roles, 60–61, 67–68; public communications, 55–56; relationships with public and deputy ministers, 54–55. *See also* cabinet government

minorities: about, 98–101; constitutional protections for, 99–100; democratic input by, 63, 98; entrenched rights, 100–101; harms from failure to protect, 98–99; minority vs. majoritarian democracy, 79, 93–100. *See also* LGBTQ people; marginalized people; race and ethnicity

Moe, Terry, 113

Molson, Melissa, 220

Morgentaler, R v (1988), 190, 191, 192

Mounk, Yascha, 122

MPs. *See* members of Parliament (MPs)

Mulroney, Brian, 147, 148, 190

multiculturalism: about, 15–16, 26–28; Blakeney's views, 26–28; Eastern Europeans, 25, 27–28; People's Party of Canada on, x, 202; prejudice and discrimination, 25, 31; provincial legislation, 27; UNESCO principles, 27. *See also* equality; race and ethnicity; social equality

Multiculturalism Act, 27

municipal government. *See* local governments

Muslims. *See* Islam; religion and democracy

National Indian Brotherhood, 174

natural resources: economic diversification, 4–5; provincial jurisdiction, 4; tax policy, 4–5, 21–22; uranium industry, 8, 17, 43–44, 173. *See also* oil and gas

industry; potash industry; resource wars (1970s and 1980s)
Natural Resources Transfer Agreement (1930), 4, 20, 171
NDP (New Democratic Party): about, 147–49; CCF roots, 137; diversity of candidates, 161; federal vs. provincial policies, 145; influence on Liberal policy, 137, 138–39, 141–43, 147, 149; middle class, 148–49; *niqab* controversy in Quebec, 199; political ideology, 136–37; welfare state, 136–37, 144–49; women candidates, 161–62. *See also* social democracy; welfare state
NDP (New Democratic Party) (Saskatchewan): Blakeney's leadership, 38; gender issues, xvii, 151; *New Deal for People* election platform, 41–42; Regina Manifesto, 38, 139, 140, 141; uranium mining controversy, 44; Waffle, 38; Winnipeg Declaration of 1956, 38. *See also* Blakeney, Allan, career as premier (1971-1982); Douglas, Tommy
neoliberalism: about, 126–32; economic inequality, 130–32; government distrust, 126–28; market competition, 126; privatization of social programs, 146–47; reduction of state role, 48; tax cuts, 129–30; vulnerable citizens, 131–32. *See also* economy; tax policy
New Democratic Party. *See* NDP (New Democratic Party)
Newman, Dwight: contributor, 319–20; on rights and the notwithstanding clause, xv, xix, 71–82, 239
North, Douglas, 108
northern Saskatchewan, 43–45, 172–73. *See also* Saskatchewan

Notley, Rachel, 162, 165, 274n67
notwithstanding clause (s.33 of *Charter*): about, xv, 72–73, 87–93, 239; abortion law, 74; academic skepticism of, 74; Blakeney's views, xv, 73, 75–82, 89–93, 239; conflicts of rights, 73, 77–79; constitutional negotiations, 74–75, 86–89; court decision on Doug Ford's threat to use, x; delegitimations of, 73–75; five-year renewal of use, 72–73; historical roots, 74–77; judicial vs. citizen powers, 78, 81; moral vs. *Charter* rights, 75–76; to override rights (s.2 and ss.7 to 15), x, 72–73, 87–89; parliamentary vs. judicial supremacy, xv–xvi, 73, 74, 78–82, 89–93; Quebec's restrictions on religious symbols, 198; revitalization of democracy, xix; same-sex marriage, 74; uses and proposed uses, x, xix, 81–82, 91–92; Waldron's views on, 77–79. *See also* Charter of Rights and Freedoms
"The Notwithstanding Clause, the *Charter*, and Canada's Patriated Constitution" (Blakeney), 75–77

Obama, Barack, 189, 201
Oil and Gas Conservation, Stabilization, and Development Act (1973), 42
oil and gas industry: about, 42; *CIGOL* case, 11–12; crown corporations (SaskOil), 42–43, 47; federal oil export tax, 7; historical background, 5; resource wars (1970s), 5–7, 20–21, 42. *See also* resource wars (1970s and 1980s)
Ontario: assisted dying issue, 196; electoral boundaries, 211, 218, 218(t), 220; notwithstanding clause and municipal elections,

81; political finance system, 224; social charter proposal, 147; social democracy, 145–48

Page, Benjamin, 113
Pal, Michael, 220
palliative care, 196. *See also* assisted dying issue
parliamentary system: decision making, 116–17, 119, 154–55; diversity and representation, 153–54, 165–66, 241; gendered political processes, 154–55, 159; populism, 62. *See also* constitutions and democracy; democracy; elections; electoral boundaries; members of Parliament (MPs); ministers; voters
Parti Québécois (PQ), 24–25
Pearson, Lester, 143, 146
People's Party of Canada, x, 202
physician assisted death. *See* assisted dying issue
Picard, André, 196
political finance systems: about, xviii, xx, 206, 223–25, 235–36; advertising, 224, 234; American model, 225–26; assessment of current system, 232–34; Blakeney's views, 224, 236; competition, electoral, 226–29; consumerist model, xviii, 225, 231, 235; contribution limits, xviii, xx, 224–25, 229–31, 233–35; corruption and scandals, 224; cultural values, 225; democratic impact of design of, 228–29, 232–36; disclosure level, 224, 227, 230, 232; equality, political, 226–27; European model, 225–26; extraparliamentary unregulated organizations, 233–34; historical background, 229–32, 235; ideological polarization, xviii, 225, 233, 235; incentives for political engagement, 165–66; informed choices and deliberation, 226–29, 235; new and small parties, barriers for, xviii, 224–25, 226, 232, 234, 235, 236; permanent campaign, 225, 234, 235; public funding for parties, xviii, xx, 224–25, 228, 230–36; purposes, 227–29; reform proposals, 235–36; revitalization of democracy, xx; spending limits, xviii, 224, 229–32, 234; supply and demand of funding, 227. *See also* elections
political parties: about, 160–61; electoral district associations (EDAs), 161, 230; fundraising, 233; gender differences, 160–61, 164; women candidates, 160–61, 164, 165–66. *See also* political finance systems; women and politics
Political Management in Canada (Blakeney and Borins), xiv, 48, 54, 57
populism: about, ix–x, 62, 239–40; Blakeney's views, xi, xx, 62, 239–40; global trends, ix–x, 201, 242; group identity vs. policy, 111, 120; immigration views, x; logical incoherence, 110; mistrust as fertile ground, 133; People's Party of Canada, x, 202; prairie populism, 62; strongman authoritarians, ix–x, 98, 119, 239; terminology, 62
post-secondary education, 18–19, 30, 45. *See also* education
Potash Corporation of Saskatchewan (PCS), 9
Potash Corporation of Saskatchewan Act, 11
Potash Development Act, 11
potash industry: about, 4–7, 43, 47; Blakeney's views, 4–6, 9–11; Central Canada Potash (CCP) case, 5–7, 11–12, 43; crown corporation (PCS),

6, 8–11, 43; nationalization, 8–12; pro-rationing program, 5–6, 11–12; reserve tax on windfalls, 6–8, 43; resource wars (1970s), 4–8; tax and royalty regime, 43. *See also* resource wars (1970s and 1980s)
Potter, Andrew, 132–34
Powell, G. Bingham, 58
premier, Blakeney as. *See* Blakeney, Allan, career as premier (1971-1982); Blakeney, Allan, principled pragmatism
prescription drug programs, xix, 18, 45, 47–48
principled pragmatism. *See* Blakeney, Allan, principled pragmatism
pro-choice and pro-life debates. *See* abortion rights issue
provincial governments: agencies, boards, and commissions, 166; Medicare shared jurisdiction, 144–45; resource wars (1970s and 1980s), 4, 8–9; welfare state shared jurisdiction, 140, 144–47
public administration: about, 33–38, 46–49; Blakeney's views, 48, 54; civil servants and ministers, 39, 54–55; communicative model, 55–57; systematic approach, 35–36, 39. *See also* accountability; Blakeney, Allan, principled pragmatism; cabinet government; ministers
public opinion: about, 58–59, 64–65; congruence between policies and public, 58; deliberated opinion polls, 64; deliberative democracy, 52–54; education for participation, 30; election platforms, 37, 41–42, 238–39; Habermas on, 52, 64; impact of inequalities on, 16; models of citizen-representative relationship, 52; public acceptance of policy, 57; research issues, 58–60, 63–65; risks to, ix, 16; talk-centric vs. vote-centric, 53–54. *See also* democratic deficiencies; democratic input; populism; voters
public opinion, issues: abortion rights, 193; disdain for government, 106, 126; equality issues, 15–16, 30–32; same-sex marriage, 64, 188–89; tax policy, 125–26; trust in government, 123–28, 240; what people want, 124; women's underrepresentation in politics, 152–53

Quebec: Bouchard-Taylor Commission, 67, 198; Catholic Church's social doctrine, 139–40; *Charter*'s notwithstanding clause, 92, 198; constitutional negotiations, 88, 91–92; electoral boundaries, 218–20, 218(t); Islamophobia, 200; Quebec Charter of Human Rights and Freedoms, 75; regional inequality, 24–25; religious symbols in public sector, 67, 92, 198–99; secularization (laïcité), 198–99; social democracy, 148
Quirk, Paul, 112

race and ethnicity: anti-immigrant campaigns, 186; *Charter* voting rights, 155; Eastern European ethnic minorities, 25, 27–28; heritage languages, 28; minority vs. majoritarian democracy, 79, 93–100; representation in House of Commons, 155–56; secular vs. transcendent metanarratives, 201–2; Syrian refugees, 199–200. *See also* Indigenous peoples; marginalized people; religion and democracy

Rae, Bob, 145
regional equality: about, 15, 20–25, 31–32; agriculture, 22–23; block funding vs. cost sharing, 24; democratic issues, 31–32; equalization payments, 32, 66–67; federal policies, 20–24; resource wars, 20–21; suppression of regionalism, 31; transfer payments, 24; western alienation, xi, 15, 20–21, 24–25, 31. *See also* economic equality; resource wars (1970s and 1980s)
Reich, Robert, 127
religion and democracy: about, xvii–xviii, xix, 185–87, 200–203; competing rights, 186–87, 193, 196–97; conscientious objection, 191, 193, 194–97; culture wars, 201–3; notwithstanding clause, 81, 92, 198; political violence, 200; power of religion, xix, 185–86; religious pluralism, 67, 187, 197; religious symbols in Quebec, 67, 92, 198–99; secular vs. transcendent metanarratives, xvii–xviii, 186–87, 189, 192–93, 200–203; social gospel, 139, 142, 185–86, 202–3; threat of non-Christian/Judaic other, 200–201. *See also* abortion rights issue; assisted dying issue; Christianity; Islam; Judaism; same-sex marriage
Report on Social Security for Canada (Marsh), 140–41
resource wars (1970s and 1980s): about, 4–7, 20–22, 238; Blakeney's views, 10–14; crown corporations, 8–10, 12–13, 21–22; export taxes, 21; OPEC crisis, 42; Potash Corp. of Sask. (PCS), 4, 9–10; provincial jurisdiction, 4, 8–9; regional inequality, 4–7, 21–22; tax policy, 4–8, 21
"A Rights-Based Critique of Constitutional Rights" (Waldron), 77–79
Roach, Kent, 48
Robarts, John, 143
Rodriguez v British Columbia (1993), 193–94
Roman Catholic Church. *See* Catholic Church
Romanow, Roy: about, 320; crown corporation (potash), 11; cutbacks to social programs, 146–47; introduction by, ix–xx; patriation debates, 74; political career, 34, 38, 74, 320; premier, 146–47, 149; on principled pragmatism, xiv, xviii, 3–14, 119–20, 238–39
Rothstein, Bo, 108
Rousseau, Guillaume, 74
Rowell-Sirois Royal Commission, 66
Royal Commission on Aboriginal People, 29–30
Royal Commission on Electoral Reform and Party Financing (Lortie Commission), 220
Royal Commission on the Status of Women, 151, 164
royal commissions, xix, 66–68
rule of law: Blakeney's principled pragmatism, 12–13, 172; conditions for democracy, 84, 108. *See also* Blakeney, Allan, principled pragmatism
Runciman, David, 106

Sabl, Andrew, 57
same-sex marriage: cultural shift, 64–65, 189, 192; marriage as institution, 189; notwithstanding clause, 74; public opinion, 64,

188–89; religion vs. politics, 187–89, 192–93, 200–201. *See also* LGBTQ people; religion and democracy
Saskatchewan: agriculture, 22–23, 28; Blakeney's Canadianism, 22–23; collectivist values, 17, 28; Depression's impact, 42; multicultural roots, 26–28; northern region, 43–45, 172–73; religious school funding, 92; western alienation, xi, 4, 15, 20–21, 24–25. *See also* Indigenous peoples; natural resources
Saskatchewan, Blakeney's government. *See* Blakeney, Allan, career as premier (1971–1982); Blakeney, Allan, principled pragmatism; cabinet government
Saskatchewan, politics. *See* CCF (Cooperative Commonwealth Federation); elections; electoral boundaries; NDP (New Democratic Party) (Saskatchewan); political finance systems
Saskatchewan Indian Federated College, 45, 173
SaskOil (Saskatchewan Oil and Gas Corp.), 42–43, 47
SCC. *See* Supreme Court of Canada
Schäfer, Armin, 123
schools. *See* education
Schreyer, Ed, 145
Schumpeter, Joseph, 60, 61
Scott, Frank, 142
Selinger, Greg, 145
Sen, Amartya, 106
sexual orientation. *See* LGBTQ people
Shoyama, Tommy, 35, 118, 143
small vs. big governments, 107, 125, 127–29. *See also* economy, government intervention; neoliberalism; tax policy; welfare state
social democracy: about, 105, 136–37, 148–49; activist state, 46, 118, 238, 240, 241; Blakeney's principled pragmatism, 13–14, 119–20; Blakeney's views, 34, 105, 238; British influences, 137; contemporary needs, 147–49; democratic deficiencies, 118–20; equality of conditions vs. opportunities, 141; equity-seeking groups, 148; historical background, 138–49; national institutions in support of, 116; needs of disadvantaged, 107; opposition to, 148–49; political ideology, 136–37, 140–41; privatization of social programs, 146–47; recent trends, 148–49; social gospel, 139, 142, 185–86, 202–3; social justice goals, 105, 107, 120, 136–37. *See also* Blakeney, Allan, principled pragmatism; economy, government intervention; welfare state
social equality: about, 15–16, 25–32; relation to legal equality, 25–26. *See also* feminism; social democracy
social justice. *See* human rights; social democracy
social media: electoral boundary input, xviii, 211, 216–17, 221; online comments, 166; sexism, 164, 166. *See also* media and communications
social welfare. *See* social democracy; welfare state
Sophocles, *Antigone*, 186–87
St. Laurent, Louis, 137, 140
Steuart, David, 10
Stiglitz, Joseph, 132
Strayer, Barry, 75
Streeck, Wolfgang, 123

strongman state. *See* authoritarianism and totalitarianism
suicide, assisted. *See* assisted dying issue
Supreme Court of Canada: abortion (*Morgentaler*), 190, 191, 192; assisted dying (*Carter* and *Rodriguez*), 193–94; fair elections (*Dixon*), 207; impact of *Charter* cases, 86–87; Indigenous peoples, duty to consult (*Haida, Mikisew Cree, Taku River*), 175, 177, 180, 183; parliamentary vs. judicial supremacy, xv–xvi, 73, 74, 78–79, 89–93; resource taxes (*CIGOL* and *Central Canada Potash*), 5–7, 11–12, 43. *See also* courts and judges

Taku River v British Columbia (2004), 175
Tansley, Don, 35
tax policy: about, xvi–xvii, xix–xx, 121–23, 132–34, 241; austerity, 127–30, 240; Blakeney's views, 126, 133–34, 241; child benefits, 131; *CIGOL* and *Central Canada Potash* cases, 11–12; corporate benefits, 130; GST reduction, 124–25; Harper's tax cuts, 124–25, 128, 132; impact on economic inequality, xvi, 17; neoliberalism, 126–32; payment of "fair share," 125, 133–34; personal taxes, 17–18; progressive taxation, xvi–xvii, 17; property taxes, 17; public opinion, 125–26; public trust issues, xvi, 122–30, 133–34, 240; resource wars (1970s), 5–7, 21–22, 42; revitalization of democracy, xix–xx; royalties, 17, 21–22; small vs. big governments, 107, 125, 127–30; tax avoidance, xix; tax cuts, xix, 124–29, 132–34; tax loopholes, xix; 2008 financial crisis, 128–29. *See also* economic equality; economic inequality; resource wars (1970s and 1980s)
Taylor, Charles, 198
Tchorzewski, Ed, 17, 27
Thatcher, Ross, government: Blakeney in opposition, 38; health user fees, 45; Indigenous relations, 172; potash policies, 5–6, 11–12
Thomas, Melanee: contributor, 320; on gender and democratic deficit, xvii, xx, 151–66, 241
totalitarianism. *See* authoritarianism and totalitarianism
treaties. *See* Indigenous peoples, treaties
Trudeau, Justin: abortion rights issue, 191; assisted dying legislation, 195; NDP influence on policies, 149; Syrian refugees, 199–200
Trudeau, Pierre: constitutional negotiations, 86, 89; family allowances, 146; LGBTQ rights, 188; multiculturalism, 26, 28; notwithstanding clause, 74, 89; resource wars (1970s), 7, 31
Trump, Donald, 96, 189, 190, 198, 201, 239
trust in government, 122–28, 240. *See also* public opinion; tax policy
truth, defined, 51. *See also* accountability
Truth and Reconciliation Commission, 30
Tupper, Charles, 138

UNESCO *Declaration of Principles of International Cultural Co-Operation*, 27
United Kingdom: Fabian Society, 16–17, 140; social policy model, 137; Thatcher's tax cuts, 126–27; workers' compensation, 138

United States: abortion rights, 190–91; business influence on foreign policy, 58; culture wars, 201–3; economic inequality, 131; *The Federalist*, 96; framing and public opinion, 64–65; immigration as threat, 201; Islamophobia, 197–98, 200; neoliberalism, 126–27; New Deal's influence, 139; policy influence by socio-economic class, 113; political finance system, 225, 282n2; ratification of Constitution, 95–96; Reagan's tax cuts, 126–27; same-sex marriage, 64, 188–89; secular vs. transcendent metanarratives, 201–2; voter deficiencies, 111–12; workers' compensation, 138
uranium industry, 8, 17, 43–44, 173

Verba, Sidney, 63
Vermeule, Adrian, 116–17
voters: about, 206; "active misinformed," 111–12; *Charter* rights (s.3), 155, 207; civic literacy, 110–12; consumerist model, xviii, 225, 231, 235; decline in turnout, 32, 124, 132; deficiencies in, 110–12; dialogues with, xiii, xvi, 239, 241; impact of socio-economic status on turnout, 32; Indigenous peoples, 153; key questions, 206; political finance and informed choices, 226–27, 228; populist theory, 111; trust in government, 123–24, 132, 240; vote aggregation, 109–11, 118–19. *See also* democratic input; elections; electoral boundaries; public opinion
vulnerable citizens. *See* marginalized people

Waldron, Jeremy, 73, 77–79
Walker, Katherine: contributor, 320–21; on the duty to consult First Nations, xvii, xix, 167–84, 241
Wall, Brad: Indigenous consultation (2010), 178–82
Webb, Sidney and Beatrice, 16–17
Weber, Max, 55
welfare state: about, xvii, xix, 18–19, 135–36, 147–49, 241; Blakeney's views, 146–47, 241; CCF-NDP influence, xvii, xix, 139–43, 147, 149; child care, xix, 135–36, 142, 145–46; citizen participation, 145; contemporary needs, 147–49; dental care, 144–45; drug insurance, xix, 18, 136, 144–45; elder care, 135; employment supports, 19; family allowances and child benefits, 131, 135, 141, 143, 146; historical background, 135–36, 138–47; home care, 145; national identity, 147–48; national institutions in support of, 116; opposition to, 145; pensions and social security, 138–41, 143, 146; political ideology, 136–37, 140–41, 146; privatization of programs, 146–47; provincial/federal jurisdiction, 140, 144–47; revitalization of democracy, xix; Saskatchewan as laboratory, 144; self-development, 19; social assistance, 19, 145–46; social charter proposal, 147; social housing, 135–36, 143, 145; unemployment insurance, 135, 138, 140; universality principle, 146; workers' compensation, 138. *See also* economic inequality; Medicare; social democracy
Whitaker, Reg: contributor, 321; on religion and pluralist democracies, xvii–xviii, xix, 185–203, 241

Whyte, John D.: contributor, 321; on human rights regime, xv, xix–xx, 83–101; introduction by, ix–xx; notwithstanding clause, 74, 78, 79, 239

Wilson, Michael, 10

Wiseman, Nelson: contributor, 321–22; on social democracy and the welfare state, xvii, xix, 135–49, 241

women: about, 15–16, 25–26; Blakeney's views, 25–26, 45, 151; democratic participation, 31–32; discrimination against, 25–26, 31; equality issues, 25–26; gender differences, 158–60; labour force participation, 157; maternity leave, 26, 274n67; pay equity, 26, 151, 157; property rights, 26, 45; public opinion on gender roles, 152; revitalization of democracy, xx; socio-economic resources, 157–58; voter participation, 157. *See also* abortion rights issue

women and politics: about, xvii, xx, 151–52, 163–66; *Charter* rights (s.3), 155; diversity of experience, 154; elections by party vs. non-party system, 161–62; family responsibilities, 159, 163–64, 274n67; gendered policy processes, 154, 163; media portrayal of women, xx, 159–61, 163–64; ministers, 155; occupational backgrounds, 145, 156; participation rates, 157; political engagement, 158–61, 165–66; quotas for women's representation, 165–66; recruitment by parties, 161, 165–66; representation in House of Commons, 155–56; revitalization of democracy, xx; role models, 158–59; sexism, 163–64; socio-economic resources, 157–58; statistics, 152–53; stereotypes, 154, 159–61; strategies to remove barriers, 165–66; supply vs. demand, 156–63; systemic barriers, 162–66; underrepresentation of women, xvii, 152–57, 165–66; women premiers, 154

Woodsworth, J.S., 138, 141, 185

Wynne, Kathleen, 224

Young, Lisa, 230

youth. *See* children and youth